P9-BJE-507

The *Home Orchard*

Growing Your Own Deciduous Fruit and Nut Trees

Chuck A. Ingels, Pamela M. Geisel, and Maxwell V. Norton

Technical Editors

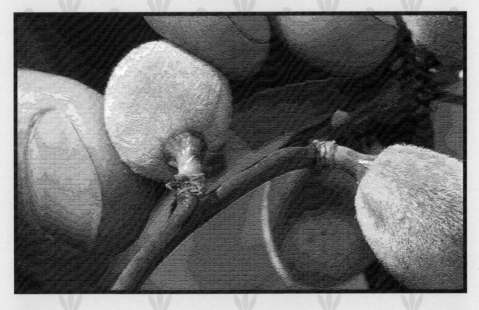

University of California
Agriculture and Natural Resources
Publication 3485
2007

UC
PEER
REVIEWED

ORDERING

To order or obtain ANR publications and other products, visit the ANR Communication Services online catalog at http://anrcatalog.ucdavis.edu or phone 1-800-994-8849. You can also place orders by mail or FAX, or request a printed catalog of our products from

University of California
Agriculture and Natural Resources Communication Services
1301 S. 46th Street, Building 478 - MC 3580
Richmond, CA 94804-4600

Telephone 1-800-994-8849 or 510-665-2195
FAX 510-665-3427
E-mail: danrcs@ucdavis.edu
Publication 3485

ISBN-13: 978-1-879906-72-3
ISBN-10: 1-879906-72-4
Library of Congress Control Number: 2006938000

©2007 The Regents of the University of California
Agriculture and Natural Resources
All rights reserved.

Cover photograph by Jack Kelly Clark.
Back cover photograph by Chuck Ingels.

The University of California prohibits discrimination or harassment of any person on the basis of race, color, national origin, religion, sex, gender identity, pregnancy (including childbirth, and medical conditions related to pregnancy or childbirth), physical or mental disability, medical condition (cancer-related or genetic characteristics), ancestry, marital status, age, sexual orientation, citizenship, or service in the uniformed services (as defined by the Uniformed Services Employment and Reemployment Rights Act of 1994: service in the uniformed services includes membership, application for membership, performance of service, application for service, or obligation for service in the uniformed services) in any of its programs or activities.

University policy also prohibits reprisal or retaliation against any person in any of its programs or activities for making a complaint of discrimination or sexual harassment or for using or participating in the investigation or resolution process of any such complaint.

University policy is intended to be consistent with the provisions of applicable State and Federal laws.

Inquiries regarding the University's nondiscrimination policies may be directed to the Affirmative Action/Equal Opportunity Director, University of California, Agriculture and Natural Resources, 1111 Franklin Street, 6th Floor, Oakland, CA 94607, (510) 987-0096. For information about ordering this publication, telephone 1-800-994-8849.

To simplify information, trade names of products have been used. No endorsement of named or illustrated products is intended, nor is criticism implied of similar products that are not mentioned or illustrated.

UC PEER REVIEWED This publication has been anonymously peer reviewed for technical accuracy by University of California scientists and other qualified professionals. This review process was managed by the ANR Associate Editor for Pomology, Viticulture, and Subtropical Horticulture.

Printed in Canada on recycled paper

5m-rep-10/10-WJC/RW   Second printing, 2010

WARNING ON THE USE OF CHEMICALS

Pesticides are poisonous. Always read and carefully follow all precautions and safety recommendations given on the container label. Store all chemicals in their original labeled containers in a locked cabinet or shed, away from foods or feeds, and out of the reach of children, unauthorized persons, pets, and livestock.

Confine pesticides to the property being treated. Avoid drift onto neighboring properties or gardens containing fruits and/or vegetables ready to be picked.

Dispose of empty containers carefully. Follow label instructions for disposal. Never reuse the containers. Make sure empty containers are not accessible to children or animals. Never dispose of containers where they may contaminate water supplies or natural waterways. Do not pour down sink or toilet. Consult your county agricultural commissioner for correct ways of disposing of excess pesticides. Never burn pesticide containers.

PHYTOTOXICITY: Certain chemicals may cause plant injury if used at the wrong stage of plant development or when temperatures are too high. Injury may also result from excessive amounts or the wrong formulation or from mixing incompatible materials. Inert ingredients, such as wetters, spreaders, emulsifiers, diluents, and solvents, can cause plant injury. Since formulations are often changed by manufacturers, it is possible that plant injury may occur, even though no injury was noted in previous seasons.

HOW TO USE THIS BOOK

This publication is intended for use by backyard orchardists, rare fruit growers, and small-scale growers. It focuses on methods that can be used by hobbyists, some of which are not practical for the commercial grower. The book offers a fairly comprehensive look at "standard" growing methods as well as some unique practices that enthusiasts have developed in recent years. Extensive photographs, diagrams, and tables are employed to help explain the practices and clarify your options. You will learn how trees grow, which species grow best in particular regions and soils, what varieties are available (and how to select the right one), and how to prepare the soil, plant the trees, water and fertilize, prune and graft, thin the fruit, diagnose problems, control pests, and harvest the fruits of your labors.

Deciduous fruit trees generally require more time and effort to grow than most landscape trees and shrubs. This is because they are susceptible to more insect pests and diseases, they require more specialized pruning, the fruit usually need thinning (and harvesting), and you have to be able to reach the top of the tree to manage and pick the fruit. Nut trees may be less labor intensive than fruit trees, but their height makes it difficult for most home orchardists to prune and control pests on these trees. However, the reward for growing fruits and nuts at home is a wider selection of varieties, control over how pests are managed, and, at least for fruit trees, the ability to harvest at the preferred degree of ripeness.

For further information on growing fruit and nut trees in the home orchard, you can find a wealth of information on commercial and small orchard production and pest management available in University of California publications. Visit the UC Agriculture and Natural Resources Catalog online at http://anrcatalog.ucdavis.edu or call 1-800-994-8849. Also, the University of California's "California Backyard Orchard" Web site (http://homeorchard.ucdavis.edu) offers additional information and resources in an easy-to-use format. If you have questions about growing fruit or nut trees, contact the UC Cooperative Extension Master Gardeners in your county. The address and phone number for your Cooperative Extension county office are listed in the county government pages of your telephone book under "University of California," or you can find them online at the UC Agriculture and Natural Resources Web site (http://anrcs.org).

We hope this publication provides you with greater knowledge and extra incentive to grow your own fruits and nuts.

Chuck Ingels
Pam Geisel
Maxwell Norton

CONTRIBUTORS AND ACKNOWLEDGMENTS

Technical Editors
Chuck A. Ingels, Pamela M. Geisel, and Maxwell V. Norton

Contributing Authors
Harry L. Andris, Farm Advisor, University of California Cooperative Extension, Fresno County

Mary Louise Flint, Education and Publications Director, University of California Statewide Integrated Pest Management Program, UC Davis

Pamela M. Geisel, Academic Coordinator, University of California Statewide Master Gardener Program, UC Davis

Chuck A. Ingels, Farm Advisor, University of California Cooperative Extension, Sacramento County

R. Scott Johnson, Extension Pomologist, Department of Plant Sciences, UC Davis

Edward D. Laivo, Sales Manager, Dave Wilson Nursery, Inc.

Maxwell V. Norton, Farm Advisor, University of California Cooperative Extension, Merced County

Terry L. Prichard, Extension Irrigation and Water Management Specialist, Department of Land, Air, and Water Resources, UC Davis

Lawrence J. Schwankl, Extension Irrigation Specialist, University of California Kearney Agricultural Center, Parlier

Beth L. Teviotdale, Extension Plant Pathologist Emerita, UC Davis

Paul M. Vossen, Farm Advisor, University of California Cooperative Extension, Sonoma and Marin Counties

Special Thanks
We offer our special thanks to Steve Barnett (UC ANR Communication Services) for undertaking the initial writing of several of the book's chapters. Thanks also to Cathy Coulter, Mike Cunningham, Phil Damewood, Judy Lee, Gail Pothour, Art Ruble, and Luke Shenoy, and to photographer Jack Kelly Clark and our production team at ANR Communication Services.

Production & Design
Robin Walton, ANR Communication Services

Editing
Jim Coats, ANR Communication Services

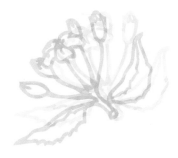

Table of Contents

1. Climate and Soils 1

Climate 1
Growing Areas 1
Chilling Hours 2
Heat Units and the Ripening Period 3
Frost 4

Soils 5
Soil Texture 5
Soil Structure 6
Soil Profile 6
Soil Physical Problems 6
Soil Chemical Problems 6
Mulch 7

References 8

2. Growth and Development 9

Tree Organs and Their Functions 9
Roots 9
The Trunk: Where Scion Meets Rootstock . . . 10
Shoots, Branches, and the Vascular Cambium . . 10
Buds 12
Leaves 13
Flowers 13
Fruit 15

Biology of Plant Growth 16
Photosynthesis and Respiration 17
Uptake and Movement of Water and Nutrients . . 18

Growth Cycle in Deciduous Fruit Trees . . . 18
Winter 19
Spring 19
Summer 20
Fall 20

References 20

3. Varieties and Rootstocks 21

Pome Fruits 21
Apples 21
Pears 24

Pomegranates 26
Quinces 26

Stone Fruits 27
Apricots 27
Cherries 28
Nectarines 29
Peaches 30
Plums and Prunes 31
Plumcots 33

Nut Crops 33
Almonds 33
Chestnuts 34
Filberts (Hazelnuts) 34
Pecans 35
Pistachios 35
Walnuts 35

Miscellaneous Temperate Fruits 36
Figs 36
Persimmons 37

References 38

4. Planting and Care of Young Fruit and Nut Trees 39

Planting 39
Tree Selection 39
Site Selection 40
Preparing the Planting Site 41
Planting the Tree 41
Pruning the Newly Planted Tree 42
Sunburn Protection at Planting 43
Irrigation 43

Care of Young Trees 43
Training Young Trees 43
Irrigation 44
Weeds 44

References 46

5. *Irrigation* 47

Importance of Good Irrigation 47

Irrigating Trees 47

Tree Water Use Units 48

Estimating Tree Water Use 48
  Tree Size 49
  Climatic Conditions 49
  Applying the Right Amount of Water 50

Irrigation Methods 50
  Garden Hose 50
  Permanent Sprinklers 51
  Drip and Microsprinkler Systems 53
  Soaker Hose Systems 54

Evaluating Your Efforts 54
  Feel Method 55

References 56

6. *Fertilization* 57

Nutrients and Their Roles in Plant Development . 57
  Macronutrients 57
  Micronutrients 58

Soil Fertility Management 59
  Nutrient Recycling 59
  Salinity 59
  Soil pH 60

Types of Fertilizer 60
  Compost, Mulch, and Organic Fertilizers . . . 60
  Synthetic (Inorganic) Fertilizers 61

Nutrient Deficiencies and Toxicities 61
  Diagnosing Nutrient Deficiencies and Toxicities . 61

Using Fertilizers 66
  Calculating How Much Fertilizer to Apply . . . 66
  Soil Application 67
  Foliar Application 67
  Recommended Timing and Rates 69

References 70

7. *Training and Pruning* 71

Fundamentals of Pruning Fruit Trees 71
  Making Pruning Cuts 71
  Apical Dominance and the Effects of Heading
    vs. Thinning Cuts 74
  Branch Spreaders to Reduce Pruning 75
  Bearing Habits of Fruit and Nut Trees 76

Summer Pruning vs. Dormant Pruning 76

Standard and Dwarfing Tree Types 78
  Genetic Dwarf Trees 78
  Full-Sized and Semidwarf Trees 78

Specific Training Systems 79
  Open-Center System 79
  Perpendicular **V** System 82
  Central Leader and Modified Central
    Leader Systems 86
  "Fruit Bush" System 88
  Espalier Training 90
  Pruning of Unique Species 93

Pruning Overgrown Trees 97
  Method 1: Maintain the Tree Height and
    Make Mostly Thinning Cuts 97
  Method 2: Reduce the Tree Height Slowly
    Over a Three-Year Period 97
  Method 3: Drastically Cut Back Most of
    the Main Branches 98

References 98

8. *Budding and Grafting* 99

Grafting Supplies 101
  Knives 101
  Wrapping and Waxing Materials 102

Key Points for Budding and Grafting 102

Budding (Bud Grafting) 103
  T-Budding 103
  Chip Budding 108
  Determining Whether the Bud Graft Has Taken . 109
  Forcing Bud Growth 109

Grafting 110
  Whip Grafting 110

Topworking 115
  Bark Grafting 115
  Cleft Grafting 117

Care of Budded and Grafted Plants 119

Grafting Shoots to Create Structures 120

References 122

9. *Fruit Thinning* 123

Natural Fruit Drop 123

Species That Require Thinning 123

Timing for Thinning 124

How Much Fruit to Thin 124

Methods of Thinning 126

References 128

10. Harvesting Fruit and Nuts 129

General Rules of Harvest 129

Storage 130

Harvesting and Storing Specific Fruits and Nuts . . 131
Apples 131
Apricots and Apriums 132
Cherries 132
Figs 132
Peaches and Nectarines 132
Pears 133
Persimmons 134
Plums, Prunes, Plumcots, Pluots, and
Cherry-Plums 135
Pomegranates 135
Quinces 135

Nut Crops 135
Almonds 136
Pecans 136
Pistachios 137
Walnuts 138

References 138

11. Integrated Pest Management for Backyard Orchards 139

What Is Integrated Pest Management? 139
Pest Management Methods 139
Types of Pests 142

Common Insect and Mite Pests 142
Aphids 142
Scale Insects 146
Codling Moth 147
Peach Twig Borer 152
Oriental Fruit Moth 152
Leafrollers and Other Leaf-Feeding Caterpillars . . 153
Walnut Husk Fly 154
Spider Mites 156
Borers 157
Other Insects 160

Common Diseases in Backyard Orchards 161
Powdery Mildew 161
Peach Leaf Curl 163
Brown Rot 165
Fire Blight 168
Apple Scab 169
Shothole Disease 171
Bacterial Canker and Blast 172

Eutypa Dieback 174
Walnut Blight 174
Armillaria Root Rot 174
Phytophthora Root and Crown Rot 175
Crown Gall 176

References 178

12. Failure to Bear and Abiotic Disorders . . . 179

Failure to Bear 179
Diagnosing Failure to Bear 179
Normal Flower and Fruit Drop 180
Planting Site 180
Pruning 180
Climate and Weather 180
Pollination 181
Alternate Bearing 181
Improper Irrigation, Root Problems, and Pests . . 182
Late to Come into Bearing 182

Physiological Disorders 182
Splitting and Cracking of Cherries 182
Splitting and Cracking of Other Fruit 183
Doubling and Spurring of Cherries 183
Split Pit of Peaches and Nectarines 183
Pit Burn of Apricot 184
Fog Spot of Apricot 184
Bitter Pit of Apple 154
Sunburn of All Fruit 185
Lack of Fruit Sweetness 185
Fall Bloom 185

References 186

Appendix: Crop-by-Crop Calendars 187
Almond 187
Apricot 188
Cherry 188
Fig 188
Peach and Nectarine 189
Pecan 189
Persimmon 189
Pistachio 190
Plum (including Cherry-Plum, Pluot,
and Prune) 190
Pome Fruit (Apple, Pear, and Quince) 191
Pomegranate 191
Walnut 191

Glossary 192

Index 197

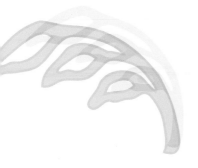

CHAPTER **1**

Climate and Soils

Maxwell V. Norton

Climate

GROWING AREAS

For the purposes of this book, we have divided California into six regional fruit growing areas for growing deciduous fruit and nut trees (Figure 1.1). These zones are approximations: each contains microclimates in which the climate can vary considerably from other areas in the zone. To get an idea of your local microclimate, consult a UC Master Gardener or your local UC Cooperative Extension farm or horticulture advisor. You can also pay attention to which fruit and nut trees grow in your area and you can ask your neighbors and knowledgeable local nursery staff. Publications such as the *Sunset Western Garden Book* (Brenzel 2001) also contain useful climate maps. You can even have distinct microclimates in your own garden or backyard, along the southern side of a house or in the shade of a building or trees, for example.

What follows is a general description of the growing zones shown in Figure 1.1 and the types of fruit and nut trees that are grown successfully in each. For information on varieties of these types of fruits and nuts, see Chapter 3.

Regions 1 and 2: San Joaquin and Sacramento Valleys

The San Joaquin Valley consists of the southern portion of the Central Valley, south of Sacramento. Its cities include Bakersfield, Fresno, Merced, Modesto, and Stockton. The Sacramento Valley consists of the northern portion of the Central Valley along the Sacramento River. Its cities include Sacramento, Yuba City, Marysville, and Redding. Certain basic seasonal weather conditions apply throughout the Central Valley: the summer is hot and dry and the winter is cool and damp. Very little rain falls from May through September and dense fog can form in December and January. Strong, dry winds are common in spring and fall. Virtually all deciduous fruits and nuts grow well in the Central Valley.

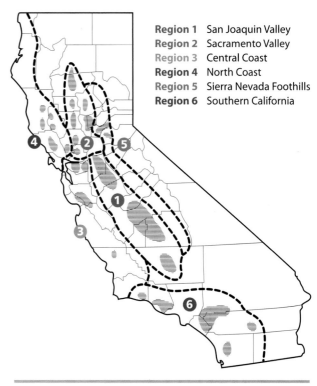

Region 1 San Joaquin Valley
Region 2 Sacramento Valley
Region 3 Central Coast
Region 4 North Coast
Region 5 Sierra Nevada Foothills
Region 6 Southern California

Figure 1.1. Primary regions for growing temperate-zone fruit and nut trees in California. Shading indicates major commercial production areas. *Source:* Adapted from Vossen 2002, p. 464.

Region 3: Central Coast

The Central Coast region extends from the Golden Gate Bridge south to Point Conception and reaches inland to include the southern portion of the Coast Range. Its cities include San Francisco, Oakland, San Jose, Concord, Santa Cruz, Monterey, San Luis Obispo, and Santa Maria. Right on the coast, the summer is cool and foggy and the winter is mild and damp. Strong sea breezes are common; frost, though rare, can occur. In the interior portions of the region, the summer is warmer and less foggy and the winter is cooler than on the coast, but the summer and winter extremes are generally less severe than in the neighboring San Joaquin Valley. Exceptions might be the King City, Paso Robles, and Cuyama areas, where in some years the temperature extremes may exceed those of the San Joaquin Valley. Deciduous fruits and nuts that grow well here, particularly in the interior areas, include almond, apple, apricot, cherry, fig, nectarine, peach, pear, plum, pomegranate, prune, and walnut.

Region 4: North Coast

The North Coast region extends from the Golden Gate Bridge to the Oregon border and reaches inland to encompass the northern portion of the Coast Range. Its cities include Novato, Santa Rosa, Ukiah, Mendocino, and Eureka. The northern end of this zone is the wettest part of California. Both summer and winter are cooler than on the Central Coast, and the area also receives more rainfall. Strong sea breezes are common on the coast, and frost can occur. The inland, higher-elevation areas of the zone are similar to those of Region 5 (below), but wetter. Deciduous fruits and nuts that grow well in the warmer areas include apple, apricot, cherry, pear, plum, prune, and walnut.

Region 5: Sierra Nevada Foothills

The Sierra Nevada Foothills region corresponds roughly to what is known as the Gold Country, the lower elevations of the western slope of the Sierra. Its cities include Sonora, Jackson, Placerville, Camino, Auburn, and Grass Valley. The summer is warm with occasional rain, and the winter is cold and wet. Frost is common in winter and spring, especially at the higher elevations. Deciduous fruits and nuts that grow well here include apple, cherry, olive, peach, pear, persimmon, pistachio, plum, prune, quince, and walnut.

Region 6: Southern California

Southern California includes the coastal and inland areas from Point Conception south to the Mexican border. Its cities include Santa Barbara, Los Angeles, Riverside, San Bernardino, and San Diego. On the coast, summer is mild with some fog, and winter is mild with some rain. Strong, dry southwest winds known as Santa Anas are common in spring and fall; frost can occur, especially in the desert and higher elevations. The climate in this region's higher-elevation areas is similar to that of the Sierra Nevada Foothills. The climate in the inland desert areas is similar to that of the southern San Joaquin Valley, but with a hotter, drier summer and a warmer winter. Deciduous fruits and nuts that grow well in this zone include apple, fig, nectarine, peach, persimmon, plum, and walnut.

CHILLING HOURS

Deciduous fruit and nut trees need a certain number of hours with temperatures below 45°F (7°C) in winter if they are to bloom normally and grow well in the spring (see Chapter 2). If a fruit or nut tree does not receive enough *chilling hours* during winter, flower buds may fail to develop, leaves may appear later than usual, and the bloom period may be extended. The tree may produce little or no fruit that year, and any fruit that do appear may be deformed or smaller than normal.

Different types of fruit and nut trees require different amounts of chilling (Table 1.1). When selecting fruit or nut trees for your home garden, choose species and varieties that are compatible with the average number of chilling hours in your area. You can find a comprehensive tabulation of chilling hours to date for the current year for many locations in the state at the University of California Fruit and Nut Research and Information Center's *Pomology Weather Services* Web site (http://fruitsandnuts.ucdavis.edu/weather). Table 1.2 presents historical data from this Web site for selected locations in each climate zone.

For example, assume that you live in Riverside and you want to grow pears in your back yard. From Table 1.1 you can see that most standard pears require between 700 and 800 chilling hours; now, looking at Table 1.2 you see that Riverside had only an average of 339 chilling hours in the winters of 2000–2001 through 2003–2004. This is fewer chilling hours than standard pear varieties need in order to reliably bear fruit. To grow pears successfully in Riverside, you will have to plant a low-chill pear variety that will bear fruit after approximately 300 chilling hours. Note that chilling in this region is more than adequate for a low-chill plum variety in some years, but in other years the number of chilling hours was even lower, and inadequate for some fruit and nut species and varieties.

HEAT UNITS AND THE RIPENING PERIOD

Once fruits and nuts reach their mature size, the period of time they take to become ripe enough to harvest is known as the ripening period (for more information on ripening and maturity, see Chapter 10). The usual length of the ripening period varies for different species and varieties and the actual length and timing of the ripening period in a given year for a given species and variety is influenced in part by the number of heat units that accumulate during the period. Heat units can be thought of as the number of hours at or above a designated temperature: the opposite of chilling hours. As with chilling hours, different climate zones in the state receive different numbers of heat units. This means, for example, that a fruit that has a long ripening period (i.e., that needs a large number of heat units) may not ripen properly in a cool part of the state. Many peach varieties require prolonged heat for the fruit to develop its best flavor, and these varieties would not be appropriate for planting in some cool coastal areas.

When choosing fruit and nut varieties, look for a variety with a ripening period that is compatible with the climate in your area (for more information on the ripening and harvest period of selected varieties, see Chapter 3). If fall rains are common in your area you may want to avoid late-maturing varieties. If you select varieties that ripen over a longer period of time, you may be able to harvest the fruit over a period of days or even weeks rather than all at once.

Table 1.1. Chilling requirements of selected deciduous fruit and nut trees

Type of fruit/nut	Approx. hours at 45ºF (7ºC) needed to break dormancy
almond	250–500
apple[*]	500–1,000
apple (low-chill)	400–600
apricot[*]	300–800
cherry, sour	1,200
cherry, sweet	700–800
chestnut	400–500
fig	100
filbert (hazelnut)	800
kiwifruit[*]	300–800
olive	200–300
peach/nectarine[*]	500–800
pear[*]	700–800
pear (Asian)	350–450
pecan	250
persimmon	100–200
pistachio	800
plum, American[*]	300–600
plum, European[*]	600–800
plum, Japanese	250–700
plumcot	400–600
pomegranate	100–150
quince	300
walnut, Persian	500–700

* May have low-chill varieties that have been reported to require fewer than 300 hours of temperatures below 45ºF (7ºC) to break dormancy.
Source: Vossen 2002, p. 455.

Table 1.2. Historical accumulations of chilling hours for selected locations in California, November 2000 through February 2006

Location*	Accumulated chilling hours, Nov. 1 through Feb. 28[†]					
	2000–2001	2001–2002	2002–2003	2003–2004	2004–2005	2005–2006
Zone 1						
Fresno	1,268	976	841	884	947	836
Zone 2						
Sacramento	1,103	698	647	717	819	617
Zone 3						
San Luis Obispo	543	436	192	367	379	251
Zone 4						
Santa Rosa	1,438	1,002	1,061	964	1,093	1,034
Zone 5						
Camino	1,647	1,401	1,011	1,591	N/A	1,097
Zone 6						
Riverside	439	421	200	383	240	218

*For location of zones, see Figure 1.1.

[†]Chilling calculation method: 1 unit = 1 hour below 45°F (7°C).

Source: University of California Fruit and Nut Research and Information Center Pomology Weather Services Web site, http://fruitsandnuts.ucdavis.edu/weather/

Frost

While you cannot control whether frost occurs, you can select fruit and nut tree varieties that are hardy enough for the low temperatures in your climate zone (see Chapter 3, and also the *USDA Plant Hardiness Zone Map* listed in this chapter's References). You can also take various steps to reduce the incidence and severity of frost damage to the trees' young green tissues.

There are two types of frosts or freezes: *advective* and *radiation*. Advective freezing occurs when wind moves a cold air mass whose temperature is below freezing into an area, displacing warmer air. This type of freezing is common in America's Midwest as cold fronts move quickly over the land. Radiation frosts occur on calm, clear nights as heat is lost from the earth's surface into the atmosphere, causing cold air to collect near the soil surface. In California, springtime radiation frost is the most common type of damaging frost.

Cold air, being heavier than warm air, will "drain" from a higher place to displace warmer air at lower sites. Orchards planted in valleys and low spots are more susceptible to frost than those planted on sloping terrain. A hillside may have better air drainage and may therefore be a little warmer than the floor of the valley into which it drains. River bottom areas can be frost prone because that's where the coldest air settles. At the same time, though, the temperature of air decreases with increasing altitude, so higher-elevation areas such as the upper foothills and mountains are generally colder than the surrounding lower-elevation areas. Long-time residents and the staff of local garden shops can give you good information about frost hazards in your neighborhood.

Sensitive species such as figs, even when they are dormant, can be seriously damaged by the low temperatures that occur in California's high-elevation and desert areas. Sensitive trees planted close to the south side of a house can benefit from heat that radiates from the building. Heat escaping from a household air vent may be just what a sensitive plant needs at night.

The U.S. National Weather Service issues a frost warning whenever frost is likely. Take steps to protect your trees if frost is predicted and your trees are susceptible to damage (see Chapter 11).

Soils

Soil is composed of minerals, organic matter, air, and water. Mineral particles in soil are defined by their size: sand particles are large enough to be detected by sight and touch, silt particles are medium in size and are too small to be seen individually, and clay particles are microscopic. The organic matter in soil consists of humus (the decayed residues of plants and animals), organisms that live in the soil, and substances such as carbon and nitrogen from decomposed living things. The air in soil is, for the most part, the same as the air in the atmosphere, although it can contain gases produced naturally or as a result of human activity. In some areas the soil is only a few inches deep; in others it can reach depths of 100 feet (30 m) or more. Minerals and organic matter form the solid parts of soil; air and water exist in the pores, the spaces between the solid particles. A soil's texture, structure, and profile should have a significant impact on how you select, plant, irrigate, and care for deciduous fruit and nut trees.

SOIL TEXTURE

The relative proportions of sand, silt, and clay in a soil determine the soil's texture (Figure 1.2). Soil scientists have defined twelve soil textures and have grouped them into three categories:

- *coarse:* sand and loamy sand

- *medium:* sandy loam, loam, silt loam, silt, clay loam, sandy clay loam, and silt clay loam

- *fine:* clay, sandy clay, and silt clay

SOIL CLASSES

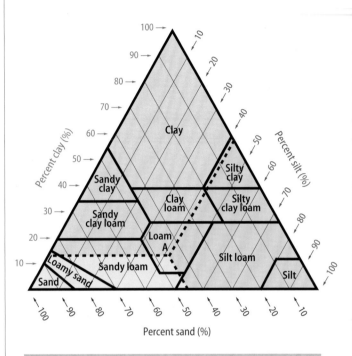

Figure 1.2. The soil texture triangle. The dotted lines indicate the percentages of clay, silt, and sand in loam, a good all-around gardening soil. *Source:* adapted from Wildman and Gowans 1975, p.3.

Coarse soils are often called *light* soils, and fine soils are often called *heavy* soils: these terms refer to how easy or difficult it is to work the soil. A practical way to identify soil texture, as well as moisture, is by the "feel test" (see Figure 5.6). Both the texture and the moisture level of the surface soil can be completely different from those of the soil a few feet deeper.

Loam, sandy loam, and silt loam are good all-around soils for gardening, and they are also good soils for growing fruit and nut trees. Fine-textured clay soils retain water and mineral nutrients well, but they do not allow water and air to move easily, and this makes them prone to waterlogging. Coarse-textured sandy soils drain well and warm quickly in spring, but they do not retain minerals or water well, and fruit and nut trees planted in such soils can be prone to water stress or nutrient deficiencies.

SOIL STRUCTURE

The arrangement of the sand, silt, and clay particles in a soil determines the soil's structure. Individual particles of silt and clay combine in soil to form aggregates, clumps of various sizes and shapes that are held together by organic matter and the binding forces of clay. Soils that lack well-defined aggregates have a structure known as *massive*, with poor water infiltration and percolation.

Soil structure is largely determined by the size of the pores between aggregates. Coarse, single-grained soils like pure sand have large pores that do not retain water or nutrients well. At the other extreme are massive soils, in which the pores are so small that they only allow water and air to move very slowly, if at all. The best soil for plant roots has a granular structure where roots can easily penetrate the pores between the aggregates, yet the pores are still able to hold water, nutrients, and air. This type of soil is said to have good *tilth* and is often associated with a relatively high organic matter content.

SOIL PROFILE

Whereas an annual plant has a root system only a few inches deep, trees can have root systems several feet deep, so they perform best on deep, well-drained soils. Any sudden change in soil texture or any physical impediment such as a claypan, siltpan, or hardpan can restrict root growth and prevent water from percolating deep into the soil profile. As soils age, they form layers known as *horizons*. The uppermost horizon, *topsoil*, may be only a few inches or several feet deep. The topsoil is home to the greatest number of roots and microorganisms and usually is darker than the lower horizons. Under the topsoil is the subsoil, which has fewer roots and microorganisms. The subsoil accumulates clay particles, minerals, and salts that have leached down from the topsoil; it can also become compacted and form a barrier to water and plant roots. Construction work and other digging can disturb the original soil profile by bringing subsoil or rock to the surface.

SOIL PHYSICAL PROBLEMS

Physical problems include soils that are too gravelly or have too heavy a clay texture. There is little you can do to change a soil's texture. If you import sand to mix with the surface soil, you will make it easier to plant annuals but do little to help the deep root system of a tree. The presence of claypans, siltpans, or hardpans will impede both roots and water. If possible, penetrate the barrier pan and mix the pan soil into the soil above and below it. To correct these impervious layers, you may need to use a backhoe or trencher. If you find yourself unable to disrupt them, you may have to install raised beds or drain tubing to carry away excess water.

Soil stratification can impede water movement and root formation in the same way as a pan. A layer of coarse sand, for instance, can impede water percolation just as effectively as a clay layer. Try to mix these layers up before planting, if you can.

Driving on wet soils and working soils when they are wet can break down the soil structure and slow water and air infiltration. Compaction is easier to prevent than to cure. Mulching, adding soil amendments (such as compost or manure), and growing fibrous-rooted cover crops (such as legumes or grasses) can improve the structure, biological activity, and water penetration of a topsoil. If possible, prevent compaction by only plowing and cultivating in the garden when the soil is relatively dry. Keep vehicle activity under the trees to a minimum.

SOIL CHEMICAL PROBLEMS

A soil can have any of a number of chemical problems, including high or low pH, total salt levels that are too high, or excess levels of toxic elements such as sodium, boron, and chloride. Soil analysis can be a useful tool for diagnosing these problems. Nutrient levels in the soil, however, are not a reliable indicator of the nutrient status of the trees and shrubs planted there. UC Cooperative Extension county offices do not offer soil analysis services, but you can ask your local UC Master Gardener program or UC Cooperative Extension county office for the names of commercial laboratories that perform soil analysis if you suspect some kind of chemical toxicity.

Soil reaction, expressed as *pH* on a scale of 0 (acidic) to 14 (basic or alkaline), refers to the acidity or alkalinity of soil. Most plants grow best at a pH of 5.5 to 7.5. You can improve overly acidic soil (pH < 5.5) by adding lime (calcium carbonate) to the soil; alkaline soils (pH > 7.5) can be improved through the addition of soil sulfur or an acidifying nitrogen source such as ammonium sulfate. If your soil has excess levels of toxic elements or salts, you cannot remedy the situation with soil chemical amendments, although gypsum can help displace excess sodium in the soil and thereby improve soil structure. Regardless, it is imperative that you improve the soil's drainage so that the offending chemicals can leach out of the root zone. Fortunately, this type of toxicity is rare in garden soils.

MULCH

A *mulch* is any opaque material that is spread on top of the soil surface. Mulch application may well be the best way to improve a soil's chemical and physical properties and create a soil environment that promotes plant growth. You can use any ground or chopped organic material, including eucalyptus leaves or pine needles. Properly applied, mulch can

- *prevent light from reaching the soil surface, and so suppress weeds*

- *help the soil retain moisture*

- *enhance root growth in the topsoil*

- *encourage earthworms and other beneficial soil organisms*

- *insulate the soil from extremes of heat and cold*

- *prevent soil crusting and new compaction (but not reduce existing compaction)*

- *improve water penetration*

- *provide habitat for natural enemies of pests (see Chapter 11)*

- *create attractive landscaping and good surfaces for walking*

- *over time, improve soil structure and add a small amount of nutrients*

Although a mulch can be made up of many types of material, including straw (green manure), sawdust, decomposed grass clippings, compost, shredded bark, rice hulls, and sheets of black plastic, one of the most effective and economical mulches for fruit and nut trees is wood chips. Wood chips can often be obtained for free from tree trimmers or arborists, or you can make them at home from trimmings using a mechanical chipper or shredder. If you get your chips from a tree trimmer or arborist, make sure before the product is delivered that it is well chipped, without large fragments such as sticks, logs, or palm fronds. Wood chips resist decomposition and are coarse enough to last through at least one growing season, and because they are not incorporated into the soil, they do not tie up soil nitrogen. Unlike black plastic, they do not eventually become a nuisance and wind up in the trash. You can also use compost as a mulch, but it will decompose much more rapidly than coarse materials and will have to be reapplied sooner. Manure-based compost can contain fairly large amounts of salt, which can cause poor growth and cause leaves to burn at the edges.

Before you apply wood chips or other mulching materials, make sure that the garden soil is free of weeds, especially perennial weeds. Thoroughly remove or spray perennial weeds such as bermudagrass, field bindweed, and nutsedge, since all of these will grow through mulch. You can use a preemergent herbicide before applying mulch to reduce weed seed germination, but this step is not necessary if the mulch layer is thick enough and coarse enough to last through the growing season.

Apply mulch in a layer 4 to 6 inches (10 to 15 cm) deep. It is preferable to keep the mulch several inches back from the trunks of the trees, since mulch can trap moisture in the root crown area, encouraging crown rot.

Although the use of mulch has many benefits, it also has some disadvantages. For example, a layer of mulch on the soil can make it harder for you to tell when you need to irrigate. A load of wood chips may also contain weed seeds from trees or shrubs; pull these weeds out as soon as they appear. Sometimes a mulch can encourage gophers and slugs. Also, mulch does break down, so you will have to reapply it as it decomposes.

References

Brenzel, K., ed. 2001. Sunset western garden book. Seventh ed. Menlo Park, CA: Sunset Books.

Faber, B., L. Clement, D. Giraud, and D. Silva. 2002. Soil and fertilizer management. Pages 29–68 in D. Pittenger, ed., California master gardener handbook. Oakland: University of California Division of Agriculture and Natural Resources, Publication 3382.

LaRue, J. H., and R. S. Johnson, eds. 1989. Peaches, plums, and nectarines: Growing and handling for fresh market. Oakland: University of California Division of Agriculture and Natural Resources, Publication 3331.

University of California Fruit and Nut Research and Information Center. Pomology Weather Services Web site. http://fruitsandnuts.ucdavis.edu/weather/ (accessed September 15, 2005)

USDA. 1990. USDA plant hardiness zone map. USDA Miscellaneous Publication 1475. Washington, DC: Government Printing Office. Also available online: http://www.usna.usda.gov/Hardzone

Vossen, P., and D. Silva. 2002. Temperate tree fruit and nut crops. Pages 449–530 in D. Pittenger, ed., California master gardener handbook. Oakland: University of California Division of Agriculture and Natural Resources, Publication 3382.

Wildman, W. E., and K. D. Gowans. 1975. Soil physical environment and how it affects plant growth. Oakland: University of California Division of Agriculture and Natural Resources, Leaflet 2280.

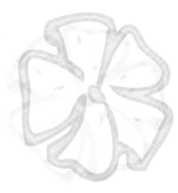

CHAPTER 2

Growth and Development

Chuck A. Ingels

If you want to grow fruit or nut trees successfully, you will need to have some understanding of how they grow and how the environment and various cultural practices influence their development. Although you don't need to be a fruit tree expert, a basic understanding of the main issues involved may save you time and frustration. Because of the many differences between the species and varieties available to a gardener, it is difficult to generalize about all aspects of growth and development. Instead, we will try to introduce you to the key aspects of tree structure and growth processes. With this information, you should be able to understand the rationale for practices described further on in this book.

Tree Organs and Their Functions

ROOTS

Roots serve a crucial role in the vitality of fruit trees and poor root health is a common cause of stunted tree growth. The root system performs multiple functions, including anchorage, water and nutrient absorption, nutrient and carbohydrate storage, and hormone production. For healthy growth and function, roots require water and oxygen from the soil as well as food materials produced in the aboveground shoots.

A root system consists of roots of several different types. Figure 2.1 shows the parts of new *fine roots,* including root tips. Only the portion at the end, beyond the root hair region, actually elongates through the soil. Elongating and recently matured new roots persist for varying lengths of time, but many are short-lived: they live only a few weeks to several months. These new roots are part of the fine root system. Most are 2 millimeters or less in diameter. They are often called *feeder roots.* A small proportion of these roots survive and grow to become part of the large, permanent root system.

APICAL MERISTEMS OF ROOTS

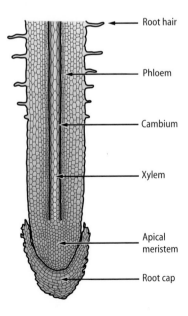

Figure 2.1. Fine root showing temporal root hairs and apical meristem with root cap. *Source:* Pittenger 2002, p. 9.

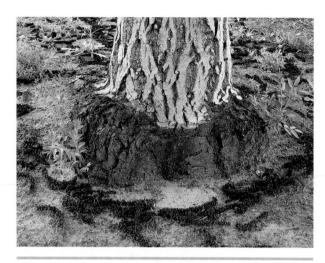

Figure 2.2. Graft union of older English walnut tree with black walnut rootstock. Photo by Maxwell Norton.

Rather than simply being a mirror image of a tree's top growth, root growth for a fruit or nut tree is lateral and relatively shallow. Roots can extend as far as two to three times the width of the canopy's drip line, or even further if soil moisture is available. Taproots, if present, are shallow and branched. Branching (lateral) root formation does not follow a regular pattern, and roots are not uniformly distributed in the soil. In general, the larger the tree, the larger the root mass. Normally, 75 percent or more of the roots of fruit and nut trees can be found in the upper 2 to 3 feet of soil.

THE TRUNK: WHERE SCION MEETS ROOTSTOCK

Most fruit and nut trees purchased in the nursery have been grafted onto rootstocks. Unlike the fruiting variety that makes up the top of a grafted tree, the tree variety used as new rootstock is well adapted to a wide range of soil conditions, it is resistant to soilborne diseases, and in many cases, it determines the mature size of the tree. The fruiting variety grafted onto the rootstock is referred to as the scion (pronounced "sigh'-en"). Most fruit and nut tree species are difficult or impossible to propagate from cuttings, and simply planting the seeds of a desirable variety almost always results in trees that produce fruit of inferior quality. Grafting provides a way to combine the qualities of the best fruit or nut varieties with those of the best roots. (See Chapter 3 for recommended rootstock and scion

varieties.) Figs, pomegranates, and olives usually are not grafted; like home garden grapes, they are usually grown from cuttings.

The *graft union* (also called a *bud union*) can usually be seen on the lower trunk of a young tree. This is the point where a bud from the desirable variety, such as Suncrest peach, was grafted in a field nursery onto a rootstock, such as Nemaguard peach (see Chapter 8). The nursery worker then forced the bud to grow by cutting off the rootstock shoot above the new bud. A newly grafted bud usually begins growing outward but then shifts to growing upward, so fruit and nut trees that you buy at the nursery sometimes have a crook on the trunk (see Chapter 4, Figure 4.6), although most nurseries now stake the trees to make the crook less obvious. After a few years' growth, the crook is almost unnoticeable, although differences in color or size above and below the union are often apparent (Figure 2.2). When you plant a fruit tree, it is important to plant it relatively high in the ground to keep the graft union from going below ground. If the scion is in continual contact with soil, it becomes susceptible to the soilborne diseases that it was grafted onto a rootstock to resist (see Chapter 4). A scion left in contact with the soil may even form its own roots, defeating the purpose of a size-controlling rootstock.

The trunk forms the structural support of a tree. It produces shoots that later form structural scaffold branches, and these in turn form lateral, fruit-bearing branches. Water and nutrients move up through the trunk and some of the carbohydrates produced through photosynthesis move downward to provide nutrition to the roots. A healthy trunk is very important to a tree because any injury to the trunk, such as sunburn or string trimmer damage, can affect the health of the entire tree.

SHOOTS, BRANCHES, AND THE VASCULAR CAMBIUM

Shoots are the new, vegetative growth that trees develop during the growing season, and are also called *current season's growth*. After their first growing season, these shoots and older wood are usually referred to as *branches*, and large branches are often referred to as *limbs*. Shoots generally become either upright and vigorous or lateral and less dominant. Both types serve a useful purpose: upright shoots of young trees often become main limbs, whereas lateral shoots often become fruiting branches. A tree will usually produce more shoots and branches than it needs, and these can then be pruned to optimize fruit production and tree size control. When pruning, you can *head* a shoot or branch (cut a portion off) or *thin* the branch (remove it entirely). Heading stimulates shoot growth below the cut and thinning defines branches and allows more light to penetrate to lower fruiting branches (see Chapter 7 for more information on pruning).

Like the trunk, branches are made up of wood on the inside and bark on the outside. Water and dissolved mineral nutrients are conducted up the active *xylem* tissues of the outer portion of the wood, known as the *sapwood*. The inner wood, known as *heartwood*, consists of inactive xylem cells. These dead xylem cells no longer conduct substantial amounts of water, but they provide structural strength for the trunk and branches and provide a food storage area. Products of photosynthesis (mainly carbohydrates) are transported away from the leaves and throughout the tree and roots through tissues known as the *phloem*. Active phloem tissues can be found on the inner bark, near the vascular cambium (see below). Phloem and xylem together are known as the vascular tissues. They usually form a continuous, multibranched system reaching from a tree's root tips to its leaf tips (Figure 2.3).

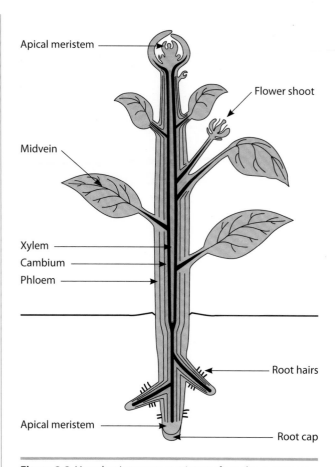

Figure 2.3. Vascular tissues are continuous from the root tips to the shoot tips. *Source:* Pittenger 2002, p. 10.

Growth by Meristems

Parts of a tree grow both by elongating and by thickening. Both forms of growth occur by means of active cell division in connected tissues known as *meristems,* which are only a few cells in thickness. Cells of the meristem divide to reproduce, grow, and develop new tissues. The two most common meristems are the apical meristem, which forms terminal (lengthwise) growth, and the vascular cambium, which forms lateral (widthwise) growth.

Apical meristems are found in root tips, shoot tips, and buds and are responsible for the lengthening of these plant parts. Aboveground apical meristematic tissues may produce shoots (vegetative growth) or flowers (reproductive growth).

The vascular cambium, often simply called the cambium, is a thin layer of actively growing cells found between the outer wood and the inner bark.

The cambium produces the tissues for lateral growth of a tree's trunk and limbs as it gives rise to xylem on the inner (wood) side and phloem on the outer (bark) side. The seasonal additions of cambial growth can be seen as concentric rings in a cross-section of a trunk or branch (Figure 2.4). If you were to pound a nail part way into the trunk, the nail would appear to grow shorter and shorter over passing years as the cambium would grow outward. Eventually, the nail would become completely embedded within the trunk. Also, the nail would not move upward but would remain at the same height, since trunk growth is only outward, not upward. The cambium layer is critically important when you are budding and grafting trees, since these tissues must be properly matched and their cells must actively divide to form connective tissues between the existing tree and the newly grafted plant part (see Chapter 8).

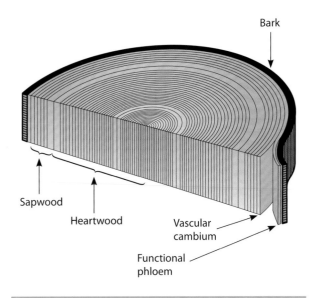

Bark

Sapwood

Heartwood

Vascular
cambium

Functional
phloem

Figure 2.4. Cross-section of a typical deciduous fruit tree trunk, showing vascular cambium, xylem (wood) tissue, and phloem (bark) on the outside. The seasonal cycle of cambial growth can be seen as concentric rings. *Source:* Pittenger 2002, p. 10.

Buds

Trees produce flower buds, which form flowers, and vegetative buds, which form shoots. Both types of bud contain apical meristems. Vegetative buds are found at shoot tips (terminal buds) and laterally along the sides of current-season shoots, tucked between the leaf stem (petiole) and the shoot in the *leaf axil*. Another type of vegetative bud is the *adventitious* bud, which can form on older wood where no bud previously existed or where a bud has become buried by thick bark. Adventitious buds can give rise to strong upright shoots that arise from roots or the rootstock *(suckers)*, main branches *(watersprouts)*, and below large pruning cuts. A shoot that grows from an adventitious bud on the scion can usually be trained into a major fruit-bearing branch, although its point of attachment to the limb is often weaker than that of other branches because the bud develops on the outer layers of the wood.

From late fall through early winter, all buds are dormant. During the growing season, not all of the vegetative buds grow into shoots. Some buds remain at rest, essentially dormant, and are sometimes referred to as *latent buds*. Latent buds are kept from growing by

an inhibiting hormone known as auxin or indoleacetic acid (IAA). Auxin is produced in shoot tips and leaves and it moves down the shoot through the phloem, preventing lateral bud growth. This phenomenon is more pronounced in *apically dominant* upright species such as cherry, pear, and pistachio, whereas far more natural branching occurs with less apically dominant species such as peach, almond, and pomegranate. You can temporarily suspend the inhibiting effect of auxin by cutting off a portion of a shoot or branch *(heading)* or simply removing *(girdling)* or filing *(notching)* a small strip of bark above a bud whose growth you wish to encourage, such as a bud grafted onto a shoot (see Chapter 8). Because auxin is strongly influenced by gravity, the practice of bending the branches of an apically dominant tree outward is a strategy for producing more lateral shoots, particularly fruiting shoots (see Chapter 7).

Flowers and shoots that grow in the spring originate from buds that started forming the previous summer. In a year with especially heavy fruit production, a tree may initiate far fewer flower buds. Under these conditions, the tree produces hormones that send a chemical message to the developing buds telling them not to initiate flower buds. Also, the heavy use of carbohydrates to produce a large crop load reduces the availability of carbohydrates for both shoot growth and flower bud formation. The overall result is that there are fewer flowers and fruit the following year, which in turn allows the tree to grow more vigorously and produce more flower buds. This is the basic mechanism of an *alternate bearing* cycle. Some species and varieties exhibit alternate bearing more strongly than others. Only appropriate pruning and early fruit thinning can bring fruit production and tree vigor into balance. Dormant pruning after a small crop season should be relatively heavy to remove more of the flower buds, whereas pruning after a large crop year should be relatively light to leave more buds on the tree and encourage flowering and fruit formation the next year.

To grow fruit and nut trees successfully, you need to be able to balance crop load and vegetative growth. On newly planted trees, however, you should remove any fruit that form during the first year after planting so the tree can use its energy (carbohydrates) to create a well-developed structure of branches and roots.

Excessive fruit production in the first three years can debilitate a tree for many years afterward because the tree's energy has been directed into the fruit rather than into shoot growth. Vegetative growth on many young standard and semidwarf fruit trees is often substantial, though, so you should encourage the maximum number of flower buds to develop on particularly vigorous trees, even in the second and third years. The way to promote flower buds on young trees is by allowing lateral shoots to grow. You can accelerate tree development and flower bud formation by practicing judicious summer pruning and tipping during the first few years (see Chapter 7). Some tree types, such as lateral-bearing walnuts and some dwarf and spur-type apples, need heavier dormant pruning to encourage vegetative growth lest they settle into excessive fruit production with little tree growth.

LEAVES

Leaves are the structures where the tree collects sunlight and conducts photosynthesis, producing food in the form of carbohydrates for the tree. The underside of the leaves has tiny openings called *stomates* (also known as stomata). The stomates open in daylight to allow free movement of gases such as carbon dioxide and oxygen, but they also cool the leaf by allowing water vapor to escape.

Most fruit and nut tree leaves are *simple* in form, with a distinct blade and petiole (leaf stem). Some species, such as walnut, pecan, and pomegranate, have *compound* leaves in which each leaf is divided into several leaflets along a central stem.

FLOWERS

Flowers are the structures in which plants sexually reproduce after pollination, forming offspring that differ genetically from the parents. The principal male structure of a flower is the *stamen*, at the tip of which is the pollen-bearing *anther* (Figure 2.5). The principal female structure is the *pistil*, which contains the *ovary* at its base, the elongated *style* or *styles* above the ovary, and the pollen-receiving *stigma* at its tip. In most species, it is the ovary that enlarges to form the fruit or nut.

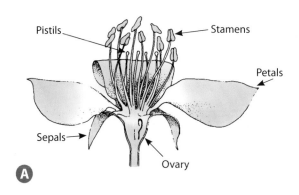

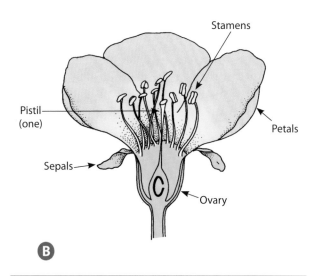

Figure 2.5. (A) Generalized diagram of a pome fruit flower *(apple shown here)*. *Source:* Westwood 1993, p. 220. **(B)** Generalized diagram of a stone fruit flower. *Source:* Westwood 1993, p. 220.

A. Pome

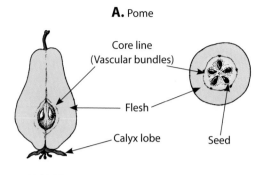

Core line
(Vascular bundles)

Flesh

Calyx lobe

Seed

B. Drupe or stone fruit

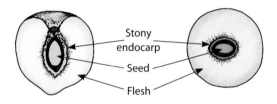

Stony
endocarp

Seed

Flesh

C. Nut

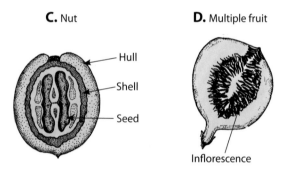

Hull

Shell

Seed

D. Multiple fruit

Inflorescence

Figure 2.6. Cross-sections of selected fruits and nuts showing the structure of seeds: **(A)** pome fruit (pear); **(B)** drupe or stone fruit (peach); **(C)** nut (walnut); **(D)** multiple fruit (fig). *Source:* After Westwood 1993 p. 71 and Hasey et al. 1994, p. 88.

Flowers of most deciduous fruit and nut tree species are *perfect* (also called *complete*); that is, both male and female structures are present in the same flower. Some species have separate male and female flowers, and these flowers are known as *imperfect* or *incomplete*. Male flowers are termed *staminate* and female flowers are known as *pistillate.* Walnuts, pecans, chestnuts, and filberts or hazelnuts are *monoecious,* which means that they have separate male and female flowers on the same tree. In contrast, pistachios and many kiwifruit varieties are *dioecious,* with only male or only female flowers on any given tree.

Pollination and Fertilization

Pollination is the transfer of pollen from a flower's anther to the stigma of a compatible flower—whether that is the same flower or a different flower. *Fertilization* is the successful union of the pollen tube with the egg to begin development of the fruit. *Fruit set* occurs shortly after petal fall, after the egg has been fertilized. When fertilization fails to occur, the fruit usually falls off.

Most deciduous fruits and almonds require pollination by insect *pollinators,* mainly honey bees but also other insects such as mason orchard bees. *Parthenocarpic* fruit, such as Bartlett pear in many areas of California, set fruit without pollination or seed development. With *self-fruitful* species and varieties, bees visiting flowers of a single variety can pollinate any flower on that tree, and that flower will develop into fruit. With *self-unfruitful* types, bees must carry pollen from a tree of a different, compatible variety (the *pollinizer*) to the fruiting tree's female flowers in order for pollination to occur. Cross-pollination of both trees may also occur when the pollen of either tree is used to pollinate the flowers of the other. *Partially self-fruitful* varieties will set some fruit when pollinated from other flowers on the same tree, but they set a better crop if pollinated from a different variety.

On trees that produce a lot of blossoms, only a small proportion of the blossoms need to set fruit in order to provide a full crop. In some years, adverse weather during bloom may greatly reduce pollination or fertilization. Proper pruning to provide an adequate number of blossoms will ensure a good crop of fruit in most years, since you can also use fruit thinning to regulate the number of fruit in a heavy set year. Of course, if you prune very little and leave an excessive number of flowers, you may have to deal with a large amount of time-consuming fruit thinning after fruit set.

Walnuts, pecans, chestnuts, pistachios, and filberts are wind pollinated. The male flower structure of these nut crops (except for pistachio), called a *catkin*, is elongated and sheds large amounts of pollen. The female flowers of walnuts and pecans are small and inconspicuous, consisting primarily of an ovary and two elongated, curved stigmas (see Figure 2.9). These flowers appear at the tips of current-season shoots after leaves begin to grow in the spring. In filberts, the female flowers in the winter look like small red tufts (stigmas) protruding from the bud. Female chestnut flowers are attached to the lower portion of some of the catkins. The stigmas of all of these nut trees, when moist, receive whatever pollen happens to land on them. With the exception of pistachio, these species are self-fruitful, but the catkins' period of pollen shedding does not completely overlap with the female flowers' period of receptivity. For this reason, growers generally provide a different variety whose male flowers complete the overlap with the main variety's female flowers, and often vice-versa.

Fruit

A tree's fruit functions to help disperse seeds when it is eaten by animals or when it rolls on the ground, floats in water, or blows in the wind to a new growing site. From a human perspective, their primary purpose is to provide a nutritious food source. Propagation by seed is mainly seen as a practice used to develop new fruit or nut varieties.

There are a few basic types of fruit that represent most of the tree fruits and nuts that we eat. *Pome fruits* include apple, pear, pomegranate, and quince. Their five stigmas arise together above the ovary, and the fruit is derived from the fusion of the ovary, calyx cup (sepals), and floral tube (Figure 2.6A). The fleshy part of the pome fruit that is eaten is not the ovary, as with stone fruits, but the calyx and receptacle tissue.

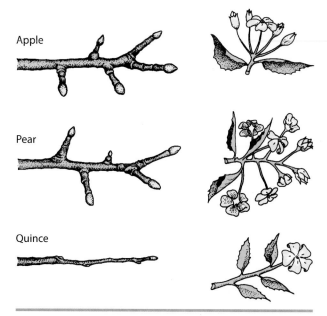

Figure 2.7. Pome fruit flowering habits. *Source:* After Westwood 1993, p. 220.

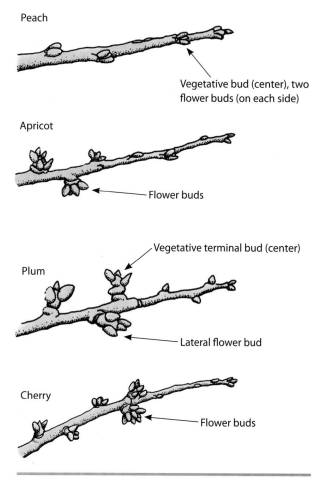

Figure 2.8. Stone fruit flowering habits. *Source:* After Westwood 1993, pp. 220–221.

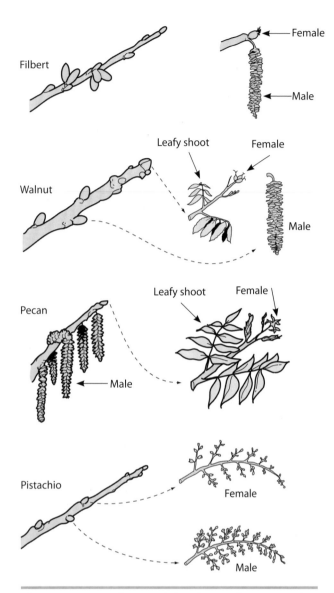

Figure 2.9. Nut crop flowering habits. *Source:* After Westwood 1993, pp. 224–225.

Stone fruits (apricot, cherry, nectarine and peach, and plum) (Figure 2.6B), almonds, and pistachios, as well as olives, are known botanically as *drupe* fruits. The drupe is a one-seeded fruit derived entirely from an ovary with a stony endocarp (pit) containing the seed.

Tree nut crops, except for almond, are hard, usually one-seeded fruit derived from the fusion of ovary, petals, and sepals (Figure 2.6C; see also Figure 2.9). The primary nutrient content of fleshy fruits consists of sugars, vitamins, and fiber, whereas the nutrition derived from a nut is primarily fat (oil) and protein. Most nuts have a high oil content and low carbohydrate content, but the edible portion of the chestnut is a high-carbohydrate, low-oil-content nut.

The flower structure of the fig (Figure 2.6D) is known as a *syconium.* The structure is cup shaped and the flowers develop on the interior surface of the cup, with a small opening at the tip. The fig is a multiple fruit derived from the fusion of ovaries and receptacles.

Beyond these general characteristics, fruit and nut tree species have a wide variety of flowering and fruiting habits. See Figures 2.7 through 2.11 and Table 7.1 in Chapter 7 for more detailed information.

Biology of Plant Growth

Fruit and nut tree growth is a process of cell division and cell growth that results in the development of new or expanded plant tissues, organs, and other structures. Tree growth requires sunlight and a source of water and mineral nutrients. The woody framework of a tree provides the structural support for the exposure of a maximum number of leaves to light in order to capture the sun's energy. The tree's success as a solar energy collector depends on its ability to efficiently capture and convert light energy into chemical energy (that is, carbohydrates, mainly sugar) and then to transport, store, and utilize that chemical energy. Wood and bark provide the vascular tissue that transports water and nutrients to leaves and transports sugar and hormones away from the leaves to other parts of the tree. Woody tissues also provide a site for carbohydrate and nutrient storage through the winter.

Photosynthesis and Respiration

Photosynthesis is the process by which the sun's energy is trapped in the green pigments of leaves *(chlorophyll)*, converted into chemical energy, and used to convert carbon dioxide and water into simple sugars. A by-product of this reaction is oxygen, which is released into the atmosphere. Photosynthesis is a complex set of reactions involving many of the nutrients required by a plant, including nitrogen, phosphorus, potassium, magnesium, iron, and manganese. These nutrients are also (1) combined with carbohydrates to synthesize the more-complex compounds needed to produce new cells for growth, (2) used in the conversion to more-complex carbohydrates (complex sugars and starch) or fats and stored in fruits, seeds, stems, or roots, or (3) involved in the biological combustion that releases the chemical energy needed for cells to function (see Respiration, below).

Carbon dioxide diffuses through specialized pores called stomates on the underside of leaves, which open and close based on environmental conditions. For photosynthesis to occur, the stomates must be open, adequate light must be striking the leaf, and water must be available to the plant. The opening of the stomates represents a trade-off for the plant, as it allows carbon dioxide to enter the leaf for photosynthesis but allows water to escape through evaporation.

Adequate sunlight—at least 6 to 8 hours of full sunlight per day—is crucial for sufficient photosynthesis to produce flower buds and ripen fruit. Also, if interior leaves in canopies become excessively shaded, those leaves gradually lose their capacity to carry on high rates of photosynthesis. Such leaves gradually become thin and yellow and, unless the canopy is opened up to allow more light in, they drop prematurely and the branch may die. For this reason, proper pruning, especially summer pruning, is often important to the health of lower fruiting branches.

Respiration is the process in which carbohydrates are biologically broken down (oxidized) and energy is released. In simple terms, it is the reverse process of photosynthesis. Respiration takes place in cells through a series of reactions in which complex carbohydrates are broken down into simple carbohydrates, carbon dioxide, and water. The energy thus released is used to carry on metabolism in various parts of the tree. Respiration

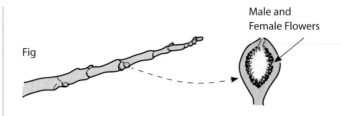

Figure 2.10. Fig flowering habit. *Source:* After Westwood 1993, p. 222.

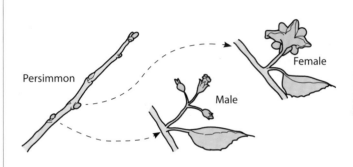

Figure 2.11. Persimmon flowering structure. *Source:* After Westwood 1993, p. 223.

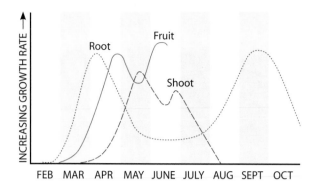

Figure 2.12. Generalized diagram of root, shoot, and fruit growth throughout the year.

occurs at all times in plants, even in harvested fruits and nuts. Respiration rates are highest in rapidly growing tissues and lowest in dormant tissues.

UPTAKE AND MOVEMENT OF WATER AND NUTRIENTS

Adequate water and mineral nutrients are crucial for the production of healthy, fruitful trees. Nearly all of the water and mineral nutrients are absorbed from the soil through the fine root system. Most of the soil water moves into the plant passively through diffusion (see below), whereas most nutrients are taken up by the roots through active transport across root cell membranes. Soils contains large amounts of nutrients, but only a fraction of these nutrients are available to plants, since roots can only take up nutrients that are dissolved in the soil water.

The opening of stomates to allow carbon dioxide into the leaf also exposes the water within the leaf to air, where it can evaporate. This is the first step in the process of *transpiration.* Water evaporation creates a tension or suction in the leaf. The combined suction of the tree's many leaves is transmitted along a gradient through the plant so that it ultimately pulls the soil water out of the soil and up through the plant. This creates a continuously flowing column of water in the xylem for as long as the stomates are open and water is available in the soil. When trees suffer from lack of water, their stomates tend to close, inhibiting photosynthesis by reducing the availability of both

carbon dioxide and water in the leaf. The fact that the amount of water and the amount of carbon dioxide in a leaf depend on the same mechanism is what ties tree water use so closely to tree growth: stomate closure reduces carbohydrate production, which is essential for shoot growth and fruit development.

The rate of transpiration depends on environmental factors that affect the evaporation rate and the degree to which stomates open, as well as the amount of available soil water. For example, stomates are often fully open and evaporation (and photosynthesis) is greatest on warm, sunny days with low relative humidity. Transpiration also helps to cool trees on hot days and serves to transport minerals absorbed from the soil and organic compounds produced in the roots to aboveground plant cells via the xylem. Transpiration virtually ceases at night because the stomates close.

Translocation is the movement of mineral nutrients, carbohydrates, plant hormones, and other dissolved compounds from one part of the plant to another. It can occur from cell to cell in the space between cells, but for the most part it takes place in the xylem and phloem tissues (see Figure 2.3). Through translocation, essential mineral nutrients from the roots are distributed to other tissues and carbohydrates produced in the leaves are moved to meristematic areas (shoot and root tips, cambium, and buds), storage organs (fruits, seeds, stems, and roots), and other tissues.

Growth Cycle in Deciduous Fruit Trees

You can see a generalized graph of root, shoot, and fruit in stone fruits in Figure 2.12. The roots of fruit trees begin growing a week or more before buds begin to swell. Root growth is very active in early spring and then slows during fruit enlargement, but it increases again in late summer or early fall. Shoot growth is most active in spring and then slows or ceases in summer. Shoot growth may continue through the summer for young trees or topped fruit bushes (see Chapter 7). A graph of the rate of fruit growth for many species follows a sigmoid (S-shaped) curve; in some species, a lag phase makes it into a double-sigmoid curve.

WINTER

In winter, deciduous trees go through their dormant stage. Fruit tree species require varying amounts of winter chilling in order to break dormancy and grow properly, flower, and produce quality fruit over the following year (see Chapter 1). Late in the dormant period, buds begin to swell as the weather warms. Buds may begin to swell as early as January if there is a period of warm weather.

Winter is also the time to prune—or to do touch-up pruning if you primarily use summer pruning—to manage the canopy. With no leaves on the trees, it is easy to see the branch structure and therefore easier to see where to make cuts than during the growing season.

Carbohydrates and nutrients, particularly nitrogen, are stored in the tree's roots and other woody tissues to be used for springtime flower and shoot growth. For this reason, and because trees take most of their nitrogen up with the flow of water during the growing season, winter is not the time to fertilize with nitrogen.

Root growth nearly ceases during the early dormant period, but a very small amount of growth does occur (Figure 2.12). Carbohydrates and nutrients, particularly nitrogen, are stored in roots and other woody tissues for later use in springtime flower and shoot growth. Active root growth begins one or more weeks before bud swell. A well-drained soil is especially important at this time of year because the new roots of many species can be killed by waterlogging (low soil oxygen), and this initial root growth period comes at a time when rains are frequent in many areas of California.

SPRING

Although almonds and many stone fruits often bloom before the official first day of spring (March 21), pomologists usually consider spring to begin with flowering and growth. Flowering of almonds, stone fruits, and pome fruits usually occurs just before or simultaneously with the beginning of vegetative growth, whereas flowering of persimmons, pomegranates, and walnuts comes after growth begins.

Species that flower very early, such as almonds and plums, are more susceptible to frost damage, lack of pollination, and, because rainfall is often more abundant, disease infection.

Spring is the time of maximum vegetative growth. Shoot elongation is most rapid then, and the leaves quickly develop and mature for maximum photosynthesis. When leaves mature, they develop a waxy or leathery texture that inhibits the inward and outward movement of water—for this reason, foliar nutrient applications are often made by mid-spring. Typically, a mature tree's shoot growth will cease or greatly slow by late spring or early summer, at which time a terminal bud will set at the shoot tip; this cessation of growth occurs earliest in the year on stressed trees. For most species, some further growth may occur during the summer, but overall growth at that time is far less than in the spring. Spring is the time to begin summer pruning to shape young trees or to remove or tip unwanted vigorous shoots on mature trees. You can identify these shoots at a fairly early stage since they usually grow straight up and are more vigorous than lateral shoots. Left unchecked, these shoots will often branch out and shade lower fruiting wood by summer.

For most species, spring is also the period of maximum fruit growth. In the early stages, fruit growth is caused mainly by cell division, whereas in the later stages most fruit growth is by cell expansion. Some varieties of apricots, cherries, and peaches ripen in late spring, especially in warmer regions. During late spring and summer, flower buds begin to form for the next spring's flowers. Excess fruit set in the spring may cause hormonal signals telling the tree to produce more vegetative buds and fewer flower buds. For this reason, fruit thinning is necessary in many species to prevent alternate bearing patterns (see Chapter 9).

Root growth is reduced during mid- to late spring because most of the tree's chemical energy is directed toward shoot and fruit growth. One or more flushes of root growth can occur in late summer as shoot growth diminishes and fruit are harvested.

SUMMER

Summer is the time of reduced vegetative growth and of fruit ripening for almonds and many fruit species. You should, however, prune unwanted vigorous upright shoots and train young tree shoots at least once in early to midsummer. Summer pruning allows more sunlight to reach the leaves of lower fruiting wood, and that improves their flower bud development and consequently fruit production. Summer pruning can also help reduce tree vigor—an important practice if you have trees with excess shoot growth.

Much of the tree's carbohydrate energy is directed into fruit growth and ripening during the summer. Flower bud formation for the next year's flowers occurs mainly during summer. If there is too much fruit production, correspondingly fewer flower buds will form; by the same token, more flower buds will often form if the current season's fruit production is low. Root growth is usually less in early summer, but increases again in late summer.

FALL

Fall is harvest time for late apples, walnuts, pecans, chestnuts, and some late-maturing fruit such as figs, persimmons, and pomegranates. The late summer flush of root growth experienced by many species may continue into early fall. By late fall, shoot growth ceases completely and terminal buds appear at the tips of virtually all shoots: this is technically the beginning of dormancy. The translocation of nitrogen and other nutrients back into woody tissues for overwinter storage comes before leaf fall and triggers the cessation of chlorophyll production in the leaves. With the disappearance of chlorophyll, other pigments already in the leaves become visible and the leaves turn yellow or other fall colors.

References

Kourik, R. 1986. Designing and maintaining your edible landscape naturally. Santa Rosa, CA: Metamorphic Press.

LaRue, J. H., and R. S. Johnson, eds. 1989. Peaches, plums, and nectarines: Growing and handling for fresh market. Oakland: University of California Division of Agriculture and Natural Resources, Publication 3331.

Micke, W. C., ed. 1996. Almond production manual. Oakland: University of California Division of Agriculture and Natural Resources, Publication 3364.

Pittenger, D. 2002. Introduction to horticulture. Pages 5–28 in D. Pittenger, ed., California master gardener handbook. Oakland: University of California Division of Agriculture and Natural Resources, Publication 3382.

Ramos, D. E., ed. 1998. Walnut production manual. Oakland: University of California Division of Agriculture and Natural Resources, Publication 3373.

Vossen, P., and D. Silva. 2002. Temperate tree fruit and nut crops. Pages 449–530 in D. Pittenger, ed., California master gardener handbook. Oakland: University of California Division of Agriculture and Natural Resources, Publication 3382.

Westwood, M. N. 1993. Temperate zone pomology: Physiology and culture, 3rd ed. Portland, OR: Timber Press.

CHAPTER 3

Varieties and Rootstocks

Paul M. Vossen

Your selection of the proper type and variety of fruit or nut tree for your home garden plays a vital role in determining whether that tree will grow well and bear fruit. A fruit or nut tree planted in a situation for which it is not suited may not perform successfully no matter how well you take care of it: it may grow too much or too little, fail to bloom or set fruit, and be susceptible to diseases and attack by insects or other pests.

In this chapter you will find information on selected fruit and nut tree varieties that are commonly grown in home gardens in California. The relative harvest periods indicated in this chapter (early, midseason, and late) are broad, general classifications. They may vary from year to year and can be influenced by many factors, especially the climate in your area. Also, in any given climate zone, home gardeners typically harvest later in the season than commercial growers do because they have the luxury of letting home fruit ripen fully on the tree.

The information in this chapter is adapted from the temperate tree fruit and nut crops chapter of the *California Master Gardener Handbook* (UC ANR Publication 3382) and other reliable sources. Also, comments on the flavor, texture, and overall quality of fruits and nuts reflect the authors' tastes and should be taken as general guidelines only. Please note that we do not cover grapes or kiwifruit in this book; for information on growing these crops in the home garden, see Chapter 15 of the *California Master Gardener Handbook* (UC ANR 3382).

Pome Fruits

APPLES (*MALUS DOMESTICA*)

Apples are adapted to many areas of California. Most red-skinned varieties require a cool climate to achieve their characteristic coloration. Winter chilling requirements for most varieties are 500 to 1,000 hours below 45°F (7°C); low-chill varieties need about 300 to 600 hours below 45°F (see Tables 1.1 and 1.2 in Chapter 1). Foggy days and dews can cause heavy cosmetic russetting on fruit. There are hundreds of apple varieties, and some varieties have several strains, each with its own characteristics. Spur-type varieties (short shoot growth and abundant spur production) do poorly on dwarfing rootstocks; they are best grown on seedling rootstocks. Several of the available rootstocks impart dwarfing and pest resistance (see below). Apple varieties exhibit considerable genetic diversity. Some require as few as 70 days to mature; others take 180 days or more. Some varieties are very cold hardy; others are tender. Nearly all apple varieties require cross-pollination from another variety that blooms at the same time and produces abundant, viable pollen. Many varieties are self-unfruitful and have sterile pollen; others are partially self-fruitful (not all of their pollen is viable); a few actually are self-fruitful. The best time to plant apple trees is from January to March.

Rootstocks

Listed below are the main apple rootstocks used in California, from least to most dwarfing:

Seedling (from any source). *Used for nonirrigated sites, low-vigor sites, spur-type varieties, or weaker varieties. Very vigorous, produces large, full-sized trees that come into bearing late (in 7 to 10 years). Susceptible to woolly apple aphid. A tree on this rootstock can fill a 30-by-30-foot (9-by-9-m) space and grow to 20 feet (6 m) tall.*

M111. *Semidwarf rootstock. Usually produces a tree 80 percent of the size of the same variety grown on seedling rootstock. Tolerates many soil conditions. Reportedly resistant to woolly apple aphid. Imparts earlier bearing than seedling rootstock, but not as early as more dwarfing rootstocks. Requires irrigation. Vigor is difficult to control.*

M106. *Semidwarf rootstock. Usually produces a tree about 65 to 75 percent of the size of the same variety grown on seedling rootstock. Provides good anchorage. Imparts early bearing of fruit and is easily propagated. Reportedly resistant to woolly apple aphid. Requires irrigation. Tree spacing ranges from 6 by 12 feet to 10 by 18 feet (2 by 3.5 m to 3 by 5.5 m).*

M7a. *Semidwarf rootstock. Usually produces a tree about 60 percent of the size of the same variety grown on seedling rootstock. Performs well in irrigated replant situations, but tends to sucker. Spacing is same as for M106.*

M26. *Semidwarf to dwarfing rootstock. Usually produces a tree 30 to 50 percent of the size of the same variety grown on seedling rootstock. Performs poorly in most California locations. May need a trellis and is highly susceptible to fire blight disease.*

M9. *Dwarfing rootstock. Usually produces a very small tree, less than 30 percent of the size of the same variety grown on seedling rootstock. This is the most commonly planted rootstock in commercial plantings, worldwide. It can be a poor performer, however, if not adequately managed. Poorly anchored, has brittle root system. Must be trellised.*

Standard Varieties

Following are the apple fruiting varieties used in California, from earliest to latest ripening:

Gala. *Early. Small to medium-sized, conical red apple with excellent flavor and keeping qualities. The best variety for the early season. Will not cross-pollinate Golden Delicious.*

Gravenstein. *Early. Medium-large fruit with short, fat stem. Skin color is greenish yellow overlaid with red stripes. Excellent flavor when fully ripe. Crisp, sub-acid, and aromatic. A good sauce and pie apple. Stores and ships poorly. High percentage of windfalls. Sterile pollen. Popular on California's North Coast, but not suited to the heat of the Central Valley.*

Jonathan. *Midseason. Round, red apple with pure white flesh. Crisp, juicy, and slightly sub-acid. Excellent for eating fresh or making sauce or juice. Highly susceptible to mildew, fire blight, and Jonathan spot. Nice red color, but is somewhat tart and gets soft on the tree in the heat of the Central Valley.*

McIntosh. *Midseason. Flat-shaped red fruit with white flesh. It has a great aromatic flavor when harvested at its peak. Macoun is a new and improved McIntosh type. The original (McIntosh) almost never develops the same quality of fruit in California as it does when grown in the East and Midwest. Fruit becomes soft easily in the hot, dry California climate. Susceptible to fire blight, mildew, and scab.*

Golden Delicious. *Midseason. Conic-shaped apple with a long stem, yellow to green skin, yellow flesh, and russet dots. Sweet, juicy, fine-textured. Number one on the North Coast for fresh eating quality and for processing. Stores well, but is susceptible to bitter pit, bruising, and russetting. Erratic in self-fruitfulness.*

Red Delicious. *Midseason. Conical apple with tapered base and five distinct lobes. Skin color varies from solid red to a mixture of red and green stripes. Crisp, sweet, mild-flavored yellow flesh. Many strains. Used fresh. Stores well. Colors very poorly in the Central Valley heat.*

Fuji. *Late. Round to flat apple with a very sweet yellow-orange flesh. Skin color is red if given enough sunlight and cool temperatures. One of the best sweet eating apples. Stores well. Very susceptible to fire blight.*

Granny Smith. *Late. Round, green- to yellow-skinned apple that is quite firm. Keeps very well. Crisp flesh. If harvested early, it is green and tart. Late-harvested fruit are yellow-skinned and sweet.*

Pink Lady. *Late. A very crisp, conical apple with pink skin and very white flesh. Excellent, sweet-tart flavor. Fruit is firm, keeps well, and is very late maturing (15 days after Granny Smith). Very susceptible to fire blight.*

Rome Beauty. *Late. Round fruit with a deep cavity, no lobes, and little russet. Several strains, including the old standard and several new, solid red-skinned strains, such as Taylor and Law. Stores moderately well. Tree leafs out late, flowers late, and produces flowers and fruit on long spur growth that requires modification in pruning. Good for baking. Colors very poorly in the heat of the Central Valley.*

Newtown Pippin. *Late. A greenish yellow apple that is grown primarily in the Central Coast area. It usually has distinctive russetting on the shoulder. It is self-fruitful, but does better with cross-pollination, and produces a very good-tasting fruit if allowed to fully mature.*

Spur-Type Varieties

Strains (mutations) of the original varieties that have shorter internodes and are naturally dwarfing. Best on seedling rootstock.

Golden Delicious Spur: Starkspur, Goldspur.

Red Delicious Spur: Bisbee Spur, Red Chief, Arkansas Black Spur.

Low-Chill Varieties

These varieties are more suitable for the lower latitudes of Southern California because they have low winter chilling requirements (fewer than 300 hours).

Anna, Beverly Hills, Dorsett Golden, Einshemer, Fuji, Gala, Gordon, Tropical Beauty.

Antique Varieties

These varieties do well in much of California if there is adequate chilling and if summer heat is not too intense. They are hard trees to find because they lack commercial value. Many have excellent flavor and perform well in home gardens.

Arkansas Black, Black Twig, Wagner, Baldwin, Cox's Orange Pippin, E. Spitzenburg, Winter Banana, Northern Spy, Winesap, Smith Cider, Red Golden, Rhode Island Greening, Staymen Winesap, Sierra Beauty, Golden Russet, Hudson's Golden Gem, Ashmead's Kernel.

Early Summer Varieties

These varieties do not have the same high quality characteristics of standard varieties, but they ripen early when no other fresh apples are available. They are excellent for eating fresh right off the tree and make a good cooking apple.

Anna. *An early season, low-chill variety with red-pink skin. Usually harvested in June.*

Gravenstein. *See above, under Standard Varieties.*

Vista Bell. *Terminal bearing habit, white-fleshed fruit with red skin, stores well.*

Paulared. *High-quality, white flesh; stores fairly well; tree requires fruit thinning.*

Akane. *Similar to Jonathan but earlier; good, solid red color, white flesh; good for eating fresh and making juice.*

Jonamac. *Similar to McIntosh but has better color, firmness, and storage life.*

Williams Pride. *See comments below, under "Disease-Resistant Varieties."*

Disease-Resistant Varieties

Several scab-resistant apple varieties have been developed in breeding programs for the Eastern U.S. where this disease is quite severe due to summer humidity and rain. Some have received limited testing here under California growing conditions. In growing districts with extended spring rains, these varieties will have few or no disease problems.

Enterprise. *A large-fruited, late-maturing, dense, crisp variety that has good keeping qualities. The color is dark red over a yellow-green background. This is one of the best of the scab-resistant varieties.*

Freedom. *A late-season variety with large, red fruit and mild flavor; not completely immune to scab.*

Goldrush. *A scab-immune selection with Golden Delicious parentage. Fruit is late-maturing, medium-sized, firm-textured, and tart, with an excellent flavor and golden skin. Stores well.*

Pristine. *This moderate to large, tart, yellow apple is immune to scab and resistant to fire blight and mildew.*

Liberty. *One of the best-quality apples of the disease-resistant varieties, Liberty is very productive and requires heavy early thinning to achieve good fruit size. It ripens in midseason and has an attractive red color with some striping and a good sweet flavor.*

Priscilla. *A late-season variety with small red fruit, soft flesh, and mild flavor.*

Williams Pride. *An early-maturing, scab-immune variety that is also resistant to fire blight and mildew. The fruit is medium to large with a round to oblong shape. It has an attractive coloration of red stripes on a green-yellow background.*

PEARS (*PYRUS COMMUNIS, PYRUS SEROTINA*)

Of all the deciduous fruit tree species, pears are the most tolerant of wet soil conditions, but they perform best on deep, well-drained sites. Pears are also the most pest-ridden of all fruit trees and generally require more spraying than other types of fruit to keep them free of pests and diseases. Pear trees get very large, requiring a spacing of 18 by 18 feet (5.5 by 5.5 m) if not planted on dwarfing rootstock and not pruned in summer. Pear trees have a tendency toward very upright growth and must be trained to develop a spreading growth habit.

Most pear varieties are self-unfruitful and require cross-pollination from another variety to set a good crop. An exception is Bartlett pear in most areas of California, where the trees are self-fruitful, setting crops of parthenocarpic fruits. Fire blight (a bacterial disease) is a serious problem in pears. Bartlett, which makes up 75 percent of the world's pear production and acreage, has a chilling requirement of about 800 hours. Days from full bloom to harvest range from about 115 to 165 for European and Asian pears.

Rootstocks

Several different species are used for pear rootstocks, but they vary only slightly in size control and their tolerance to "wet feet." Quince is the only dwarfing rootstock available, and it is incompatible with some pear varieties.

Quince. *Several strains available. Semidwarfing rootstock. Resistant to root aphid, root rot, and most nematodes. Trees are 50 percent of standard size and are very productive. Compatible with D'Anjou, Comice, Flemish Beauty, and Swiss Bartlett, but incompatible with Bartlett, Bosc, Seckel, and Clapp; these varieties require an interstem of Old Home. On poor sites with shallow soil or where the trees are not well irrigated, trees grafted onto Quince tend to be runty. Fruit are of lower quality than those grown on other stocks.*

French Seedling. *Seeds from Bartlett or Winter Nelis are used for this rootstock, which withstands both wet feet and dry conditions. This rootstock is resistant to oak root fungus and trees are very susceptible to fire blight. Good for general use.*

Calleryana. *Moderately vigorous rootstock. Resistant to wet feet, root aphid, and most nematodes, and confers fire blight resistance to the tree. Not the best stock for Asian pear varieties. Produces a tree a bit larger than French seedling.*

Betulaefolia. *Best rootstock for most Asian pears. The most vigorous of the pear rootstocks, producing the largest tree on any site. Best tolerance of wet and drought conditions. Resistant to pear decline, fire blight, root aphid, and root rot. Poor rootstock for D'Anjou.*

Old Home × Farmingdale. *A P. communis rootstock propagated from cuttings or by layering. Somewhat dwarfing. Compatible with most varieties. Resistant to fire blight. Many strains are available.*

European Pear Varieties

European varieties (*Pyrus communis*) mostly have the traditional pear shape and are harvested green when they begin to drop off the tree. They are then stored at 33° to 45°F (1.5° to 7°C) for several weeks. As the fruit is brought up to room temperature, it softens and turns buttery. If allowed to ripen on the tree, certain cells within the fruit called stone cells develop and make the fruit gritty.

Bartlett. *Early. The best-quality pear fruit. Fruit are bell-shaped and have white flesh and excellent flavor. Tree is susceptible to fire blight. Fruit keep relatively well, up to 2 months after maturing in August. The variety "Sensation" is a red Bartlett.*

Bosc. *Late. Bears heavy crops regularly. Fruit are long and tapering, with a long neck and stem. Skin is golden russet brown.*

Comice. *Late. Inconsistent bearer. Excellent-quality fruit, green color with red blush. Delicate skin, chubby shape. Very vigorous tree, does best on Quince rootstock.*

D'Anjou. *Late season. Good-quality pear with excellent keeping qualities. A large, vigorous tree. Egg-shaped fruit with a small shoulder. Light green to yellow-green color with a white flesh. French origin. There is a red strain called Red Anjou, which is very popular. Poor fruit quality in the hot Central Valley.*

Seckel. *Midseason. A small fruit with reddish green skin and a very dense, sweet, and flavorful flesh. Excellent quality for the home orchard. It is resistant to fire blight and pear scab.*

Winter Nelis. *Late. Medium-small, almost round fruit with light russetting over a green skin. Resistant to fire blight. Large tree. Regular producer.*

Low-Chill Pear Varieties

These pear varieties are adapted to the lower latitudes of Southern California because they have a low winter chilling requirement (fewer than 300 hours).

Baldwin, Florida Home, Fan Stil, Hood, Kieffer, Orient, Pineapple.

Asian Pear Varieties

Asian pears (*Pyrus serotina*) are round fruit that remain very firm, crisp, and juicy when eaten ripe. Also known as salad pears or pear-apples. The best rootstock for these varieties is Betulaefolia. Generally require cross-pollination. Fruit must be heavily thinned in May or June in order to size properly, and the largest fruit are produced if flowers are thinned during or shortly after bloom. Harvest by taste and pick exposed fruit first. Unlike European pears, Asian pears ripen on the tree. They are immune to apple scab disease, but very susceptible to fire blight (at least as susceptible as European pears).

Chojuro. *Early. Greenish brown russet skin. Coarse, tasty flesh.*

Hosui. *Midseason. Brown skin, juicy white flesh with a sweet aromatic flavor.*

Kikusui. *Midseason. Yellow-green skin. White flesh, excellent flavor. Fruit drop from the tree when ripe.*

Shinseiki. *Midseason. Amber yellow skin. White flesh that is crisp but softens rapidly; less flavor than other varieties.*

Nijisseiki. *Midseason. Also known as **Twentieth Century**. Excellent quality. Very popular variety with yellow-green skin.*

Shinko. *Late. Brown russet skin, firm, crisp flesh, and very aromatic flavor.*

Niitaka. *Late. Very large fruit, juicy, with an aromatic flavor.*

Tsu Li. *Late. Blooms early. Use Ya Li as pollinizer. Chinese type (pear-shaped). Light green color, crisp, tasty flesh.*

Ya Li. *Late. Blooms early. Use Tsu Li as pollinizer. Chinese type (pear-shaped). Light, shiny yellow color, crisp, tasty flesh.*

POMEGRANATES (*PUNICA GRANATUM*)

Pomegranates are exotic fruits that grow on a small tree or shrub 15 to 20 feet (4.5 to 6 m) tall that has shiny foliage and a long flowering season. The tree is very long-lived. It is sensitive to frost in fall and spring and does not mature well in cool climates. The tree tolerates wet, heavy soils, but performs better in deep, well-drained loams. The fruit crack open with the first fall rains. Propagated from cuttings. Requires only a short chilling period. Resistant to oak root fungus (*Armillaria mellea*). Not attacked by codling moth or twig borers. Unharvested ripe fruit attracts ants and fruit flies.

Standard Varieties

Wonderful. *Late. Large, deep red fruit. Large, juicy, red kernels. Small seed. Matures late. Juice is made into grenadine syrup.*

Granada. *Late. Deep crimson fruit color. Needs heat to mature.*

Ruby Red. *Late. Matures late (with **Wonderful**), but not as sweet or colorful as **Wonderful**. All fruit mature at once.*

Ambrosia. *Late. Huge fruit, pale pink skin; similar to **Wonderful**.*

Eversweet. *Late. Very sweet, almost seedless fruit. Red skin, clear juice. Good for southern coastal areas.*

QUINCES (*CYDONIA OBLONGA*)

Quince fruit grow on a small tree or shrub 8 to 12 feet (2.5 to 3.5 m) tall with twisted, bumpy branches. Gardeners grow it as a flowering ornamental or for fruit processing. Adapted to many climates, quince tolerates wet feet better than most other deciduous fruit trees. Quince trees bloom late, which means that they are generally unaffected by spring frosts. Quince has many of the same pest problems as apple and pear. All varieties are self-fruitful. Quince is used as a dwarfing rootstock for some pear varieties, but it is very susceptible to fire blight.

Orange. *Midseason. Orange-yellow flesh, golden skin, rich flavor, low-chill fruit.*

Pineapple. *Late. The preferred variety. Pineapple flavor, white flesh, golden skin, low-chill fruit.*

Smyrna. *Late. Large fruit with brown pubescence. Light, tender flesh, yellow skin, low-chill fruit.*

Stone Fruits

ALMONDS (*PRUNUS DULCIS*)

Almonds, though technically stone fruit, are consumed as nuts. Information on almond varieties is listed under *Nut Crops* later in this chapter.

APRICOTS (*PRUNUS ARMENIACA*)

Apricots bloom in February and early March, a time of year when cold rainstorms are not uncommon along the North Coast; this combination of timing and environmental conditions makes consistent crops unlikely from year to year in North Coast counties. Apricots perform best in climates with dry spring weather. They are susceptible to late spring frosts. Bacterial canker is a common disease of young trees in California. Plant your apricot trees at a spacing of about 10 to 20 feet (3 to 6 m). Apricots are mostly self-fruitful. Some varieties set better with cross-pollination, especially in years with wet, cool weather during bloom. Apricots ripen in late June to July, 100 to 120 days from full bloom. The hot weather characteristic of most areas of the Central Valley often causes the fruit to "pit burn" (soften and turn brown around the pit), which lowers fruit quality.

Rootstocks

The main apricot rootstocks used in California, from least to most dwarfing:

Myrobalan 29C Plum. *A cutting selection that is immune to root knot nematodes; susceptible to oak root fungus, root rot, and root lesion nematode. Produces a tree with more vigor than Mariana 2624.*

Citation. *Peach-plum hybrid. One of the best rootstocks for apricots. Slightly dwarfing. Less susceptible to bacterial canker; tolerant of wet feet. Does not tolerate drought, but helps produce larger fruit.*

Marianna 2624 Plum. *Somewhat resistant to oak root fungus. Tolerates wet feet much better than apricot or peach root.*

Lovell Peach. *Imparts some resistance to bacterial canker. Susceptible to oak root fungus. Not as tolerant of wet soils as other apricot rootstocks.*

Prunus besseyi. *Semidwarfing rootstock. Short-lived. Suckers profusely. Produces inferior fruit in the scion variety.*

Standard Varieties

The main apricot fruiting varieties used in California, from earliest to latest ripening:

Royal (Blenheim). *Early. Large, very flavorful, used for eating fresh and drying.*

Harcot. *Early. A large orange fruit with a slight red blush, blooms late, self-fertile.*

Tilton. *Midseason. Large fruit, heavy producer. Mild flavor. Used for canning.*

Moorpark. *Midseason. Excellent flavor, ripens unevenly, highly colored.*

Patterson. *Midseason. Medium-sized fruit. Used for eating fresh, drying, or canning.*

Autumn Royal. *Late. Blenheim sport. Ripens in late summer to fall.*

Low-Chill Varieties

These apricot varieties are adapted to the lower latitudes of Southern California because they have low winter chilling requirements (fewer than 400 hours).

Goldkist, Katy, Early Golden, Newcastle.

Other Varieties to Consider

Castlebright. *Very early. Medium-sized firm fruit with tart flavor.*

Chinese. *Early. Medium-sized fruit, good flavor, cold hardy, heavy bearer.*

Royalty. *Early. Very large, light-colored fruit with mild flavor.*

Golden Amber. *Midseason. Large fruit, good flavor, light colored.*

Puget Gold. *Late. Large fruit, good flavor and color, reliable producer.*

CHERRIES (*PRUNUS AVIUM, PRUNUS CERASUS*)

There are two basic types of cherry that you can grow: sweet cherries for eating as fresh fruit and sour cherries for cooking in pies and processing for preserves. Cherry trees in general are the most difficult fruit trees to keep alive. They do not tolerate wet feet and are very susceptible to brown rot, bacterial canker, cytospora canker, root and crown rots, and several viruses. Trees on standard rootstocks should be planted 14 to 20 feet apart in well-drained soil and up on a small mound, raised bed, or berm. Sweet cherries require cross-pollination (many varieties are self-sterile and intrasterile, as noted below). Sour cherries are self-fertile and do not require a pollinizer. Both types require fewer than 100 days to mature their fruit. Cherries have a high chilling requirement and are not suitable for most parts of Southern California.

Rootstocks

Mazzard. *Good rootstock for cherries in coastal California. Produces a large, vigorous tree that is delayed in coming into bearing. Less susceptible to root rots and gophers than Mahaleb but more susceptible to bacterial canker.*

Mahaleb. *Very susceptible to root and crown rots. Some resistance to buckskin virus, bacterial canker, and root lesion nematode.*

Colt. *Somewhat dwarfing rootstock. Also somewhat resistant to root rot. Sensitive to drought.*

Gisela Series. *These dwarfing rootstocks are relatively new and in most cases produce trees that are small in stature, 8 to 10 feet (2.5 to 3 m) tall. They also tend to impart early bearing. The smaller trees are easier to cover with netting in order to keep birds from eating all of the fruit. Trees can be spaced about 10 to 12 feet (3 to 3.7 m) apart.*

Sweet Varieties

Early Burlat. *Early. Moderate-sized fruit. Ripens two weeks before Bing. Soft flesh. Pollinized by Bing and Black Tartarian.*

Tulare. *Early. Large, firm, heart-shaped fruit. Red skin and pink to red flesh. Fruit stores well. Pollinizers include Brooks, King, and Bing.*

Bing. *Early. Industry standard variety for sweet cherries. Deep, mahogany-red fruit. Heavy producer. Highly susceptible to bacterial canker. Pollinized by Van, Black Tartarian, or Sam. Bing, Lambert, and Royal Ann do not pollinate each other (they are intrasterile).*

King. *Early. Medium to large, dark red fruit. Tree is willowy and spreading. An effective pollinizer for Brooks and Tulare.*

Lambert. *Midseason to late season. Dark, large, firm fruit. Pollinized by Van. Lambert, Bing, and Royal Ann do not pollinate each other.*

Brooks. *Early. A large, dark red fruit with good flavor. It is a good producer with few doubles even in hot climates.*

Royal Ann. *Early. Yellow fruit with a red blush. Pollinized by Van. Late season. Royal Ann, Lambert, and Bing do not pollinate each other.*

Van. *Early. Large, dark fruit. Pollinized by Bing or Lambert.*

Black Tartarian. *Early. Small, black fruit. A good pollinizer for Bing and most other varieties.*

Stella. *Midseason. Dark-fleshed fruit. Matures just after Bing. Self-fruitful.*

Lapins. *Midseason. Fruit resembles that of Lambert, but larger, firmer, and self-fruitful. Produces some crop in the higher-elevation areas of Southern California.*

Rainier. *Early. Yellow-red blush. Large, crack-resistant fruit.*

Early Ruby. *Early. Large, dark red fruit. Prolific. Fruit hold on tree.*

Utah Giant. *Early. A very large fruit that does not double very much; outstanding flavor.*

Craig Crimson. *Early. Dark fruit with excellent flavor. Genetic semidwarf. Self-fruitful.*

Low-Chill Sweet Varieties

None available.

Sour ("Pie") Varieties

Montmorency. *Early. The leading sour variety. Medium-sized, dark red fruit, clear juice.*

Early Richmond. *Early. Bright red fruit, clear juice.*

North Star. *Early. Semidwarf. Self-fruitful, red juice.*

Meteor. *Early. Semidwarf with clear juice.*

English Morello. *Early. Red flesh. Sets some crop in Southern California, but not along the coast.*

Low-Chill Sour Varieties

None available.

NECTARINES *(PRUNUS PERSICA)*

Nectarines are fuzzless peaches. They do well in most of California if given the proper growing conditions. Nectarines require a very well-drained soil, abundant soil nitrogen, plenty of summer water, fruit thinning, heavy annual pruning, and pest control sprays to prevent peach leaf curl and brown rot. There are many very good varieties. Trees can bear in their second year. Nectarines (like peaches) are self-fruitful and do not require a pollinizer tree. In freestone nectarines, the stone detaches fairly easily from the flesh of the fruit; in clingstone nectarines, the stone is more difficult to remove. Due to the smooth skin of nectarines, they are very susceptible to scarring and deformation from western flower thrips. Trees should be spaced about 5 to 14 feet (1.5 to 4 m) apart.

Rootstocks

Lovell Peach. *The best choice for coastal California and the Sacramento Valley. A seedling that tolerates wet winter soils better than any other peach rootstock, but still requires good drainage. Produces a full-sized tree, but one that is managed easily. Plant 8 to 14 feet (2.5 to 4 m) apart.*

Nemaguard Peach. *The best choice for the San Joaquin Valley. A nematode-resistant rootstock best adapted to sandy, dry sites that never get too wet. Produces a full-sized tree.*

Prunus besseyi. *Semidwarfing rootstock. Suckers badly. Produces inferior fruit on the scion variety. Has not performed well. Somewhat incompatible with most varieties.*

Citation. *A new peach-plum hybrid that provides some dwarfing to most varieties. Tolerates wet winter conditions. Produces trees that are smaller in trunk diameter without any height reduction in some scion varieties. Does not tolerate drought.*

Standard Varieties

Flamekist. *Late. Excellent quality. Large, firm, yellow clingstone.*

Independence. *Early. Excellent quality, red skin, yellow flesh freestone that requires less chilling.*

Panamint. *Midseason. Medium-sized fruit. Red skin, golden flesh. Freestone, low-chill variety.*

Flavortop. *Midseason. Large; excellent flavor. Yellow freestone.*

Fantasia. *Late. Large, brightly colored yellow freestone.*

Mericrest. *Early. Late-blooming, large, yellow-fleshed freestone with red skin. Excellent tart flavor.*

Double Delight. *Early. Excellent flavor, yellow freestone with red skin, heavy bearing.*

Goldmine. *Late. Large; great flavor. White flesh. Freestone.*

Arctic Glo. *Early. Small; excellent flavor. White flesh.*

Heavenly White. *Midseason. Large; excellent flavor. White flesh. Fruit cracking is common.*

Arctic Rose. *Midseason. Old favorite. White clingstone with excellent flavor and low chilling requirement.*

Snow Queen. *Early. Early season white freestone; juicy and tasty.*

Low-Chill Varieties

These nectarine varieties are adapted to the lower latitudes of Southern California because they have low winter chilling requirements (fewer than 500 hours).

Arctic Star, Desert Dawn, Desert Delight, Rose, Panamint, Pioneer, Silver Lode, Snow Queen.

PEACHES *(PRUNUS PERSICA)*

Peaches are very popular fruit trees that can be grown successfully in many parts of California. They require adequate summer watering, a deep, well-drained soil, relatively high soil nitrogen, fruit thinning, heavy annual pruning, and pest control sprays to prevent peach leaf curl and brown rot. Peach trees are short-lived (15 to 20 years). Like nectarines, peaches are self-fruitful. In freestone peaches, the stone detaches fairly easily from the flesh of the fruit; in clingstone peaches, the stone is more difficult to remove. Trees should be spaced about 5 to 14 feet (1.5 to 4 m) apart.

Rootstocks

Lovell Peach. *The best choice for coastal California and the Sacramento Valley. A seedling that tolerates wet winter soils better than any other peach rootstock, but still requires good drainage. Produces a full-sized tree, but one that is managed easily. Plant 8 to 14 feet (2.5 to 4 m) apart.*

Nemaguard Peach. *The best choice for the San Joaquin Valley. A nematode-resistant rootstock best adapted to sandy, dry sites that never get too wet. Produces a full-sized tree.*

Prunus besseyi. *Semidwarfing rootstock. Suckers badly. Produces inferior fruit on the scion variety. Has not performed well. Somewhat incompatible with most varieties.*

Citation. *A new peach-plum hybrid that provides some dwarfing to most varieties. Tolerates wet winter conditions. Produces trees that are smaller in trunk diameter without any height reduction in some scion varieties. Does not tolerate drought.*

Standard Varieties

Thousands of peach varieties have been developed worldwide. Some perform better in warmer areas; others have better fruit quality when grown in cooler climates along the coast of California. Four listed below (Veteran, Loring, Red Haven, and La Feliciana) are more trouble free; Frost and Indian Free are somewhat more resistant to peach leaf curl. These varieties are listed in approximate order of ripening:

Earligrande. *Early. Excellent flavor. Yellow-red blush. Semi-freestone, low-chill variety.*

Springcrest. *Early. Medium-sized fruit. Yellow flesh. Excellent flavor.*

Strawberry Freestone. *Early. Medium-sized fruit with white flesh and sweet, mild flavor.*

Babcock and Giant Babcock. *Early. Medium-sized. White flesh. Freestone, low-chill varieties.*

La Feliciana. *Midseason. Medium-sized. Firm, red. Excellent flavor.*

Red Haven. *Midseason. Yellow. Semi-freestone. Needs heavy thinning.*

Suncrest. *Midseason. Large fruit. Yellow flesh. Freestone. Excellent flavor.*

Veteran. *Midseason. Red blush. Freestone. Dependable, heavy producer. Excellent flavor.*

Nectar. *Midseason. White flesh. Pink skin. Excellent flavor.*

Loring. *Midseason. Very large fruit. Red skin. Yellow flesh. Freestone. Excellent quality.*

Forty-Niner. *Midseason. Large fruit. Yellow flesh. Freestone.*

Fay Elberta. *Midseason. Large fruit. Yellow flesh. Freestone. Good producer. Excellent flavor.*

O'Henry. *Midseason. One of the best-flavored peaches. Large fruit. Yellow flesh. Freestone.*

Snow Giant. *Midseason. One of the Snow series varieties that is white fleshed and has excellent flavor.*

Doughnut. *Also called* **Saucer** *or* **Peento.** *Midseason. Unique, white-fleshed fruit with a sunken center (shaped like a doughnut). Sweet, with a mild flavor described by some as almondlike.*

Frost. *Midseason to late. A yellow-fleshed freestone.*

Rio Oso Gem. *Late. Very large fruit. Yellow flesh. Freestone.*

Indian Free. *Late. Freestone peach. Red skin and flesh. Tart until fully ripe. Prolific. Highly resistant to peach leaf curl. Another nectarine or peach variety needed as pollinizer.*

Autumn Gem. *Late. Medium-large fruit. Yellow flesh. Keeps well.*

Fairtime. *Late. Large fruit. Yellow, firm flesh. Excellent flavor.*

Low-Chill Varieties

These peach varieties are adapted to the lower latitudes of Southern California because they have low winter chilling requirements (fewer than 500 hours).

August Pride, Babcock, Bonita, Desertgold, Early Amber, Earligrande, FlordaPrince, Midpride, Red Baron, Tropi-berta, Eva's Pride, Tropic Snow.

PLUMS AND PRUNES (*PRUNUS DOMESTICA, PRUNUS SALICINA*)

Plum trees are among the best-adapted fruit tree species for almost anywhere in California. They are easy to grow. Available rootstocks are very tolerant of wet winter soils. They bloom late enough to avoid most spring frosts, and they have few pest problems. Plum trees get relatively large and require 12 to 18 feet (3.5 to 5.5 m) of space. Most plums require cross-pollination to set an adequate crop; plan to plant two different varieties. There are two basic kinds of plums: Japanese (*Prunus salicina*), and European (*Prunus domestica*). European types are either very sweet fresh plums or prunes used for drying. Both European and Japanese plums require about 140 to 170 days to mature the crop. Most Japanese plums bloom earlier and so mature earlier. They typically require less chilling than European plums.

Rootstocks

Myrobalan Seedling. *The largest and most vigorous of the plum or prune rootstocks. Hardy, long-lived, adapted to most soils. Tolerates wet winter soil conditions. Susceptible to oak root fungus and nematodes, but somewhat resistant to root and crown rots.*

Myrobalan 29C Plum. *A cutting selection that is immune to root knot nematodes. Susceptible to oak root fungus, root rot, and root lesion nematode. Somewhat more resistant to bacterial canker. Produces a tree with a little less vigor than the seedling Myrobalan.*

Marianna 2624 Plum. *The overall best choice. It is resistant to oak root fungus, root rots, root knot nematodes, and crown gall, but susceptible to bacterial canker and root lesion nematode. This cutting is shallow-rooted and produces a smaller tree. It is the rootstock best adapted to poor, wet soil conditions, but it does tend to sucker from the roots.*

Lovell Peach. *Less susceptible to bacterial canker, but the most intolerant of heavy soils, wet feet, oak root fungus, nematodes, and root rots. Produces a moderately large tree that fruits earlier and sets more consistent crops. Compatible with most plum or prune varieties.*

Prunus besseyi. *Semidwarfing rootstock. Suckers badly. Produces inferior fruit quality on the scion variety. Partially incompatible with most varieties.*

Citation. *A new peach-plum hybrid that produces a full-sized tree. Tolerates wet soils, but is not tolerant of drought.*

Standard Japanese Plum Varieties

Japanese plum varieties used in California, in approximate order of ripening:

Beauty. *Early. Green skin, amber flesh, heart-shaped. Poor keeper.*

Santa Rosa. *Early. Purple skin. Amber flesh. Excellent flavor.*

Shiro. *Early. Light green-yellow skin. Yellow flesh.*

El Dorado. *Midseason. Purple skin. Amber flesh. Large, oblong.*

Mariposa. *Midseason. Green-yellow skin. Red flesh. Large, heart-shaped.*

Wickson. *Midseason. Green-yellow skin. Yellow flesh. Large heart.*

Friar. *Midseason. Black skin. Amber flesh. Very mild flavor. Old variety.*

Kelsey. *Midseason. Green-yellow skin and flesh.*

Laroda. *Midseason. Red-purple skin. Yellow flesh.*

Nubiana. *Midseason. Purple-black skin. Yellow flesh. Oblong.*

Burgundy. *Midseason. Red skin and flesh. Self-fertile. Ripe fruit holds well to tree. Good pollinizer.*

Satsuma. *Midseason. Red skin and flesh. Small, round.*

Late Santa Rosa. *Midseason. Large fruit with purple flesh and tart flavor.*

Howard Miracle. *Midseason. Large, pink skin. Yellow flesh. Also called* **Howard Wonder.**

Elephant Heart. *Late. Purple skin. Large, heart-shaped.*

Golden Nectar. *Late. Large. Yellow flesh. Tender skin. Great flavor.*

Autumn Rosa. *Late. Large. Purple skin. Self-fertile.*

Standard Prune (European Plum) Varieties

European plum or prune varieties used in California, in approximate order of ripening:

French Improved. *Midseason. Medium-sized fruit. Self-fertile. Late-maturing.*

Imperial. *Midseason. Large fruit. Requires cross-pollination. Late maturing.*

Italian. *Midseason. Large fruit. Purple skin. Yellow flesh.*

Green Gage. *Midseason. Greenish-yellow skin. Amber flesh. Old variety.*

Stanley. *Midseason. Vigorous, self-fruitful, heavy bearing, freestone. Very popular all over the United States.*

Blue Damson. *Midseason. Small sweet plum with greenish yellow flesh and blue skin with a heavy bloom. Good for jam and jelly.*

President. *Late. Large. Blue skin. Yellow flesh. Very sweet. Can be dried into extra-large prunes.*

Standard Cherry-Plum Varieties

The original cherry-plum was made in the early 1800s as a cross of sandcherry and Japanese plum. Cherry-plums primarily exhibit plum features. Varieties used in California are listed here in approximate order of ripening:

Sprite. *Midseason. Hybrid of cherry-plum and Japanese plum. Freestone fruit with black, sweet skin. Exotic* *flavor. Small. Should be grown with the Delight cherry plum variety for cross pollination.*

Delight. *Midseason. Hybrid of cherry-plum and Japanese plum. Clingstone fruit with black, sweet skin. Small. Pollinizer required.*

Low-Chill Plum Varieties

These plum varieties are adapted to the lower latitudes of Southern California because they have low winter chilling requirements (fewer than 500 hours).

Beauty, Burgundy, Howard Miracle, Kelsey, Mariposa, Methley, Santa Rosa, Satsuma, Sprite.

PLUMCOTS *(PRUNUS DOMESTICA AND PRUNUS SALICINA ✕ PRUNUS ARMENIACA)*

A plumcot is a cross between a plum and an apricot. When the breeding creates a 50-50 mix, the result is a plumcot. A three-quarter plum is a pluot and its fruit and tree are very plumlike. A three-quarter apricot is an aprium, which is very apricotlike in tree type and fruit. Plumcots are extremely flavorful fruits that tend to bear poorly for the first few years. Plumcots should be planted with other plumcot or plum varieties nearby and apriums should be planted with other aprium varieties or apricots nearby for good cross-pollination. Apriums use apricot rootstocks and pluots use plum rootstocks.

Standard Varieties

Flavor Supreme Pluot. *Early. Red-fleshed, large, plumlike fruit with deep red to greenish purple skin. Pollinated by Santa Rosa plum or Late Santa Rosa plum, or by another pluot.*

Flavor Delight Aprium. *Early. Resembles an apricot but with a distinctive flavor and texture. Bigger crops if pollinized by any apricot.*

Plum Parfait Plumcot. *Early. Pinkish orange skin. Crimson and amber flesh. Self-fruitful.*

Flavor Grenade Pluot. *Midseason. Elongated, green fruit with red blush. Crisp texture and "explosive" flavor. Pollinize with Japanese plum.*

Dapple Dandy Pluot. *Midseason to late. Creamy, large, white and red-fleshed freestone with outstanding flavor. Skin greenish-yellow with red spots, turning to a maroon and yellow dapple. Pollinized by Flavor Supreme pluot or Santa Rosa plum or Burgundy plum.*

Flavor King Pluot. *Midseason to late. Reddish purple skin, sweet red flesh. Outstanding flavor. Naturally small tree. Pollinized by Flavor Supreme pluot, Santa Rosa plum, or Late Santa Rosa plum.*

Flavor Queen Pluot. *Late. Golden-fleshed, deep yellow-golden skin, plumlike fruit with excellent flavor. Very sweet. Pollinized by plum or another Pluot, but not Flavor King. Difficult to get good fruit set.*

Nut Crops

ALMONDS *(PRUNUS DULCIS, FORMERLY P. AMYGDALUS)*

Almonds are stone fruits that are eaten as nuts. Nearly all almonds that are produced commercially in the United States are grown in California. Among stone fruit they are the earliest to bloom (February) and they generally do poorly in North Coast counties. Almonds bloom when the weather there is cold and rainy, and the trees are very susceptible to spring frosts. Almonds do not tolerate wet soils. The Central Valley and drier regions of the southern coast are very favorable for almonds because they require little chilling—only 100 to 300 hours. Trees are very susceptible to bacterial canker disease, which kills the tree. Most varieties are self-sterile and require cross-pollination (All-in-One is self-fruitful); some pairs of varieties are cross-unfruitful. Almonds are harvested by shaking the trees when hulls begin to split. It takes 180 to 240 days from bloom to mature the nuts. The nuts (embryo and shell) are dried down to a minimum moisture content after harvest.

Standard Varieties

Nonpareil. *Late. The most popular paper-shelled variety. Interfruitful with Price, Mission, and Carmel.*

Price. *Late. Very similar to Nonpareil. A good pollinizer.*

Carmel. *Late. Excellent quality. A well-sealed nut in the shell. Excellent pollinizer.*

Mission. *Late. Late-blooming, productive tree. Hard shell, short kernel.*

Ne Plus Ultra. *Late. Large, soft-shelled nut. Long, flat kernel. Good pollinizer.*

All-in-One. *Late. Produces heavy crops of soft-shelled nuts that mature late. Self-fruitful.*

Hall's Hardy (Texas Mission). *Frost-tolerant blossoms. Bittersweet kernels. Self-fruitful. Pink flowers; often grown as an ornamental in cold climates.*

CHESTNUTS *(CASTANAEA SPP.)*

Chestnuts are monoecious (separate female and male flowers are borne on one plant, like walnuts), and some cultivars are self-unfruitful; you should grow two different varieties for cross-pollination in order to produce consistent crops. Trees reach a height of 80 feet (24 m) and spread to 60 feet (18 m) wide under ideal conditions. The chestnut is an excellent, fruitful shade tree if grown in very well-drained soil. The chestnut tree is almost pest free in California, although it is susceptible to root rot in poorly drained soils. Seedling is the only known rootstock. Edible chestnuts should not be confused with the poisonous horse chestnut or California buckeye (*Aesculus californica*). Fresh chestnuts contain about 50 percent moisture. Unlike other nuts, chestnuts have a low oil content (8%). Store them in the refrigerator like apples.

Standard Varieties

Colossal. *Late. The industry standard. Large-fruited. Excellent quality. Best choice. Parentage unknown.*

Nevada. *Late. Large nut. Good pollinizer for Colossal.*

Seedling. *Late. Not a "named" variety. Each tree is genetically different. Unknown fruit quality. Tree shape and fruit size are unknown. Chestnuts are always grown on a seedling rootstock.*

Dunstan. *Late. A cross of American and Chinese varieties. Medium to small nuts. Sweet; blight resistant. Late flowering.*

Other Varieties to Consider

There are many chestnut varieties that are being evaluated in California for the first time. These four offer the most promise, to date:

Marrone di Maradi, Castel del Rio, Montesol, Fowler.

FILBERTS (HAZELNUTS) *(CORYLUS SPP.)*

These plants grow naturally as suckering shrubs but can be trained as trees if you continually remove the suckers. They reach a height of 15 to 20 feet (4.5 to 12 m) with an equal spread. Filberts are monoecious (separate male and female flowers on the same plant, like walnuts) but self-unfruitful. Cross-pollination is required to set fruit, so you have to plant two different varieties. Crop production is not consistent in California, maybe because summer heat causes the catkins (male flowers) to fall off prematurely. Filberts are grown on their own roots. They need a 180-day growing season.

Standard Varieties

Barcelona. *Late. The old industry standard. Use Davianna or Du Chilly as a pollinizer.*

Davianna. *Late. Use Barcelona or Du Chilly as a pollinizer.*

Du Chilly. *Late. Use Barcelona or Davianna as a pollinizer.*

Ennis. *Late. A new variety that has better quality than Barcelona. Use Butler as a pollinizer.*

Butler. *Late. Pollinizer for Ennis.*

PECANS (*CARYA ILLINOENSIS*)

Pecans are not a good choice for Northern California, but they can be grown in the southern San Joaquin Valley. They require a deep, well-drained soil, a hot climate to mature the nuts properly, and adequate soil moisture. You have to plant at least two different varieties for good pollination: even though pecans are largely self-fruitful, the flowers are dichogamous, which means that there is little overlap in the times for pollen shedding and stigma receptivity. Most varieties require at least 180 days for nuts to mature. Trees grow to the same size as a walnut tree. Pecans are grown on seedling stocks.

Standard Varieties

Western Schley. *Late. Early pollen shed and receptivity. Self-fruitful.*

Wichita. *Late. Late pollen shed. Early receptivity. Partially self-fruitful.*

Choctaw. *Late. Late pollen shed. Early receptivity. Partially self-fruitful.*

Mahan. *Late pollen shed.*

Mohawk. *Late pollen shed. Large nut. Partially self-fruitful.*

Pawnee. *Early pollen shed. Partially self-fruitful.*

PISTACHIOS (*PISTACIA VERA*)

Pistachio trees require long, hot, dry summers and mild winters. April frosts kill the flowers and cool summers discourage good kernel development. Adequate winter chilling and good weather are required for wind-pollination.

Pistachio trees are dioecious (separate male and female trees); male trees must be planted near to the female trees to get a good crop set. Trees become large and should be planted about 20 feet (6 m) apart. The warmest regions in the state are adapted for pistachio production in the home garden, but pistachios are a poor choice for coastal California.

Rootstocks

Pistacia atlantica. *Resistant to many nematodes, but susceptible to cold below 15° to 20°F (−9.6° to −6.5°C) and Verticillium wilt.*

P. terebinthus. *The best rootstock. Most tolerant of cold. Resistant to nematodes. Susceptible to Verticillium wilt.*

P. integerrima. *Resistant to Verticillium wilt. Very susceptible to cold damage.*

Standard Varieties

Kerman. *Late. Female. Best nut-producing variety.*

Peters. *Late. Male. Good for pollination.*

WALNUTS (*JUGLANS REGIA* [ENGLISH WALNUT], *JUGLANS HINDSII* [BLACK WALNUT])

Walnuts need a deep, well-drained soil at least 5 feet (1.5 m) deep to grow and produce well. Shoots (particularly blossoms) do not tolerate frosts. Once growth begins in the spring, rainy weather can cause severe losses due to walnut blight. Trees range in size from medium height (40 to 50 feet [12 to 15 m] tall) to very large (80 feet [24 m] tall). They require a spacing of 30 to 60 feet (9 to 18 m). Walnut culture has changed drastically in the last few years as new varieties have been introduced. Production in coastal climates should be limited to the late-leafing varieties. Walnuts are monoecious (separate male and female flowers on one tree) and dichogamous (pollen is shed when female flowers are not receptive); thus, you have to plant two different varieties to ensure that male and female bloom periods will overlap for good fruit set.

Rootstocks

English. *This rootstock is a seedling of English walnut. It is very susceptible to oak root fungus but less susceptible to blackline virus. It is the least tolerant of wet soils.*

Black. *This variety, also known as* **Northern California Black,** *has long been the standard rootstock in California. It is resistant to oak root fungus but susceptible to crown rot, root rot, root lesion nematode, and blackline virus.*

Paradox. *The best rootstock choice in general. A hybrid between Black and English (Black walnut fruit pollinized by English walnut pollen). Very vigorous. Tolerates poorer soil conditions than the others. Less susceptible to crown and root rot, but susceptible to crown gall and blackline virus.*

Standard Varieties

Hartley. *Late. The main variety grown in California. Excellent quality nuts. Huge tree, but requires little pruning; only 5 percent fruitful lateral buds. Leafs out late, blooms late.*

Scharsch Franquette. *Late. Old-time variety. Should be planted as a pollinizer for the late-blooming varieties. Poor producer. Leafs out late. Blooms late. Large tree, but requires little pruning.*

Placentia. *Late. 80 percent fruitful lateral buds. Produces a smaller tree that requires careful pruning and training to maintain vigor. Early leafing and requires less chilling than other varieties. Self-fruitful.*

Chandler. *Late. Best choice for coastal California. Newer variety; 80 percent fruitful lateral buds. Produces a smaller tree that requires careful pruning and training to maintain vigor. Blooms late. Leafs out late.*

Pedro. *Late. New variety; 80 percent fruitful lateral buds. Produces a smaller tree that requires careful pruning and training to maintain vigor. Requires less chilling. Good pollinizer.*

Tehama. *Late. New variety; 80 percent fruitful lateral buds. Produces a smaller tree that requires careful pruning and training to maintain vigor. Blooms late. Leafs out late.*

Black Walnut Varieties

Seedling. *Late. Seedlings of Northern California Black walnut trees that do not come true from seed. Each tree is different.*

Eastern Black Walnut Varieties

Thomas, Ohio, Meyers. *Late. Three named varieties that may be worthy of consideration.*

Miscellaneous Temperate Fruits

FIGS (*FICUS CARICA*)

Figs can be grown easily in most areas of California, but they require a protected location in the cooler parts of the state because it takes a great deal of heat to mature the fruit properly. Fig trees do best in well-drained soils, but will tolerate wet soils better than most other fruit trees. Gophers must be controlled. Figs are grown on their own roots from cuttings. Trees reach heights of 20 to 30 feet (6 to 9 m) with an equal spread, but you can prune them to a smaller size each year in the dormant season. Most varieties require no cross-pollination. Several varieties set fruit parthenocarpically, and several varieties have two crops per year (shown below as "early/late"). The "breba" (first crop) matures in early to midsummer and the second crop matures in late summer or fall. Figs require very little winter chilling. The Smyrna types require caprification (that is, pollination by caprifig wasps living nearby).

Standard Varieties

Brown Turkey. *Early/late. Large fruit. Excellent quality. Produces a small breba crop every year and a second crop in August to October. Purple-green skin. Red flesh.*

Black Mission. *Early/late. The most dependable variety for the home orchard. Purple-black skin with red flesh. The breba matures in early summer, and the second crop matures in September to October.*

Osborn Prolific. *Early/late. Performs well only in cool, coastal areas. Produces breba and second crops. Purple-bronze fruit with amber flesh. Very prolific.*

Italian Everbearing. *Early/late. Brown. Turkey-type. Very prolific.*

White Genoa. *Early/late. Good for coastal locations. Large fruit. Yellow-green, thin skin. Strawberry flesh. Ripens in years when others will not.*

Kadota. *Early/late. Requires high temperatures and a long growing season to perform well. Yellow-green fruit with amber flesh. Produces both breba and second crops with moderate pruning.*

Adriatic. *Early/late. Good fresh but especially good for drying. Yellow skin and amber flesh.*

Black Jack. *Early/late. Dwarf variety that has less vigor than others. Large, purple-brown fig with strawberry flesh.*

Panachée. *Early/late. Striped green-yellow skin with strawberry flesh.*

Calimyrna. *A commercially grown fig that has excellent quality but requires very specific cross-pollination every three to five days with wasps from the caprifig over a two- to three-week period. This type of fig is not recommended for the home garden: it is generally too difficult to obtain caprifigs and to properly time the pollination procedure.*

PERSIMMONS (*DIOSPYROS KAKI*)

The persimmon is a very good fruit tree for home planting. Persimmons bloom late, avoiding spring frosts, and they do not require much winter chilling. They perform well throughout the state. Persimmon trees do not need ideal soil. They will tolerate wet feet in winter and dry conditions in the summer. The tree and fruit are almost pest-free. Blossoms and fruit are produced on current-season's shoots that originate

from the buds near the tips of one-year-old branches. Cross-pollination is not usually necessary. Cross-pollinated fruit will have seeds, whereas fruit from a lone tree probably will not.

Rootstocks

Diospyros lotus. *Most widely used seedling rootstock. Best choice. Compatible with most varieties. Tolerates wet soil.*

D. kaki. *An adequate rootstock. Produces a long taproot and little, branching, fibrous roots.*

D. virginiana. *This U.S. native species produces a very good fibrous root system and tolerates drought and excess moisture fairly well, but may sucker badly and may not be uniform from one tree to the other.*

Standard Varieties

Hachiya. *Late. Large, deep orange-red, acorn-shaped fruit. The flesh turns brown around the seeds, and flesh should be very soft to eat. Does not need cross-pollination. Trees get large and require an area of 20 feet (6 m). The fruit is astringent until very ripe and soft.*

Fuyu. *Late. Medium to large, flat, orange-red color. Flesh is firm like that of an apple and nonastringent when ripe. Cross-pollination is not required, but when present, fruit will have seed. Trees are smaller than Hachiya, requiring a width of 14 to 16 feet (about 4.5 m). The fruit loses astringency at maturity while still firm and crunchy.*

Chocolate. *Late. Cinnamon-chocolate-colored flesh. Good pollinizer.*

Izu. *Late. Round, orange skin, medium size, nonastringent type that is eaten crisp or soft. Sweet brown flesh.*

D. virginiana. *Late. U.S. native species, not a variety. Very small, very flavorful fruit. Must be eaten when soft.*

References

Larue, J. H., and R. S. Johnson, eds. 1989. Peaches, plums, and nectarines: Growing and handling for fresh market. Oakland: University of California Division of Agriculture and Natural Resources, Publication 3331.

Micke, W. C., ed. 1996. Almond production manual. Oakland: University of California Division of Agriculture and Natural Resources, Publication 3364.

Ramos, D. E., ed. 1998. Walnut production manual. Oakland: University of California Division of Agriculture and Natural Resources, Publication 3373.

Vossen, P. 2000. Chestnut culture in California. Oakland: University of California Division of Agriculture and Natural Resources, Publication 8010. Available free online from the UC ANR Communication Services Web site, http://anrcatalog.ucdavis.edu.

Vossen, P., and D. Silva. 2002. Temperate tree fruit and nut crops. Pages 449–530 in D. Pittenger, ed., California master gardener handbook. Oakland: University of California Division of Agriculture and Natural Resources, Publication 3382.

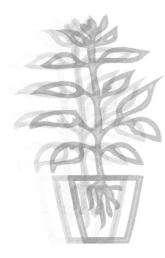

CHAPTER 4

Planting and Care of Young Fruit and Nut Trees

Chuck A. Ingels and Pamela M. Geisel

Planting

TREE SELECTION

Although you can plant containerized fruit and nut trees at any time of year, the most common time of year for buying them is during January and February when they are dormant and available as *bare-root* trees. The best bare-root trees have a trunk diameter from ½ to ⅝ inch (12.5 to 16 mm); a tree like this will usually have a better survival rate and be quicker to establish than a smaller or larger bare-root tree. If you are unable to plant bare-root trees soon after purchase, you should temporarily *heel them in* by covering the roots with soil, sawdust, or compost, and then keep them moist to prevent the roots from drying out.

At the nursery, select trees that are healthy and do not show signs of disease. The roots of a bare-root tree should be strong, healthy, and mostly unbroken (Figure 4.1). They should also be relatively straight, preferably with no sharp kinks or twists of large roots. Branch development may be useful in a bare-root tree in the nursery, but it is not essential since the trunk and most or all branches will be cut off at planting time.

For a containerized tree, the leaves and shoots should have vigorous growth and dark green color (Figure 4.2). Ideally, the branches should be spaced evenly along the trunk. Of equal importance, at least some of the branches should originate within about 2 ft. of the soil level since low branching is often desirable. If possible, inspect the roots and avoid trees that are severely root bound. Also avoid trees that were recently potted (early spring) from bare root and have not yet established enough of a root system to hold the container soil in place upon transplanting.

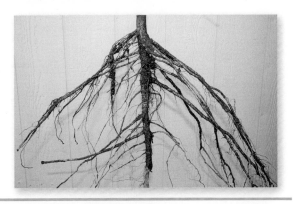

Figure 4.1. Roots of a healthy bare-root peach tree. Photo by Chuck Ingels.

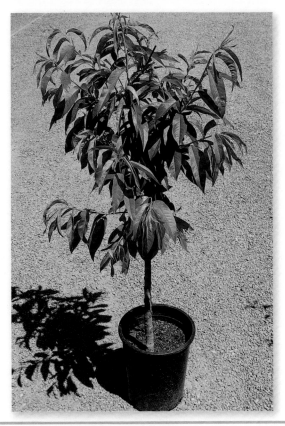

Figure 4.2. A healthy containerized peach tree in mid-spring. Note the vigorous growth, dark green foliage. Photo by Chuck Ingels.

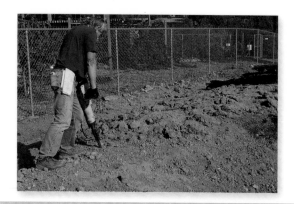

Figure 4.3. A jackhammer with a clay spade can be used to break up a soil that has been compacted by heavy equipment. Photo by Chuck Ingels.

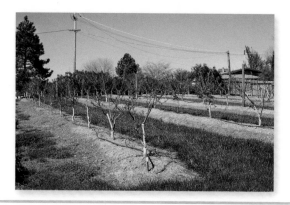

Figure 4.4. Planting on berms is an excellent way to improve drainage around the root crown and to increase the loose soil for roots to explore. Photo by Paul Vossen.

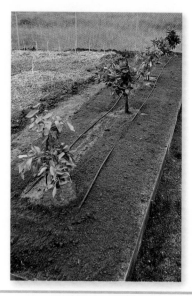

Figure 4.5. A raised planter bed with sandy loam topsoil that has been planted with dwarf citrus trees. The soil underneath is heavy clay with fractured hardpan. Photo by Chuck Ingels.

SITE SELECTION

Plant your new fruit trees where they will receive full sun for 6 to 8 or more hours per day during the growing season. A location with too much shade will reduce the amount and quality of fruit the tree can produce. Sunny exposures also encourage the best tree growth and development. Plant trees that may be susceptible to damage by wind or frost in locations where they can be sheltered and may benefit from heat retained by nearby buildings or trees.

Fruit and nut trees grow and produce best in soil that is at least 3 feet (1 m) deep and is uniform (has no compacted or stratified soil layers) and well drained (not excessively clayey). If the soil in your garden is not this deep or you have removed or compacted some topsoil during construction, your trees' growth may be stunted and the fruit may be small. Special attention to watering and fertilization, however, may make it possible for you to grow fruit trees successfully in as little as 1 to 1½ feet (30 to 50 cm) of good topsoil. Methods of improving poor soils are described in the next section.

Select a site that has a ready supply of water from a hose or from drip or sprinkler irrigation. Bear in mind how large the tree will be when mature: an unpruned standard-sized tree can reach 25 feet (7.5 m) or taller if allowed to, so avoid planting trees under power lines or other overhead obstructions. Allow enough space around the tree for pruning, spraying, harvesting, raking leaves, and other maintenance operations. Good air circulation around trees can help prevent disease. Take advantage of the fact that fruit trees can be quite beautiful when in bloom: plant them where you can see and enjoy them. If you plant a tree near a sidewalk or lawn, be prepared to harvest fruit regularly in order to keep it from dropping to the ground and creating a nuisance. A backyard or side yard may be preferable to a front yard if fruit theft is a consideration.

PREPARING THE PLANTING SITE

Many home gardens have soil that is loose and well drained. Many others, however, have less-than-ideal soil conditions for drainage and root growth, including heavy clay soil, soil that has been compacted by heavy equipment, and layers of *hardpan* (formed when mineral deposits become cemented to soil particles) beneath the soil surface. Ideally, a compacted soil should be cultivated or excavated to a depth and width that will allow adequate root exploration and movement of water through the soil. Some commercial growers use tractor-mounted, deep-ripping shanks or backhoes before planting to break through compacted zones or to mix stratified soils. For the home gardener, it may be possible to break through compacted soil or hardpan with tools that are available at equipment rental outlets, such as a pickaxe, a powered soil auger, a trencher, or a jackhammer with a clay spade attachment (Figure 4.3). Such work is best done with soil that is neither too dry nor too wet, but has the consistency of a wrung-out sponge. Another alternative is simply to create large mounds for tree planting or berms (Figure 4.4) or to build a raised bed at the planting site about 1 to 2 feet (30 to 60 cm) tall and fill it with a mix of native soil and good-quality topsoil (Figure 4.5).

If you have a deep, well-drained loam soil with good tilth, you will not have to add soil amendments or fertilizer to the soil. You may, however, want to add compost, well-rotted manure, gypsum, fertilizer, or other amendments to your soil if it is less than ideal for planting. Use a rotary tiller or a spade when working the amendment in to make sure it is mixed thoroughly into the soil. In heavy clay soils, undecomposed organic amendments may rot and become toxic to new roots, especially in heavy soils. It is best to wait until new top growth is several inches long before you apply nitrogen fertilizer: young trees do not need nitrogen immediately, and nitrogen will readily leach through the soil. Also, excessive nitrogen can burn young roots. If your soil requires added phosphorus and potassium, it is best to work it into the soil before you plant because these nutrients will not leach through the soil to the roots.

Planting the Tree

Once you have made sure that the surrounding soil is loosened and that compacted layers have been broken up, dig the planting hole just bigger than the depth and width of the roots. Unless the soil was already severely compacted beneath the hole, it is best to leave the soil directly below the root system undisturbed to help prevent the tree from settling; this undisturbed soil is sometimes referred to as a *pedestal*. If needed, dig deeper and wider just beyond the root system. If deeper soil layers were dug or augured, be sure to form enough of a mound to prevent settling and the creation of a basin, where sitting water could rot the root crown. If the sides of the planting hole are slickened by digging or augering (as can happen in clay soils), loosen the sides with a shovel to help roots grow out of the planting hole and into the native soil. Avoid planting trees in very wet soil.

Fruit trees should be planted "high" to help avoid crown rot disease (Figure 4.6). When properly planted, the soil line on the trunk (visible as a change in color where the soil surface met the trunk in the field) should be at or slightly above the level of the surrounding ground, and the bud union should be at least 4 inches (10 cm) above the soil surface. Placing a shovel handle or other straightedge across the hole can be a helpful way to check planting height during the filling process. As a general rule, after the soil has settled, the uppermost large root should be no more than an inch or two below the soil surface. Tree anchorage is not improved from deep planting, but from subsequent root growth. Gently pull the tree up if it was planted too deep. The soil should slope downward from the tree to prevent water from accumulating near the trunk. Apply a layer of mulch or wood chips a few inches thick in a radius 2 to 3 feet (60 to 90 cm) around the tree. Keep the mulch a few inches away from the trunk to minimize the likelihood of crown rot and to eliminate hiding places for insect pests. Consider the following additional strategies when planting trees:

Bare-Root Trees. Before you put a bare-root tree into the ground, examine its roots; cut off any that are broken or kinked. Avoid shortening excessively long roots; instead, dig a bigger hole to accommodate the roots and straighten them to prevent kinking (Figure 4.7). Begin backfilling loose soil and lightly tamp it down around the roots (Figure 4.8), add the remaining soil, and tamp further.

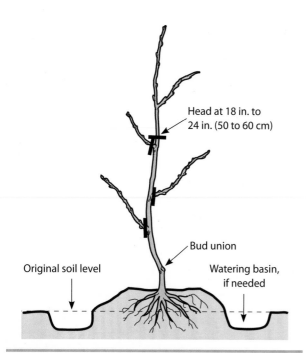

Head at 18 in. to
24 in. (50 to 60 cm)

Bud union

Original soil level

Watering basin,
if needed

Figure 4.6. How to plant and prune a deciduous fruit or nut tree. Plant the tree on a slight mound, especially if drainage is poor. The bud union should be at least 2 to 4 inches (5 to 10 cm) above the surface of the soil. The uppermost large roots should be just below the surface of the soil. Head the trunk at 18 to 24 inches. If branches below the heading cut are not well developed, cut them off at the trunk. In hot areas, paint the entire tree from 2 inches (5 cm) below the soil surface to the top of the tree with a 50-50 mixture of flat white interior latex paint and water. *Source:* Adapted from Vossen and Silva 2002, p. 486.

Container-Grown Trees. Container-grown trees may have circling or girdling roots, which should be gently pulled away from the root ball before the tree is planted (Figure 4.9). Fill the hole with soil and firm it lightly, eliminating large air pockets. Be sure to keep the top of the root ball free of backfill soil (Figure 4.10).

Holeless Planting. In poorly drained soils, plant the tree on a mound or berm to prevent crown rot. A simple method of planting on a mound is to dig soil under and around the planting site, set the tree in the middle of this cultivated soil, and pile soil over the roots (Figure 4.11). Be sure to make the mound wide enough to allow for a way to irrigate after planting.

Pruning the Newly Planted Tree

An important goal of many home orchardists is to maintain relatively small trees to facilitate pruning,

thinning, pest management, and harvesting. By heading (cutting off) the newly planted bare-root tree at knee height (about 18 to 24 inches [50 to 60 cm]), you can force the tree to develop low branches. If it's important to you to have access to the area under the tree, however, you can head the tree higher up, as far as 36 inches (90 cm) from the ground. Make sure, though, to cut the tree back by at least one-third of its original length or the shoot growth may be inadequate. You can head walnut, pecan, and chestnut trees at 5 to 7 feet (1.5 to 2.1 m).

Many bare-root trees either have no lateral branches below the trunk heading cut, or have only spindly or broken lateral branches that should be removed (see Figure 4.6). Still, some bare-root trees may have undamaged lateral branches with wide branch angles that are large enough to retain. Branches that are about $^3/_{16}$ to $^1/_4$ in. (4.8 to 6.4 mm) in diameter at the base can be shortened to stubs of two or three buds (Figures 4.12 and 4.13). You can retain well-placed, well-attached branches that are larger than about $^1/_4$ inch in diameter where they join the trunk and then cut them back by about one-third to one-half their original length (Figure 4.14). Any retained stubs or branches should be spaced vertically and radially around the trunk, if possible. Even if only one healthy branch is present, you can stub or shorten it. By retaining one or more lateral branches you can get better vertical spacing between scaffold branches; otherwise, nearly all of the branches will arise from just below the heading cut on the trunk. Just make sure that any shoots that grow from these retained lower shoots do not get shaded out by the new top growth. Later on, you should thin the shoots that grow from buds on stubs to only one shoot per stub, or as many as two shoots for longer retained branches. These shoots will later become the tree's main scaffold branches.

When purchasing containerized fruit trees, carefully consider each tree's branch height and placement. Branches at 2 feet at the time of planting will be at 2 feet at maturity unless the tree is headed back. Do not attempt to head a high-branched tree on the trunk below the branches when you plant it in spring or summer. If you would like a lower-branching tree, though, you may be able to head it back the following winter. Trunks of older trees should not be headed in this manner since the cut stump may decay before callus growth closes the wound.

SUNBURN PROTECTION AT PLANTING

The bark of your newly planted tree needs protection from sunburn, which can dehydrate the bark and lead to bark cracking, infestation with borer insects, and wood decay (Figure 4.15). Use a 1:1 mixture of flat white interior latex paint and water (the exact proportions of paint and water are not critical—dilution simply makes the paint easier to apply). You can also use tree trunk whitewash products sold at nurseries. Organically acceptable whitewashes are also available. In hot interior areas of California, extend the paint application area to 2 inches (5 cm) below the soil surface (to allow soil settling) and up the entire trunk, including over the dormant buds, or at least up to the new tree's first main branch.

IRRIGATION

Newly planted trees should be watered thoroughly to settle the soil around the roots. Form a donut-shaped ring around the outer edge of the root ball of a container-grown tree, or just beyond the spread of the roots of a bare-root tree, and fill the ring with water (Figure 4.16). If using drip irrigation, place the drip line near the tree and use two emitters per tree, about 1 foot (30 cm) from either side of the trunk (Figure 4.17), and water thoroughly.

Care of Young Trees

TRAINING YOUNG TREES

You can train a deciduous fruit or nut tree into any of a number of basic structures: open center, central leader, modified central leader, espalier, or fruit bush. The structure you choose depends on the species of tree, the height at which you wish to maintain the tree, your growing conditions, and your personal taste. If you want a tree to grow to its full size, you can simply let the tree grow without any pruning during the first growing season and then prune during the dormant season when the leaves are gone and the branches are clearly visible. You can accelerate the tree's training, though, by using summer pruning to start its structural development during the first growing season and

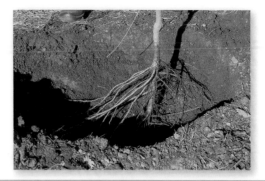

Figure 4.7. Avoid shortening roots. Instead, dig the hole larger to accommodate the roots as they are. Photo by Chuck Ingels.

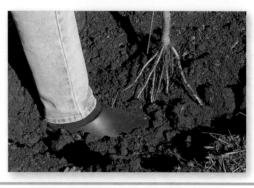

Figure 4.8. Fill the soil around the roots of a bare-root tree and lightly tamp the soil to remove air pockets. Photo by Chuck Ingels.

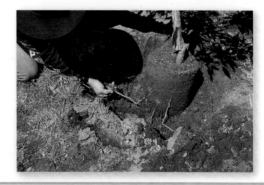

Figure 4.9. Pull any wound roots away to straighten them before planting. Photo by Chuck Ingels.

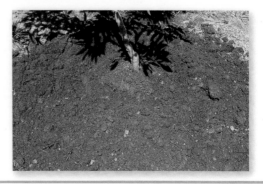

Figure 4.10. Containerized tree planted, showing no soil backfilled over the soil in the pot. Photo by Chuck Ingels.

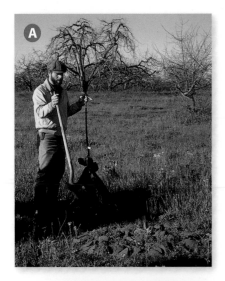

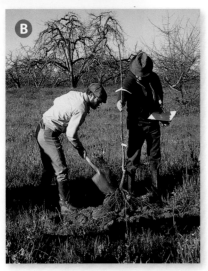

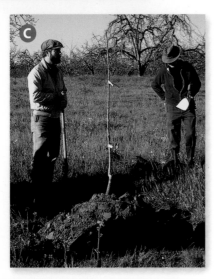

Figure 4.11. A simple method of planting a tree on a mound. **(A)** Loosen the soil in a large circle. **(B)** Set the tree in the middle of the circle. **(C)** Place soil over the roots. Be sure to allow for some soil settling and for a way to water the mound. Photos by Muchtar Salzman.

then fine-tuning the training during the first dormant season. If you want to create a fruit bush, you will have to prune about two times during the summer, and to grow espalier trees you will have to apply some training and pruning during the first season (for more information on training and pruning, see Chapter 7).

Irrigation

Newly planted trees generally do not require much irrigation until the weather turns warm and new growth is several inches to 1 foot (30 cm) long. Container-grown trees that are transplanted in the summer, however, often have a relatively large canopy and require frequent watering until their roots become established in the surrounding soil. A healthy first-year tree with no mulch requires about 5 to 15 gallons (19 to 57 L) of water per week in the summer in hot areas of California, depending on the extent of canopy growth, or less than that if you use mulch (see Table 5.1). The frequency and amount of irrigation both depend on the soil type, the irrigation method, weather conditions, ground cover, and tree size (see Chapter 5). For best growth, the soil in the root zone should be moist at all times yet never saturated, although the soil surface may be allowed to dry. To determine whether you have adequate soil moisture, periodically dig a small test hole about 8 to 10 inches (20 to 25 cm) deep with a soil sampling tube or a shovel or trowel and examine the soil in the root zone (see Figure 5.5). Use the soil moisture feel test to determine how wet the soil is (see Figure 5.6).

Weeds

Weeds compete with young trees for water and nutrients; if left uncontrolled, they can slow a tree's growth and make it more susceptible to sunburn damage. Keep the ground within at least 3 feet (1 m) of the tree trunk free of grass, weeds, and other vegetation. A layer of mulch, together with hand weeding, can provide good weed control. Avoid hoeing or using string-type weed trimmers as these may injure roots or nick the trunk and allow introduction of crown gall disease.

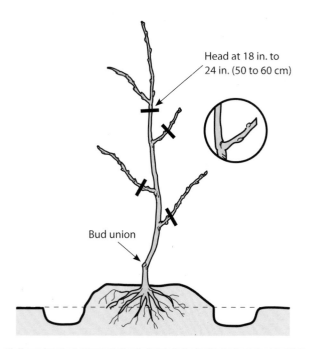

Head at 18 in. to 24 in. (50 to 60 cm)

Bud union

Figure 4.12. Pruning a tree with well developed and unbroken lateral branches below the heading cut. Retain as many as three branches spaced vertically and radially around the tree. Branches that are thinner (³/₁₆ to ¹/₄ inch) should be shortened to 2 or 3 buds (*see inset*) and thicker branches can be cut back to one-third to one-half their original size. Remove all other branches. New shoots that grow from these stubs will become main scaffold branches (*see* Chapter 7). *Source:* Adapted from Vossen and Silva 2002, p. 486.

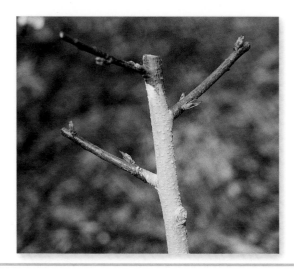

Figure 4.13. Healthy branches of this bare-root peach tree were cut back to short stubs. New shoots that grow from them or from the trunk will be selected as scaffold branches. Photo by Chuck Ingels.

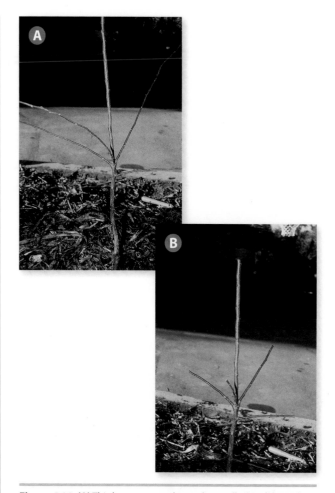

Figure 4.14. (A) This bare-root apple tree has well-placed branches. **(B)** The branches were cut back to about one-third their original length to begin developing the first tier of branches. The trunk was headed to begin to form the second tier and a new leader. Photos by Chuck Ingels.

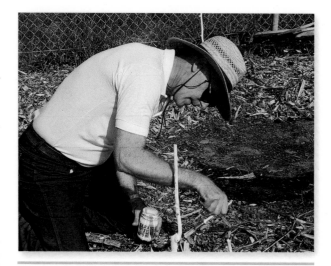

Figure 4.15. A 50:50 mix of interior white latex paint and water is painted onto the newly planted bare-root tree. You can substitute an organic-based or other whitewash material for the paint. Paint from the top of the tree to 2 inches below the soil level. Photo by Chuck Ingels.

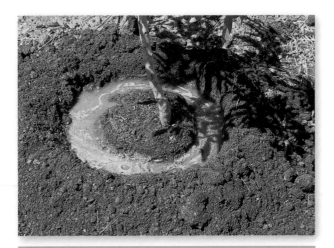

Figure 4.16. Form a doughnut-shaped ring around the root ball and flood this basin. Within a few months, construct a wider, doughnut-shaped ring or simply flatten the soil on the mound if using drip or sprinkler irrigation. Photo by Chuck Ingels.

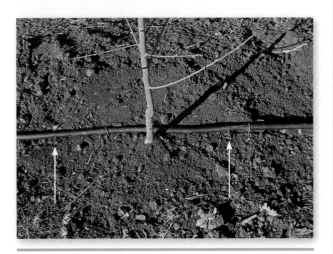

Figure 4.17. Drip irrigation added after planting the bare-root tree, with an emitter *(arrows)* placed on either side of the tree. Photo by Chuck Ingels.

References

Carson, J., G. Shimizu, C. Ingels, P. Geisel, and C. Unruh. 2002. Fruit trees: Planting and care of young trees. Oakland: University of California Division of Agriculture and Natural Resources, Publication 8048. Available free online from the UC ANR Communication Services Web site, http://anrcatalog.ucdavis.edu.

Hickman, G. W., and P. Svihra. 2002. Planting landscape trees. Oakland: University of California Division of Agriculture and Natural Resources, Publication 8046. Available free online from the UC ANR Communication Services Web site, http://anrcatalog.ucdavis.edu.

Hodel, D., and D. Pittenger. 2002. Woody landscape plants. Pages 311–336 in D. Pittenger, ed., California master gardener handbook. Oakland: University of California Division of Agriculture and Natural Resources, Publication 3382.

Vossen, P., and D. Silva. 2002. Temperate tree fruit and nut crops. Pages 449–530 in D. Pittenger, ed., California master gardener handbook. Oakland: University of California Division of Agriculture and Natural Resources, Publication 3382.

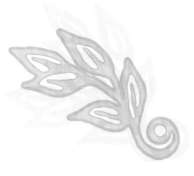

CHAPTER 5

Irrigation

Lawrence J. Schwankl, R. Scott Johnson, and Terry L. Prichard

It is difficult to irrigate trees with maximum efficiency—applying just the right amount of water—in a home landscape, since trees are often interplanted with turfgrass and other plants that have their own, different water needs. The precise water needs of many landscape plants are unknown, and beyond that the plants' growing environment (including sun exposure, surrounding vegetation, and other factors) significantly influences their water use. Even with these difficulties, though, we will present a way to estimate your trees' water needs along with some easy hints on how to determine whether the right amount of water is being applied. We will also give you information on operating your irrigation system, whether it be a garden hose or a sophisticated drip irrigation system. The ability to estimate when and how much water to apply and the knowledge of how to apply that water will enable you to improve your trees' health and make you a more efficient water user.

Importance of Good Irrigation

The proper irrigation of trees with the correct amount of water is important for a number of reasons. Trees can be killed if you apply too much water or too little. Young trees are especially susceptible to damage from poor irrigation management practices. When you under-irrigate trees, you expose them to water stress that can inhibit their growth or kill them. It can also eventually lead to greater susceptibility to pests such as mites and trunk-boring insects. Too much water, especially in a soil that is not well drained, can be equally damaging to trees. Soil that is too wet can be an ideal environment for many tree root diseases. These diseases, in conjunction with a weak root system caused by overly wet soil, can quickly kill a tree. The ideal is to have your trees growing in soil moisture conditions that allow it access to sufficient soil water without being too wet.

It is important to manage your tree irrigation in a way that does not waste water. This is being efficient with the applied irrigation water. An efficient irrigator applies just enough irrigation water to replenish the soil water that has been used by the tree and lost to evaporation. Another aspect of irrigation efficiency is to apply water only where the roots are. In general, a tree's underground roots spread out at least as far as the canopy does above ground. This means that as the tree grows and the root zone expands, you should increase the area you irrigate. If you apply all of a large tree's water right next to the trunk, much of that water is likely to soak down beneath the root zone where it will be unavailable to the tree.

Irrigating Trees

There are two irrigation decisions that you need to make—how much water to apply and how often to irrigate. Frequent (e.g., daily) irrigations can encourage a tree to develop a shallow root system. You want to encourage deeper rooting, so irrigations should be less frequent and longer in duration during the summer than in the winter for an established tree. More frequent irrigations may be needed if you are using drip irrigation. A young tree has a small root zone so it may need to be irrigated more frequently (but with a lesser amount of water) than an established tree. The amount of water needed to irrigate trees is discussed below, under *Estimating Tree Water Use.*

Finally, you also need to know how much water your irrigation system is applying. You will find a discussion of how to make this determination in each of the irrigation system sections that follow.

Tree Water Use Units

The units used to express tree water use can be confusing. Tree water use is often expressed in "inches" of water. An easy way to think of this is to see inches of tree water use as just the opposite of inches of rainfall. When someone says, "It rained a half-inch," many people have a feel for how much that is. Tree water use of ½ inch would indicate that the tree had drawn enough water out of the ground to make a ½-inch thick layer under the tree's canopy and, through transpiration, had returned it to the atmosphere—more or less reversing the process of rainfall.

The time units associated with tree water use may vary, too, ranging from daily values (e.g., inches per day) to tree water use on a weekly or even a monthly schedule. To use this information to calculate how much to irrigate, you can simply sum the daily values for tree water use from the time of the last irrigation until the time you have set for your next irrigation. This is how much water you want to apply. It is easy to determine daily tree water use information from weekly or monthly values. Assume that tree water use is uniform throughout the week or month and then divide by the number of days: seven if you are working from weekly values and thirty if you are working from monthly values.

Inches of water works well as a measure of tree water use when you are using sprinklers for irrigation. You can set out collection cups in the sprinkler area and easily judge the depth of water you have applied. Usually, sprinkler application rates are given in inches/hour. When you use a hose, drip emitters, or microsprinklers, however, application rates are measured in gallons per minute or hour, and you will have to convert inches of tree water use to gallons of water. The key to this conversion is to determine how much land area is covered by the tree. An easy way to do this is to measure the area of the tree's canopy using the standard formula for the area of a circle, πr^2 (π, or pi, is approximately equal to 3.14). The area under the canopy is then:

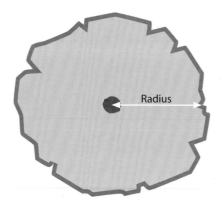

Tree Area (ft^2) $3.14 \times$ (radius of canopy [ft])^2

For example:

Given: Radius of the tree's canopy is 10 feet

Tree Area (ft^2) $= 3.14 \times (10\,\text{ft})^2 = 3.14 \times 100\,\text{ft}^2 = 314\,\text{ft}^2$

If the tree's daily water use is 0.25 in/day, you can use the canopy area to convert that value into gallons per day using the conversion factor of 0.623:

$$\frac{\text{Tree water}}{\text{use (gal/day)}} = \frac{\text{Tree water}}{\text{use (in/day)}} \times \frac{\text{Tree canopy}}{\text{area (ft}^2\text{)}} \times 0.623$$

Tree water $= 0.25\,\text{in/day} \times 314\,\text{ft}^2 \times 0.623$ use (gal/day)
$= 49\,\text{gal/day}$

You may be able to find information on plant water use from a variety of sources, presented in terms of *reference evapotranspiration*. Be careful when you use this information, since reference evapotranspiration is recorded in terms of the water use of tall fescue pasture grass, or in some places, alfalfa, not of trees. You will do better to use the tree water use information provided in this chapter or other information that has been developed specifically for trees.

Estimating Tree Water Use

The amount of water used by a healthy fruit or nut tree is dependent on many different factors. These factors can be roughly categorized into two general areas: tree size and climatic conditions. By taking into account these factors combined with occasional monitoring of actual tree and soil conditions, you should be able to determine the right amount of irrigation water to apply.

Table 5.1. Tree water use (gallons per tree per day) in California coastal and inland areas*

Canopy diameter (ft)	1	2	3	4	5	6	8	10	12	15	20	25	30
Zone and tree type													
Midsummer (June, July, and August) *gal/tree/day*													
Coastal trees	0.2	0.6	1.2	2.1	3.2	4.5	7.9	12.2	17.7	27.7	49.0	76.5	110.2
Inland trees	0.4	1.0	2.1	3.5	5.4	7.6	13.4	20.7	30.0	47.0	83.0	129.7	186.8
Spring and fall (April, May, and September) *gal/tree/day*													
Coastal trees	0.2	0.4	0.9	1.4	2.2	3.1	5.5	8.5	12.4	19.4	34.3	53.6	77.1
Inland trees	0.3	0.7	1.5	2.5	3.8	5.3	9.4	14.5	21.0	32.9	58.1	90.8	130.7

*Water use of olive and citrus trees is about 65% of table values. Following harvest, water use of all trees can be reduced to 75% of table values.

TREE SIZE

The greater the sun-exposed leaf area on a tree, the greater will be its water use. You can get a good estimate of a tree's sun-exposed leaf area simply by measuring the diameter of the tree canopy and dividing that in half to find its radius (r). Then apply the common formula for the area of a circle (area $= \pi r^2$). This works for most fruit and nut trees since their canopies develop in a roughly spherical shape, but you will have to make adjustments for odd-shaped trees. For example, a tall espalier tree would use more water than its canopy diameter would indicate.

CLIMATIC CONDITIONS

The weather affects evaporation from stomates much as it affects evaporation from an open body of water. This means that a tree's water use increases with an increase in light, daylength, temperature, or wind speed, or with a decrease in humidity. Detailed computer models have been developed to estimate daily (and even hourly) plant water use based on current weather conditions. California weather conditions are generally consistent enough from year to year to allow growers to use long-term averages to estimate tree water use for a typical spring or summer day. Table 5.1 gives a summary of these estimates. Because the cool, moist conditions of California's coast are quite different from the hot, dry conditions further inland, separate estimates are listed for these two zones. For areas in between these two extremes, you can make your own estimate somewhere in the middle.

APPLYING THE RIGHT AMOUNT OF WATER

Table 5.1 provides a good starting point for how much to irrigate your trees, but you may have to make some modifications to fit your local conditions. Here are a few basic things to consider.

A tree shaded by a building or other trees will use less water than a tree in full sun. As a general rule, shaded trees use about one-third as much water. Therefore, if the tree is shaded all day, multiply the values in Table 5.1 by ⅓; if shaded for half the day, multiply by ⅔.

Light reflections off of cement, asphalt, and metal can increase the temperature of (and therefore the water loss from) trees. A tree's water use can be as much as 40 percent higher if it is exposed to such conditions.

The use of organic or fabric mulches around the tree can be very beneficial, reducing water lost to evaporation from the soil surface, cooling surface roots, and reducing weed growth. Unwanted weed growth under the tree can increase irrigation water use by as much as 30 percent.

Don't start irrigating too early in the spring. When trees first leaf out, they do not use much water, conditions are cool, and there is generally water stored in the soil from winter rains. As a general rule, you don't need to start irrigating until one month after bud break unless it has been a particularly dry winter. In a dry winter, irrigate the tree's root zone one month before bud break to encourage good root growth.

Some soils are considered problem soils and can be particularly difficult to manage. For instance, if your soil has a shallow, impervious hardpan layer, simple weekly irrigations may waterlog the root zone for long periods of time, leading to the death of your trees. In this situation, it would be better to irrigate more frequently with less water to keep the tree from dying.

Monitor the tree's health. A healthy, vigorous tree is a good sign that your irrigation management is correct. A stressed tree will stop growing and start to lose its leaves. The growing shoot tips of a stressed tree may wilt and older leaves may look droopy. Trees with too much water may show those same symptoms. Many of their roots may have died from waterlogging, leaving the root system insufficient to keep the tree supplied with water. In either case, it is important that you check the water status of the soil and the health of the roots. Healthy roots are white under the bark and generally exhibit signs of new growth. Dying roots are brown with no new growth and often have a fermented or "swampy" smell.

Irrigation Methods

GARDEN HOSE (USED ALONE OR SUPPLEMENTING ANOTHER IRRIGATION SYSTEM)

The simplest method of watering a backyard tree is to use a garden hose. Whether you have a sprinkler attached to the hose end or you simply allow the water to run onto the ground, you should apply the water where the tree can take it up from the soil. Apply water under the canopy of the tree to make it available to the roots.

Advantages

- *The major advantage to the use of a garden hose for irrigating trees is its simplicity. It is low-cost and low-maintenance.*

Disadvantages

- *Use of a garden hose for irrigation is labor-intensive. You must remember to start the hose running, remember to move it, and, often the most difficult, remember to turn it off.*

A good way to determine how much water the hose is applying is to see how long it takes for the hose, set at a flow rate you will be using to irrigate, to fill a 5-gallon bucket (make sure it holds 5 gallons). Use this equation:

$$300 \div (\underline{\hphantom{xx}} \text{ seconds to fill a 5-gallon pail}) = \underline{\hphantom{xx}} \text{ gal per minute}$$

For example:

If it takes 45 seconds to fill a 5-gallon pail, then:

$$300 \div 45 \text{ seconds} = 6.7 \text{ gal/min}$$

Once you know the hose's flow rate in gallons per minute and the number of gallons you want to apply, you can determine how many minutes to run the hose. Bear in mind that it is difficult to return accurately and repeatedly to any faucet setting other than fully open.

If you have no other irrigation system to irrigate surrounding vegetation, all of the tree's irrigation requirements will need to be supplied from the garden hose. Even if you have other vegetation surrounding the tree (e.g., turfgrass irrigated with automatic sprinklers), it may be beneficial to use the hose periodically for deep watering. Keep turfgrass or groundcovers at least 6 inches away from the tree trunk to keep water competition to a minimum.

An excellent way of controlling hose applications is to use a control device (Figure 5.1) between the faucet and the hose. You can set the device with the number of gallons you want to apply and it will shut off the water after that much water has run through it. Because this type of device measures the actual amount of water, you do not have to worry about opening the faucet to a consistent level each time you water the tree.

An alternative hose control device is one which works like a kitchen timer. The controller runs for a set number of minutes, and at the end of that time the device shuts off the water. While this works well, you still need to know the hose's discharge rate if you want to apply a specific number of gallons.

If there is other vegetation (e.g., turfgrass or ground cover) around the tree, it is more difficult to determine how much water to apply to the tree. You may have to apply 25 to 30 percent more water to the area around a tree if additional vegetation is growing there. If, on the other hand, this other vegetation is irrigated regularly, it can be difficult to know how much (if any) additional water the tree needs. Assuming that the irrigation of the other vegetation is done well, the tree will probably benefit from some infrequent, deep irrigations, say every week or two.

PERMANENT SPRINKLERS

Permanent irrigation sprinklers are sprinklers that have been installed into the ground and operate when the watering cycle is initiated either manually or by an automatic controller and solenoid valve(s). Many gardeners equip their sprinkler systems with pop-up sprinkler heads that automatically extend upward when irrigating and then drop back underground when the water turns off. If you install permanent sprinklers near your home orchard, it's important to choose sprinkler heads that will not apply water to the tree foliage and trunk and cause disease problems. Low-angle sprinklers are preferable as are pop-up sprinklers that can be adjusted manually to lower the angle of water "throw."

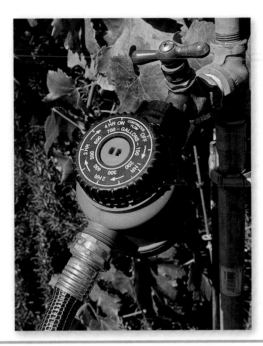

Figure 5.1. This flow control device shuts the water off based on the number of gallons applied. This model can also be set to shut off after a set period of time. Photo by Chuck Ingels.

Fruit trees will require a separate valve and program so that the frequency and length of irrigation can be separated from that of the rest of the landscape. Fruit trees require less frequent irrigation than turf and garden plantings.

Advantages

- *The water application rate of permanent sprinklers is fairly easy to determine.*

- *Permanent sprinklers can be automated using solenoid valves and an electronic controller. This makes irrigating easy. Automation also allows you to schedule early morning irrigations when evaporation losses may be lower.*

Disadvantages

- *Automatic sprinklers can be a problem if you fail to adjust the operation times on the controller to match changing tree water demands. You could end up wasting water and your tree could be over- or under-watered.*

- *Sprinklers that operate when no one is home or awake may develop leaks and other damage that may go undetected. Periodically, you should turn the sprinklers on manually so you can check for leaks.*

Many permanent sprinkler systems are designed so that some areas receive water from more than one sprinkler. If your trees are irrigated this way, the best method to determine the sprinkler system's application rate is to put out six to ten straight-sided containers (empty cat food or tuna cans work well) here and there around the tree to collect water during irrigation. Operate the sprinklers for the usual amount of time, or for at least 15 minutes. Make a note of how long the sprinklers operate. Using a thin ruler, measure the depth of water in each container. To determine the average depth of water applied, add up the depths of water from all of the containers and divide that sum by the number of containers.

For example:
Irrigation time = 30 minutes (0.5 hr)
Water collected in each container:

Container	Amount of water collected (inches)
1	½ (= $\frac{8}{16}$)
2	⅜ (= $\frac{6}{16}$)
3	$\frac{7}{16}$
4	$\frac{9}{16}$
5	$\frac{11}{16}$
6	⅝ (= $\frac{10}{16}$)
7	⅛ (= $\frac{2}{16}$)
8	½ (= $\frac{8}{16}$)
9	⅜ (= $\frac{6}{16}$)
10	$\frac{9}{16}$

Sum of depths (inches) in containers = ($\frac{8}{16}$ + $\frac{6}{16}$ + $\frac{7}{16}$ + $\frac{9}{16}$ + $\frac{11}{16}$ + $\frac{10}{16}$ + $\frac{2}{16}$ + $\frac{8}{16}$ + $\frac{6}{16}$ + $\frac{9}{16}$) = $\frac{76}{16}$ in = 4.75 in

Average depth of water applied = Sum of container depths ÷ Number of containers

= 4.75 in ÷ 10 containers = 0.475 in

Application rate (in/hr) = Avg. depth of water applied (in) ÷ sprinkler test operation time (hr) = 0.475 in ÷ 0.5 hr = 0.95 in/hr

To convert a sprinkler application rate given in in/hr to the number of gallons per minute, use the following formula:

$$\left(\begin{array}{c}\text{Application}\\\text{Rate (in/hr)}\end{array}\right) \times \left(\begin{array}{c}\text{Tree canopy}\\\text{diameter (ft)}\end{array}\right)^2 \times 0.0083 = \left(\begin{array}{c}\text{Application}\\\text{Rate (gal/min)}\end{array}\right)$$

For example:
Sprinkler application rate = 0.95 in/hr
Tree canopy diameter = 10 ft
0.95 in/hr x (10 ft)² x 0.0083 = 0.79 gal/min

Compare the water application rate (in/hr) from the example above to the tree's water use (gal/day) from Table 5.1 to determine how long you need to irrigate (see example below). Remember, it's better to give trees deep, infrequent irrigations than to irrigate them often with shallow irrigations.

Example:
An inland deciduous tree 10 feet in diameter uses 20.7 gallons of water per day during midsummer. Using the sprinkler system described above (application rate = 0.79 gal/min), how long should the irrigations be?

If water were to be applied daily, the operation time of the sprinklers should be

20.7 gal/day ÷ 0.79 gal/min = 26.2 min/day (round to 26 min/day)

Instead of irrigating each day, it would be better to irrigate every few days in order to encourage deeper watering and deeper root growth. If irrigations were scheduled every 3 days, the irrigation time should be

13 min/day × 3 days = 39 min

As the irrigation times get longer, runoff may become a problem, so you should take it into account when choosing a sprinkler irrigation time.

DRIP AND MICROSPRINKLER SYSTEMS

Drip and microsprinkler irrigation systems (Figure 5.2) apply water to a localized area and are well-suited to irrigating trees and other stand-alone plants. The discharge rates from drip emitters range from ½ to 4 gallons per hour (gal/hr), depending on which model you use. Microsprinkler discharge rates are higher, ranging from 6 gal/hr up to 30 gal/hr. In order to irrigate a tree adequately with drip emitters, you have to place multiple drip emitters around each tree and make sure to conduct frequent, long irrigations to meet the midsummer water needs of mature trees. Microsprinklers, with their higher flow rates, can more easily meet the midsummer water demands of a mature tree. One or two microsprinklers per tree are often sufficient. Avoid hitting the tree trunk with the spray.

Advantages

- *Water can be applied accurately to the tree's root zone.*

- *Drip emitters can be used underneath mulches, minimizing the water lost to evaporation.*

- *Drip and microsprinkler systems are easily expanded and changed to adapt to a changing landscape.*

- *Weed growth may be less of a problem because you are only wetting a portion of the soil surface.*

- *Because young trees require more frequent irrigations than mature trees, they do especially well under drip or microsprinkler irrigation.*

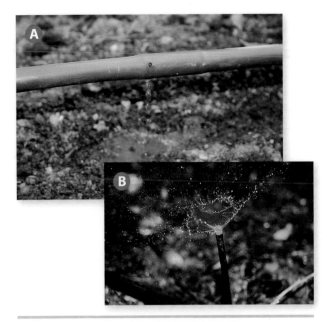

Figure 5.2. (A) Inline drip tubing has built-in emitters and is available in different flow rates and emitter spacings. **(B)** A microsprinkler system puts out more water with less tubing than an inline drip tubing system. Photos by Chuck Ingels.

Disadvantages

- *Depending on the irrigation water quality, maintenance of drip irrigation systems can be a problem. Drip emitters and microsprinklers, with their small emission openings, can plug easily.*

- *Drip irrigation systems can be damaged by animals, insects, digging, and human traffic.*

- *Under a thick organic mulch, tree roots may grow over drip lines, making repairs difficult.*

Drip and microsprinkler systems are "high-frequency" irrigation systems. They apply water slowly and must be run frequently to keep up with the tree's water needs. A large tree may use over 50 gallons of water per day. To replace this soil moisture, a drip irrigation system using 1 gal/hr drip emitters would need to have multiple drip emitters under the tree and would have to be operated for many hours. For large trees, microsprinklers or permanent sprinklers may be more appropriate than drip emitters.

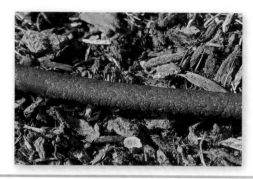

Figure 5.3. A soaker hose can be useful in irrigating narrow plantings. Photo by Chuck Ingels.

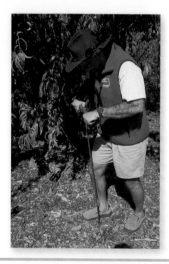

Figure 5.4. By pushing a metal rod into the soil, you can judge how deeply the soil has been wetted (in this photograph, a handle has been welded onto the rod). You will be able to push the rod easily into moist soil, but not into dry soil. Photo by Chuck Ingels.

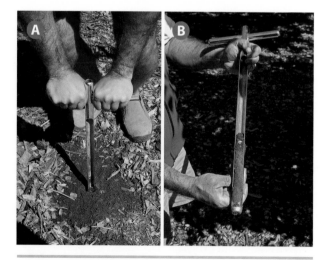

Figure 5.5. (A) A soil sampling tube can help you determine soil condition and soil moisture content. **(B)** The removed soil core. Photos by Chuck Ingels.

SOAKER HOSE SYSTEMS

A soaker hose (Figure 5.3) is a specialized form of drip irrigation. Soaker hoses can be effective for irrigation of narrow plantings that are difficult to irrigate with sprinklers or microsprinklers. You can also run the soaker hose in a circle under the tree's canopy to form a ring of irrigation around the tree.

There are three main problems with soaker hoses. First of all, unless you have a flow meter connected to the soaker hose, it is hard to determine how much water you are applying with each irrigation. Second, like other drip irrigation systems, water contaminants can easily clog soaker hoses. If you use good filters you can keep this problem to a minimum. Finally, you should not try to use lengths of soaker hose greater than approximately 50 feet. The pressure losses in a soaker hose can be high, with the result that the tail end of the hose will get much less water than the head end.

Evaluating Your Efforts

A good way to find out how deep water has penetrated into the soil following an irrigation is to push a metal or plastic rod (Figure 5.4) into the soil. It will easily push into wet soil but it will not penetrate easily into dry soil. A day or two after a thorough irrigation, the soil around a mature tree should be moist to a depth of at least 2 to 3 feet. If your tree is planted over a hardpan or compacted layer of soil, you may not be able to use a push probe.

If you have access to a soil sampling tube or an auger (Figure 5.5), you can evaluate soil moisture using your hand as a measuring device. See the following paragraph and Figure 5.6 for details of how to use the *feel method* to determine soil moisture and texture.

FEEL METHOD

As a first step in learning to determine soil moisture by the feel method, get an idea of how a handful of the soil feels at its extremes of soil moisture: wet and dry. The wet limit (its *field capacity*) is the soil moisture after the area has been allowed to drain following an irrigation. This is usually 2 to 3 days after a thorough irrigation. Determine the soil's dry limit by sampling and feeling soil away from the planted area that has gone a long period (weeks) since it was last irrigated. This soil will be at what is termed the "permanent wilting point." For healthy trees, you want to have your soil moisture somewhere between these wet and dry limits. See Figure 5.6 for help in determining soil texture and soil moisture content.

Coarse-textured soil (Hanford sandy loam)

Dry

Medium

Wet

Medium-textured soil (San Joaquin loam)

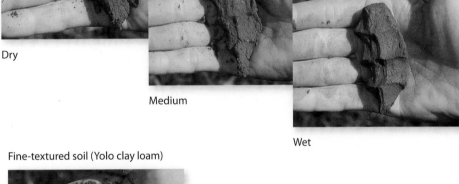

Dry

Medium

Wet

Fine-textured soil (Yolo clay loam)

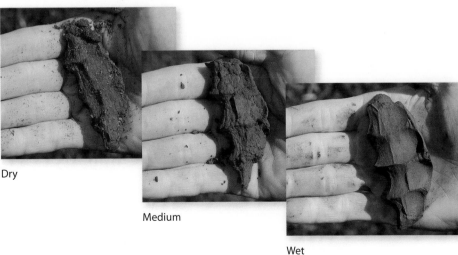

Dry

Medium

Wet

Figure 5.6. Determining soil texture and moisture by the *feel method*. Photos by Jack Kelly Clark.

References

California Department of Water Resources. 2000. A guide to estimating irrigation water requirements of landscape plantings in California. Sacramento: California Department of Water Resources.

Hanson, B., L. Schwankl, and A. Fulton. 1999. Scheduling irrigations: When and how much. Oakland: University of California Division of Agriculture and Natural Resources, Publication 3396.

Hickman, G. W., and P. Svihra. 2002. Planting landscape trees. Oakland: University of California Division of Agriculture and Natural Resources, Publication 8046. Available free online from the UC ANR Communication Services Web site, http://anrcatalog. ucdavis.edu.

Schwankl, L., B. Hanson, and T. Prichard. 1997. Micro-irrigation of trees and vines: A handbook for water managers. Oakland: University of California Division of Agriculture and Natural Resources, Publication 3378.

Schwankl, L., and T. Prichard. 1999. Drip irrigation in the home landscape. Oakland: University of California Division of Agriculture and Natural Resources, Publication 21579.

Snyder, R. L., B. L. Lanini, D. A. Saw, and W. O. Pruitt. 1987. Using reference evapotranspiration (ETo) and crop coefficients to estimate crop evapotranspiration (ETc) for trees and vines. Oakland: University of California Division of Agriculture and Natural Resources, Publication 21428.

Snyder, R. L., W. O. Pruitt, and D. A. Shaw. 1987. Determining daily reference evapotranspiration (ETo). Oakland: University of California Division of Agriculture and Natural Resources, Publication 21426.

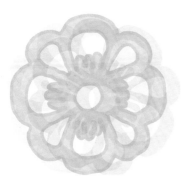

CHAPTER 6

Fertilization

Maxwell V. Norton

Nutrients and Their Roles in Plant Development

Deciduous fruit trees require several nutrients for optimal growth and fruit production. Elements required in relatively large amounts (macronutrients) include nitrogen (N), phosphorus (P), potassium (K), calcium (Ca), magnesium (Mg), and sulfur (S). Elements required in relatively small amounts (micronutrients) include iron (Fe), manganese (Mn), zinc (Zn), boron (B), copper (Cu), chlorine (Cl), and molybdenum (Mo). These nutrients are absorbed primarily by the roots from the soil, although some may also be absorbed through the leaves or other plant surfaces.

In order to be absorbed by the roots, nutrients must be dissolved in water in a plant-available chemical form, usually inorganic *(mineral)*. For example, roots absorb most nitrogen in the form of nitrate (NO_3^-) and some in the form of ammonium (NH_4^+). They absorb potassium in its ionic form, K^+. As soil microorganisms decompose organic matter, they convert many nutrients to plant-available forms. Other nutrients become available through chemical reactions in the soil. You can also supply plant-available forms by applying organic and synthetic (chemical) fertilizers.

Although deciduous fruit trees require many nutrients for tree growth and fruit production, those grown in backyard settings in typical sandy loam to clay loam soil with proper irrigation rarely need to be fertilized. Nutrient deficiencies, when encountered, are generally limited to nitrogen, potassium, iron, and zinc, and, on rare occasions, boron. Unless your soil has a known nutrient deficiency, regular applications of fertilizer usually are not necessary in a mature orchard.

MACRONUTRIENTS

Nitrogen (N)

Fruit trees use nitrogen in large amounts. It is used in building new cells through photosynthesis and is especially needed for the growth and development of shoots and leaves. Nitrogen is taken up by the roots from soil. Most of the nitrogen in soil exists in an organic form in living organisms and decaying organic matter. This organic nitrogen is slowly converted to plant-available inorganic forms, mostly nitrate (NO_3^-), as soil microorganisms decompose the organic matter. Nitrate is mobile and moves with water in the soil. It can easily leach out of the root zone, especially in sandy soils; the use of excess nitrogen fertilizer can lead to leaching of nitrate into groundwater.

Backyard fruit trees do not need heavy applications of nitrogen. If you suspect nitrogen deficiency, watch for yellowing of leaves, particularly the older leaves since nitrogen is mobile in plant tissues and is drawn toward fruit and new shoot growth. Yellowing of leaves can have a variety of other causes, however, including drought, poor soil condition, and waterlogging. If you do need to fertilize, divide the total nitrogen requirement for the year into two or three smaller quantities applied during the growing season. Too much nitrogen will cause the tree to produce excessive new growth, which will shade the lower parts of the tree and lead to fewer fruit, poor fruit color and flavor, and delayed maturity. Excess nitrogen also increases the tree's susceptibility to insect pests and diseases and can lead to nitrate pollution of groundwater.

Phosphorus (P)

Phosphorus deficiency has very rarely been observed in California fruit or nut trees, except in some Sierra Nevada foothill soils that may be deficient. Phosphorus is an essential plant growth nutrient, especially for the growth of roots and the development of seeds. It is available to plants primarily in the form of phosphate. Phosphorus reacts very readily with many elements in the soil and in doing so it can become unavailable to plants. It is most available at a pH of about 6.0 and when nitrogen is plentiful.

Potassium (K)

Potassium is abundant in most California soils but is often in an unavailable form. This is especially true in soils that contain large amounts of clay. Potassium does not readily leach out of the soil. It is taken up by plant roots as a positively charged ion (*cation*), K^+; unlike nitrogen and phosphorus, it is not synthesized into complex molecules, but remains as a simple ion in solution in the plant.

Calcium (Ca)

Calcium is abundant in California soils and is absorbed by roots in an ionic form (Ca^{++}). Calcium does not readily leach out of the soil. Its deficiency in deciduous fruit trees is rare. Excess calcium in the soil can reduce the availability of micronutrients such as iron, manganese, and zinc. Excess lime (calcium carbonate) in the soil raises the soil pH and can induce a disorder known as lime-induced chlorosis, in which the ends of the shoots turn yellow as they do with iron deficiency.

Magnesium (Mg)

Magnesium deficiency is rare in fruit trees in California. Magnesium is not easily leached from the soil. Like calcium, it is taken up from the soil in the form of an ion (Mg^{++}).

Sulfur (S)

Deciduous fruit trees are only rarely deficient in sulfur. It exists in soil organic matter and is released as sulfate (SO_4^-) as that matter is decomposed by soil microorganisms. It also exists in the atmosphere as sulfur dioxide (SO_2). Plants absorb sulfur mainly through their roots, but they can also absorb it through leaves and other plant surfaces. Gardeners generally add sulfur to the soil to lower the soil's pH.

MICRONUTRIENTS

Iron (Fe)

Iron deficiency can be relatively common in deciduous fruit trees in California and is usually caused by waterlogged, compacted, or alkaline soils. Roots absorb iron primarily in an ionic form (Fe^{+++}); it can also be absorbed by leaves. Although iron is one of the most abundant elements in soil, most of it is bound up in minerals and so is unavailable to plants. A plant's ability to absorb the small amount of iron that actually is available can be greatly reduced by poor aeration (too much water in the soil), a soil pH value above 7.5, or physically damaged or diseased roots. Iron is not mobile in the soil or in plant tissues.

Manganese (Mn)

Deciduous fruit trees in California rarely suffer manganese deficiency. Roots absorb manganese from the soil in its high-pH ionic form (Mn^{++}); it is relatively immobile in the soil and in plant tissue.

Zinc (Zn)

Zinc deficiency is fairly common in fruit trees in California. Zinc is taken up by a tree's roots and absorbed through its leaves in an ionic form (Zn^{++}). Like iron, manganese, and many other minerals, zinc combines readily with other elements. Relatively little free (ionic) zinc is available to plants in most California soils. Many factors can reduce its mobility in soil, such as a low level of zinc in the soil or a high pH. It is often tied up and unavailable if excess manure has been applied to the soil. Zinc is immobile in plant tissue. Although plants use zinc in small amounts, a deficiency can be immediately noticeable on leaves and can severely damage buds, twigs, and stems. Zinc-deficient leaves are often small and have interveinal chlorosis.

Boron (B)

Most California soils have an adequate supply of boron, and its deficiency is relatively uncommon in fruit trees. Deficiencies may occur on very sandy soils and Sierra Nevada foothill soils. Boron is not easily leached out of the root zone in clay soils but may be leached out of a sandy soil if its internal drainage is good. It is immobile in plant tissues. An excess of boron (boron toxicity) can be a problem in arid regions of the state or where the water contains boron. Boron toxicity has been observed on the west side of the San Joaquin Valley and in the Cache Creek watershed in Yolo County.

Soil Fertility Management

A good soil has an appropriate balance of mineral nutrients, organic matter, living organisms, air, and water (see Chapter 1). Maintaining soil fertility largely consists of maintaining this balance and correcting it when necessary.

NUTRIENT RECYCLING

In a mature backyard landscape, little or no fertilizer needs to be added to trees and shrubs each year if you recycle leaves, clippings, and prunings back into the soil. In the home landscape, many nutrients are naturally recycled: as leaves, twigs, and other plant debris are decomposed by soil microorganisms, the nutrients tied up in them are released into the soil to be taken up by plants. The recycling process can take from a few weeks to several years. You can greatly enhance the process by adding ground-up or chopped prunings, leaves, and clippings to the soil as mulch. This returns many nutrients to the soil to be used again by the trees. Over time, you can increase the soil's overall fertility in this way.

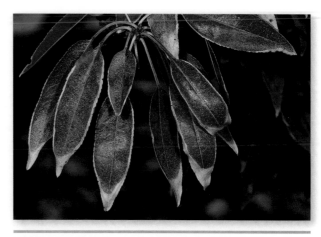

Figure 6.1. Marginal necrosis of almond leaf margins caused by excessive soil salinity. Photo by Jack Kelly Clark.

SALINITY

A soil's salinity (salt level) refers not only to common table salt (sodium chloride [NaCl]), but to many chemical compounds in which sodium, calcium, or magnesium combine with chloride, sulfate, or bicarbonate to form a salt. High levels of salts in the soil can break down the soil's structure, raise its pH, reduce its fertility, and kill plants.

Plants absorb salts through their roots and leaves. Salts occur naturally in soils; other sources include synthetic (chemical) fertilizers, manures, manure-based composts, poor-quality water used for irrigation, and de-icing materials used by road departments in cold-winter areas.

Many California soils in low rainfall areas have naturally high salinity. In all soils, the excessive use of fertilizers, composts, or manures, and irrigation with poor-quality water can raise salinity to damaging levels. Salinity injury symptoms may appear similar to those of nutrient deficiencies and other problems, but more severe salt damage leads to burning of leaf tips and margins (Figure 6.1). If you suspect salinity injury, take a soil sample from the root zone and have it tested by a laboratory. Such analyses are expensive and you should try to rule out other causes first. The best way to avoid problems related to salinity is to prevent them: apply fertilizers sparingly and in the proper amounts, use fertilizers with a high nutrient content when possible, exercise caution when applying manures and compost made from manure, and irrigate with good-quality water if possible.

In some areas the water supply will contain salts if it comes from a well. River water can be either very low or very high in salt. For example, municipal water from the Sacramento River Delta and water from the Colorado River may be high in salts, depending upon exactly where it is pumped from and the time of year. Salts come from a variety of sources, which can include irrigation water, fertilizers, manure, compost, and the soil itself. "Total salts" is not the same thing as "water hardness." Water hardness is usually descriptive of the amount of calcium, magnesium, bicarbonates, and carbonates in the water. The best water, of course, is rainwater. Capture as much of it on your property as you can.

Once high salinity develops in a soil, it is difficult to correct. No chemical or material added to the soil can correct it, and products specifically marketed to eliminate it are not effective. The only practical remedy is to leach (drain) the salts out of the root zone using good-quality water, but even this can only be done if the soil at the site has good drainage. Rainwater is the best water available for keeping salt levels low. Try to keep rainwater on your property rather than lose it to the storm drain system.

Soil pH

The acidity or alkalinity of a substance is expressed as its pH on a scale of 0 to 14. Acid soils have low pH values (less than 7); alkaline soils have high pH values (greater than 7). The optimal pH for deciduous fruit trees is between 6.0 and 7.5. A very low (acidic) pH below 5.5 reduces the availability of calcium, magnesium, phosphorus, nitrogen, and other nutrients, encourages aluminum and manganese toxicity, and makes trees more susceptible to certain fungal and bacterial diseases. An exception is blueberries, which require a very acidic soil (pH 4.5 to 5.5). A very high (alkaline) pH in excess of 7.5 reduces the availability of iron, zinc, copper, and manganese.

Maintaining the soil at the proper pH helps you maintain your soil's fertility. In rare cases you may find it useful to have your soil tested before you plant. If the soil pH is too low (acidic), you can raise it by incorporating lime, dolomite, or wood ashes into the soil. If the pH is too high (alkaline), you can lower it by incorporating soil sulfur or let it go down as a side effect of the use of fertilizers such as ammonium sulfate. Both of these processes are relatively long-term solutions that can take several months or even years. For more information, consult your local UC Cooperative Extension Master Gardener.

Types of Fertilizer

Compost, Mulch, and Organic Fertilizers

Composts, mulches, and organic fertilizers constitute an important part of fertility management in backyard fruit culture. Their nutrients are released slowly during the growing season and converted into a form that the tree can use. Composts and mulches also serve to recycle waste, and that may reduce the amount of material sent to landfills. Because organic fertilizers release their nutrients slowly, they are not useful in treating acute nutrient deficiencies; faster-release materials should be used for this purpose. Compost, mulch, and organic fertilizers supply the same nutrients as synthetic fertilizers. The difference between them is that the nutrients in synthetic fertilizers are more concentrated and are released more quickly whereas composts and mulches, in addition to supplying nutrients, may also improve the soil's tilth and water penetration. Compost, mulch, and organic fertilizers can be used in conjunction with synthetic fertilizers. When correcting a nutrient deficiency, check the guaranteed analysis of any fertilizer to make sure it has the nutrients you need.

Compost is made up of partially decomposed organic material and is often incorporated into the soil where its nutrients gradually become available to roots, but it can also be used as a mulch on the soil surface. It can be a good source of nutrients and can improve soil structure and tilth. You can make your own compost using waste materials from your house, yard, and garden. Publications on making compost are available at your local UC Cooperative Extension office or online (http://anrcatalog.ucdavis.edu). Make sure that the compost is fairly well decomposed before you incorporate it into the soil. Plant-based compost contains virtually all of the nutrients needed for tree growth. In rare cases compost alone may not supply enough nitrogen for optimal tree growth.

Mulch, strictly speaking, is not a fertilizer—it is any material put on top of the soil to conserve moisture, suppress weeds, encourage beneficial organisms, reduce erosion, and other useful functions. Yet applying organic mulches such as chopped leaves, clippings, twigs, and other organic waste to the soil can help improve soil fertility by improving its tilth, encouraging beneficial organisms such as earthworms, and reducing the number of weeds that compete with trees for nutrients. Also, over time, the bottom of the mulch layer—the part that touches the soil—will decompose and gradually become part of the soil, much like a compost. You can make mulch at home by chopping leaves, clippings, tree prunings, and other yard waste and spreading them on top of the soil.

Organic fertilizers are commercially produced materials that include various manures or organic concentrates such as bone meal or fish meal (Table 6.1). Purchased on a retail basis, organic fertilizers are more expensive per unit of nutrient than synthetic fertilizers. Manures, which often are mixtures of composted animal waste and plant matter, can be used to supply nitrogen and other nutrients to trees, but they must be used with caution since they may contain weed seeds and high levels of salts. Manures, depending on the source, have varying levels and ratios of nutrients and are viewed mostly as soil amendments. Manures usually do not have a guaranteed analysis printed on the bag.

Table 6.1. Approximate analysis of some organic fertilizers*

Fertilizer	Nitrogen[†] (N %)	Phosphorus[‡] (P_2O_5 %)	Potassium[§] (K_2O %)
Straight manures and composts (some store-bought materials are blends of manure and compost)			
Chicken (dry)	2.0–4.5	4.6–6.0	1.2–2.4
Dairy (dry)	0.6–3.5	0.5–1.1	2.4–3.6
Horse (fresh)	0.7–3.0	0.3–1.2	0.5–2.2
Poultry (dry)	2.0–5.0	1.0–2.3	1.6–2.3
(fresh)	1.0	0.9	0.5
Sheep (dry)	3.0–5.0	0.4–1.6	2.0–4.0
(fresh)	1.1	0.4	1.0
Steer (dry)	1.0–2.5	0.9–1.9	2.4–3.6
Organic concentrates			
Bat guano	10.0	3.0	1.0
Bone meal	3.0	15.0	0
Cottonseed meal	6.0	0.4	1.5
Dried blood	13.0	1.5	2.5
Feather meal	12.0	0.0	0.0
Fish meal	10.0	6.0	0
Soybean meal	7.0	1.2	1.5
Wood ashes[¶]	0	2.0	6.0

Source: Faber et al. 2002, p. 59.

*For more extensive information, see *Organic Soil Amendments and Fertlizers* (UC ANR Publication 21505). Analysis reported in this table is an average for primary nutrients without accounting for losses caused by leaching or decomposition. One cubic foot of air-dry manure weighs about 25 lb.

[†]Analysis based on dry weight except for fresh manures, which contain about 65% to 85% water.

[‡]Analysis based on dry weight except for fresh manures, which contain about 65% to 85% water. Phosphoric acid (P_2O_5) actually contains 43% phosphorus. The percentages given for the oxide can be converted to percentages of the element by multiplication: $P = P_2O_5 \times 0.43$.

[§]Analysis based on dry weight except for fresh manures which contain about 65% to 85% water. Potash (K_2O) actually contains 83% potassium. The percentages given for the oxide can be converted to percentages of the element by multiplication: $K = K_2O \times 0.83$.

[¶]Burning eliminates organic matter and forms inorganic compounds.

Table 6.2. Examples of synthetic fertilizers for soil application

Fertilizer*	Formula	Nitrogen (N %)	Available Phosphorus (P$_2$O$_5$ %)[†]	Potassium (K$_2$O %)[‡]	Effect on soil pH	Comments
Ammonium sulfate "sulfate of ammonia"	(NH$_4$)$_2$SO$_4$	21	0	0	strongly acidic	
Calcium nitrate	Ca(NO$_3$)$_2$	16	0	0	basic	also a source of calcium
Potassium chloride (old term: "muriate of potash")	KCl	0	0	60	neutral	high hazard from chloride
Potassium nitrate	KNO$_3$	13	0	44	slightly basic	
Potassium sulfate (old term: "sulfate of potash")	K$_2$SO$_4$	0	0	50	almost neutral	
Superphosphate	Ca$_2$H$_2$(PO$_4$)$_2$	0	20	0	neutral	
Urea	CO(NH$_2$)$_2$	45	0	0	moderately acidic	
12-12-12	—	12	12	12	varies, usually acidic	
16-16-16	—	16	16	16	varies, usually acidic	

Source: Adapted from Faber et al. 2002, p. 56.

*Other synthetic materials used as fertilizers include zinc sulfate (ZnSO$_4$·H$_2$O, 36% zinc) and chelates of iron and zinc. Chelation increases the stability of the nutrients in the soil, making them available to plants for longer periods of time.

[†]Phosphoric acid (P$_2$O$_5$) actually contains 43% phosphorus. The percentages given for the oxide can be converted to percentages of the element by multiplication: P = P$_2$O$_5$ x 0.43.

[‡]Potash (K$_2$O) actually contains 83% potassium. The percentages given for the oxide can be converted to percentages of the element by multiplication: K = K$_2$O x 0.83.

SYNTHETIC (INORGANIC) FERTILIZERS

Synthetic fertilizers, also known as inorganic, chemical, mineral, or "commercial" fertilizers, are concentrated minerals or elemental salts (Table 6.2). The nutrients they contain (nitrogen, phosphorus, potassium, etc.) are the same as those found in organic fertilizers, but synthetics are derived from chemical sources rather than natural sources. For the most part, the nutrients in synthetic fertilizers are rapidly available to plants, although slow-release synthetic fertilizers are available.

Synthetic fertilizers are sold in bags or packages that may be labeled with the name of the chemical form of the nutrient and must have a guaranteed analysis—that is, the percentage of nitrogen, phosphorus, and potassium. The analysis generally consists of three numbers that describe the chemical content of the fertilizer: the first represents the percentage of nitrogen, the second, the percentage of phosphorus as P_2O_5, and the third, the percentage of potassium as K_2O. For example, ammonium nitrate contains 34 percent nitrogen by weight and has no phosphorus or potassium, so it is labeled "34-0-0." A "complete" synthetic fertilizer contains some amount of all three nutrients. The term "complete" does not mean that the fertilizer supplies all of the nutrients needed by a plant nor that they are present in the correct relative amounts, only that all three are present. Since complete fertilizers are mixes, they are named after their analysis, such as 16-16-16, instead of being named after the chemicals they contain. A 16-16-16 fertilizer is termed "complete," but it certainly does not supply the complete set of nutrients needed by fruit trees: for example, they rarely need phosphorus but they do require zinc.

Take special care in the use of synthetic fertilizers. Since synthetic fertilizers are salts, they can increase the salinity of the soil if misapplied and they can burn leaves or fruit if they come in contact with them. Also, when you apply one nutrient you may reduce the tree's ability to take up some other nutrient: for example, excess phosphorus can tie up zinc and magnesium may compete with calcium. Too much nitrogen can cause excessive growth, and ammonium sulfate or sulfur may increase the soil's acidity to damaging levels.

Nutrient Deficiencies and Toxicities

Plants can be harmed by too little of a nutrient (deficiency) or too much of a nutrient (toxicity). In most California backyard environments, deciduous fruit trees seldom develop nutrient deficiencies or toxicities. The most commonly deficient nutrients are zinc, potassium, and in sandy soils nitrogen; deficiencies of boron, manganese, and magnesium can also occur. Other nutrient deficiencies are rare. Iron deficiency symptoms are common, but they almost never result from a lack of iron in the soil. Instead, the symptom usually results from excess soil moisture, which prevents the roots from taking up sufficient iron. Iron deficiency symptoms can also be an indication of excess lime or high soil pH.

DIAGNOSING NUTRIENT DEFICIENCIES AND TOXICITIES

Many nutrient deficiencies and toxicities produce relatively distinctive visual symptoms on leaves and shoots (Table 6.3). A good place to begin diagnosis is with an attempt to eliminate other causes of the symptoms, such as insect damage or disease (see Chapter 11), too much or too little water, or damage from wind, sun, heat, or cold (see Costello et al. 2003). If the plant is healthy and no other causes of damage are apparent, determine whether the problem affects new growth or old growth first. Nitrogen and potassium are mobile in the plant, so deficiencies in these nutrients tend to affect older leaves first. Zinc and iron are immobile in plants, so deficiencies in these tend to affect younger leaves first. Also, consider the location or pattern of symptoms—for example, whether leaves are turning brown on the tips and edges or are yellowing between the leaf veins. Symptoms of several nutrients are shown in Figures 6.2 through 6.7.

Even with the most careful examination, nutrient deficiencies and toxicities cannot be conclusively diagnosed on the basis of visual symptoms alone: laboratory analysis of plant tissues (leaves and petioles) may be needed as well. Because it can cost $10 to $15 per element per sample, tissue analysis is generally too expensive for the backyard orchardist unless a tree is very valuable. Soil analysis is expensive but can be

Table 6.3. General symptoms of nutrient deficiency and toxicity in deciduous fruit and nut trees

Nutrient	Deficiency symptoms	Toxicity symptoms
Nitrogen (N)	Deficiency symptoms are similar for peach and plum, showing pale green leaves near the terminal of shoot and yellow leaves at the base. In peach and nectarine, leaf midribs and stems are characteristically red. As the season progresses, red and brown spots develop in leaves. Shoot growth and leaf size are reduced, but not so much as with zinc deficiency. Premature leaf drop often occurs. Fewer flower buds are produced for the next season and if very severe, the resulting fruit may be smaller and have more color.	Excessive growth of dark green leaves; few fruits; delayed maturity of fruits; reduced fruit size and quality; leaf tips and margins may turn brown and die.
Phosphorus (P)	Leaves on peaches and nectarines are dark green, eventually turning bronze and developing a leathery texture. A purple or red coloration appears on the leaves, petioles, and young shoots. Leaf size may be reduced and premature defoliation may occur, beginning with the basal leaves. Yield and fruit size are reduced. Fruit are more highly colored and ripen earlier but exhibit surface defects. Slow growth, stunting, and purplish or dark green leaves, eventually turning bronze and developing a leathery texture (sometimes with cupping), chlorosis between leaf veins (interveinal) and at leaf edges (marginal). Extremely rare.	
Potassium (K)	Slow growth; pale green leaves; leaves curl and roll upward along margins; leaf tip and marginal browning ("burn") and necrosis. Symptoms usually do not show up until midsummer and often are first observed in the middle of the shoot. Older leaves may fall off. You may observe fewer flower buds and fruits. Fruit is often smaller. On pears and walnuts the leaves may have a bronze color. Apples often have burning on the edge of the leaves. In almonds the tip of the leaf will curl up.	None, but excess K can cause Mg deficiency symptoms.
Calcium (Ca)	Reduced terminal (end) growth of shoots; may have twig dieback and leaf drop; chlorotic patches may develop on leaves before they fall; pits on apples, pears. Very rare.	

Table 6.3. General symptoms of nutrient deficiency and toxicity in deciduous fruit and nut trees, cont.

Nutrient	Deficiency symptoms	Toxicity symptom
Magnesium (Mg)	Marginal chlorosis leaving an inverted V-shaped pattern around the midrib; leaves curl upward along margins; marginal yellowing with green area along midribs of leaves; older leaves are affected first and it then progresses out the shoot. Tree usually remains vigorous and yield and fruit size usually are not affected. Very rare.	
Sulfur (S)	Similar to nitrogen deficiency, generally showing on young leaves first. Very rare.	
Iron (Fe)	Loss of chlorophyll, leading to interveinal chlorosis (veins remain green); young leaves affected first; twig dieback; reduced growth and leaf drop in severe cases. The ends of shoots often turn a bright gold color and may even turn white.	
Manganese (Mn)	Interveinal and marginal chlorosis (no sharp distinction between veins and interveinal areas as with iron deficiency); chlorosis develops into a herringbone pattern; in contrast to other plants, fruit trees show symptoms on older leaves first. Unless severe, shoot growth, yield, and fruit size are unaffected.	
Zinc (Zn)	Leaves remain very small ("little leaf"); decrease in stem length; rosetting of terminal leaves, interveinal chlorosis on young leaves; fewer fruit buds form; delayed bloom; smaller crop; twig dieback after first year. Terminal leaves will have a wavy margin. Small leaves may form rosettes on the shoot tips and young spurs.	
Boron (B)	Death of terminal growth; growth of many shoots at the end of twigs ("witches' broom"); thickened, curled, wilted, chlorotic leaves; young leaves affected first; soft, necrotic spots on fruits; reduced flowering. Rare.	Small necrotic (dead) spots on underside of leaves; yellowing of leaf tip; edges of leaves turn blackish and die. Cankers may develop along midrib, petiole, and young twigs. Rare except in arid inland areas with water containing high levels of boron. Fruit can be distorted and have sharp, sunken areas. Peach and nectarine are very sensitive.

Sources: Costello et al. 2003; Faber et al. 2002; Johnson and Uriu 1989; Perry and Asai 1983.

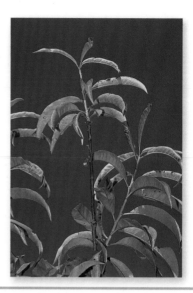

Figure 6.2. Symptoms of nitrogen deficiency on a peach tree, showing overall yellowing of leaves, including the veins. Photo by Jack Kelly Clark.

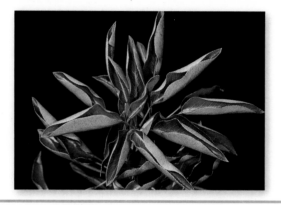

Figure 6.3. Phosphorus deficiency symptoms of pear, showing cupping of leaves. Photo by Jack Kelly Clark.

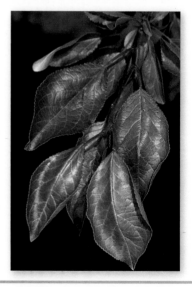

Figure 6.4. Potassium deficiency symptoms of prune, with pale green-yellowing of the leaves and a curling inward (boating) and sometimes burning along the margins and tips. Photo by Harry Andris.

helpful, as it will determine the pH of the soil as well as the levels of salts and potentially toxic elements such as boron, sodium, and chloride; it does not, however, indicate the levels of nutrients in plants. For information on preparing plant tissue and soil samples, the locations of commercial testing laboratories, and help interpreting test results, contact your local UC Cooperative Extension Master Gardener. Note that Cooperative Extension offices *do not* provide tissue or soil testing.

Using Fertilizers

Different fertilizers release nutrients at different rates. If a tree is acutely deficient in nitrogen, an application of compost or organic fertilizer will not solve the problem quickly and the nitrogen deficiency may lead to overall tree decline. Do not over-fertilize: select the fertilizer that will apply the minimum amount of nutrients necessary to correct the deficiency. Besides wasting your money and time, an excess application of fertilizer can harm trees, the soil, and the overall environment. Follow all instructions on the fertilizer label regarding timing, rates, mixing, method of application, and disposal of unused material.

CALCULATING HOW MUCH FERTILIZER TO APPLY

Fertilizer recommendations are often given in terms of the amount of the needed element rather than the amount of the fertilizer product required. In Table 6.4, however, we actually indicate the amount of fertilizer required, so no further calculations are needed. To determine how much of a particular fertilizer it would take to apply a given amount of the needed element, divide the amount of the element by the percentage of that element in the fertilizer. For example, assume that you need to apply 1 pound of actual nitrogen using ammonium sulfate fertilizer. The analysis of ammonium sulfate (as printed on the bag) is 21-0-0, meaning that it contains 21% nitrogen (or 0.21 lb N for every 1 lb of fertilizer), 0% phosphorus, and 0% potassium. The calculation would be: 1 lb N ÷ 0.21 lb N in fertilizer = 4.8 lb, which equals about 4 lb 13 oz of fertilizer.

Soil Application

Nitrogen, phosphorus, and potassium fertilizers are applied to the soil, usually in a dry (granular or powdered) form. Spread the fertilizer evenly on the soil, avoiding clumps and uneven spots, in a circular area around the tree, but coming no closer than two feet from the tree trunk. When fertilizing a young tree, do not concentrate the fertilizer on top of the root ball. After spreading the fertilizer, it helps to rake it into the top inch or so of soil. For individual trees, you apply the fertilizer in a narrow band around the tree near the drip line (Figures 6.8 and 6.9). Nitrogen fertilizers are best applied in the spring and summer when uptake of water and nutrients is greatest. Water the fertilized soil thoroughly to move the nitrogen into the tree's root zone. You can also place fertilizer material conveniently right under a drip irrigation emitter so the applied water can dissolve it and carry it into the root zone.

Foliar Application

Micronutrient fertilizers (mainly iron and zinc) can be applied to a tree's leaves. The usual method is to spray them on in a liquid form. Check the guaranteed analysis of nutrients on the label. Verify that the formulation is safe for application to leaves (foliar application) and dilute it according to instructions. Foliar applications are best made in the spring before hot weather causes leaves to become thick and waxy. If the leaves are heavily coated with dust, wash the tree off and let it dry prior to application. Spray the fertilizer evenly and make sure that all leaves are fully wetted. The spray should be applied to the point where the liquid begins to run off. Foliar sprays provide an immediate but short-term response; they are often used in conjunction with soil-applied fertilizers. Some people use various organic foliar sprays, such as fish and kelp products, to add small amounts of nutrients, vitamins, minerals, and hormones. Little formal research has been conducted to determine the value of such treatments. Do not combine foliar fertilizers with pesticide sprays, since some combinations can damage leaves.

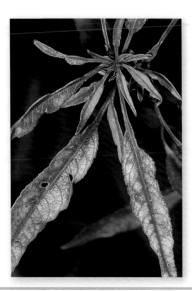

Figure 6.5. Zinc deficiency, showing the classic "little leaf" symptom. Photo by Jack Kelly Clark.

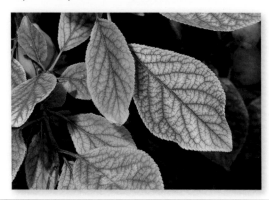

Figure 6.6. Iron deficiency symptoms include a characteristic interveinal chlorosis, with sharply defined green veins. It usually occurs in soil that has a high pH or is overwatered. Photo by Jack Kelly Clark.

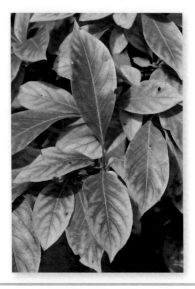

Figure 6.7. Manganese deficiency symptoms, showing interveinal chlorosis and with broad green bands around the veins. Usually caused by high-pH soil. Photo by Harry Andris.

Table 6.4. Approximate amounts of fertilizer to apply per year to correct a deficiency*

Deficiency and fertilizer type	Dosage to correct deficiency			
Nitrogen	Large fruit trees	Small fruit trees or fruit bushes	Large nut trees	Small nut trees
	pounds per year			
Actual nitrogen	1.0	0.5	2.0	1.0
Ammonium sulfate	4.8	2.4	9.5	4.8
15-15-15	6.7	3.4	13.3	6.7
16-16-16	6.6	3.1	12.5	6.3
16-20-0	6.6	3.1	12.5	6.3
20-27-5	5.0	2.5	10.0	5.0
	Apply half of the nitrogen in midspring and the rest right after harvest.			

Deficiency and fertilizer type	Dosage to correct deficiency	
Potassium	Large fruit and nut trees	Small fruit and nut trees and bushes
	pounds per year	
Potassium sulfate applied to clay soil	15	8
Potassium sulfate applied to sandy soil	7	4

Deficiency and fertilizer type	Dosage to correct deficiency
Zinc	
Zinc sulfate	2 oz per gallon of water as a foliar spray in early to mid-November. Thoroughly soak all the leaves on the trees. This will cause the leaves to burn and drop off, but this will not hurt the tree.

*Trees younger than four years old should receive the small tree rate. For other specialty fertilizers not listed here, follow the label directions.

Table 6.5. Approximate weight of ammonium sulfate fertilizer and actual nitrogen held in some commonly available containers that you can use for measuring

Container	Ammonium sulfate (21-0-0) fertilizer	Actual nitrogen
	ounces	
6.5 fl oz tuna can	8	1.7
14 fl oz soup can	16	3.4
12 fl oz frozen juice can	14	2.9
24 oz coffee can	70	14.7

RECOMMENDED TIMING AND RATES

As stated earlier, trees and shrubs in a mature yard usually need very little in the way of routine fertilizer applications. In loam and clay loam soils, few added nutrients are needed. Very sandy or gravelly soils have a low nutrient-holding capacity, so trees planted there may benefit from preventive application of certain nutrients. Zinc and potassium are the most likely to become deficient; zinc sulfate and potassium sulfate applied every other year will prevent deficiencies. Because zinc and potassium are immobile in the soil, you have to apply them in a concentrated band where the roots can grow through the treated zone. You can also apply nitrogen fertilizer in the same band. The band does not need to extend all the way around the tree. It can be as short as a foot or two in length on two sides of a small tree (Figure 6.10) or four sides of a large tree.

The amount of nitrogen to apply depends on the condition of the tree. If the tree is growing well and its foliage is dark green, no extra nitrogen is needed. If growth is weak and leaves are uniformly pale, the tree may need some more nitrogen, although other factors can also cause these symptoms. Follow the guidelines in Tables 6.4 and 6.5. The type of nitrogen to use depends upon whether your soil is typically acidic (low pH) or basic (high pH). Table 6.2 shows the soil's reaction, or effect on soil pH, of the fertilizer. You can influence the pH of your soil with the reaction of the fertilizer you choose. Ammonium sulfate acidifies the soil slightly more than other fertilizers and benefits acid-loving plants like blueberries, azaleas, camellias, and hydrangeas.

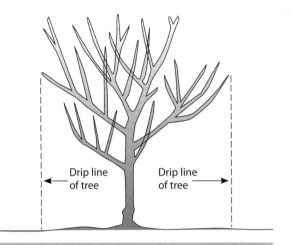

Figure 6.8. Location of the drip line or canopy edge of a tree. This is a good area for applying fertilizer and water.

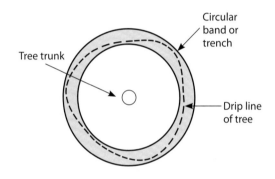

Figure 6.9. Location of the circular band or trench around the drip line in which you can apply fertilizer.

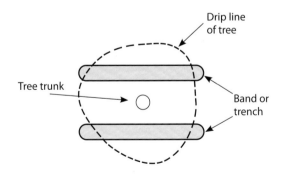

Figure 6.10. Location of straight bands or trenches for fertilizer application.

References

Chaney, D. E., L. E. Drinkwater, and G. S. Pettygrove. 1992. Organic soil amendments and fertilizers. Oakland: University of California Division of Agriculture and Natural Resources, Publication 21505.

Costello, L. R. 2003. Abiotic disorders of landscape plants. Oakland: University of California Division of Agriculture and Natural Resources, Publication 3420.

Faber, B., L. Clement, D. Giraud, and D. Silva. 2002. Soil and fertilizer management. Pages 29–68 in D. Pittenger, ed., California master gardener handbook. Oakland: University of California Division of Agriculture and Natural Resources, Publication 3382.

Geisel, P. M., and C. L. Unruh. 2001. Compost in a hurry. Oakland: University of California Division of Agriculture and Natural Resources, Publication 8037.

Johnson, R., and K. Uriu. 1989. Mineral nutrition. Chapter 13 in J. H. LaRue and R. S. Johnson, eds., Peaches, plums, and nectarines: Growing and handling for fresh market. Oakland: University of California Division of Agriculture and Natural Resources, Publication 3331.

Perry, E., and W. Asai. 1983. Fertilizing home fruit trees, nut trees, and grapevines. Oakland: University of California Division of Agriculture and Natural Resources, Publication 21329.

Pittenger, D., ed. 2002. California Master Gardener handbook. Oakland: University of California Division of Agriculture and Natural Resources, Publication 3382.

Raabe, R. D. 1981. The rapid composting method. Oakland: University of California Division of Agriculture and Natural Resources, Publication 21251.

Van Horn, M. 1995. Compost production and utilization: A grower's guide. Oakland: University of California Division of Agriculture and Natural Resources, Publication 21514.

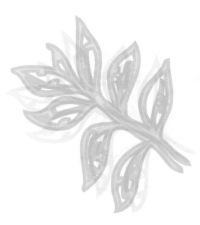

CHAPTER 7

Training and Pruning

Chuck A. Ingels, Pamela M. Geisel, Maxwell V. Norton, Harry L. Andris, and Edward D. Laivo

In order to support the weight of a potentially large fruit or nut crop, you need to use *training* in the first few years to create a strong scaffold and branch structure. Training also makes various cultural practices easier, including fruit thinning, pest management, and harvesting. There are many approaches to training a tree, such as open-center, central leader, modified central leader, espalier, and "fruit bush" training. Table 7.1 lists the training methods used for fruit and nut species.

Pruning is the most important practice used in training young trees (bending branches and tying or staking them into position can also help in tree training). Pruning is also used on mature trees to reduce tree height, improve sunlight penetration into the lower portions of the tree, rejuvenate fruiting spurs, and reduce the amount of fruit thinning that the tree will need. Pruning can be done at any time of year, but the two most common times are during the dormant season (winter), and mid-spring through summer. Table 7.1 also lists the amount of pruning that is generally used on various fruit and nut species.

If a tree receives no training or pruning after planting it will bear relatively heavy crops at an early age, but the weight of the fruit will bend or break the main branches, resulting in a poorly structured tree. Also, the fruit will be fairly small and vigor will be much less. Although fruit trees originally grew without training or pruning, their fruit were much smaller than those of modern varieties, allowing the trees to develop a strong branch structure.

This chapter provides some basic concepts and advice on specific training and pruning methods. Make sure to observe the effects of your training work in subsequent weeks or months, and remember that mistakes are for learning and they usually can be corrected.

Fundamentals of Pruning Fruit Trees

MAKING PRUNING CUTS

Use pruning loppers to cut shoots and small to medium-sized branches. There are two types of pruning loppers: bypass (two blades pass each other, like scissors) and anvil (one blade cuts down against a flat surface) (Figure 7.1). Bypass loppers are generally easier to use and better for cutting because they cut more cleanly and cause less damage to the bark of larger branches than anvil types. Use a sharp pruning saw for branches too large to be cut with loppers. Keep pruning tools sharp: dull tools make rough cuts that can tear bark, which inhibits wound healing and promotes damage by insects or disease.

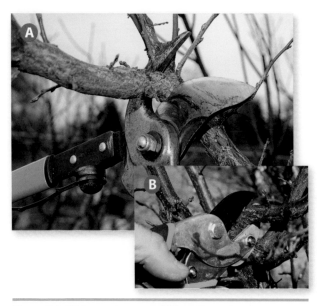

Figure 7.1. (A) Bypass lopper and **(B)** anvil-type hand pruner. Many gardeners prefer bypass loppers; anvil loppers are mainly used on small branches. Photos by Chuck Ingels.

Table 7.1. Fruiting wood characteristics and pruning of fruit and nut trees

Type of tree	Location of fruiting buds on Long branches		Short branches or spurs		Approx. life of bearing spur or branch	Type of training system	Amount of pruning for mature trees
	Laterally	Terminally	Laterally	Terminally			
Almond	minor		major		5 years	open center	light (thinning)
Apple		minor		major	8–10 years	central leader, modified central leader, open center, espalier, or fruit bush	moderate
Apricot	minor		major		3 years	open center or fruit bush	heavy
Cherry	minor		major		10–12 years	open center or fruit bush	light to moderate
Chestnut		minor		major		modified central leader	light (thinning)
Fig*	major		minor		bears on 1-year and new shoots	open center, modified central leader, or fruit bush	various
Peach/ Nectarine	major		minor		1–2 years	open center, perpendicular V, or fruit bush	heavy
Pear, Asian	minor	very minor		major	6–8 years	modified central leader, open center, espalier, or fruit bush	moderate to heavy
Pear, European	minor	minor		major	8–10 years	modified central leader, open center, multiple leader, espalier, or fruit bush	moderate

open center   central leader   modified central leader   fruit bush   espalier

Table 7.1. Fruiting wood characteristics and pruning of fruit and nut trees, cont.

Type of tree	Location of fruiting buds on Long branches		Short branches or spurs		Approx. life of bearing spur or branch	Type of training system	Amount of pruning for mature trees
	Laterally	Terminally	Laterally	Terminally			
Pecan		major		major	fruit spikes borne on tips of new shoots	central leader	light (thinning)
Persimmon[†]	major	major	minor	minor	bears on new shoots that grow near tips of 1-year-old branches	modified central leader or open center	light (mainly thinning)
Pistachio	major		minor			modified central leader or open center	light
Plum, European	minor		major		6–8 years	open center or fruit bush	moderate
Plum, Japanese	minor		major		6–8 years	open center or fruit bush	heavy
Pomegranate	minor		major		bears on short, new shoots	modified central leader or fruit bush	moderate
Quince	major	minor			bears on new shoots	modified central leader or open center	light (mainly thinning)
Walnut, terminal-bearing varieties[‡]		major		major	bears on tips of new shoots	modified central leader	light (mainly thinning)
Walnut, lateral-bearing varieties[‡]	major	major	major	major	bears on tips of new shoots	modified central leader	light to moderate; heavier if little shoot growth

*Figs bear fruit laterally on both 1-year-old branches and current-season's shoots.

†Persimmon fruit are borne laterally on new shoots that grow from 1-year-old branches. Fruiting shoots originate mainly from terminal buds and lateral buds near the tips of branches.

‡See Chapter 3 for bearing habits of walnut varieties.

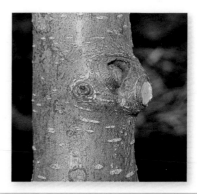

Figure 7.2. Pruning cut made just beyond the swollen branch collar. Cutting into the collar would inhibit callus formation and wound healing. Photo by Chuck Ingels.

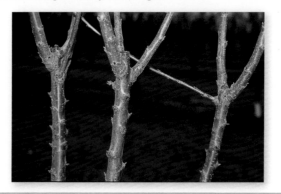

Figure 7.3. A heading cut leads to the vigorous growth of shoots from buds just below the cut as shown. With apically dominant species such as cherry, shown here, only the top two or three buds usually grow, and the shoot growth is upright. Growth of the lowest shoot is often weaker and more horizontal. Photo by Chuck Ingels.

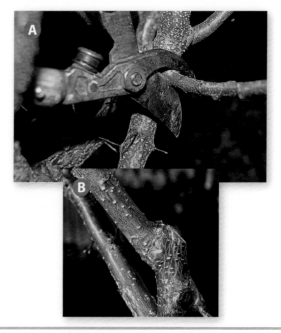

Figure 7.4. Thinning cuts: **(A)** removal of branch back to a main branch and **(B)** cutting off a branch just above a lateral branch that is at least one-third the diameter of the main branch. Photos by Chuck Ingels.

To remove a whole branch, cut just beyond the branch collar (the slightly raised area on the main branch at the point of attachment of the branch to be cut) (Figure 7.2). Do not cut into the branch collar, or the callus will not be able to grow to close the wound. Branches more than 2 inches (2.5 cm) in diameter should be removed by first sawing an undercut. With a saw, cut about one-quarter through the underside of the branch near its point of attachment. Then remove the limb with a cut on the upper side of the branch just outside the branch collar. For very large branches, you should use a three-step cut (Ingels, Geisel, and Unruh 2002).

Do not apply emulsions, paint, or other materials to pruning cuts. Leave the cuts open to the air so they can dry out and callus naturally. Emulsions and other materials can trap moisture and lead to disease. For more information on making pruning cuts, see Hodel and Pittenger (2002, p. 322) and Vossen and Silva (2002, p. 489).

APICAL DOMINANCE AND THE EFFECTS OF HEADING VS. THINNING CUTS

Proper pruning requires an understanding of the way trees respond to different types of cuts. Tree growth is controlled in part by plant hormones that are produced primarily in the apical meristems and the leaves. The plant hormone auxin (indole acetic acid [IAA]) is produced in the shoot tips and new leaves and moves down the shoot, preventing or delaying the growth of lateral buds (see Chapter 2). This hormone also influences both the rate of growth and the angles of the branches produced. This phenomenon is called *apical dominance.* Some species, such as cherry and pear, exhibit strong apical dominance; shoots of these species grow strongly upright, usually with few lateral branches, especially on young trees. Other species such as peach and almond have little apical dominance so branching readily occurs.

A *heading cut,* in which a branch or shoot is shortened (Figure 7.3), removes the short tip that regulates growth below it. Lateral buds are then freed from the effects of auxin and the buds just below the cut respond with rapid shoot growth. This response is sometimes desirable, for instance when developing scaffold branches on young trees. Often, however, excessive shoot growth from too many heading cuts will result in dense branching and shading of lower fruiting branches.

A *thinning cut* is a cut that entirely removes a whole branch or shoot at the point of attachment to a larger branch (Figure 7.4A). Cutting a branch just above a lateral branch that is at least one-third the diameter of the branch being cut is also considered a thinning cut (Figure 7.4B). Because a thinning cut does not leave a stub or short branch, it does not stimulate vigorous shoot growth but it does enhance sunlight penetration into the canopy. In general, an unheaded branch will branch naturally, develop fruiting spurs, and come into fruit production more quickly than a headed branch. There are some species, however, such as cherry, that develop long, pole-like branches unless they are either headed where branching is desired or tied in an outward position.

BRANCH SPREADERS TO REDUCE PRUNING

In some cases, you can improve and accelerate the training of trees by spreading upright shoots and branches rather than removing or heading them. You can spread branches using toothpicks, clothespins, sticks or pruned branches, or purchased spreaders (Figure 7.5). For larger branches, spreader boards can be made by notching the ends of lath or by inserting finish nails into the ends of ¾- to 1-inch-square sticks (Figure 7.6). Remember, a branch that is trained to grow into a particular position now will remain in that position for the life of the tree. Spreading branches when they are young also increases the angle of branch attachment, making the branch connection stronger. Spreaders are particularly useful with central leader training, as it reduces the chances that a branch will become co-dominant with the central leader. If a branch needs to be repositioned, you can also pound a stake into the ground and use it as an anchor to tie the branch in the desired location (Figure 7.7). You can remove spreaders and stakes after about a year or sometimes sooner.

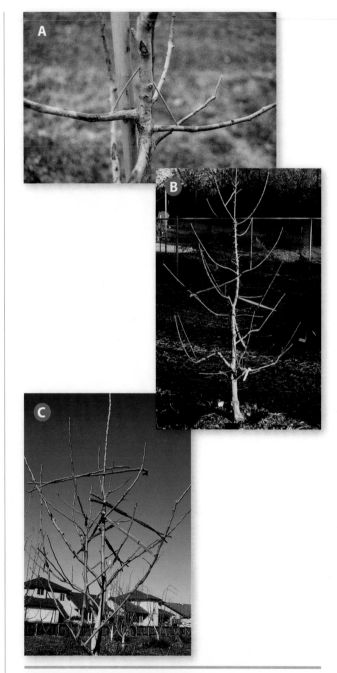

Figure 7.5. By spreading branches you can increase the branch angles, making their attachment to the tree stronger and helping form a good tree structure. **(A)** Toothpicks were placed on these two pear shoots in early spring of the previous year. The holes cause no damage to the tree. **(B)** A plastic spreader *(red)* and sticks were used to spread branches on this genetic dwarf apple. **(C)** Each of these spreaders was created by twisting two 1-year-old branches around each other (Asian pear). Photos by Chuck Ingels.

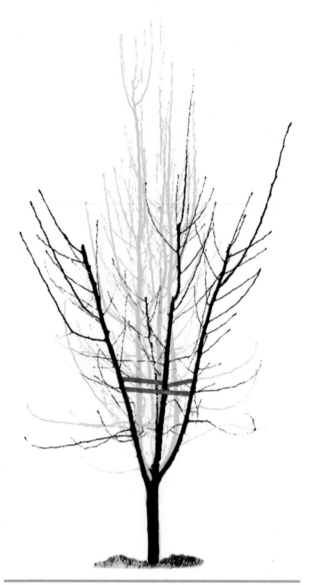

Figure 7.6. This pear tree developed an upright, narrow shape that cannot be corrected solely by pruning. An open center was developed by using spreaders. *Trees in this chapter are shown before pruning (green) and after pruning (brown). Adapted from Micke et al. 1980.*

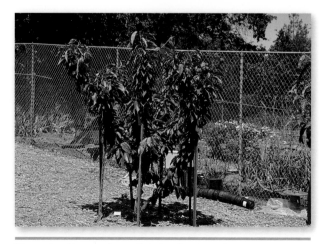

Figure 7.7. Using stakes to bend and tie branches to spread them. Photo by Chuck Ingels.

BEARING HABITS OF FRUIT AND NUT TREES

When pruning fruit and nut trees, it is important for you to know what types of branches or shoots the tree usually uses to produce fruit. For example, persimmons bear mainly on new shoots that originate from near the tips of one-year-old branches (Figure 7.8A), so you should not make many heading cuts on those trees unless strong branches are desired. Many trees produce *spurs* (short shoots specialized for fruiting, Figure 7.8B) that should be retained, and sometimes reinvigorated, in pruning. Peach and nectarine trees produce flowers and fruit on long one-year-old branches (Figure 7.8C). Table 7.1 shows the bearing habits of various fruit and nut species.

Summer Pruning vs. Dormant Pruning

The timing of pruning influences a tree's response to pruning. Dormant pruning is the most invigorating because it allows the carbohydrates that the tree has stored in its wood for the winter to be allocated to fewer growing points. Also, unlike summer pruning, dormant pruning does not remove actively growing and photosynthesizing leaves. Pruning in early spring also stimulates growth below the pruning cuts. However, pruning from mid-spring through summer reduces a tree's vigor to some extent since the tree has already expended valuable carbohydrate reserves on shoot growth, leaf development, and root growth. The removal of young leaves before they can contribute substantial carbohydrates to make up for the energy that has gone into creating them has a somewhat devigorating effect on the tree, reducing its overall growth potential. Because most fruit trees tend to grow too vigorously, summer pruning can have a beneficial effect.

Summer pruning, which actually is done any time from mid-spring through summer, typically is used to remove excessively vigorous shoots that shade lower fruiting branches. When you prune in summer, primarily using thinning cuts, you are able to prune very vigorous shoots without stimulating even more growth. Summer pruning of fruit bushes, however, does lead to vigorous shoot growth. In general, it is a good idea to do both summer pruning (in which you mostly use thinning cuts to allow more sunlight into the lower canopy) and dormant pruning.

If trees receive appropriate summer training and pruning, far less dormant pruning is necessary. Winter pruning, however, allows you a clear view of the tree's framework in the absence of leaves. In winter you can remove any crowded or unwanted branches that were not adequately pruned during the growing season.

One notable feature about apricots, and to a lesser extent, cherries, is that they are susceptible to infection by the branch-killing disease Eutypa dieback (see Chapter 11). Infection occurs on wounds made during wet weather from fall through winter, causing severe gumming at pruning wounds and branch dieback. Because they are susceptible to this disease, it is best to prune apricot and cherry trees in the summer (July or August) so that at least 6 weeks of rain-free weather are likely to follow the pruning. Pruning in August will result in less subsequent regrowth than pruning in July. This summer pruning also promotes more blossoms the following spring. Make sure to prevent sunburn by leaving enough foliage to cover limbs or by painting exposed limbs with whitewash or a 50-50 mixture of interior white latex paint and water. If summer pruning is missed, prune in the late dormant season.

No matter which training method you choose, consider doing some pruning in the spring and summer to train young trees and shorten the time to full fruit production. When necessary, bend and stake shoots of young trees to grow in the desired direction during the spring and summer. Bending branches in this manner is a quicker way to develop the scaffold structure than heading the branches and waiting for new lateral branches to form.

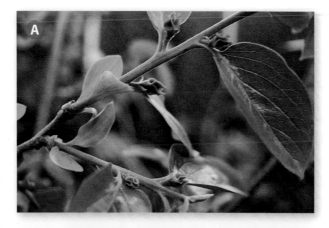

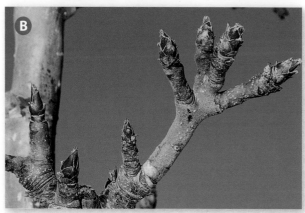

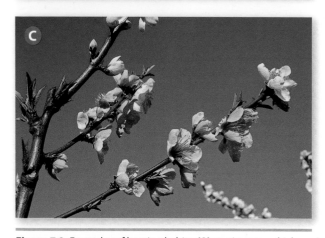

Figure 7.8. Examples of bearing habits: **(A)** persimmon, which bears on new shoots; **(B)** Asian pear spurs (which should be thinned); **(C)** one-year-old peach fruiting branches. Photos by Chuck Ingels.

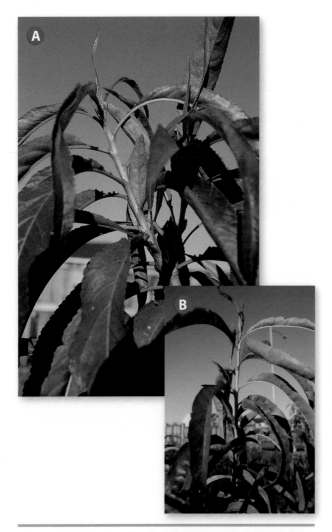

Figure 7.9. (A) Genetic dwarf peach, showing short internode distance, and **(B)** standard-sized peach, showing longer internodes. Photos by Chuck Ingels.

Standard and Dwarfing Tree Types

Genetic Dwarf Trees

Genetic dwarf trees produce shorter internodes than standard or semidwarf trees (Figure 7.9), resulting in compact branches with dense foliage. At maturity, these trees grow to 8 to 10 feet (2.4 to 3.0 m) tall and wide. They make beautiful landscape trees (Figure 7.10) that are easily managed to provide an adequate amount of fruit for a single family. Excellent varieties are available in many fruit species. The lower and interior fruiting branches of genetic dwarf trees, especially peaches and nectarines, tend to die quickly due to shading by the dense growth. The trees are small, though, so fruit production on the extremities of the higher branches is not a serious problem so long as the branches are strong enough to hold the weight of the fruit. Because genetic dwarf trees tend to overbear, substantial fruit thinning is necessary.

Pruning genetic dwarf trees mainly involves thinning the branches in the dormant season to open up the canopy and maintain the height and spread of the tree. Control tree size and strengthen limbs by removing branches at their point of attachment to the trunk or to a larger branch (thinning cuts) rather than by heading or "topping" them.

Full-Sized and Semidwarf Trees

Full-sized trees on standard rootstocks can grow to heights of 25 to 30 feet (7.6 to 9.1 m), whereas trees on semidwarf rootstock can grow 15 to 20 feet (4.6 to 6.1 m) tall. You can keep both standard and semidwarf trees relatively small by pruning them, but they still may grow too large for many backyard situations. An excellent selection of semidwarf apples is usually available, and true dwarfing rootstocks are being developed for many fruit species. Depending on the type of tree (that is, its growth habit and the location of fruiting buds), full-sized and semidwarf trees may be trained to open-center, central leader, modified central leader, fruit bush, or espalier forms.

Specific Training Systems

OPEN-CENTER SYSTEM

The open-center, or vase-shaped, system is most commonly used on almond, apricot, cherry, fig, nectarine, peach, pistachio, plum, and prune trees. Apple, pear, persimmon, and pomegranate trees can also be trained to this system. With this method, the center of the tree is kept free of large branches and vigorous upright shoots, preferably during the growing season, in order to allow sunlight to reach the lower fruiting branches.

First growing season. You may be able to hasten the development of an open-center tree by choosing and promoting scaffold branches in the first growing season, but only if the tree was headed properly (see Chapter 4) and growth is adequate. In late spring of the first growing season, select three or four shoots that will become the *primary scaffold branches* (main structural branches) and pinch back all other strong shoots to about 4 to 6 inches (10 to 15 cm) long (Figure 7.11). Avoid excessive summer pruning since it can have a stunting effect on the young tree. When possible, the scaffold branches should be spaced several inches apart vertically and should be distributed evenly around the trunk, with the lowest branch about 12 to 18 inches (30 to 46 cm) above the ground. Branches should have a wide angle of attachment to the trunk—narrow-angle branches tend to split off in later years with the weight of the fruit. If a shoot or branch grows in the wrong direction, consider tying or staking it into the correct position rather than cutting it back and waiting for a properly positioned shoot to grow.

If growth is vigorous, the selected scaffold branches should be pinched back to about 2½ to 3 feet (75 to 90 cm) long in midsummer (or when they have grown long enough) to promote side branching and the development of *secondary scaffold branches.* Continue to pinch or head back unwanted branches, but leave lateral shoots for future fruit production. The unwanted branches will be removed later, but their leaves conduct photosynthesis and provide shade for the trunk and main branches of the young tree. They also provide "spare" branches in case a scaffold branch is damaged.

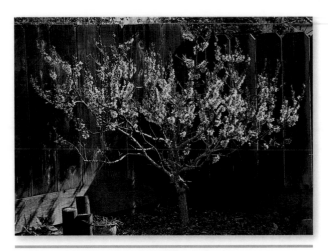

Figure 7.10. Genetic dwarf peach and nectarine trees can be featured in the landscape and are especially showy during flowering. Photo by Chuck Ingels.

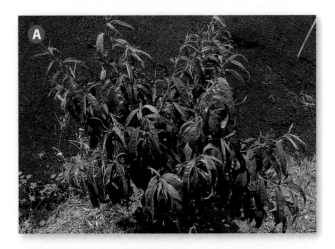

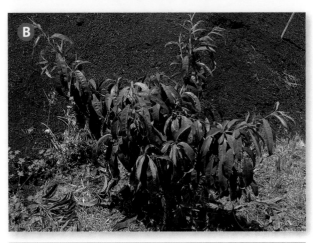

Figure 7.11. (A) Peach tree in first growing season before summer pruning. **(B)** Unwanted shoots were headed back or removed and three well-spaced shoots were selected to become the primary scaffold branches. Photos by Chuck Ingels.

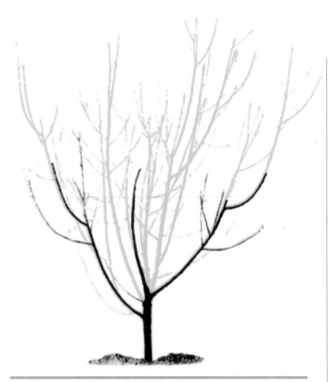

Figure 7.12. This unpruned 1-year-old peach tree had numerous potential scaffold limbs arising from its trunk. With pruning, three limbs were left, spaced about 120° apart around the trunk and several inches apart vertically. These scaffold limbs were headed slightly to promote branching at the desired points during the next growing season.

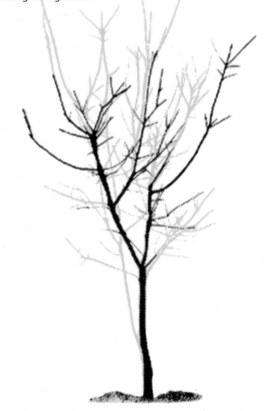

Figure 7.13. Some trees do not have three desirable scaffold limbs. In such cases, a branch arising from a primary scaffold can be selected to fill in the space and provide another scaffold limb. The third scaffold limb was selected by cutting off weak limbs in the center of the tree and leaving a strong outside branch.

Young cherry, plum, and pear trees produce very upright growth. To promote tree spread, you can bend the scaffold branches outward while they are still flexible or you can cut them back to outside lateral branches (see Figures 7.5 and 7.6). Other trees such as apricots, peaches, and almonds have a spreading growth habit and tend to produce lateral branches without heading. With these species, it is often necessary to remove flatter-angled branches and leave more upright branches, thus maintaining the upward, outward growth pattern.

First dormant season after planting. Select three or four primary scaffold branches if you did not do so the previous summer (Figures 7.12 to 7.14). The branches should be distributed evenly around the trunk and, if possible, spaced several inches apart vertically on the trunk. Leave small lateral branches along these scaffold branches and the trunk for early fruiting, tree growth, and sunburn protection.

Select three or four branches that are distributed evenly around the trunk and, if possible, spaced about 6 inches (15 cm) apart on the trunk, leaving small lateral branches along these scaffold branches and the trunk for early fruiting, tree growth, and sunburn protection. Later, head back the scaffolds to 2 to 3 feet (60 to 90 cm) long or prune them to outside laterals at this point. Almond scaffolds, however, should not be headed back.

Do not select scaffold limbs that are directly above or below one another. Avoid upright limbs that have narrow, acute angles of attachment: they tend to be weak at the point of attachment and can later split or break from the tree. Flat or horizontal limbs should also be avoided as scaffold limbs. For most species, a 45° to 60° angle (from vertical) for limb attachment is the most desirable. If the tree grows poorly the first year, head back the primary scaffolds severely to three or four buds in order to promote vigorous growth the next year, and then correct the causes of the poor growth, which often involve poor soil condition or improper watering.

Developing the mature tree. Head or pinch the primary scaffold branches to encourage the growth of secondary scaffold branches. Sometimes lateral branching will occur without heading; in that case, the primary scaffold branch can be cut off just beyond the laterals. Allow two, or in some cases as few as one or as many as three secondary branches to develop from each primary (Figures 7.15 and 7.16). Remove all other strong branches, during either the growing season or the dormant season, to reduce competition with the scaffold branches and to provide sunlight to lateral fruiting branches and spurs.

Continue training trees in subsequent dormant seasons to direct scaffold growth upward and outward and to fill open spaces with fruiting branches (Figures 7.17 to 7.19). By the end of the fourth year, a tree should have three or four primary scaffolds, with five to seven secondary scaffolds at about eye level. Above this point, additional branches should fill the periphery of the treetop. The center of the tree should be kept open to permit light infiltration for lower fruiting branches. With almonds, however, the center can fill in somewhat since spurs low in the tree are not as important, as the nuts are shaken from the tree rather than hand-harvested.

Mature trees. Pruning mature open-center fruit trees involves keeping the center free of vigorous, upright shoots, preferably during the growing season (Figure 7.20), reducing tree height, and thinning out branches to reduce crowding (Figures 7.21 and 7.22). Ensure that ample sunlight reaches the lower spurs of stone and pome fruit trees.

Remove or thin out older spurs to keep remaining spurs productive and to produce larger fruit. You do not need to thin almond spurs. Refer to Table 7.1 to determine spur life. For peaches and nectarines, which do not form spurs, select one-year-old lateral fruiting branches that originate close to main branches. Thin these fruiting branches during the dormant season (you can remove about half of them) and head the ones that remain by one-third if they are longer than about 18 inches (46 cm). Remove or cut back most two-year-old fruiting branches or cut them back to healthy one-year-old branches unless you want to retain them as branches (Figure 7.23). During the winter, circle a strong rope around the scaffold branches toward the top of the tree to support the branches as they bear the weight of the fruit (Figure 7.24).

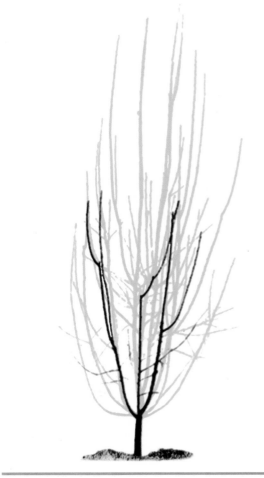

Figure 7.14. So that it would develop an open center, this 1-year-old Japanese plum tree was pruned to leave outside, spreading limbs, and was headed to promote branching at the desired locations.

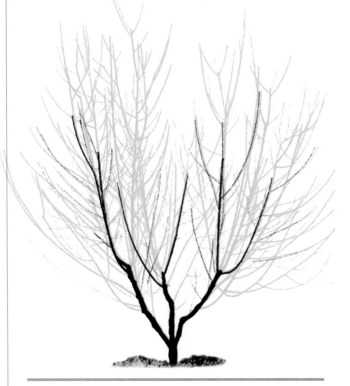

Figure 7.15. Many branches had to be removed from the vigorous 2-year-old peach tree. Low and horizontal limbs were cut off and vigorous, moderately upright limbs were selected for permanent secondary scaffolds and headed at 2 to 3 feet (60 to 90 cm) long.

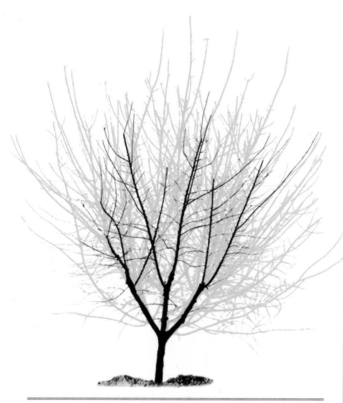

Figure 7.16. This 2-year-old almond tree had too many limbs. These were removed during pruning to leave two secondary scaffolds on each primary limb. No heading cuts were made and many small lateral branches were left for fruit wood.

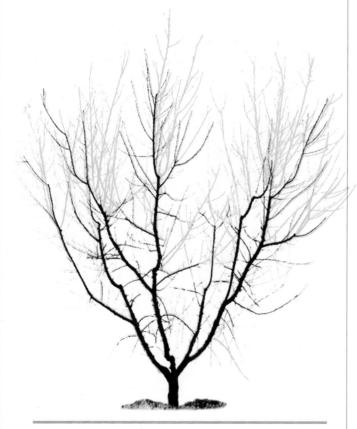

Figure 7.17. This 4-year-old peach tree should bear a substantial crop in its fifth year. Fruit wood was thinned out to adjust the crop load and reduce fuit thinning.

Perpendicular V System

With the perpendicular **V** training system, trees are grown in a **V** shape that is perpendicular to the row. The method was developed by University of California researchers at the Kearney Agricultural Center near Fresno and is used for peaches and nectarines. The main advantages of this system are close spacing (to allow multiple varieties to grow in a smaller space) and ease of management. This system is similar to open center in that the center is kept open through the growing season, but in this case only two primary scaffold branches are developed and no secondary or tertiary branches are created. All of the fruiting branches grow directly off of the two main scaffolds or off of short branches that arise from the scaffolds.

Begin by planting bare-root trees 5 to 6 feet apart in the row. A north-south row orientation works best as it allows both sides of the **V** to receive equal sunlight as the sun moves across the sky. Head the trees at about 12 to 18 inches (30 to 45 cm). Place two bamboo stakes in the ground in a **V** shape and as shoots grow, tie one strong shoot to each stake (Figure 7.25). Remove or cut back all other branches that grow from the trunk. Make sure that the angle of attachment of the two branches is wide; this will help strengthen the branches for the weight of the fruit. Continue to direct the growth of the two shoots upward and outward, and allow lateral shoots to grow off of them; these will be next year's fruiting branches and their leaves will shade the scaffolds to prevent sunburn. Do not allow vigorous upright shoots to grow in the middle or to become co-dominant with the scaffold branches.

Continue to develop the two scaffold branches and keep them topped at the desired final height, usually about 8 to 10 feet (2.4 to 3 m) (Figure 7.26). Remove or cut back competing upright shoots once or twice during the growing season. Be careful, though, not to allow west- or south-facing scaffold branches to remain bare and exposed to hot afternoon sun for more than about two hours of the day. If after pruning you can see that the branches will be exposed (considering the presence of leaves), paint the exposed surfaces with a 50-50 mix of interior white latex paint and water to prevent sunburn and borer infestation. With proper pruning practices, however, lateral fruiting branches should provide adequate protection from sunburn. The scaffold branches should be strong enough to support

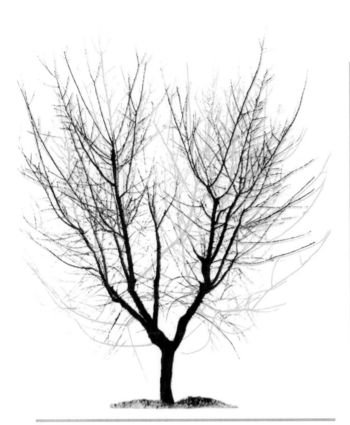

Figure 7.18. This 3-year-old plum tree was pruned by thinning the tertiary scaffolds to one or two per secondary scaffold. All interfering branches in the center of the tree were removed. By pruning to outside branches, the weight of leaves and fruit next summer will help spread this naturally upright growing tree.

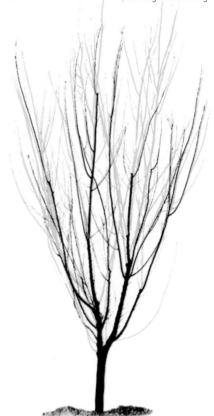

Figure 7.19. This 4-year-old almond tree was pruned by thinning out undesirable growth in the center and those limbs that had not assumed an outward-upward direction. Note that because a heavy nut set is desired on almond trees, little thinning of the young lateral branches was done. Larger interfering branches in the lower part of the tree were removed.

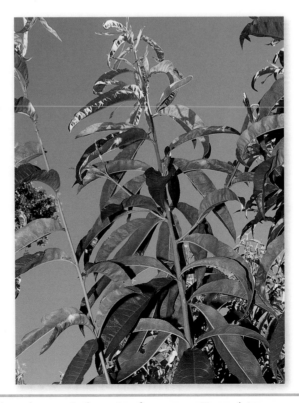

Figure 7.20. This vigorous, upright shoot that grew in the center of an open-center peach tree was removed in May. You need to remove these shoots because they shade lower fruiting branches, rendering them unproductive. Photo by Chuck Ingels.

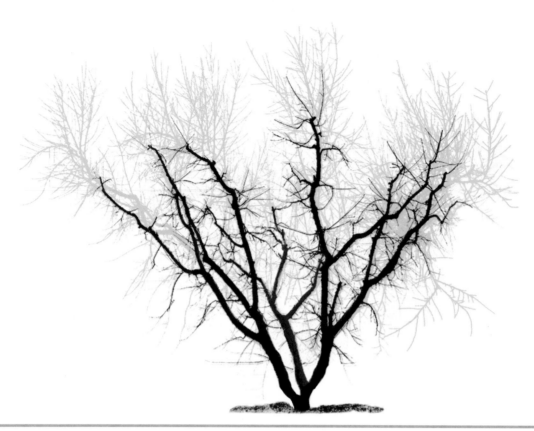

Figure 7.21. Mature peach and nectarine trees require thorough thinning out of the 1-year-old (bearing) wood.

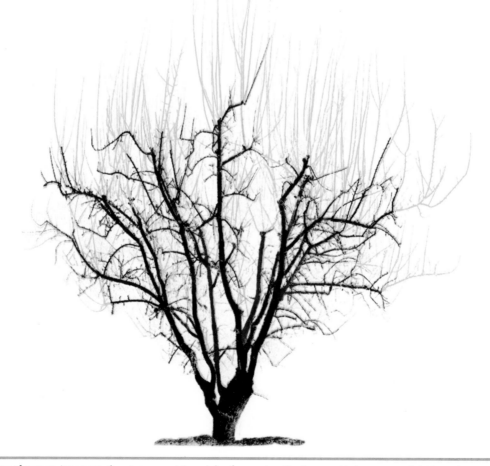

Figure 7.22. Pruning of mature Japanese plum trees consists mainly of removing the 1-year-old vigorous, upright branches. Some 1-year-old branches are left to develop spurs, while some of the old, weak spurs are removed.

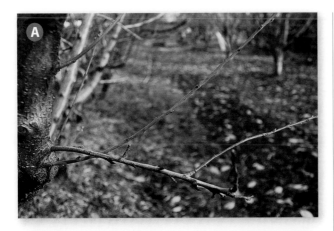

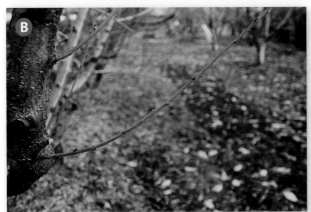

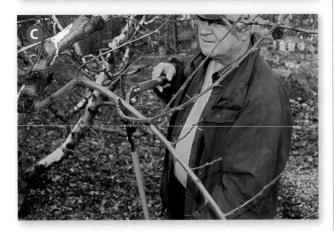

Figure 7.23. One way to prune a peach fruiting branch: **(A)** Dormant 2-year-old branch that was headed the previous winter and fruited the previous summer, bending it downward. Two new shoots grew in the summer: one on the fruiting branch and one on the scaffold branch. **(B)** After pruning, the older wood was cut off to promote 1-year-old fruiting wood near the scaffold branch. **(C)** This 2-year-old branch is being shortened back to a 1-year-old fruiting branch. Photos by Chuck Ingels.

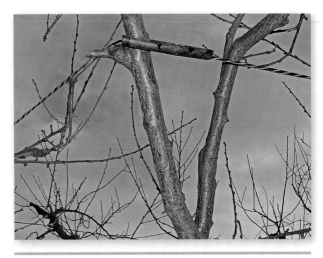

Figure 7.24. You can tie a strong rope around the tree to reduce propping and limb breakage. Photo by Chuck Ingels.

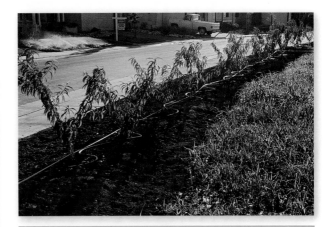

Figure 7.25. Developing perpendicular V trees. After planting, place one bamboo stake in each direction of desired growth and grow one shoot on each stake. Continue to direct shoots upward and outward and remove or cut back competing upright shoots, but leave lateral shoots to develop fruiting branches. Photo by Chuck Ingels.

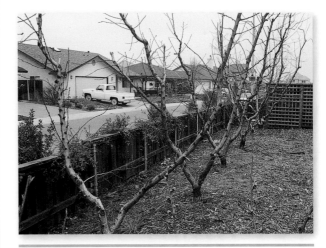

Figure 7.26. Four-year-old peach and nectarine trees trained to perpendicular V and topped at about 9 to 10 feet. Note the lateral fruiting branches that arise from the scaffold branches. Photo by Chuck Ingels.

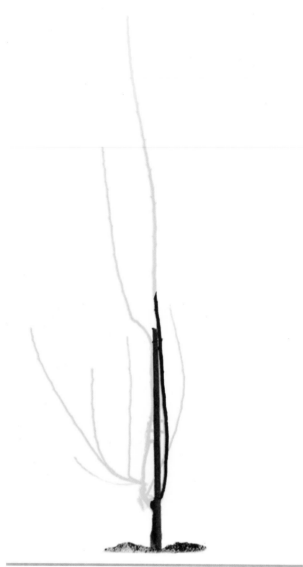

Figure 7.27. After the first growing season, all lateral branches of this walnut tree were removed and the central leader was headed about 6 inches above the stake.

the weight of the fruit, but circling a rope around them near the top of the tree will provide extra support.

Winter pruning involves thinning and shortening lateral fruiting branches, removing any competing leaders, and reducing the tree height. A sun-exposed one-year-old branch arising from the scaffold limb should produce fruit as well as several new shoots the following season. At the end of that season, cut back the lateral branches to leave one-year-old branches that arise from or near the scaffold branch (see Figure 7.23). Head by about one-third any of these branches that are longer than about 18 inches. Winter pruning should remove about half or more of the one- and two-year-old wood from the tree.

CENTRAL LEADER AND MODIFIED CENTRAL LEADER SYSTEMS

Some tree species naturally grow or are easily trained to a single central trunk with lateral branches growing upward and outward, similar to a Christmas tree, but there are several ways for a gardener to create the single-leader tree. When the leader is allowed to continue its upward growth indefinitely (central leader), it results in an excessively large tree, so this approach is only used on dwarf trees, usually dwarf apples (see Figure 7.5B). Far more often, the leader is removed beyond a selected lateral branch (modified central leader).

For large trees, such as walnut, pecan, and chestnut, the leader is allowed to grow tall with widely spaced lateral branches. Beyond about five to seven main lateral branches, the dominance of the leader fades and multiple limbs are allowed to form. For apples and pears, three or four tiers of lateral branches are often formed along the leader to facilitate harvest and management, but the leader is removed beyond the top tier. For some species, such as fig, persimmon, and pistachio, the leader is often kept much shorter and lateral branches become dominant; this system is often called delayed open center. It is used to create scaffold branches with vertical spacing along the trunk that are structurally stronger than open center but that also have a center that is kept relatively open.

Walnuts, pecans, and chestnuts are trained in a similar way. After planting the tree, head it at about 2 feet (60 cm). Place a stake next to the tree, extending about 6 feet (1.8 m) above the ground. During the first growing season, tie the most vigorous shoot to the stake as it grows and pinch back all others. In the first winter, head the staked leader about three or four buds above the stake, or just above the height desired for the lowest scaffold (Figure 7.27). If growth was insufficient, head the tree lower and continue to train the leader in the second season. Remove any long, "necked" buds near the top of the leader. In the second winter, begin selecting the scaffold branches and head back the leader and desired scaffolds (Hartley and other terminal bearing walnut varieties require no heading of scaffold limbs). Cut the scaffold branches shorter than the leader (Figure 7.28). In subsequent years continue to select well-spaced scaffold branches from the leader until four to six are established (Figure 7.29). Then simply allow the leader to become the topmost scaffold. An example of a large walnut tree with widely spaced scaffolds can be seen in Figure 7.30.

Apples and pears are often trained by forming three or four tiers of lateral branches along the leader, with three or four branches per tier (Figure 7.31). Beginning in the growing season and continuing during dormancy, select the central leader, spread the desired scaffold branches, and head back (and later remove) any other vigorous upright shoots that compete with the central leader. Create the first tier of four lateral branches by tying or staking branches outward at an angle of about 45° to 60° from vertical after they have grown 2 to 3 feet (60 to 90 cm) long. When the central leader has grown about 2 to 3 feet (60 to 90 cm) past the first tier, usually in the first dormant season after planting, head it just below this point and also head the scaffold branches (Figure 7.32). Sometimes it is not necessary to make this heading cut, as some trees may branch out at the desired locations on their own. Also, in some cases (such as with dwarf apples), it may not be desirable to head the scaffold branches.

During the next season, train a second tier of four branches outward from the leader. These second-tier branches should be offset vertically from those of the first tier; bend and tie branches in the proper direction if necessary. Allow the most vigorous upright shoot to continue its growth as the central leader. Then create the third tier in a similar manner. Avoid bending one branch directly over another branch of an adjacent tier; also, maintain the tree's pyramidal shape by keeping lower branches longer than upper branches (Figure 7.33).

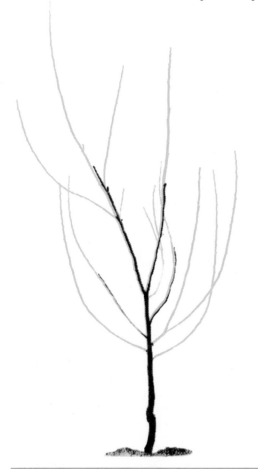

Figure 7.28. After the second growing season, three lateral branches were selected and headed back and the central leader was headed but left the longest to encourage its dominance. All other branches were removed.

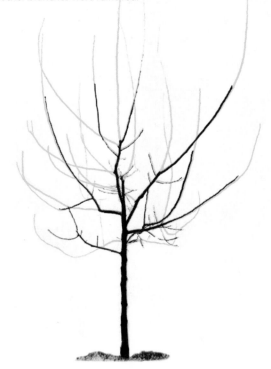

Figure 7.29. After the third growing season, additional lateral branches were selected on this walnut tree. The central leader may be allowed to bend outward and become the topmost scaffold or maintained for an additional year to develop more lateral branching.

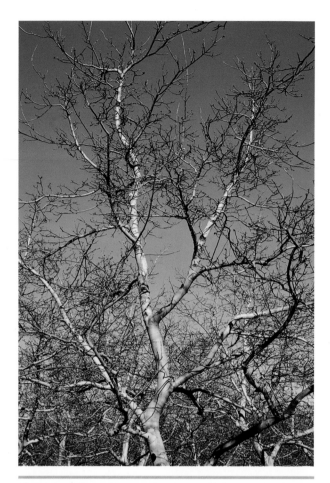

Figure 7.30. This walnut tree has a very tall, dominant leader and the scaffold branches are well spaced. Light penetration is good and the tree is structurally very sound. Photo by Bill Olson.

When the desired tree height is reached, cut the leader back to a lateral branch. The entire training process will take about 4 to 6 years, depending on tree vigor and spacing.

Another method used for creating central leader trees is to allow lateral branches to grow singly rather than in distinct tiers (see Figure 7.5 B and C). This method is simpler and can work, so long as the branches do not crowd or shade each other; sunlight must reach the lower branches for at least a portion of each day. If, as the tree grows, shading occurs, you should remove whole branches or make the upper branches narrower.

Spur development and some side branching of the main lateral branches should be encouraged. Vigorous upright shoots can be removed or headed back to only three to six buds during the growing season (summer pruning), although some or most of these shoots should be left longer for shading if fruit is exposed to very hot afternoon sun. Heading these upright shoots in the summer creates fruit-bearing spurs if the tree is not too vigorous; for this reason, dwarfing rootstocks are preferred. Heading may also encourage the growth of another set of vigorous shoots; simply remove these shoots or prune them back to create more spurs. Alternatively, you can simply remove these upright branches in the dormant season.

Fig, persimmon, and pistachio trees can be trained to a modified central leader that is essentially a delayed open center (Figure 7.34). In the first year or two, a central leader is formed and three to five scaffold branches that are separated both around the tree and vertically along the leader are selected. The scaffolds should be vertically spaced about 6 to 12 inches (15 to 30 cm) apart. Mature pruning of each of these three species is covered later in this chapter.

"Fruit Bush" System

"Fruit bushes" are standard (full-sized) trees or, preferably, trees on dwarfing rootstock. You keep them small by periodically pruning them in summer (Figure 7.35). This method can work for virtually any fruit species. The benefits of this system are that you can manage trees without a ladder and you can grow multiple species and varieties in a relatively small area. Fruit bush crop yields are generally lower than those of other training methods, however.

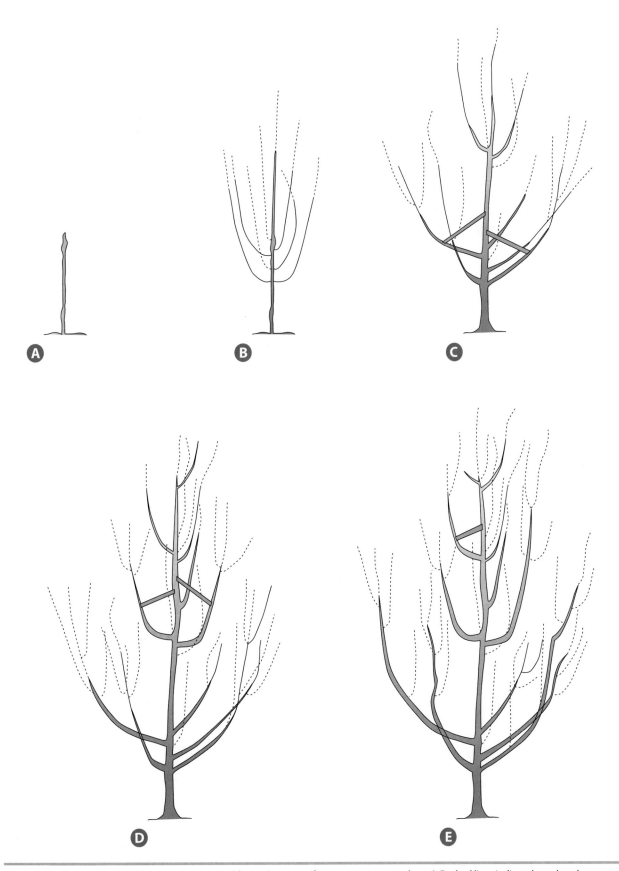

Figure 7.31. Modified central leader pruning method for apple or pear (fruiting spurs are not shown). Dashed lines indicate branches that are to be removed. **(A)** Bare-root tree at planting time. **(B)** First tier of scaffold branches and reestablished central leader. **(C)** First tier of branches staked into desired position as second tier of branches is established. Branches developed in the third **(D)** and subsequent **(E)** years are spaced evenly around and up the central leader. The leader is removed at a predetermined height. Note the 45°–60° angle of branch attachment formed by using spreaders.

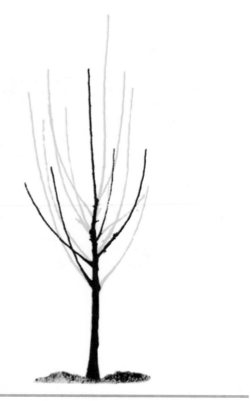

Figure 7.32. Apple trees are often trained to the modified central leader system. The first year's branches of this apple tree were thinned out to four scaffold limbs and the central leader was maintained. All scaffold limbs and the central leader were headed back with approximately one-third of last year's growth removed.

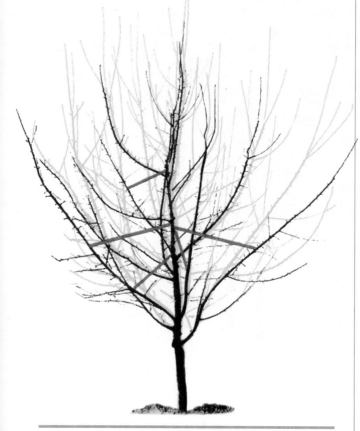

Figure 7.33. The uprights and interfering branches of this 4-year-old apple tree have been continually thinned out and the central leader maintained. Spreader boards are often used to achieve wider angles of later branches.

Pruning of newly planted trees begins in about late April or May of the first growing season, when new growth is about 2 to 3 feet (60 to 90 cm) long. At this time, cut the new growth in half, aiming for a uniform, bushy appearance. Hedge-trimming shears may be useful for this step (Figure 7.36). In about late June or July, cut the subsequent new growth in half (Figure 7.37). If new growth is vigorous, you may need to cut it once more during the season. This typically occurs with apricots, plums, and plum-apricot hybrids, for which three prunings per season are common. These cuts promote an excess of shoots, so thin them out to allow sunlight to reach the lower branches during the summer. If needed, thin out additional crowding branches in the dormant season when they are easier to see.

In the second year, continue cutting new growth in this manner until the trees reach 5 to 7 feet (1.5 to 2.1 m) tall, or a height at which you can easily prune the top. Pruning in subsequent years involves cutting off any shoots above the tree's permanent height two to three times per year (Figure 7.38). Also, periodically thin out crowding branches, especially at the top of the tree, and remove nonproductive fruiting wood in early spring when you can see which branches have no flowers. After the third year, you may find it necessary to open up the center of the tree. Fruit bushes have worked well for many home gardeners. It is easier to use with dwarfing rootstocks since they grow somewhat less vigorously. Trees with dwarfing rootstocks are not always available, however, and vigorous growth can also occur on many semi-dwarf trees. The rapid, dense growth can be especially challenging with plums and apricots.

Espalier Training

Most fruit species can be trained on a trellis, but apples, pears, and Asian pears lend themselves well to this kind of training because substantial numbers of fruit spurs develop on the horizontal branches without overly vigorous shoot growth. Although you can use nearly any variety, spur-bearing apple types on seedling rootstocks are ideal for espalier training because they set flower buds on short shoots and produce relatively few vigorous upright shoots (see Chapter 3). With proper summer pruning, tip-bearing apples on dwarfing rootstocks and pears, for which there are currently no dwarfing rootstocks, can also be trained in this way, but they require more room and diligent pruning to keep them under control.

The trellis should be rigid enough to support the tree and fruit so it won't sag. If you use wire, use 10 or 12 gauge wire for strength and attach it firmly to the posts. Plant the trees 7 to 10 feet (2.1 to 3.0 m) apart, depending on the number of wires and the expected vigor of the trees. Espalier trellises usually have two to four wires, but they could have just one or as many as five. Use fewer wires for less-vigorous trees and three or four wires where more vigor can be expected. The horizontal wires should be spaced 18 to 24 inches (45 to 60 cm) apart vertically. Also, more-vigorous trees should be planted farther apart to provide more buds and, therefore, less vigor from each shoot.

Plant the trees as described in Chapter 4. Head the trees at planting to just above the lowest wire. When spring growth begins, direct the uppermost shoot of each tree upward toward the next wire. Allow the two strongest lateral branches to grow outward and upward. For continued growth, it is best to direct the two shoots outward at a 45° to 60° angle, tying each shoot to a bamboo stake, and to bend them later to the horizontal and tie them to the wires (Figure 7.39). Shoots of vigorous trees will usually continue their growth, though, if you simply tie them to the wire as they grow. If growth is vigorous, you can head back the vertical leader to just above the second wire in the same growing season; otherwise, make this cut during the following dormant season. Continue this type of training with new shoots in the years that follow, as the uppermost shoot reaches each successive wire of the trellis. There are many other patterns of espalier training, including fans, long, single-wire hedges, and upright shoots trained to resemble a menorah (Figure 7.40).

As upright, vigorous shoots begin to grow from the horizontal branches, head them during the growing season to three or four buds each after they have grown about 8 to 12 inches (20 to 30 cm). With this treatment, spur-bearing apples usually will begin to form spurs or short shoots that end in terminal flower buds. Vigorous apples and pears may continue to produce strong upright shoots from below these cuts; thin these to leave only the weaker lateral shoots or cut them to three buds as before. During the dormant season, thin the spurs to prevent overproduction.

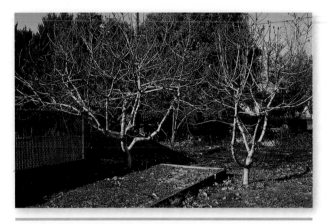

Figure 7.34. These fig trees were grown with delayed open-center training. With each tree, scaffold branches were developed off the short leader and the open center was developed low, but the center was not kept open on top. Photo by Joe Connell.

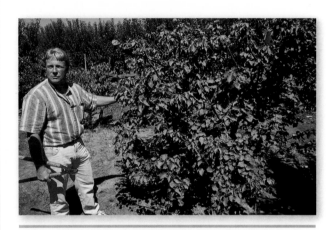

Figure 7.35. Recently pruned apricot fruit bush, which is being maintained at about head height. Photo by Chuck Ingels.

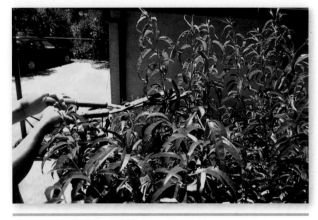

Figure 7.36. When training the young fruit bush, you can use hedge shears to cut the shoots by about half. Some selective shoot thinning will also be needed to prevent crowding and shading of lower fruiting branches. Photo by Chuck Ingels.

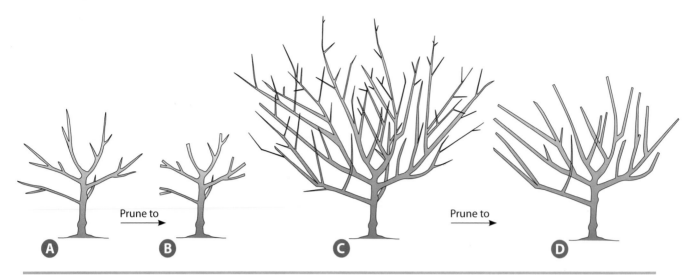

Figure 7.37. Fruit bush pruning method (leaves removed to show structure). **(A)** New growth early in first growing season (late April to early May). **(B)** Initial heading of new growth. **(C)** Subsequent new growth after heading (June or July, with some shoots removed to allow light penetration). **(D)** Additional growth headed back in summer and some branches thinned out. Growth may require pruning one or two more times during the first growing season. Continue heading back each year until the tree reaches the desired height.

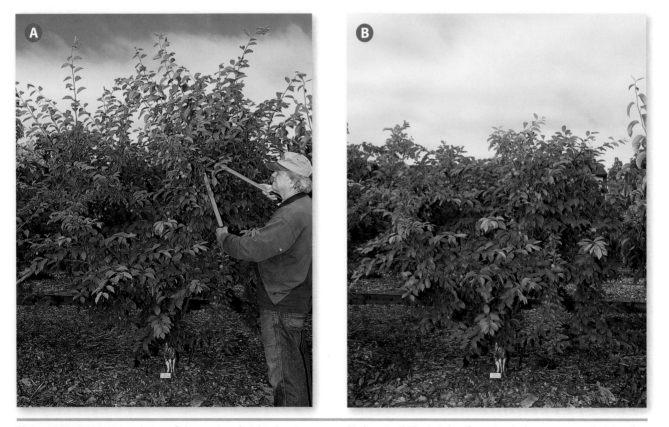

Figure 7.38. (A) Vigorous shoots of cherry-plum fruit bush to be removed in late April. The height of pruning is the permanent height of the tree. **(B)** Completed pruning of fruit bush. Photos by Chuck Ingels.

Renovate spurs on older trees by thinning and by pruning away old or unproductive sections, leaving the younger wood. To prevent shading lower down, do not allow the top tier to grow wider than lower tiers.

Pruning of Unique Species

Walnut, pecan, and chestnut. On young, vigorous walnut, pecan, and chestnut trees, some heading of long, whip-like shoots is desirable to promote strong lateral branch development. Some varieties bear large numbers of nuts at an early age, and this can stunt their growth. For example, spur-bearing walnut varieties tend to set a heavier crop than laterally bearing varieties (see Chapter 3) and the spur-bearers benefit from more severe pruning, especially from heading cuts. Pruning of mature walnut and chestnut trees is often not essential for backyard trees. For optimal growth and production, however, you should thin branches periodically to prevent crowding and allow sunlight into the tree. This helps keep the tree healthy and productive throughout the canopy. Chestnuts and some walnut varieties, such as Hartley and Franquette, bear flowers and fruit at the ends of long, one-year-old branches, so avoid making any heading cuts on these trees after the first few years of training.

Persimmon. Young persimmon trees are generally pruned very lightly to encourage the development of a large tree in as short a time as possible. Long, vigorous shoots should, however, be tipped or headed, preferably during the growing season, to promote branching and create a strong structure. Young persimmon trees tend to produce a secondary flush of growth in midsummer. This new growth does not harden off well and can freeze back in winter in cold climate areas. For this reason growers prune off this secondary growth in cold areas, but in most areas of California this is unnecessary and most growers ignore this midseason growth.

It is important to understand that, in general, only the end three or four buds on a one-year-old persimmon branch produce flowers and eventually fruit. For this reason you should only perform very light pruning. Heavy dormant season pruning stimulates strong vegetative shoot growth that will not develop flowers and fruit until the following season. This phenomenon can be used to one's advantage since persimmon trees tend to go into alternate bearing very

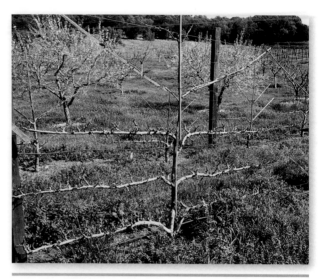

Figure 7.39. For young espalier-trained trees, it is best to train the new shoots upward and outward at an angle along a stake to provide optimal growth and fruit spur formation. Once they reach the end of the stake, tie them down to the wire.

easily. If you make a few heading cuts in the dormant season after heavy bearing years, the tree will respond by producing more fruit in the light crop years. By the same token, you should make more heading cuts after a light crop year.

Since you only want to do minimal pruning on a persimmon tree in order to maintain a continuous supply of flowers and fruit, the tree will eventually develop a spreading shape and the fruit will be borne farther away from the trunk and scaffold limbs. For this reason, you should make heading cuts periodically on some branches (cutting back a few branches each year to 10 to 25 inches [25 to 64 cm] from the larger branch) to bring them closer to the trunk and prevent the fine, spindly branches from hanging down or breaking from the weight of fruit. To maintain a healthy, productive tree and to prevent alternate bearing, cut several weaker branches back severely (to two or three buds' length). The shoots that grow from these headed branches will be rejuvenated for fruit production the following year.

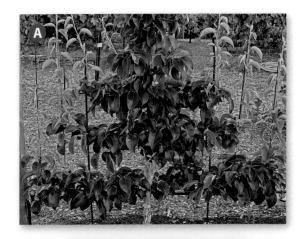

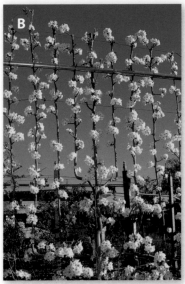

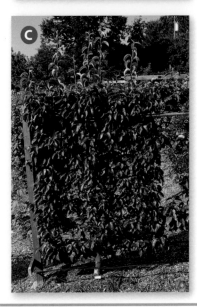

Figure 7.40. (A) Espalier-trained Asian pear with main branches being directed outward and then upward. **(B)** The tree in spring, two years later. **(C)** The tree in early summer (photo taken from a ladder). Note the strong trellis needed to support the tree. Photos **A** and **B** by Chuck Ingels. Photo **C** by Jack Kelly Clark.

Persimmon branches tend to die back fairly easily if they receive insufficient sunlight. Therefore, an open canopy must be maintained to allow sunlight to penetrate and filter through the leaf area. To achieve this open canopy, you may have to perform a heavy pruning of the scaffold limbs or larger branches at some point. Persimmon trees respond well with new growth after heavy pruning.

It is possible to maintain persimmon trees at a height of 8 to 10 feet. You must, however, remove or thin the many vigorous upright shoots that would otherwise quickly grow to shade the fruiting wood lower down. This pruning should be performed twice: once in late spring and again in summer. Trees maintained in this manner produce much less fruit than minimally pruned trees, but all of the fruit is reachable from the ground or from a 6-foot ladder.

Pomegranate. Pomegranates sucker profusely from the crown. Once the tree is trained, annual pruning consists of thinning suckers and unwanted branches and removing dead or damaged branches. Remove vigorous water sprouts during the growing season to reduce shading and promote fruit production. If a pomegranate tree is left untrained it will develop naturally into a bushy, umbrella-shaped shrub.

Pomegranates naturally grow as a bush from several suckers that grow from the root crown. To create an aesthetically pleasing and productive tree, use the open-center or modified central leader system. Remove all suckers growing from the crown and the base of the trunk. In very cold areas where killing frosts can occur, it's a better idea to develop multiple trunks from three to four suckers in case one or more trunks are killed.

Pomegranate trees can become quite large and spreading, requiring the use of tall ladders to harvest the fruit, or you can maintain a smaller tree at a height of about 8 feet. As with most species, the heading cuts required to maintain a small tree stimulate vigorous growth. Once your tree achieves the desired height, use thinning cuts to maintain its shape. After a few years, the density of the branches will make it hard for light to penetrate the canopy and the tree will become less fruitful. Heavy pruning to remove any crossing-over branches and large interior branches will help with light penetration and the rejuvenation of fruiting wood. Pomegranate trees produce long thorns that can puncture the eyes or skin, so wear protective gloves and eyewear when pruning.

Fig. A fig tree can be trained into nearly any shape or size using any of the methods discussed above. You can allow it to mature into a large, beautiful shade tree with a single trunk or multiple trunks. The branch structure can be developed from an early age to create a jungle gym for climbing or limbs to sit on. Large, well-trained trees may require only light annual pruning. Alternatively, you can also prune fig trees severely so that the fruit can be picked without use of a ladder. Figs can also be espaliered. In climates with very cold winters, fig trees may be killed back to the ground in winter, so they are trained as bushes.

To successfully prune figs, you need to understand their bearing habit. Most fig varieties bear two crops: one in early summer (known as the *breba* crop) and another in late summer and fall. Buds for the first crop form the previous fall and overwinter as expanded buds arrayed laterally along the "one-year-old" branches (see Figure 2.12). The second crop forms the following summer on current-season's shoots; this later crop usually has more fruit than the first crop. Severe winter pruning to reduce a tree's size can eliminate or severely reduce the first crop, but a tree will usually form a substantial second crop no matter how severe the winter pruning. Some cultivars have a tendency to produce better late figs and are therefore more suited to severe pruning. To successfully grow the first crop of figs, leave as many unheaded tips on the tree as possible. As a general rule, thinning out the canopy by about one-third should produce a good first crop.

Figs generally do not require summer pruning, although some thinning of shoots is warranted to reduce crowding of trees that are kept short. If you head back long shoots, the second crop will be reduced, but some summer pruning may still be useful just after the first-crop figs are harvested. Some growers use one particular method of summer pruning to produce earlier-maturing fruit of a higher quality. This technique involves the removal of the growing tip when 5 or 6 leaves have developed in the spring. This interrupts vegetative growth and diverts the plant's energy into fruit development until vegetative growth can resume. This technique may slightly alter the shape of the fruit. You can experiment in your own climatic conditions to find local limits for how early or late you can perform summer pruning, but you must allow enough time afterward for regrowth to develop and form buds for the following season's first crop, since the purpose of this method is to maximize double cropping.

Pistachio. It is very important to train pistachio trees correctly during the first 4 or 5 years because strong apical dominance can severely limit the branching of young trees. Use the open-center or modified central leader system with three or four well-spaced scaffold branches that are evenly distributed around the trunk and spaced about 6 to 10 inches apart vertically. In this case, the central leader is short, resembling the "delayed open-center system" described earlier. When these scaffold branches are about 30 inches long, pinch them back in the summer or head them to that length in the winter to stimulate lateral branching. The following winter, select two vigorous, well-spaced lateral branches near the end of each primary scaffold. Continue this process for several years until the framework of the tree is established, always heading back branches of young trees to 30 inches to promote lateral branching. Keep the center of the tree fairly open above the leader in order to admit sunlight for flower bud formation and fruiting.

After you establish the basic framework of the tree, only light pruning is necessary. Relatively few vegetative buds form laterally on shoots (most buds are flower buds), so heading cuts do not always stimulate lateral branching. If you do want to encourage rejuvenation of the tree, though, regrowth is usually satisfactory when you prune the tree back fairly severely using both heading and thinning cuts.

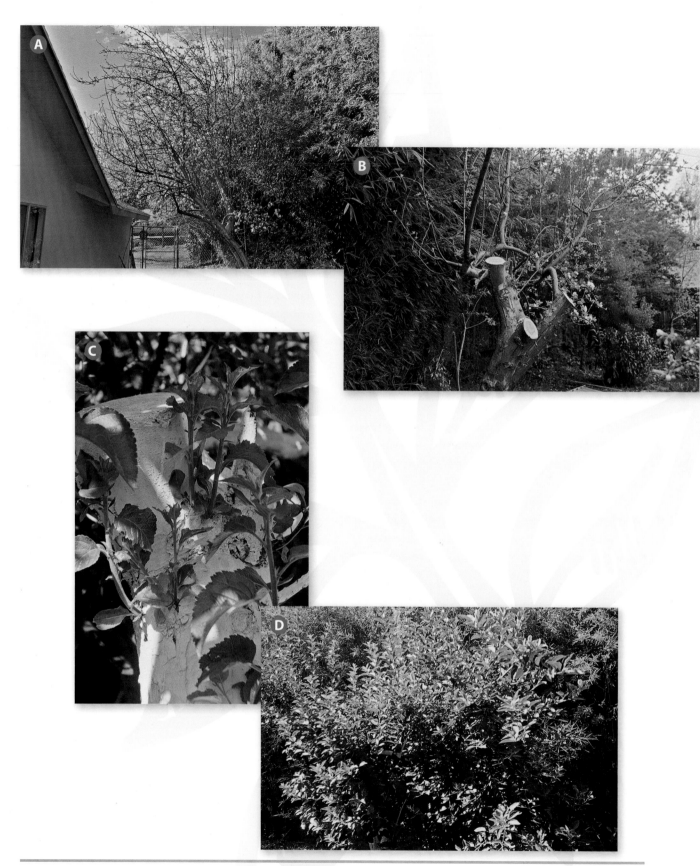

Figure 7.41. (A) This apple tree grew too tall and was unmanageable. **(B)** The main branches were cut back in late March, leaving "nurse limbs." **(C)** New shoots began to grow in April and were thinned to develop several structural limbs. **(D)** The same tree later in the season, being trained as a fruit bush. Photos by Chuck Ingels.

Pruning Overgrown Trees

Many people have one or more large, neglected fruit trees in their yard. Because the trees may be very tall, you have to pick most of the fruit using ladders; many people simply do not pick them at all. It is difficult to prune or spray these overgrown trees, and the higher branches often break from the weight of unthinned fruit. Diseases, borers, and other insect pests frequently invade these trees.

Before deciding to prune an overgrown fruit tree, you need to decide whether the tree is worth the time and effort. Ask yourself these questions:

- *Are there any serious disease or insect problems on the trunk or main branches?*

- *Do you like the fruit from the tree?*

- *Are new, improved varieties (disease-resistant, dwarf, etc.) of the tree available?*

- *Would you rather have a different type of fruit tree?*

- *Would you would rather have a shade tree instead of a fruit tree?*

If you choose to work with an existing overgrown fruit tree, use one of these three basic methods of pruning:

1. Maintain the tree height and make mostly thinning cuts.

2. Reduce the tree height slowly over a three-year period.

3. Drastically cut back all main branches except for one or two temporary scaffold branches.

If you must cut large branches, wait until about March or early April to do so—even into the flowering period—to allow the wounds to begin to close more rapidly and to reduce the chances of decay in the large wounds (see Method 2, below). When thinning a branch, cut it back to a lateral that has a diameter at least one-third the size of the diameter of the branch you are cutting. If the pruning will cause branches to be exposed to prolonged periods of hot afternoon sun (a common result of severe pruning), protect the branches from sunburn by painting them with whitewash or a 50-50 mixture of white interior latex paint and water.

METHOD 1: MAINTAIN THE TREE HEIGHT AND MAKE MOSTLY THINNING CUTS

This method assumes that the tree is structurally sound and no taller than you can easily manage with an available ladder. If the tree has been neglected, you will need to remove many branches, especially those high in the tree. Begin by removing any dead, diseased, or broken limbs. Branches that cross or rub against each other should be pruned out, as should crowded limbs and branches that grow toward the interior of the tree.

Thin enough of the remaining canopy to allow sunlight to penetrate to the lower wood, but don't create such big gaps that the main branches can be sunburned. (If branches do become exposed to afternoon sun, paint them white as discussed above.) It is preferable to remove any branches that grow beyond the height at which you are able to pick the fruit. Prune the tree to that same height every year. The tree will produce new, vigorous shoots, especially near the top of the tree, and you will have to remove them each year, preferably through at least some summer pruning.

METHOD 2: REDUCE THE TREE HEIGHT SLOWLY OVER A THREE-YEAR PERIOD

If the tree is structurally sound but taller than you can manage with an available ladder, reduce the tree's height to a manageable level over a period of about three years. Determine how tall you would like the permanent (fruit-bearing) structure of the tree to be and then reduce the excess height of the tree by one-third each year for three years in the winter until the desired height is reached. If there are no low branches, you may simply want to remove such trees, since it will be difficult to develop new limbs on the trunk.

Avoid making such major cuts during summer, as remaining shoots may be damaged when you remove the branches, tree growth may suffer excessive devigoration, and the exposed branches will sunburn and attract borers. Avoid leaving large stubs; when possible, cut back to a lateral branch that is at least one-third the size of the main branch. Because large cuts often stimulate new growth, remove or head back suckers and watersprouts once or twice during the summer to prevent shading of the lower fruiting wood. Thin additional branches as needed to allow some sunlight to penetrate into the canopy.

METHOD 3: DRASTICALLY CUT BACK MOST OF THE MAIN BRANCHES

This is an extreme method for reducing tree height in a single season in which large branches are headed or cut back to lateral branches (Figure 7.41). The cuts are made somewhere below the desired height of the tree in order to allow for new growth. Bear in mind, however, that large cuts may not callus over so the wood is likely to rot in future years.

Not all trees are capable of resprouting from large lower branches: apples and pears usually will do so, as will citrus and avocados. Old stone fruit trees, however—including peaches, cherries, apricots, and nectarines—may not resprout effectively because buds low down on the tree may not be able to grow through the thick bark. Also, many trees may not have small, low branches or twigs for you to use to form a new framework. If the tree has no main branches lower than 6 to 8 feet (1.8 to 2.4 m) from the ground, it is better to use method 1 or 2 or simply to remove the tree completely, since a major cut low on the tree would leave just a stump.

Preserve and cut back lateral branches where possible, even if the laterals are small. These laterals, along with shoots that arise from buds on the main branches, will form the framework for the new, smaller tree. A good time for this type of major pruning is March or early April, when active growth and drier weather are beginning. To prevent sunburn, paint all exposed scaffold branches with whitewash or a 50-50 mixture of white interior latex paint and water.

Because this method removes a great deal of leaf area while leaving in place a large root system, make sure to leave one or two smaller main branches or a large side branch (*nurse limb*) unpruned to absorb the tree's growth energy and provide foliage so photosynthesis can continue. You can remove the nurse branch or cut it back the following year, after new branches have arisen from the cut branches. A follow-up program of summer pruning and dormant pruning is essential to reshaping the tree in the desired manner.

If you want to grow one or more different varieties instead of the variety of the existing tree, consider topworking (grafting) the tree to a different variety. Topworking can be used at the time that you cut the main branches (see Topworking in Chapter 8).

References

Aldrich, T. M., D. E. Ramos, and A. D. Rizzi. 1982. Training young walnut trees by the modified central-leader system. Oakland: University of California Division of Agriculture and Natural Resources, Publication 2471.

Brickell, C., and D. Joyce. 1996. Pruning and training: A fully illustrated plant-by-plant manual. American Horticultural Society. New York: DK Publishing.

Crane, J. C., and J. Maranto. 1988. Pistachio production. Oakland: University of California Division of Agriculture and Natural Resources, Publication 2279.

Harris, R. W. 1999. Arboriculture: Integrated management of landscape trees, shrubs, and vines. Third ed. Englewood Cliffs, NJ: Prentice-Hall.

Hodel, D. R., and D. Pittenger. 2002. Woody landscape plants. Pages 311–335 in D. Pittenger, ed., California master gardener handbook. Oakland: University of California Division of Agriculture and Natural Resources, Publication 3382.

Ingels, C., P. M. Geisel, and C. L. Unruh. 2002. Fruit trees: Training and pruning deciduous trees. Oakland: University of California Division of Agriculture and Natural Resources, Publication 8057. Available free online from the UC ANR Communication Services Web site, http://anrcatalog.ucdavis.edu.

Micke, W., A. A. Hewitt, J. K. Clark, and M. Gerdts. 1980. Pruning fruit and nut trees. Oakland: University of California Division of Agriculture and Natural Resources, Leaflet 21171.

Vossen, P., and D. Silva. 2002. Temperate tree fruit and nut crops. Pages 449–530 in D. Pittenger, ed., California master gardener handbook. Oakland: University of California Division of Agriculture and Natural Resources, Publication 3382.

CHAPTER 8

Budding and Grafting

Chuck A. Ingels and Pamela M. Geisel, *with special assistance from professional grafter Art Ruble of Clovis, California, and plant propagation technician Judy Lee of UC Davis.*

Budding and grafting are methods of plant propagation that the home orchardist can use to grow more than one variety, and in some cases more than one species, of fruit on a single tree. For example, if you have space for only one cherry tree and you also need a pollinizer variety, you can bud or graft one or more other cherry varieties onto the single tree. Budding and grafting can also be used to extend the period of fruit harvest from a single tree, for example, by growing several peach and nectarine varieties with different harvest periods on a single tree. In addition, you can use budding and grafting to repair an existing tree that has been injured or to change over one variety to another. These practices are also commonly used by wholesale nursery staff to propagate new plants that are to be grown on rootstock.

The home orchardist will most often use budding and grafting to add one or more varieties or species to an existing tree. Different varieties of the same species (for example, one cherry variety added to another) are generally compatible: grafted properly, they unite readily and grow together. Different species (for example, peach grafted onto plum) may be incompatible because they may grow together poorly or the graft union may fail entirely. Table 8.1 gives you a list of graft compatibilities for selected deciduous fruit and nut trees. Consult a UC Master Gardener or a knowledgeable nursery employee for more information on grafting compatibility for your tree.

In order to get a scion to graft onto your tree, you need to know someone with a tree of the desired variety and it must be graft-compatible with your tree. A friend or neighbor may even want to graft your variety onto

his or her tree. There may also be an annual scion exchange at a local chapter of the California Rare Fruit Growers (online at http://www.crfg.org).

In both budding and grafting, parts of two plants are united to grow as one plant. The *scion* is the part that is removed from one plant and attached to another; the new growth from the scion remains true to type rather than blending genetically with the rootstock. The *rootstock* (also called *stock*) is the plant to which the scion is attached. A union forms as a result of the tissue connection that is formed between the stock and scion by the *vascular cambium* (also called simply the *cambium*), a thin layer of actively dividing cells located between the wood and the bark of a tree (see Chapter 2). Undifferentiated *callus* cells form at the union, and these soon differentiate into new vascular tissues that permit the passage of nutrients and water between the stock and the scion.

With *budding* (also called *bud grafting*), the scion is a single vegetative bud from the desired plant. In *grafting*, the scion is a section of a one-year-old branch that contains two or more vegetative buds. Your choice of whether to use budding or grafting will depend on the age and size of the stock, the time of year, and your comfort level and history of success with the method. Some people prefer budding because it requires smaller cuts and can be done using either of two techniques: *T-budding* or *chip budding*. Both can be done nearly all year long. Grafting is generally limited to winter and early spring, but some people prefer it because it is more versatile in that it can be used on one-year-old wood or wood that is several years old.

Table 8.1. Grafting compatibilities of common deciduous fruit and nut trees

Rootstock	Almond	Apple	Apricot	Cherry	Peach and nectarine	Pear	Plum (European and Japanese)*	Quince	English walnut
Almond	S	I	U	I	P[†]	I	P	I	I
Apple	I	S	I	I	I	U	I	U	I
Apricot	U	I	S	I	P[‡]	I	P[§]	I	I
Cherry:									
Mazzard	I	I	I	S	I	I	I	I	I
Mahaleb or Stockton Morello	I	I	I	P	I	I	I	I	I
Peach	S	I	P	I	S	I	P	I	I
Pear	I	U	I	I	I	S	I	U	I
Plum:									
Myrobalan	U	I	P	I	U	I	S	I	I
Marianna 2624	P[¶]	U	S	I	U	I	S	I	I
Quince	I	U	I	I	I	P[#]	I	S	I
Walnut:									
Northern California black or Paradox	I	I	I	I	I	I	I	I	S

Key:

S = Satisfactory for grafting.

P = Partly satisfactory for grafting: most cultivars grow and fruit normally on this rootstock, although some cultivars and some trees do not make satisfactory or permanent graft unions.

I = Incompatible combination for grafting: the grafts either do not grow or growth is weak and short-lived.

U = Unsatisfactory for grafting, although grafts may grow for a time.

Source: Geisel 2002, p. 114; Hartmann and Beutel 1994, p. 26.

*In general, many European and Japanese plums may be grafted on most European plums. Although many Japanese cultivars do well on other Japanese cultivars, European cultivars are not successful on Japanese stocks. Peaches, almonds, and apricots may sometimes be grafted on Japanese and European plums with reasonable success, but as a rule the grafts will fail to grow or do not grow satisfactorily.

[†]Peach trees are sometimes short-lived and become dwarfed on almond rootstock.

[‡]Many peach varieties fail to grow well on apricot rootstock.

[§]Some Japanese plum cultivars are compatible with some apricot rootstocks. In contrast, most European plums are not compatible with apricot rootstocks.

[¶]Some almond cultivars (such as Nonpareil) do not make a satisfactory union with Marianna 2624, so an interstock of Havens 2B plum must be used to work such cultivars on this stock. Other cultivars (such as Ne Plus Ultra and Mission) make reasonably satisfactory unions with Marianna 2624.

[#]Some pear cultivars (such as Old Home and Hardy) make good unions with quince, while others (such as Bartlett) do not and must be double-worked using one of the compatible pear cultivars as an interstock.

Grafting Supplies

KNIVES

Many types of grafting knives are available from mail-order catalogs, nurseries, and farm supply stores. Folding knives are the safest because the blade, which must be kept very sharp, is only out when you are making the cuts. Some folding knives have two blades: one used for grafting and the other for **T**-budding (Figure 8.1A). The single, straight blade is used for most grafting methods as well as for chip budding, but it is not well suited for making the long **T** cut on the stock in **T**-budding. Knives designed primarily for **T**-budding have a substantial curve at the end of the blade and a bark lifter opposite the blade (Figure 8.1A). A similar type has a single blade with a very slight curve at the tip and a bark lifter on the opposite side (Figure 8.1B). This blade can be used for both grafting and budding, but again, the long **T** cut on the stock is somewhat easier with a more curved blade. Another type of folding knife has a simple curved blade on one side and a bark lifter on the other (Figure 8.1C). Non-folding budding knives (Figure 8.1D) and grafting knives (Figure 8.1E) are also available. You can also make a grafting knife at home by grinding down a strong household knife into the correct shape.

Always keep the blade very sharp using a sharpening stone or other sharpening tool. A sharp blade is actually safest because it will make consistently clean cuts without a sudden "give" that may cause you to accidentally cut yourself. Make sure to bevel the blade on one side only, as with bypass loppers and hedge shears. The straight, non-beveled side enables the grafter to make long, straight cuts. Most grafting knives are beveled for right-hand use. Left-handed pruning knives are available, but you may have trouble finding one.

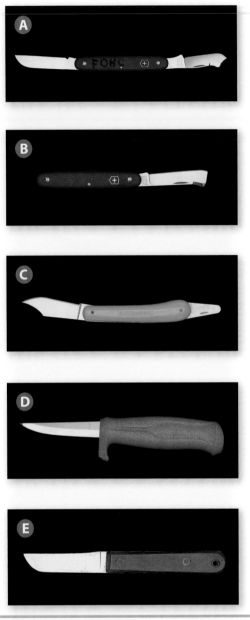

Figure 8.1. Some of the knives available for budding and grafting. **(A)** Knife with two folding blades: a straight blade *(left)* for grafting and a T-budding knife *(right)* with a curved tip and a bark lifter. These blades are also available singly on some models. **(B)** Rose-budding knife combining the T-budding and grafting blades into a single folding blade. Making a longitudinal cut (see Figure 8.4C) is slightly more difficult with this blade than with the more curved blade in (A), above. **(C)** Budding knife with separate folding blade and bark lifter. **(D)** Simple (non-folding) budding knife. **(E)** Simple (non-folding) grafting knife. Photos by Jack Kelly Clark.

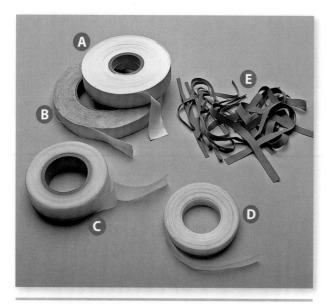

Figure 8.2. Various types of wraps used in budding and grafting. **(A)** Plastic tape with no adhesive. **(B)** Cloth tape with one adhesive side. **(C)** Parafilm tape with perforations for easy removal (Buddy Tape). **(D)** Parafilm tape. **(E)** Rubber strips. Photo by Jack Kelly Clark.

Knife Safety and First Aid

Because you have to keep the blade of a grafting knife very sharp, there is potential for serious injury when grafting. Unless you are an experienced grafter, never cut toward unprotected fingers. Avoid pushing hard with the grain of the wood, as the knife may suddenly "give" and slice into your flesh or into a branch that you don't want to cut. With some methods, such as the long, sloping cut used in whip, bark, and cleft grafting, your thumb may be perilously close to the blade, so you should make sure to wear a thumb protector or suitable glove. Gloves generally increase safety, but they may be cumbersome. Better yet, always cut away from your body. When not in use, always close a folding knife or sheath a non-folding knife. If you do cut yourself, seek prompt medical attention. Have a first aid kit available when you are grafting.

WRAPPING AND WAXING MATERIALS

Different types of wrapping and waxing products are available to hold grafts in place and to provide an airtight seal. The type of wrap to use depends on which grafting method you use and the size of the wood. Wraps include cloth and plastic grafting tape, with or without one sticky side; parafilm stretch tape, which sticks to itself; and rubber strips, also called budding rubbers or budding strips (Figure 8.2A-E). Some products, especially parafilm tape and rubber strips, begin to break down within a few weeks, so you usually will not have to cut them off later. Other tapes may not break down before branch thickening occurs, so you may have to cut them to prevent girdling of the branch.

Waxing is necessary with several grafting methods, especially if the wrap does not form an airtight seal. Most products are paste-like or creamy even in cold weather, but others must be softened by working them with your warm hands. When properly used, any sealing product designed for grafting should form an adequate seal, but remember to check for cracks at least once a week for a few weeks and to re-seal if cracks form.

Key Points for Budding and Grafting

- *Use disease-free scions and rootstock.*

- *Position the scion so that at least a portion of the cambium of the scion touches the cambium of the rootstock — the more contact, the better.*

- *Use a sharp budding or grafting knife or other sharp, single-beveled knife (i.e., sharpened on one side only).*

- *Keep scions cool after you collect them and during the grafting.*

- *Make clean, straight cuts, and have extra scion wood available.*

- *Do not leave cut surfaces exposed to sunlight or wind — or at least keep such exposure to a minimum.*

- *Do not touch the cut surfaces and do not allow them to dry out.*

- *Label each graft with the variety name, and later mark or paint where the graft was made.*

- *If you use wax, make sure to re-wax whenever cracks appear.*

- *If necessary, cut binding strings or tapes once the grafts or buds have healed.*

- *Stake new shoots, if necessary, and remove suckers and unwanted shoots that shade out desirable shoots growing from the graft.*

Budding (Bud Grafting)

There are two primary methods of bud grafting. Historically, **T**-budding has been the most widely used technique for grafting fruit trees and some ornamentals, but chip budding is increasing in popularity because some people find it easier and more successful. **T**-budding is usually performed in the spring and early summer and chip budding can be used from midsummer through fall as well as during the dormant season.

T-BUDDING

With **T**-budding, you insert a shield-shaped piece of the desired (scion) variety into a **T**-shaped cut in the bark of the stock. For this reason, it is sometimes called shield budding. **T**-budding is best done with a specially designed budding knife (see Figure 8.1). If no budding knife is available, you can use an unused single-edge razor blade or a very sharp knife such as an X-Acto hobby knife instead.

Because **T**-budding involves cutting and peeling back the bark of the stock, you have to do it when the bark is *slipping* (when it can easily be peeled away from the wood), which happens most when the tree is actively growing. Depending on the species, the bark of a one-year-old branch can begin slipping as early as late February in southern California and later as you go north, and bark may continue to slip through early fall. Bark of a water-stressed tree does not slip easily.

T-budding is usually done on current-season's shoots, but it can also be done on one-year-old branches. The shoot or branch should be at least as thick as a pencil at its base. Budding that is done in the spring is known as *spring budding* or *June budding* (even if done in April or May); budding done in late summer or early fall is called *fall budding*.

Steps in making a T-Bud

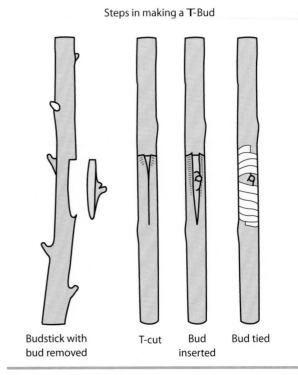

Budstick with bud removed · T-cut · Bud inserted · Bud tied

Figure 8.3. Overview of T-budding method. *Source*: Adapted from Hartmann and Beutel 1994.

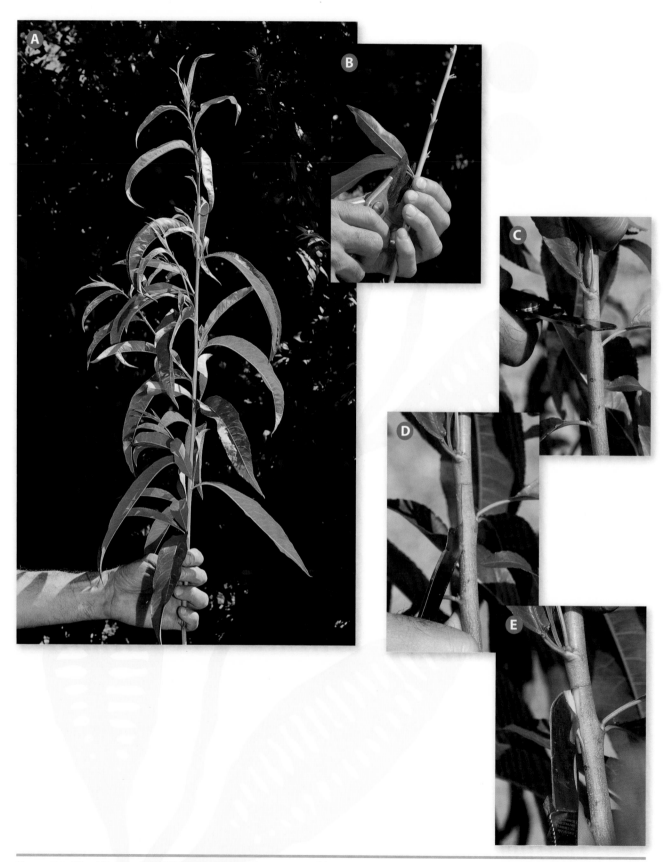

Figure 8.4. T-budding method: **(A)** Vigorous peach shoot removed from tree. **(B)** Budstick with leaves being cut off but petiole portion remaining for handling. **(C)** Transverse cut through the bark of the stock. **(D)** Longitudinal cut through the bark of the stock. **(E)** Using the bark lifter to separate the bark of the stock from the wood. Photos by Jack Kelly Clark.

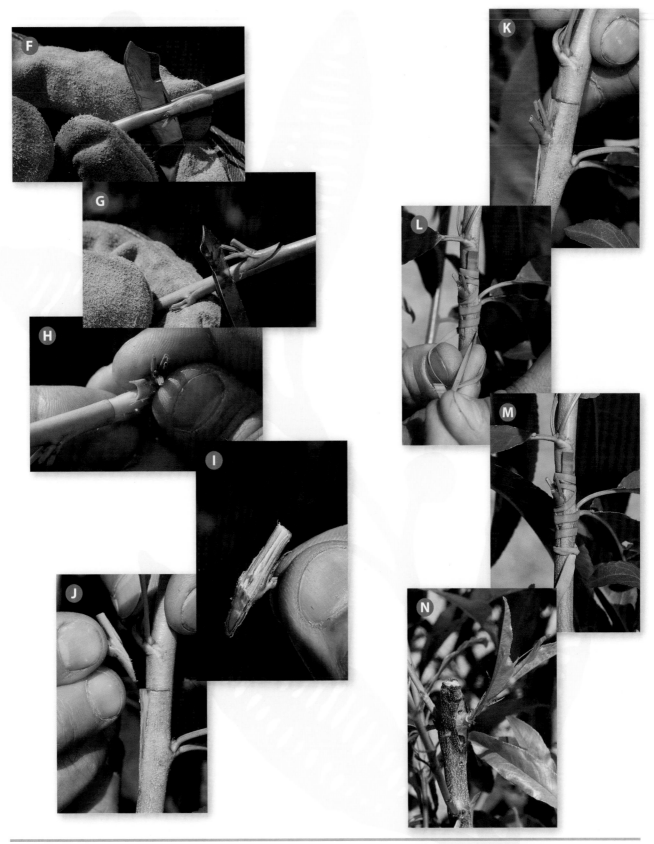

Figure 8.4. cont: **(F)** Undercutting the bud on the budstick. **(G)** Horizontal cut through the bark of the budstick. **(H)** Bud shield removed from budstick wood. **(I)** Optional method of including the wood with the bud. **(J)** Inserting the bud shield into the T cut on the stock. **(K)** Bud shield inserted under the flaps of the T cut. **(L)** Wrapping and final tie-off of rubber strip around the stock to secure the bud shield. **(M)** Wrapping with rubber strip completed. **(N)** Growth of new shoot. Photos by Jack Kelly Clark with the exception of **I** and **N**, photographed by Chuck Ingels.

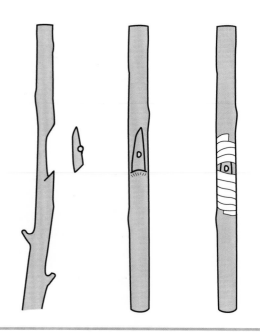

Figure 8.5. Overview of the chip budding method.

T-Budding Method *(see Figures 8.3 and 8.4)*

1. To collect bud wood, cut off a vigorous current-season shoot that is about ¼ to ⅜ inch (6 to 10 mm) thick from the bud source tree (Figure 8.4A). This shoot is called the budstick or budwood. Immediately cut off the budstick's leaves by cutting the leaf stalks (petioles) in half (Figure 8.4B); this reduces water loss through the leaves and also provides you with a short handle (the half stem) by which to hold the bud after it is removed. Also, cut off the top portion of the budstick, where there will be buds that are not mature enough to graft. If you will not graft the buds immediately, wrap moist paper towels or newspaper around the budstick and put it in a plastic bag. Keep it refrigerated, preferably at 36° to 40°F (2° to 4°C), until you use it; it will remain viable for 2 to 3 weeks when cut and stored in this manner.

2. Choose a current-season shoot on the stock tree that is the same size as or slightly bigger around than the scion shoot. If budding to a young rootstock tree or a rootstock sucker, choose an area on the trunk about 6 to 12 inches (about 15 to 30 cm) above the ground. Make a transverse cut through the bark only, running about halfway around the shoot (Figure 8.4C). Then finish the capital **T** by making a longitudinal cut perpendicular to the first cut and extending downward about 1½ inches (38 mm) (Figure 8.4D). (Some prefer to make an inverted **T**, with the longitudinal cut extending upward from the transverse cut. In this case, the bud cuts [see below] would also be reversed.) Use the bark lifter on the budding knife (a butter knife will work, too) to separate the bark from the wood on both sides of the second cut, beginning at the top and working downward (Figure 8.4E). Avoid using a sharp blade for lifting: it will tend to cut the bark rather than lift it.

3. Hold the scion budstick by the bottom and remove a lower bud from the scion in the following manner. Beginning about ½ inch (13 mm) below the bud, make a shallow cut beneath the bud, cutting toward the top of the budstick. Continue the cut upward to just over ½ inch (13 mm) above the bud, cutting about one-third to one-half the thickness of the shoot (Figure 8.4F). Then make a horizontal cut about ½ inch (13 mm) above the bud, through the bark only (Figure 8.4G). Remove the bud by squeezing the sides of the cut bark just above the bud. This squeezing should separate the bark from the wood, taking the bud with the bark. Only a sliver of wood will remain attached to the budstick (Figure 8.4H).

Some sources say to include the wood sliver with the bud rather than remove the bark from the wood (Figure 8.4I). If you do this, make sure you are grafting onto stock that is larger than the budstick in order to ensure a good contact between the edge of the bud piece (the cambial area) and the cambium of the stock. The larger stock is usually necessary because the flat surface of the scion's wood sliver is being placed against the round surface of the stock.

4. Hold the bud by the leaf stalk and insert the point (bottom) of the bud shield into the **T** cut on the stock (Figure 8.4J). Gently slide the bud shield downward until the top cut of the bud piece is just under and touching the top of the **T** cut. If necessary, use the flat part of the knife to help push the bud into place. The bud should be centered between the bark flaps (Figure 8.4K).

5. To secure the bud, firmly wrap the cut areas with a rubber strip or parafilm tape around the bud, beginning at the top and working downward (Figure 8.4L). Begin and end the wrapping by tucking the ends of the rubber strip or tape under the wrap. With a rubber strip, it is not essential to completely cover the cut area; that is, there can be some space between the spiral wraps of rubber strip, as long as the bark flaps firmly cover and seal the bud piece (Figure 8.4M). If you are using parafilm tape, pull the tape as you wrap it to stretch it tightly over the cut areas, but preferably not over the bud. Within a few weeks, you can cut the branch off above the bud to force the shoot to grow (Figure 8.4N).

Chip Budding

Chip budding is a method that is often used at times of year when you cannot use **T**-budding (when the bark is not slipping), such as in late summer to early fall and during the late dormant season. When the bark is slipping (in spring and early to midsummer), **T**-budding is often used instead.

Grape growers sometimes plant rootstocks in the vineyard, let them grow all summer, and then use chip budding in the fall on the young rootstock plants. A bud of the desired variety is grafted at the base of each vine and then covered with soil for several weeks to keep the bud cool and moist.

Chip Budding Method (see Figures 8.5 and 8.6)

1. Choose budwood about ¼ to ⅜ inch (6 to 10 mm) in diameter and choose a rootstock that is the same size or slightly larger, but no bigger than about ¾ inch (19 mm) in diameter. If you are chip budding in the summer or fall, your budstick should be a current-season shoot the base of which is starting to turn brown and woody. Choose only healthy shoots that were exposed to substantial sunlight on the tree. Immediately remove the leaves from the budstick, leaving a petiole stem to hold the bud (Figure 8.6A).

2. Remove a "chip" with a bud from the budstick:

    a. Make the first cut about ½ inch (13 mm) below the bud, transversely across the shoot or branch and at a downward angle of about 45° (Figure 8.6B). Sometimes a narrower angle may be better because it will permit the bud to fit more deeply into the stock, allowing a tighter fit.

    b. Start the second cut about 1 inch (25 mm) above the first, cutting downward under the bud until your cut intersects with the first cut (Figure 8.6C). The bottom of the chip is **V** shaped (Figure 8.6D).

3. Remove a chip of a similar size from the stock (Figure 8.6E).

4. Place the chip with the scion bud into the cut you have made in the rootstock (Figure 8.6F).

5. For best success, the chip should match in size and shape so the bud chip's cambium layer matches with that of the stock. If the cut on the stock is wider than on the bud chip, place the chip to one side or the other so the cambium layers match on that side (Figure 8.6G).

6. Securely wrap the cut areas with parafilm tape and rubber strips (Figures 8.6H and I). If you use a rubber strip alone, seal all cut edges with grafting wax, but avoid waxing over the bud.

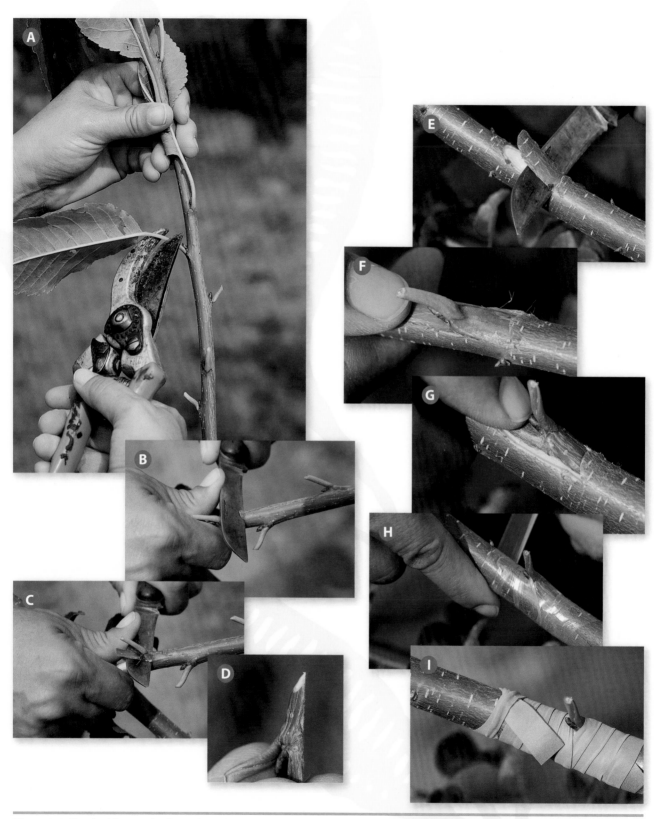

Figure 8.6. Chip budding method: **(A)** Cherry budstick with leaves being cut off but petiole portion remaining for ease of handling. **(B)** Transverse cut across scion below bud at about a 45° angle. **(C)** Downward cut on scion intersects with the end of the first cut. **(D)** Removed chip being held upside down to show **V** cut at base. **(E)** Identical cuts being made in stock. **(F)** Chip of desired variety inserted into cut on stock. **(G)** Cambium layers of chip of a smaller size than the stock cut should match on one side (cambium layer of stock can be seen on cut surface). **(H)** Wrapping with parafilm tape; double-wrap the parafilm, but use a single layer on the bud. **(I)** Budding rubber secured over the parafilm. Photos by Jack Kelly Clark.

DETERMINING WHETHER THE BUD GRAFT HAS TAKEN

You can tell that the graft was successful if the bud remains plump and the bark piece remains green. To be certain, you can nick the bark of the bud patch with a knife: if it is green underneath, the graft was successful (although the bud could still be dead); if brown, the graft was not successful.

FORCING BUD GROWTH

Buds that are grafted in late summer through early fall should not be forced to grow until the following spring; otherwise, fall frost may kill the tender, young shoot. You can, however, force buds grafted from early spring through midsummer to grow about 2 to 3 weeks after grafting, or when you are confident the graft was successful. To force a bud to grow, cut off the shoot or branch onto which the bud was grafted, about ¼ inch (about 6 mm) above the top of the cut. As the desired shoot grows, remove any nearby competing shoots that might shade it.

If you don't want to cut the branch off above the bud, you can sometimes force the bud to grow by *girdling* or *notching* (also called *scoring*) the branch above the bud. To girdle a branch to stimulate bud growth, remove a strip of bark about ³⁄₁₆ to ¼ inch (5 to 6 mm) wide and running crosswise, halfway around the branch just above the top cut of the bud graft (Figure 8.7). You can girdle any time from early spring (after the bark begins to slip) through early summer. The practice is most successful on current-season or one-year-old wood, but it often works on older wood as well. The girdle can even extend all the way around the branch; it will quickly callus over after the bud begins to grow.

A quicker way to force the bud is notching: you pull a ⅛-inch (3 mm) round "rattail" file in a single stroke across the branch just above the bud, filing through the bark only (Figure 8.8). Besides being quicker, notching can be done in the late dormant season to force a bud to grow in early spring. Girdling and notching work by interrupting the downward movement of the plant hormone auxin through the phloem. Auxin is a plant hormone that is produced in the shoot tips and leaves

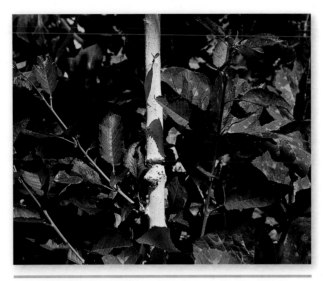

Figure 8.7. Girdling above a grafted bud may force it to grow without heading the branch or trunk. Here, two vertically separated half-girdles were made in the spring on the trunk of this young cherry tree, forcing new shoots to grow below the cuts. Photo by Chuck Ingels.

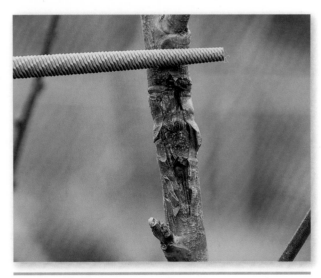

Figure 8.8. Notching above a grafted bud to force shoot growth. Photo by Chuck Ingels.

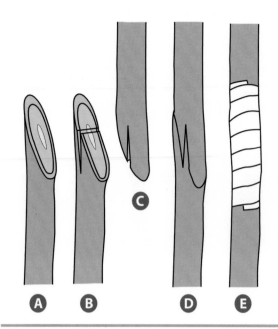

Figure 8.9. Overview of whip grafting method. *Source*: Adapted from Hartmann and Beutel 1994, p. 5.

and moves down the phloem, preventing the growth of lateral buds (see Chapter 2). When you interrupt the flow of auxin, the bud or buds immediately below the girdle or notch cease to be influenced by the auxin and will usually begin to grow.

Grafting

Grafting, which includes topworking (see next section), consists of attaching a one-year-old scion branch with two or three buds to the rootstock, rather than attaching only a single bud. Grafting is best done from dormancy through early spring. As with budding, specially designed cutting tools are available, but you can use any small, sharp knife—preferably one that is beveled on one side only.

WHIP GRAFTING

Whip grafting, also known as *whip-in-tongue grafting*, is often used on one-year-old rootstock wood that is about ¼ to ¾ inch (6 to 19 mm) in diameter. For best results, the scion and rootstock should be about the same diameter. The practice can also be successful when the stock is larger than the scion, as long as the cambiums of the stock and scion match on at least one side. Whip grafting usually provides excellent cambial contact and results in a strong graft union.

Whip Grafting Method (see Figures 8.9 and 8.10)

1. Collect the scion wood in the dormant season before buds begin to swell (Figure 8.10A). Graft it immediately or wrap it with moist paper towel or newspaper and store it in a plastic bag in the refrigerator for later use.

2. Make a sloping cut 1 to 2 inches (25 to 51 mm) long at the top of the rootstock and a matching cut at the base of the scion (Figure 8.10B and C). The straightest cut is made by one swift movement rather than rocking or slicing with the knife. The cut will be longer with larger diameter wood and shorter with smaller diameter wood.

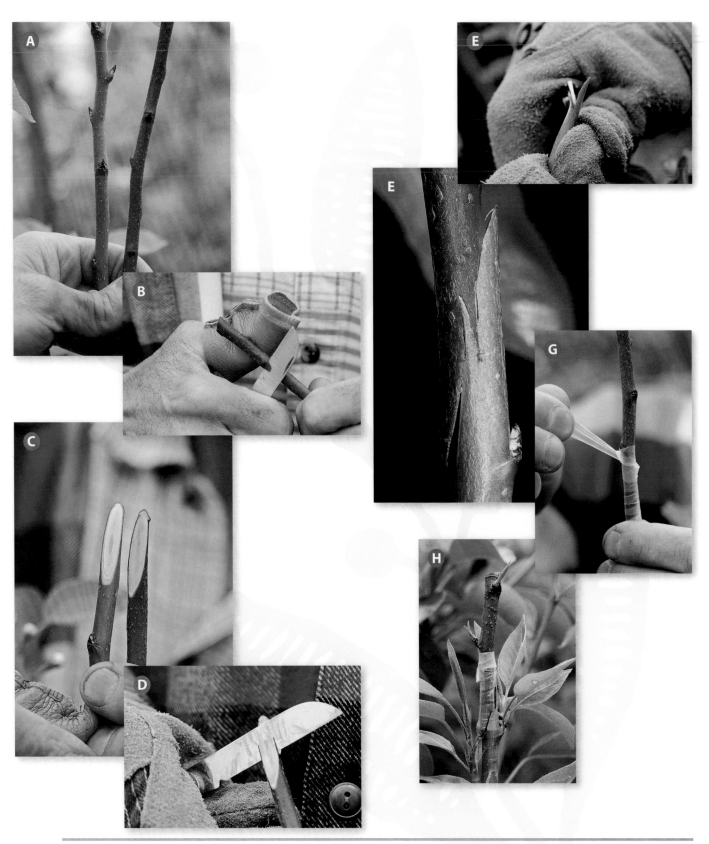

Figure 8.10. Whip grafting method: **(A)** Pear scion wood *(right)*, collected in January and stored in refrigerator until early April, is matched in size with 1-year-old branch *(left)*. **(B)** Beginning the long, sloping cut (exercise caution). **(C)** Matching cuts of the stock *(left)* and scion *(right)*. **(D)** Downward cut through the wood of both the stock and the scion, one-third of the distance from the tip. **(E)** Gently twist the knife away from the tip to create an opening; try not to split the wood. **(F)** Slide the scion into the stock so the cuts interlock and cambium layers match. **(G)** Union wrapped with parafilm tape. **(H)** Shoots starting to grow and tape breaking several weeks later. Photos by Jack Kelly Clark.

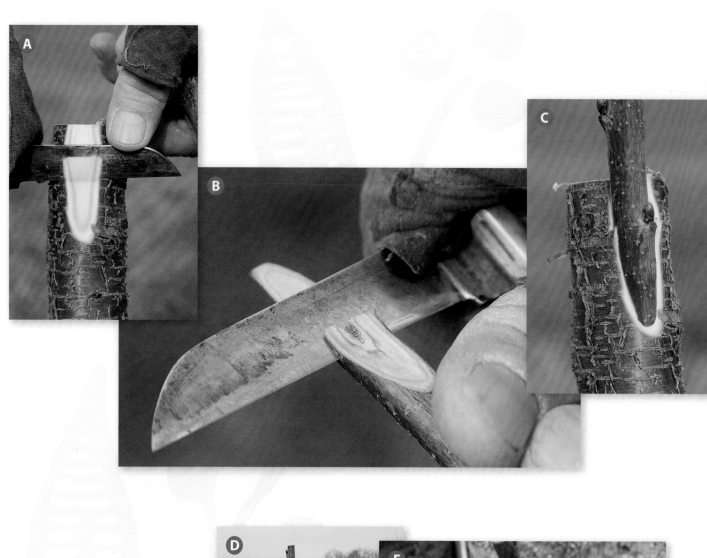

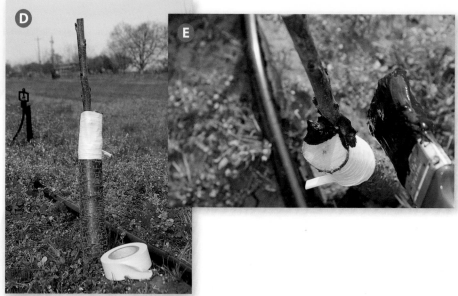

Figure 8.11. Whip grafting method for large stock: **(A)** Make a slicing upward cut on the stock and then make a downward vertical cut, starting one-third the distance from the tip. Notice the highly visible cambium layer. **(B)** Make a long, sloping cut at the base of the scion and then make the vertical cut starting halfway between the ends of the sloping cut. **(C)** Lock the scion into place in the stock, matching cambium layers on at least one side. Notice that a portion of the thick bark of the stock is visible but the cambium layer of the scion is in contact with that of the stock. **(D)** Graft wrapped with plastic tape. **(E)** Painting a thick coat of grafting wax. Photos by Jack Kelly Clark.

3. Make a cut downward into the stock starting about one-third of the distance from the tip; the cut should be about ¼ to ⅜ inch long (6 to 10 mm) (Figure 8.10D). The cut is made going with the grain of the wood; avoid cutting at an angle or the remaining tip will be flimsy. With the knife still in place, slightly twist the knife away from the tip of the stock to create an opening (Figure 8.10E). Bending the knife in this manner will make it easier to interlock the stock and scion. Make a similar cut in the scion, one-third the distance from the tip. There is potential for injury here: use caution when making these cuts.

4. Slide the two vertical cuts together so the pieces interlock tightly (Figure 8.10F).

5. Wrap the union tightly with parafilm tape (Figure 8.10G) or grafting tape. Wax the union if the wrap is not airtight. If the tape is airtight (e.g., parafilm tape), no wax is needed. Shoot growth of the scion may be delayed in comparison with the stock (Figure 8.10H).

Whip Grafting Method for Large Stock (see Figure 8.11)

A variation of the whip graft can be used on stocks as large as about 2 to 3 inches (3 to 8 cm).

1. Cut off the stock and make an upward slicing cut in the stock. Then make a downward vertical cut, starting about one-third the distance from the top (Figure 8.11A).

2. Make a sloping cut at the base of the scion, then make the vertical cut starting this time in the middle of the sloping cut (Figure 8.11B).

3. Insert the scion so that it locks tightly into the stock (Figure 8.11C). Make sure the cambium layers match on at least one side. Because the bark of the stock is much thicker than the bark of the scion, the scion will be set in from the edge of the stock cut.

4. Wrap with tape and cover all cut surfaces with grafting compound (Figures 8.11D and 8.11E).

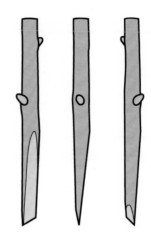

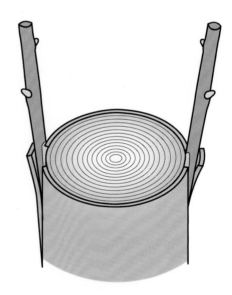

Figure 8.12. Overview of the bark grafting method. *Source:* Adapted from Hartmann and Beutel 1994, p. 7.

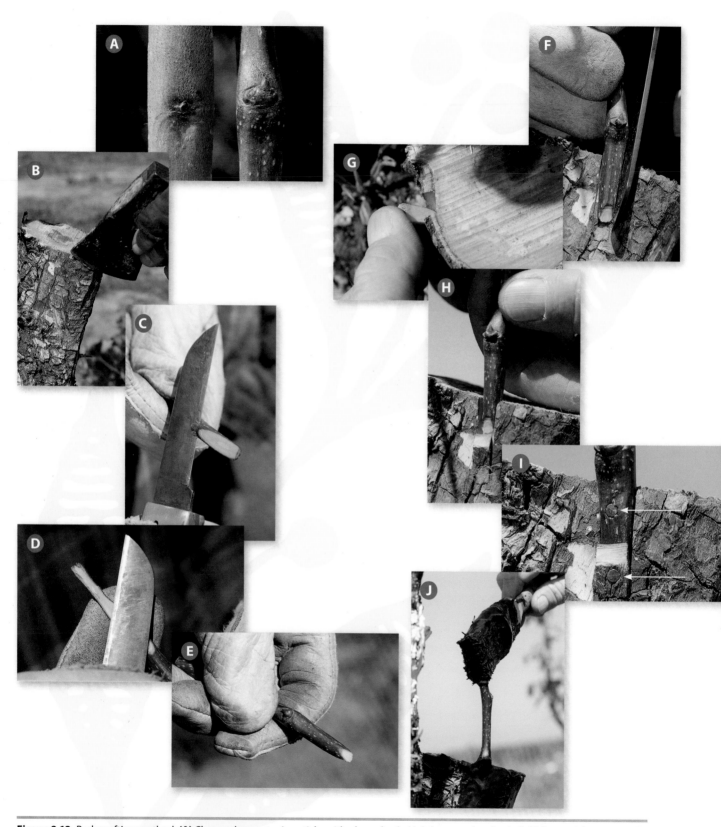

Figure 8.13. Bark grafting method: **(A)** Choose dormant scion sticks with plump buds *(right)*, not sunken buds *(left)*; keep sticks moist and cold until the spring. **(B)** In the spring, cut off a limb of the stock and scrape off the dead bark where grafting is to be done. **(C)** Make a long, sloping cut on one side of the bottom of scion wood. **(D)** Cut off the "tail," if present. **(E)** Make a short, diagonal cut on the other side. **(F)** Make two parallel cuts, slightly shorter than the scion cut, into the bark of the stock. **(G)** Peel back the bark strip. **(H)** Cut off the top half of the bark strip and slide the stick between the bark and the wood of the stock (the short cut on the back of the scion is visible). **(I)** Pound one wire nail through the bark strip and the scion and into the wood of the stock, and pound another nail above the first, through the scion and into the stock. **(J)** Apply grafting compound over all cut surfaces to seal in moisture. Photos by Jack Kelly Clark.

Topworking

Topworking, also known as *grafting over*, is a method of grafting in which you cut off a fairly large branch of a mature tree and graft one or more one-year-old, dormant scion wood sticks onto the cut branch. Growers use this technique to change the variety of a whole orchard if marketing conditions change. In the home orchard, it can be used to replace an undesirable variety or to add a pollinizer. Topworking connects the scion to a tree's fully developed root and main branch systems, so the new cultivar should begin bearing within 2 years. In this chapter we discuss two methods of topworking: bark and cleft grafting.

To prepare the tree for topworking, cut back the branches to be grafted but leave one or two smaller limbs uncut. These *nurse limbs* will continue to provide carbohydrates (from photosynthesis in the leaves) to the large root system until the new grafts have grown.

If topworking grafts fail, you may still be able to bud graft or whip graft onto shoots that grow below the large cut. If you do this, thin to only two or three outward-growing shoots when they are several inches long and then graft them when they are at least pencil thick.

BARK GRAFTING

Bark grafting, like cleft grafting, can be used on relatively large limbs. The technique requires that the bark be slipping (separating readily from the wood), so you can only do it in the spring after the rootstock has started active growth. Bark grafting is also called rind grafting.

Bark Grafting Method (see Figures 8.12 and 8.13)

1. Collect one-year-old scion sticks about ⅜ to ½ inch (10 to 13 mm) in diameter in late January or early February when the tree is fully dormant. Use wood with plump buds (Figure 8.13A, right) on stout branches (see Figure 8.16A). Store the scions wrapped in moist paper towel or newsprint in a plastic bag in the refrigerator.

2. In the early spring when the bark is easy to separate from the wood, saw off the limb or trunk of the rootstock at a right angle to create a stump and scrape off dried outer bark (Figure 8.13B).

3. Make a 1- to 1½-inch (25 to 38 mm) sloping cut on the bottom of the scion (Figure 8.13C) and if a "tail" was created, place the blade flat against the cut and slice off the tail so the sloping cut is straight (Figure 8.13D). Cut a much shorter diagonal cut on the other side (Figure 8.13E). Cut the scion to 2 buds long.

4. Make two parallel cuts through the bark of the stock to match the diameter of the scion (Figure 8.13F). Make the cuts slightly shorter than the long diagonal cut on the scion. Pull back the cut strip (Figure 8.13G) and cut the strip off just below its halfway point.

5. Slide the scion into the remaining cut strip (Figure 8.13H) and push it down so it is firmly held. Pound a thin wire nail about 1 inch long through the bark strip and the base of the scion and into the wood of the stock. Pound another nail above the first one, into the scion and the wood of the stock (Figure 8.13I).

6. Thoroughly wax all cut surfaces, including the top of the scion, with a thick layer of grafting compound (Figure 8.13J).

Alternative Bark Grafting Method (see Figure 8.14)

Some grafters prefer an alternative method, but it requires two angled scion cuts that can be difficult to make correctly. The method also uses no nails so there is no danger of splitting the scion, but it requires strong grafting tape.

1. Make a single cut through the bark of the stock. The cut should be slightly shorter than the scion cuts. Push the knife sideways to scrunch the bark to one side (Figure 8.14A).

2. Make a long, sloping cut at the bottom of the scion stick. Make a second sloping cut such that the **V** on one side is larger than the **V** on the other side (Figure 8.14B). In doing so, you cause the bottom edge of the scion to slope toward the narrower cut.

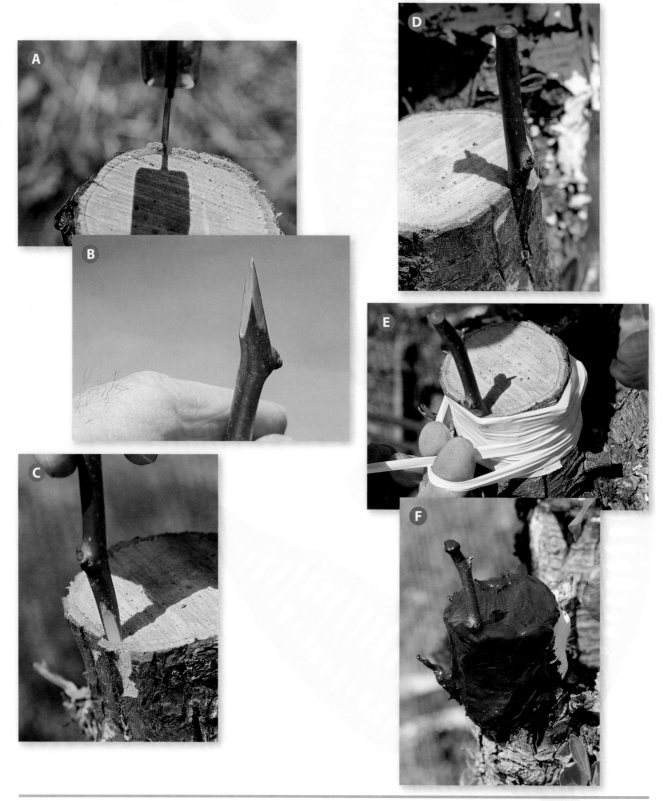

Figure 8.14. Alternative bark grafting method: **(A)** Cut off branch, make a single cut in bark, and push knife sideways to separate bark from wood. **(B)** Make two sloping cuts at bottom of scion stick so that the V on one side is narrower than the V of the other side. **(C)** Insert the scion between the bark and the wood so that the wider V faces the cut in the bark. **(D)** Scion fully inserted. **(E)** Wrap the stock with strong tape. **(F)** Apply grafting compound to all cut surfaces. Photos by Jack Kelly Clark.

3. Slide the bottom edge of the scion into the space created between the bark and the wood of the stock so that the wider **V** of the scion is facing the bark cut of the stock (Figure 8.14C and D). Push the scion down so it is held firmly in place.

4. Tie strong grafting tape around the stock and pull the final wrap through to cinch it (Figure 8.14E).

5. Thoroughly wax all cut surfaces, including the top of the scion, with a thick layer of grafting compound (Figure 8.14F).

CLEFT GRAFTING

Cleft grafting is a challenging method for some people. It requires the use of a fairly thin, heavy knife. You can purchase cleft grafting tools, but make sure the blade is not too thick or it will cause the bark to split rather than cut cleanly. Inexperienced grafters often have a low success rate with this method, probably because it matches only one side of the scion cambium with the stock cambium and the cambium layers are not easy to align. Cleft grafting must be done in the winter, before the sap begins to flow and the bark begins to slip. The scion wood can be collected and then used immediately for grafting or the wood can be wrapped in a moist paper towel in a plastic bag and stored in a refrigerator until the day of grafting. On a larger stock, you can use two scions, one on either side of the stock, but use only one scion when grafting onto a smaller stock.

Cleft Grafting Method (see Figures 8.15 and 8.16)

1. Collect scion wood about ⅜ to ⅝ inch (10 to 16 mm) in diameter. Select wood that is stiffened and does not bend easily (Figure 8.16A).

2. Saw off a limb or trunk of the stock and pound a cleft grafting knife through the center of the stump (Figure 8.16B and C).

3. Insert a screwdriver in the center to open the split wood (Figure 8.16D).

4. Prepare scion stick: Make a 1½- to 2-inch (38 to 51 mm) sloping cut at the base of the scion.

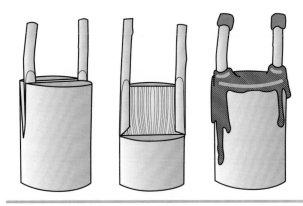

Figure 8.15. Overview of the cleft grafting method. *Source*: Adapted from Hartmann and Beutel 1994, p 7.

Make a second cut on the other side of the stick; the second cut should not be parallel to the first, but at a slight angle to it (Figure 8.16E). This creates a wider bark section (Figure 8.16F), which will be placed to the outside. Make an angled cut through the wood (Figure 8.16G).

5. Insert the scion at the outer edge of the cut in the stock, with the pointed (wider) part to the outside (Figure 8.16H). Make sure that the outer cambium layer of the scion aligns with the cambium layer of the stock (Figure 8.16I). Note that the scion is inset slightly because its bark is thinner than the bark of the stock.

6. Remove the screwdriver, wrap the union tightly with strong tape, and place a thick coating of wax or grafting compound on all cut surfaces and over the tape to seal in moisture (Figure 8.16J).

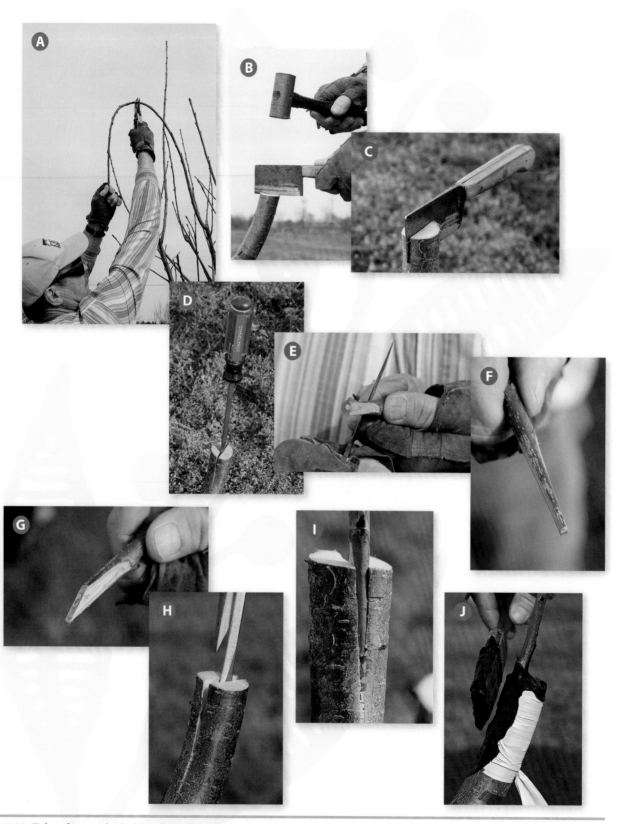

Figure 8.16. Cleft grafting method (cherry shown here): **(A)** Bend a one-year-old branch and select scion wood below the portion that easily bends; discard the terminal end. **(B)** Pound a thin cleft grafting knife through center of cut branch (knife shown here is homemade). **(C)** Homemade cleft grafting knife pounded into branch. **(D)** Insert a screwdriver to slightly open the split. **(E)** Make two long, sloping cuts at the base of the scion, with the second cut at a slight angle to the first cut. **(F)** The bark section shown on the top is slightly narrower than the other side. **(G)** Make a sloping cut through the wood so that the wider side is longer. **(H)** Insert the scion stick into the stock, with the wider side to the outside. **(I)** Scion stick inserted so that the stock and scion cambiums align. The outer edge of the scion stick will be set in from the outer edge of the stock because their bark thickness differs. **(J)** Wrap stock tightly with tape and apply grafting compound to all cut surfaces and over the tape. Photos by Jack Kelly Clark.

Care of Budded and Grafted Plants

Follow-up care is required for all grafts. Here is a checklist to help you ensure good growth of recently grafted plants.

- *On older trees that you have topworked, one or two limbs of the old variety that were not selected for grafting should be maintained as nurse limbs for one year. Reduce the total leaf surface of the old variety as the graft grows. After one year, the new variety should be strong enough for you to remove or graft over the nurse limbs.*

- *Wax is a sealant that excludes air and prevents drying. If you use wax, check for cracks about two days after you graft and then weekly for several weeks and apply additional wax if necessary.*

- *With some grafting methods, you will want to paint or whitewash the union to prevent sunburn damage. It is an especially good idea to paint the graft union or stock branch if you used black grafting wax or if you topworked a main limb. Use a commercially prepared tree whitewash or a 50-50 mix of interior white latex paint and water.*

- *When you cut a branch off for grafting, one result is the growth of many shoots below the cut. Once you know that the graft is successful, remove these shoots to prevent them from shading out the desired (grafted) variety (Figure 8.17). It is best simply to break the shoots off when they are several inches long rather than cut them off when they are fully grown branches. If the graft is not successful, thin the new growth down to two or three well-placed shoots and try bud grafting to them.*

- *When vigorous scion growth begins, cut or remove the tape if necessary so that it will not girdle the branch.*

- *If necessary, tie new shoots to a stake or head them back if they grow too long in order to prevent them from snapping or from growing in the wrong direction.*

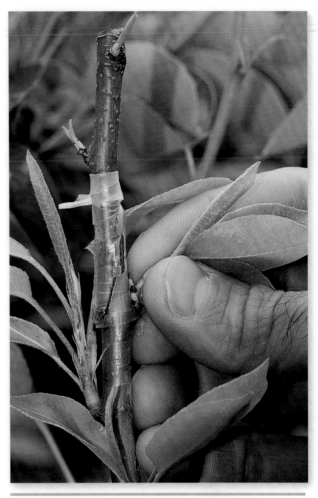

Figure 8.17. When the grafted bud or branch grows, cut or break off undesired shoots when they are young to prevent them from shading out the grafted variety. Photo by Jack Kelly Clark.

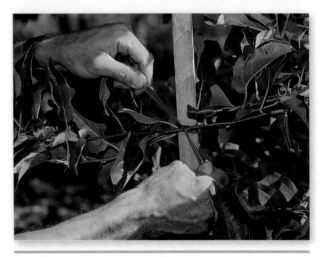

Figure 8.18. The shoot beyond the graft must be held firmly in place to prevent movement at the graft union. Photo by Jack Kelly Clark.

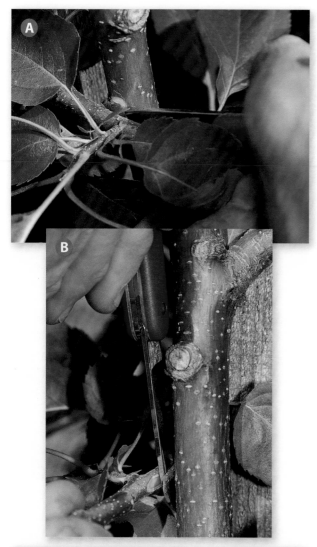

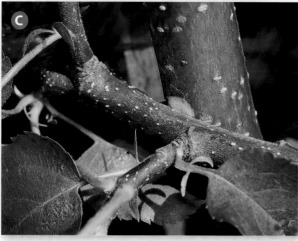

Grafting Shoots to Create Structures

When shoots are young, they are pliable and you can direct their growth into unusual structures and shapes and then graft them onto other shoots, branches, or nearby compatible trees. This is considered by some to be an art form and has been called *arborsculpture* or *tree trunk topiary* (Reames 1995). Although the technique is practiced mainly for aesthetic purposes, it can also have some practical uses, such as a living ladder or chair.

Before attempting to create a particular structure, envision the ultimate shape and size that you want to achieve, and design the final plant before you plant the tree or trees. Because branches must be held firmly in place after grafting, consider creating a solid framework or tree stakes or a trellis on which you can direct and tie the shoots to prevent movement. Bear in mind that shoots of many species stop growing or only grow very slowly when bent horizontally, especially if they are shaded by upper growth, so make sure to allow shoots to grow upward at an angle until they are long enough to bend and graft.

Grafting in this manner is most successful on vigorous current-season shoots of at least pencil thickness, but you can also graft one-year-old or older branches. The best period for this kind of grafting is from mid-spring through midsummer, when shoot growth or callus formation is active. You can also do it in the late dormant season on one-year-old wood.

Before you graft, the branch or shoot beyond the graft must be held immobile (Figure 8.18), even if there are strong winds and even after the shoot has grown to a substantial length, if you can allow it to do so. The cuts you will want to make on the two shoots are simple vertical slicing cuts through the bark and into the wood, or at least to the cambium layer (Figure 8.19). The goal is to make flat surfaces so you can hold the two cut sections firmly together, with cambium-to-wood connections along the edges

Figure 8.19. When cutting grafts for arborsculpture, make simple slicing cuts on the two branches to be grafted (**A** and **B**) through the bark and into the wood. In (**C**), the two cuts are placed together in preparation for tying. Photos by Jack Kelly Clark.

and cambium-to-cambium connections in the corners of the square created at the union (Figure 8.20). Two shoots of equal diameter are easier to graft, although shoots of different thicknesses, such as a shoot grafted to a small branch or trunk, can also be successful. The graft must be tied firmly together using green tie tape of an appropriate thickness for smaller shoots (Figure 8.21) and string for larger branches, both of which should be cut away a few months after grafting in order to prevent girdling. After you make the graft, seal the entire union with grafting wax to prevent the union from drying out (Figure 8.22).

Check for cracks in the sealant once a week for about a month and apply more wax if necessary. As the shoots expand, make sure the tape or string does not choke or girdle the union. A knot or burl may form at the union; that is only a growth of undifferentiated callus cells that eventually is hidden by branch thickening as the tissues differentiate into bark and wood. The shoot beyond the union will continue to grow and form large branches, or if one shoot is shaded it may die (Figure 8.23). If you only plan to retain one of the shoots, remove the other shoot only after you know that the graft is well connected. Alternatively, you can shorten (head) the shoot somewhat to reduce movement in the wind. The branch that is cut off will continue to thicken below the graft union because it has formed xylem and phloem connection with the branch to which it was grafted.

Creating tree structures is fun and they can add a striking feature to a landscape. Tree structures can also add great strength and stability to a tree. Two or more trees can be planted near each other and their branches grafted into unusual shapes. Examples of tree structures include circles (Figure 8.24) or other shapes incorporated into the trunk, such as ladders, lattice enclosures, and jungle gyms, as well as multi-trunked trees that merge into a single trunk.

More information on arborsculpture can be found on the Internet at Arborsmith Studios (http://www .arborsmith.com) and Bonfante Gardens Family Theme Park (http://www.bonfantegardens.com).

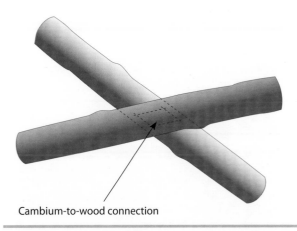

Cambium-to-wood connection

Figure 8.20. Make cambium-to-wood connections along the edges and cambium-to-cambium connections in the corners of the square that is created at the union.

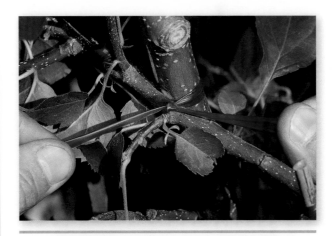

Figure 8.21. The graft must be held together firmly using green tie tape of an appropriate thickness for smaller shoots and string for larger branches. Photo by Jack Kelly Clark.

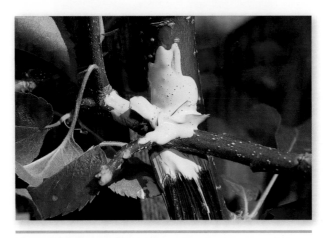

Figure 8.22. Thoroughly seal the graft union to prevent drying. Photo by Jack Kelly Clark.

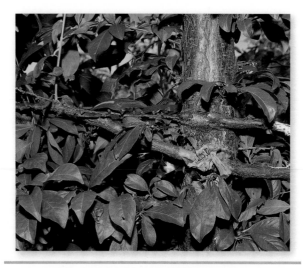

Figure 8.23. Three pluot trees were planted in a triangle and their branches were bent over to create a three-sided ladder. Here, two rungs of the ladder, coming from different trees, were grafted into the trunk of one of the trees. The shoot beyond (to the left of) the top graft died due to shading, but the branch beyond the bottom graft continues to grow; it can also be cut off. Photo by Chuck Ingels.

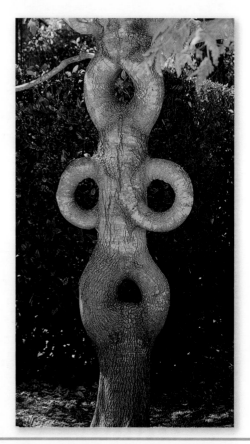

Figure 8.24. Loops or other designs can be created in a tree trunk by bending and grafting shoots when the tree is young. This and other living tree structures are growing at Bonfante Gardens in Gilroy, California. Photo by Chuck Ingels.

References

Geisel, P. M. 2002. Plant propagation. Pages 91–120 in D. Pittenger, ed., California master gardener handbook. Oakland: University of California Division of Agriculture and Natural Resources, Publication 3382.

Hartmann, H. T., and J. A. Beutel. 1994. Propagation of temperate-zone fruit plants. Oakland: University of California Division of Agriculture and Natural Resources, Publication 21103.

Hartmann, H. T., D. E. Kester, and F. T. Davies Jr. 1990. Plant propagation: Principles and practices. Fifth ed. Englewood Cliffs, NJ: Prentice Hall.

Reames, R., and B. H. Delbol. 1995. How to grow a chair: The art of tree trunk topiary. Williams, OR: Arborsmith Studios.

Toogood, A., ed. 1999. Plant propagation. American Horticultural Society. London: DK Publishing, Inc.

Useful Web Sites

California Rare Fruit Growers (http://www.crfg.org)

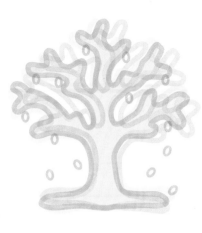

CHAPTER 9

Fruit Thinning

Chuck A. Ingels

Fruit trees often set more fruit than they can adequately support or develop to optimal size, especially if the trees did not have adequate pruning during the previous season. A tree's leaves supply energy for growth; if there are not enough leaves on the tree to support the number of fruit that set, the fruit will, in effect, compete with each other for carbohydrates and so remain small. Too much fruit on a tree can also lead to limb breakage or alternate bearing patterns (see Chapter 2). If you thin immature fruit at the proper time, you can help correct these problems and allow each remaining fruit to develop to its maximum size. Although thinning reduces the number of fruit and total yield, it improves the size and quality of fruit. It may also increase the sugar content of individual fruit so they end up tasting sweeter.

Fruit thinning can also reduce the spread of some diseases. Where two fruit are touching on a tree, moisture is trapped between them, providing better conditions for disease development. Also, diseases such as brown rot can quickly spread from one fruit to another just before harvest. Air movement around separated fruit is greater, which means that the surface of thinned fruit dries more quickly, reducing the chances for multiplication and spread of disease organisms. Certain insect pests, such as leafrollers, also prefer to feed in fruit clusters.

Natural Fruit Drop

Flowers and fruit naturally thin themselves, often at distinct developmental stages (see Chapter 2). Blossoms that are not pollinated turn yellow and drop off just after flowering. Later, small, immature fruit often drop naturally during what is known as *June drop,* which in most parts of California usually occurs in late April or May. Fruit or nuts that are diseased (such as walnuts with walnut blight) or infested with insects (such as apples or pears with codling moth) may also drop prematurely.

In some types of trees, this sort of natural thinning is sufficient; other species need additional thinning to produce high-quality fruit. Cherries, figs, pomegranates, citrus, and nut trees do not usually require thinning.

Species That Require Thinning

Most stone fruit trees (peach, nectarine, apricot, and plum) other than cherry require thinning in most years. Of pome fruits, all apples and Asian pears and most European pears require thinning. Bartlett pears often thin themselves, and if you harvest larger, more mature fruit early you will allow the smaller fruit to increase in size for a second pick 1 to 2 weeks later. Fruit of other species can and should be thinned if the crop is excessive, relative to the vigor of the tree. As mentioned earlier, nut crops do not need to be thinned.

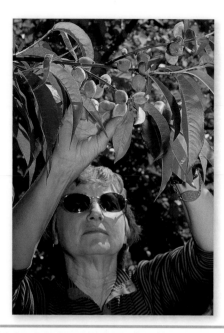

Figure 9.1. Peach and nectarine trees form large numbers of fruit along 1-year-old branches. These fruit should be thinned to about 5 to 7 inches apart, which would leave only about three fruit on the branch shown here. Photo by Jack Kelly Clark.

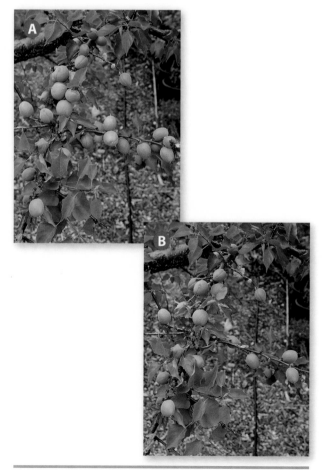

Figure 9.2. Immature apricots **(A)** before thinning and **(B)** after thinning. Note that about half the fruit were removed and even more fruit could have been thinned. Photos by Jack Kelly Clark.

Timing for Thinning

Fruit can be thinned anytime from right after bloom until a few weeks before harvest. It is a good idea, though, to wait until natural drop has occurred so you can assess the crop load before you thin. Also, it is difficult to identify and remove defective fruit when they are very small, and thinning too early can occasionally result in split pits in stone fruits, especially peaches. On the other hand, if you wait too long to thin you run the risk of reducing final fruit size and increasing the chances of limb breakage. For these reasons, you should thin fruit when they are fairly small, typically from early April (for early ripening fruit) to mid-May (for late-ripening fruit). Stone fruit are thinned when they are about ¾ to 1 inch (1.9 to 2.5 cm) in diameter and pome fruits (apples and pears) are thinned at ½ to 1 inch (1.3 to 2.5 cm) in diameter, or within about 30 to 45 days after full bloom.

How Much Fruit to Thin

The amount of fruit to thin depends on the species (and sometimes variety) and the overall fruit load on the tree. If a tree is excessively vigorous, less thinning (more fruit) will slow the growth but may still result in broken limbs. Poorly growing trees should be thinned far more and the causes of the poor health should be corrected. Many home gardeners are apprehensive about fruit thinning and often leave too much fruit on the tree. In some cases, little to no thinning may result in large fruit and healthy trees, but too often the trees or fruit will suffer and they may tend toward alternate bearing (see Chapter 12).

The recommendations that follow will usually result in healthy trees and adequate amounts of large fruit. When a range is given, use the closer spacing for varieties with smaller fruit and the wider spacing for larger-fruited varieties. You can still use closer spacing, but to do so may be to sacrifice fruit size and quality.

If you have had ideal spring conditions for pollination, excessive fruit may have set, and the tree may require even more thinning. If the overall fruit load is light, but one or two branches have a large amount of fruit, the tree may require less thinning because the total number of fruit on the tree is low.

Peaches and nectarines, which produce fruit on long, one-year-old branches instead of spurs, should be thinned to about 5 to 7 inches (13 to 18 cm) apart along the branch (Figure 9.1). Long lateral fruiting branches, such as those over about 1.5 to 2 ft (46 to 61 cm) long, should have been shortened by about one-third to one-half their original length during the dormant season in order to reduce the amount of time you spend on thinning (see Chapter 7). If a lateral fruiting branch is long and it produces fruit along its entire length, thin it more heavily, especially near the terminal end. Remove "doubles" (two fruit fused together) and small, disfigured, or damaged fruit.

Apricots, plums, and apricot-plum hybrid varieties are generally smaller, so they can be spaced closer together. Thin apricots and apriums to 3 to 5 inches (8 to 13 cm) apart on the branch (Figure 9.2) and thin plums and pluots slightly farther apart, to about 4 to 6 inches (10 to 15 cm) apart. On short spurs, thinning may leave only one or two fruit per spur (Figure 9.3).

Unlike stone fruits, which produce one fruit per bud, apples and pears produce a cluster of flowers and fruit from each bud. Thin to one fruit per cluster (Figure 9.4). If the overall crop is light, you can leave two fruit per cluster. Retain the largest fruit whenever possible. If the crop is heavy, fruit should be spaced no less than 6 to 8 inches (15 to 20.5 cm) apart.

Quince do not require thinning. Persimmons are often not thinned, but thinning increases fruit size. Also, a large fruit load may break branches, so you may want to thin them to 6 inches (15 cm) apart. Any tree with excessive fruit load and poor growth will benefit from fruit thinning (Figure 9.5).

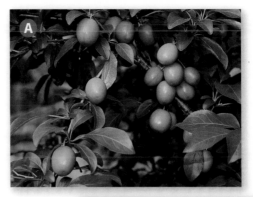

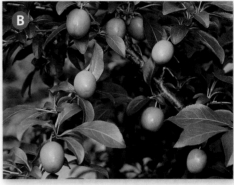

Figure 9.3. Fruit on plum spurs **(A)** before thinning and **(B)** after thinning. Photos by Chuck Ingels.

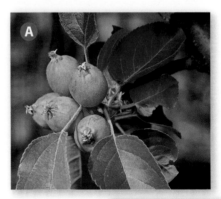

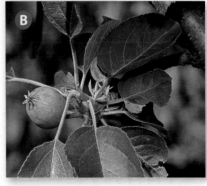

Figure 9.4. Thin apples and pears to one fruit per cluster. **(A)** Before thinning and **(B)** after thinning. Photos by Jack Kelly Clark.

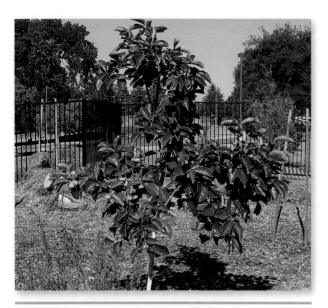

Figure 9.5. Scaffold branches of young trees, like the persimmon shown here, may bend over or break if the fruit load is heavy. Photo by Chuck Ingels.

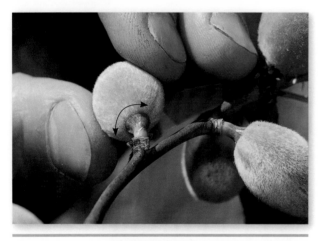

Figure 9.6. Hand-thin stone fruit by twisting the fruit rather than pulling. This prevents damage to the branch or spur. Photo by Jack Kelly Clark.

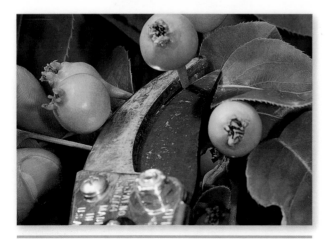

Figure 9.7. Asian pears and other pome fruits should be thinned using hand clippers. Photo by Jack Kelly Clark.

Methods of Thinning

For the home orchardist, there are two main ways to thin fruit: by hand or by pole. Hand thinning is more thorough and accurate than the pole method, but it is also much slower and may not be practical with larger trees. Whichever method you use, thinning is easiest if the trees have been adequately pruned the previous winter or summer.

Hand thinning should be done carefully—do not simply pull the fruit off or you may end up breaking off the entire spur with it. Instead, remove the fruit by twisting (Figure 9.6), cutting the stem with fingernails between the thumb and index finger, or using clippers (Figure 9.7), especially with apples and pears, which are hard to remove otherwise. When hand thinning, avoid leaning a ladder against the trunk or branches of a tree, as it may become unstable or damage the bark or branches. Also, avoid climbing fruit trees—branches break easily, and if you fall you can be seriously injured.

Pole thinning generally cannot be used on apples or pears because they are very difficult to remove, so pole thinning would do excessive damage to the remaining fruit. Pole thinning is used mainly on large stone fruit trees where hand thinning would be cumbersome, impractical, or dangerous. It can also save a lot of time since it is much faster than hand thinning, and although it is less precise, the results are often acceptable once you have mastered the technique. The pole can be made of a long dowel rod, rigid plastic pipe, bamboo, or other lightweight material. Attach a short length of rubber hose, cloth, or thick tape to the end of the pole to minimize scarring or bruising to remaining fruit. Strike individual fruit or clusters or the base of the branch to remove some of the fruit (Figure 9.8). With experience, you will be able to strike a cluster or branch once or twice with just enough force to thin the right number of fruit.

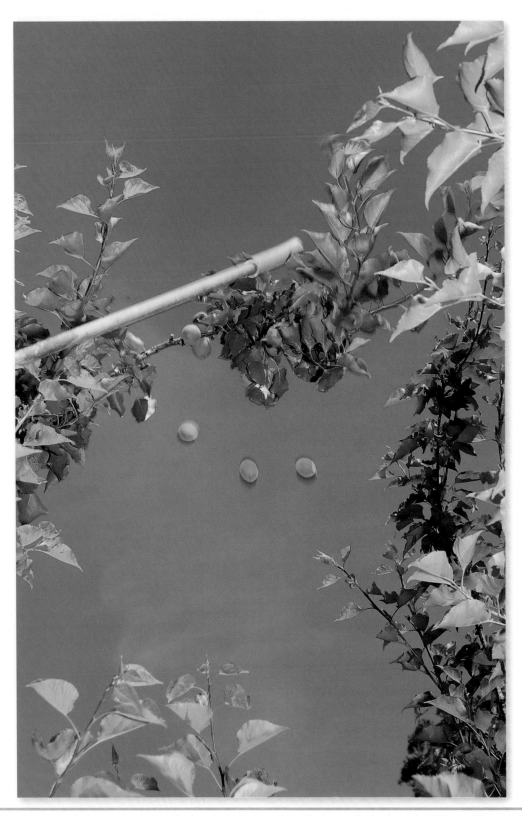

Figure 9.8. You can use a pole thinner consisting of a dowel with a short piece of hose attached to its end to thin stone fruits (apricot is shown here) by carefully whacking the cluster or branch. Pole thinning is quicker than hand-thinning, but is harder to do accurately. Photo by Jack Kelly Clark.

References

Ingels, C., P. M. Geisel, and C. L. Unruh. 2001. Fruit trees: Thinning young fruit. Oakland: University of California Division of Agriculture and Natural Resources, Publication 8047. Available free online from the UC ANR Communication Services Web site, http://anrcatalog.ucdavis.edu.

Yoshikawa, F. T., and R. S. Johnson. 1989. Fruit thinning. Pages 56–59 in J. H. LaRue and R. S. Johnson, eds., Peaches, plums, and nectarines: Growing and handling for fresh market. Oakland: University of California Division of Agriculture and Natural Resources, Publication 3331.

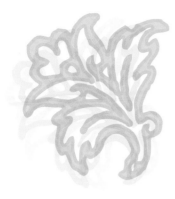

CHAPTER **10**

Harvesting Fruit and Nuts

Pamela M. Geisel

A great deal of effort goes into growing fruit and nut trees so that we can harvest crops of the best possible quality. We prune, thin the fruit, water, fertilize, and manage pests, yet we often ignore the most critical and timely task of harvest, sometimes until it is too late to salvage a quality crop. In addition to having a timely harvest, it is important to provide the optimum storage conditions to maintain the fruit quality for as long as possible or until the fruit can be either eaten or processed for longer-term storage.

General Rules of Harvest

Each crop has an optimum period and method for harvest, but the harvest period can vary, depending on the individual tastes of the gardener, physiological characteristics of the fruit, and planned use for the fruit. Fruit and nuts ripen by degrees, and they can be harvested over a range of maturity and ripeness.

Some species are harvested when fully ripe and ready to eat; others when simply physiologically "mature," meaning that they will continue to ripen after harvest. For those that do not ripen further after harvest, the sugar they have at harvest is all they ever will have; it will not increase after harvest. These species may seem to get sweeter as their acidity decreases, but sugar content itself does not increase. They may also soften after harvest, but this is more a manifestation of decay and breakdown than of ripening. Fruit in this category include blackberries, cherries, grapes, citrus, raspberries, and strawberries.

Other species of mature-harvested fruit may further change in color, texture, and juiciness, but will not improve in sweetness or flavor. These fruit include apricot, blueberry, fig, nectarine, peach, and plum.

Some fruit, such as apples, European pears, cherimoyas, kiwifruit, mangoes, and papayas, do increase in sugar and sweetness after harvest. These fruit contain starch that can be converted to sugars whether the fruit are on or off the tree.

Nut crops such as almond, walnut, and pecan can be harvested late without significant loss of quality to the nut itself. All the same, a timely harvest when the hulls begin to split will prevent other creatures, such as squirrels, ants, and navel orange worms, from getting to the crop before it can be harvested.

In all cases, waiting too long to harvest will render fruit overripe and very susceptible to birds, dried fruit beetles, or rot. Overripe fruit does not store well and fruit that is harvested mature-green does not taste the best. Fully tree-ripe fruit flavor cannot be beat.

The harvest stage you choose for your fruit also depends on how you plan to use the fruit. For immediate fresh eating, fully ripe is ideal. For canning, the fruit should be more firm than soft; for drying, fully ripe fruit will yield a full-flavored dried fruit. That is the advantage of growing your own fruit—you get to harvest it when it is at the peak stage for your preference. Notations on your calendar that indicate the ripening period for your individual trees will help remind you to prepare for the harvest. The exact date of harvest will vary from year to year, however, depending upon factors such as weather and water stress.

It is also important to note that most species are harvested over a period of time, since ripening usually occurs over one or more weeks. You may have to harvest every 3 to 5 days in order to get all of the fruit right when it is ready. While more time-consuming than one-time harvesting, this extended harvest period allows you to process a smaller quantity of fruit at one time instead of processing the whole tree all at once. The ripening period also varies with the growing region. Fruits of the same variety tend to have a later harvest period in cooler climates.

Finally, what is considered "optimum ripeness" will vary with your own individual preferences. Some people prefer a bit more tang or acidity to their fruit, so they harvest their fruit less ripe. Others prefer a bit more sugar, and so harvest fruit when it is more ripe. Commercial growers follow maturity standards that are based on indices such as the amount of sugar or acid in the fruit, firmness of the fruit, or splitting or browning of nut tissue. In the home garden, however, that determination is up to the individual.

When harvesting fruit by hand, treat it gently. Avoid throwing or dropping the fruit into bags and boxes. Rather, place it gently where it won't get bruised. Also, avoid stacking the fruit too deep in containers as the weight of the fruit on top can contribute to bruising the fruit on bottom.

It is also a good idea to wear cotton gloves in order to reduce bruising and cutting of the fruit. Any opening or wound in the fruit will reduce its shelf life. Pay attention to the methods of harvest described for each fruit species. With some species and varieties, improper harvesting can cause damage to the fruiting spurs and destroy the crop in following years.

Storage

A single large tree may produce several hundred pounds of fruit. For a small family, this may be more than the family can use. In this type of situation, you can give excess fruit to neighbors or to a local food bank instead of dumping it in the trash. Planning for the harvest and storage is just as important as planning which variety to plant. Do you have a large enough freezer to store the fruit or sufficient time to can or dry it? If not, consider growing "fruit bushes" or small genetic dwarf trees that produce a smaller quantity of fruit and are easier to manage.

Even if you don't plan on freezing, drying, or canning, you will still need to be able to provide some cold storage for your fruit. The capacity to get fruit cold and keep it that way is the next most important quality control tool, right after timely harvest. The focus on keeping it cool begins when you choose to pick fruit in the morning when it is cool and continues

when you get the freshly harvested tree-ripe fruit into a refrigerator as soon after harvest as possible. Most kitchen refrigerators cannot handle the large amount of fruit that may come from a single harvest in addition to normal household food storage needs. Having a spare "fruit fridge" can be a good idea, but try to get a newer, energy-efficient model and only use it during fruit harvest. Look for one that has wide doors for ease of loading and unloading and has uniform distribution of cold air. Make sure its temperature controls are functioning accurately.

Temperature is the most crucial factor that determines how fast fruit will degrade in storage. For every 18°F (−7.8°C) above the fruit's optimum temperature, its rate of deterioration increases two to three times (Thompson 2002). Deciduous fruit are not as sensitive to chilling injury as the tropical-type fruit. For example, most deciduous tree fruit such as apricot, cherry, fig, nectarine, peach, and plum are not chilling sensitive and are best stored at just above freezing, from 32°F up to 35°F (0° to 1.7°C). For optimum ripening, however, temperatures between 68° and 77°F (20° and 25°C) are best. The more tropical-type fruit such as olive, citrus, cherimoya, mango, papaya, avocado, and feijoa tend to be much more sensitive to chilling injury and are best stored between 50° and 59°F (10° and 15°C), with optimum ripening temperatures between 68° and 77°F (20° and 25°C).

It is difficult to maintain lower temperatures in a home-type refrigeration unit. Test your fruit refrigerator with a thermometer at the different settings and on the various shelves to determine what setting is best for your particular harvest. Most can be maintained around 45°F (7.2°C) or somewhat lower. If you are dedicating one refrigerator to fruit storage, it would be better to set its temperature at 35°F for all temperate fruits.

When you load the fruit into the refrigerator, try to stack it in a way that allows adequate air circulation around each fruit. Keep fruit away from the walls. Avoid rot by not putting wet fruit into the refrigerator. Layer the fruit in clean newspaper to reduce the amount of fruit-to-fruit infection from decay fungi (Figure 10.1).

Harvesting and Storing Specific Fruits and Nuts

Most firm or green-ripe fruit can easily be ripened off the tree. Commercially produced fruit-ripening bowls are available (Figure 10.2), but you can also use a brown paper bag. Place the fruit you would like to ripen more fully into the bag and place a high-ethylene-producing fruit, such as an apple, avocado, peach, plum, or passion fruit in the bag as well. Ethylene is a natural gas given off by ripening fruit, and it has an effect on the aging and ripening of fruit and other horticultural crops that are exposed to it. In some cases, too much ethylene can be a problem, but in this instance it is helpful as it encourages the ripening of green-ripe fruit.

APPLES

Harvest

Apples require relatively low nighttime temperatures and high light intensity during the ripening period for the best development of skin color on the tree. Low light, high temperatures, or conditions such as summer fog tend to reduce color development. To determine ripeness, taste is the best indicator. If the fruit tastes good to you, it is ready for harvest. In addition, if the fruit has full color both inside and out as is appropriate for that variety, that is a good indication of maturity. Apples that are to be stored into winter should be harvested when "firm ripe"—physiologically mature but firm for cold storage. Winter-stored apples can then be brought out and allowed to ripen at room temperature.

Apples that are ready to harvest should break easily away from the fruit spur. Avoid pulling down on the apple, since that may break the fruit spur. Gently twist the fruit upward, rotating it slightly.

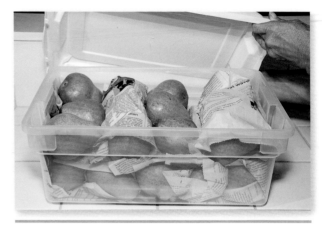

Figure 10.1. Storing harvested fruit in layers of newspaper in the refrigerator. Photo by Mike Poe.

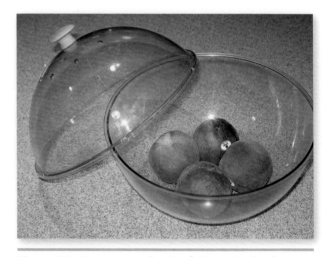

Figure 10.2. Ripening stone fruit in a fruit-ripening bowl.

Storage

Apples require relatively high humidity during cold storage to reduce moisture loss from the fruit. You can place a moist towel in the bottom of your fruit fridge to increase the humidity. Apples should not be stored with other produce or where odd odors may exist, since they tend to pick up external odors and produce "off-flavors." Also, apples give off some ethylene, so they can increase the ripening rate of other fruit.

Apples can be eaten fresh, dried, or made into apple cider, applesauce, apple butter, or apple leather.

APRICOTS AND APRIUMS

Harvest

Apricots and similar fruit develop the best flavor when allowed to fully ripen on the tree. An individual tree will bear fruit that ripen over a period of one to three weeks. For canning and drying, the fruit is best harvested when firm ripe. To harvest, gently pull the fruit from the spur with a slight upward twist.

Storage

Apricots can be stored under refrigeration for about three weeks before their quality begins to deteriorate. They are best eaten fresh. You can also dry them, can them, make them into jam, freeze them, or make them into fruit leather.

CHERRIES

Harvest

Cherries are harvested when fully ripe and usually over a period of two weeks or so. They are most often harvested with the stems attached because they store best that way (Figure 10.3). Grab the stem or stems and twist upward. Be very careful not to break the fruit spur when you harvest. If you are planning to use the fruit for canning or for further processing, you can harvest without the stems, which is much faster.

Storage

Cherries can be eaten fresh or cooked and can be stored by canning, freezing, or drying. It is important that cherries be rapidly cooled after harvesting if processing is to be delayed for some reason. The longer they are exposed to warm temperatures and pressure in the harvest container after harvest, the more rapidly they will begin to break down.

FIGS

Harvest

The optimum harvest period for figs is when the neck of the individual fruit begins to bend down over the stem and the fruit begin to crack. They should be soft for fresh eating or firm ripe if they are to be used for pickling. If beads of milky white sap (latex) ooze from the stem end after picking, the fruit is not yet ready to harvest.

Storage

Figs can be eaten fresh or they can be frozen, pickled, or dried for future use. For optimum flavor of dried figs, allow them to partially dry on the tree and then complete the drying process on drying trays. You can also let them fall naturally to the ground, but be sure to pick them up quickly to avoid insect and disease problems in the fruit (Figure 10.4). For longer storage of fresh fruit, optimum storage temperatures range from 32° to 35°F (0° to 1.7°C). Storage below 32°F (0°C) may subject the fruit to freeze injury.

PEACHES AND NECTARINES

Harvest

Peaches and nectarines for fresh eating are at their most flavorful when they are tree ripened. Allow the fruit to develop full color on the tree, but harvest when they are still fairly firm to the touch. It is important that you harvest them before they become too soft. Soft-ripe fruits are sweeter, but they tend to break down very quickly and are more predisposed to bruising and injury. Fruit that are to be stored before eating or processing should be harvested when firm-ripe and stored under refrigeration (between 32° and 35°F [0° and 1.7°C]). Then you can bring them out of refrigeration a few days before you want to eat them, so they can finish ripening.

Clingstone fruit that are to be canned should be harvested when they break away from the stem easily yet are still firm. Allow them to sit out for a day or two before processing. This will make the skin much easier to peel.

Storage

Peaches can be stored under refrigeration for several weeks when harvested firm-ripe. Optimum storage temperatures range from 32° to 35°F (0° to 1.7°C). Below 32°F (0°C) they will be susceptible to chilling injury. Peaches and nectarines can be eaten fresh or they can be stored frozen, dried, or canned.

PEARS

Harvest

To harvest pears, lift fruit gently upward (Figure 10.5). Do not twist or pull to avoid breaking the fruit spur. If the fruit does not separate easily from the stem, then wait a few more days to begin to harvest. European pears are best ripened off the tree. If allowed to ripen on the tree, they will be mealy. Asian pears are an exception to this rule and are harvested when firm-ripe and sweet. Harvest European pears when the fruit is still hard and green but has reached the fully developed size for the variety. Pears can then be ripened on the shelf at room temperature to full flavor and maturity.

Storage

Store pears under refrigeration between 32° and 40°F (0° and 4.4°C). They can be stored for many weeks and brought out as needed for ripening at room temperature. Winter pear varieties will store much longer and actually produce a better-flavored pear when exposed to refrigeration for six weeks or so before you bring them out to ripen at room temperatures. The winter varieties include Bosc, Winter Nelis, Comice, d'Anjou, and Seckel.

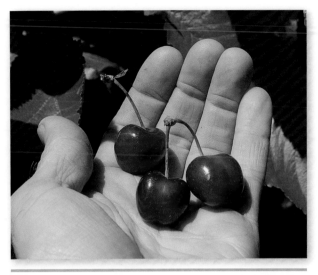

Figure 10.3. Keep stems on cherries for harvest to help them last longer in storage. Photo by Chuck Ingels.

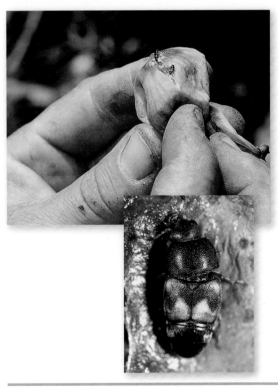

Figure 10.4. Dried fruit beetles on a fig. Photos by Richard Coviello (top) and Jack Kelly Clark (bottom).

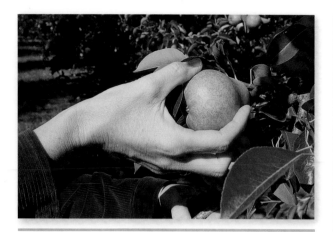

Figure 10.5. Lifting a pear off the spur to harvest. Photo by Mike Poe.

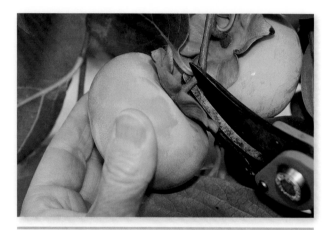

Figure 10.6. Use pruning shears to harvest persimmons *(shown here)* and pomegranates. Photo by Chuck Ingels.

Asian pears can be stored for two to three weeks at room temperature and longer under refrigeration. These are best used for fresh eating only.

European pears can be eaten fresh, baked, canned, dried, or made into preserves and fruit leather. The quality of frozen pears is not great, so that is not a recommended storage method.

Persimmons

Harvest

Persimmons, both the astringent and non-astringent types, begin to ripen in late September to November. The astringent types (e.g., Hachiya) can be allowed to become soft-ripe on the tree but are usually harvested when firm-ripe and then allowed to become very soft and ripe at room temperature. The non-astringent types, (e.g., Fuyu) are harvested when they develop their full orange color for the variety. Fuyu persimmons are eaten when firm (crisp) like an apple. To maintain their crispness, protect from exposure to ethylene produced by other fruit.

To harvest the fruit, use hand pruning shears to cut the stem and allow the calyx (the green collar on the fruit) to remain attached to the fruit (Figure 10.6).

Storage

Fruit will store for a month or more under refrigeration. You can pull them out of refrigeration as required and allow them to ripen more fully at room temperature. You may find, however, that the fruit lose flavor and that their texture deteriorates slightly with cold storage. Persimmons are often frozen for up to a year before being used in persimmon puddings and cakes.

Persimmons can be eaten fresh or they can be frozen or dried for storage. Dried persimmons have an outstanding flavor and sweetness.

PLUMS, PRUNES, PLUMCOTS, PLUOTS, AND CHERRY-PLUMS

Harvest

To harvest a plum, prune, plumcot, pluot, or cherry-plum, gently lift the fruit off the fruit spur. It should separate easily. For fresh eating, the optimum harvest time is when the fruit are firm-ripe and full flavored. In many varieties, this period may last for several weeks; for others, the harvest may occur all at one time. Usually the early maturing varieties are harvested two or three times, picking only the ripe fruits each time. Later-maturing varieties tend to hang on the tree longer before they become soft-ripe, so they can be picked over a longer period.

Prunes that are to be dried should be allowed to stay on the tree until they are fully ripe and easily knocked from the tree. You can wait until a few of the fruit begin to fall naturally and then pick them all for drying.

Storage

Fresh plums and prunes are best stored under refrigeration between 32° and 40°F (0° and 4.4°C). You can also store them in a cool, dry place for several weeks, but in that case they should be harvested a little less ripe than if they are going to be used immediately.

Plums and prunes can be processed for long-term storage by canning, drying, or freezing them, or making them into jams and jellies.

POMEGRANATES

Harvest

Optimum fruit quality is attained when the pomegranate fruit has developed full color, but before it starts to split. The splitting significantly reduces its storage life. The best time to eat fresh pomegranates, however, is in the early splitting period. To harvest, cut the fruit from the stem with shears. Avoid pulling the fruit from the tree as you are likely to break fruit spurs.

Storage

Pomegranates will shrivel if stored at room temperature for extended periods. The arils (the fruit surrounding each seed) will remain edible after the husk has dried, but the flavor will decline over time without cold storage. Avoid storing split or damaged fruit. You can juice the fruit and freeze the juice in ice cube trays. Remove the frozen cubes from the trays and store the cubes in plastic bags. You can also can the juice.

QUINCES

Harvest

Quince fruit are ready in the fall once they begin to lose their green color and develop a full yellow color. The fruit will not soften on the tree and are harvested while still firm. Handle the fruit gently to prevent bruising.

Storage

Quince store well on the tree, but they tend to break down within a few weeks under refrigeration. The woolly outer layer should be retained if the fruit are to be stored. The fruit of most varieties of quince are not edible unless cooked. Quince is most often processed into jams and jellies.

Nut Crops

Nut crops have an external hull (or husk), which may be somewhat fleshy prior to harvest. Just under the hull is the shell, which hardens and protects the edible kernel inside. For most nuts, the hull must be removed before the crop is dried or processed.

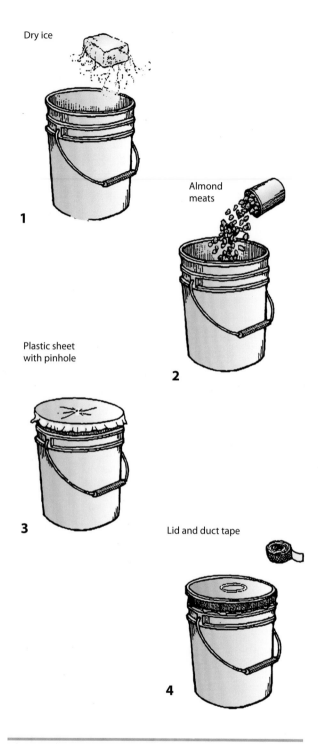

Dry ice

1

Almond meats

2

Plastic sheet with pinhole

3

Lid and duct tape

4

Figure 10.7. If handled properly, solid carbon dioxide (dry ice) can provide safe, economical control for some pests in stored almonds. **(1)** Put ½ pound of dry ice in the bottom of a 5-gallon bucket. **(2)** Fill the rest of the bucket with almond kernels (about 23 pounds). **(3)** Cover the bucket with a sheet of plastic (such as plastic wrap or part of a plastic trash bag) secured with a large rubber band, and prick a pinhole in the middle of the sheet to let oxygen escape as the bucket fills with heavier carbon dioxide gas from the dry ice. **(4)** After 8 hours or so, when all of the dry ice has had time to turn to gas, seal the bucket with a tight-fitting lid (leaving the plastic sheet in place) and further seal the edges of the lid with duct tape.

ALMONDS

Harvest

Almonds are ready to harvest once the outer hull begins to split, although you can allow them to stay on the tree until the hulls are dry and the nuts begin to drop on their own. The kernels are only partially dry at hull split and need a few more weeks of drying after harvest in order to cure completely. Once the nuts are ready to harvest, they should be knocked or shaken from the tree rather than allowed to fall naturally. This will avoid problems with insect pests, diseases, and birds that may otherwise get the crop before you do. Once you collect the nuts, remove the hulls and allow them to cure fully for a week or more in a dry, well-ventilated location. Avoid overly hot locations such as driveways, since excessively high temperatures can damage the kernel. Make sure to protect the nuts from squirrels, ants, and birds as well. The nuts are dry when the kernel rattles in the shell and the dried kernel will snap in two and has a nutty taste with no bitterness.

Storage

Pest-free, in-shell almonds will store for up to six months in a cool, dry, well-ventilated location. Once the almonds have been shelled, though, they should be stored frozen. To kill any pests that may be inside the in-shell almonds, place them in a freezer for 48 hours below 32°F (0°C), and store them afterward at room temperature in a sealed container. You can kill insect pests in larger quantities of almonds by exposing the nuts to carbon dioxide in a large, sealed container (Figure 10.7)

PECANS

Harvest

Pecans should be harvested once the green hull begins to split. It is best to knock the nuts from the tree rather than allow them to fall naturally. That way birds and other pests will not be able to get to the crop before you do. Collect the nuts and remove the hulls (not the shells) as soon as possible after harvest. It is a good idea to wear gloves to avoid staining your hands during the hulling process. Wash the hulled nuts and then spread them out in the sun for a few days to complete the curing process. Protect the nuts from birds and squirrels while they are drying. The nuts are fully cured when the kernel of a cracked nut will break cleanly rather than bending.

Storage

Pecans in the shell may be stored in a cool, dry, well-ventilated location for many months. Once the nuts are shelled, you can store them frozen (at 32° to 35°F [0 to 1.7°C]) for up to a year, or under refrigeration for up to about three months.

PISTACHIOS

Harvest

Pistachios are ready to harvest when the outside of the hulls begins to change from glossy to dull, indicating that the kernels inside are fully developed. The hull that surrounds the shell will loosen and will be slightly yellow at the stem end. In some cases, the shell will begin to split. To harvest the nuts, shake them from the tree onto a tarp that you have spread underneath. Remove the hulls as soon as possible after harvest. Use a screen made of ½-inch mesh hardware cloth or expanded metal (Figure 10.8) to remove hulls: lay the nuts on the screen and gently rub the nuts over the screen. The hulls will fall through the screen, away from the nuts in their shells.

Many of the pistachios may be what are called "blanks": they develop a hull and a shell, but not a kernel. You can easily cull out the blanks after hulling. Just place the hulled nuts in a bucket of water. The blanks should float, and you can separate them out and discard them.

Storage

You can process pistachios further after hulling by boiling the hulled, unshelled nuts in salted water for a few minutes to "salt them in the shell." The nuts are then dried in a dry, well-ventilated location and then stored. The dried nuts can be stored under refrigeration for 6 weeks or so and frozen to last up to 1 year or so.

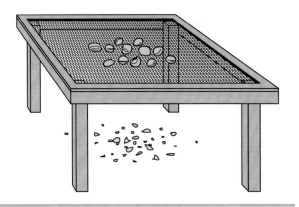

Figure 10.8. A table fitted with an expanded metal top can be used for hulling pistachios, pecans, or walnuts.

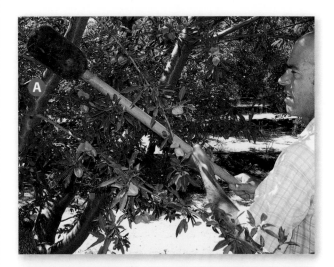

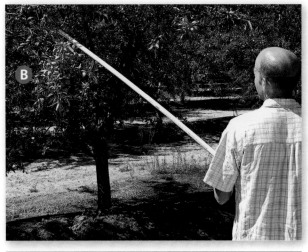

Figure 10.9. Nut crops (almond shown here) should be knocked **(A)** or poled **(B)** from the tree to harvest. Photos by Maxwell Norton.

Walnuts

Harvest

Walnuts should be harvested once the green hulls begin to split and the packing tissue between and around the kernel halves has just turned brown. It is best to knock the nuts from the tree rather than allow them to fall naturally (Figure 10.9). That way you can keep insects and other pests from getting to the crop before you do. Collect the nuts and remove the hulls as quickly as possible after harvest. You can use a knife to hull small quantities of walnuts. For larger quantities, use a screen made of expanded metal to remove hulls: lay the nuts on the screen and gently rub the nuts over the screen (see Figure 10.8). The hulls will fall through the screen, away from the nuts in their shells. If hulls stick tightly to the shells, moisten them and cover with a moist tarp or burlap sheet for several days to loosen. Hulls may be composted and used in the garden; the composting process degrades any natural toxins present in the hulls.

It is a good idea to wear protective gloves during the hulling process to avoid staining your hands. Wash the hulled nuts and then spread them out in a shaded, well-ventilated location for a few days to complete the curing process. Protect the nuts from birds and squirrels while they are drying. The nuts are fully cured when the kernel of a cracked nut will break cleanly rather than bending and the kernel has developed a nutty taste. If your nuts have had a problem with walnut husk fly, the hulls may stick to the shells. Place a moist burlap bag over the unhulled nuts overnight to soften the hulls and make removal easier.

Storage

Unshelled walnuts may be stored in a cool, dry, well-ventilated location for many months. Once the nuts are shelled you can store them frozen for up to a year or up to about 3 to 4 months under refrigeration.

References

Perry, E., and G. S. Sibbett. 1998. Harvesting and storing your home orchard's nut crop: Almonds, walnuts, pecans, pistachios, and chestnuts. Oakland: University of California Division of Agriculture and Natural Resources, Publication 8005. Available for free downloading at the UC ANR Communication Services Web site, http://anrcatalog.ucdavis.edu.

Thompson, J. F. 2002. Psychrometrics and perishable commodities. Pages 129–134 in A. A. Kader, ed., Postharvest technology of horticultural crops. Third ed. Oakland: University of California Division of Agriculture and Natural Resources, Publication 3311.

Useful Web Sites

UC Davis Postharvest Technology Research & Information Center (http://postharvest.ucdavis.edu)

Produce for Better Health Foundation (http://www.5aday.org)

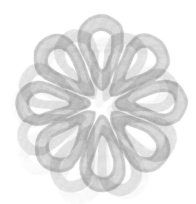

CHAPTER 11

Integrated Pest Management for Backyard Orchards

Mary Louise Flint and Beth L. Teviotdale

You will find a wide array of organisms in any backyard orchard. Only a small number of them are pests. Many are considered beneficial because they decompose organic matter (such as dead leaves or fruit), pollinate crops, prey on pests, provide shelter or food for natural enemies of pests, or perform other useful functions. Still others are just incidental, having little or no impact on the landscape. The first step in managing pest problems is to identify pests and their damage symptoms and distinguish them from beneficial or non-damaging organisms and from problems such as inappropriate cultural care. Many pest species are damaging only at certain stages of plant growth or when their numbers are high, so a good knowledge of pest biology is essential before you choose any pest management practices.

Gardeners can select from a variety of nonchemical and chemical methods to prevent, reduce, or eliminate pest problems. Cultural practices, physical barriers and devices, biological control agents, and pesticides all are tools that are commonly used. Choosing the right tool and applying it properly and at the right time are the keys to success. Integrated pest management (IPM) is a strategy for combining various environmentally sound, effective pest management techniques to protect plants and people from pests.

What Is Integrated Pest Management?

With integrated pest management, you use your knowledge about how the garden ecosystem works in order to find environmentally sound solutions to pest problems. The goal is long-term prevention of pests or their damage through a combination of techniques such as biological control, habitat manipulation, modification of cultural practices, and use of resistant crop varieties and rootstocks. Pesticides are used as a last resort when careful monitoring indicates they are needed, and treatments are made with the goal of removing only the target organisms. Pest control materials are selected and applied in a manner that minimizes risks to human health, beneficial and nontarget organisms, and the environment.

PEST MANAGEMENT METHODS

The first-choice methods in IPM are those that keep pests from becoming established or abundant in the first place. Although most gardeners are looking for a single silver bullet to solve their problems easily, a combination of methods is usually more effective over the long term than any single method. Some preferred methods in an IPM program include

- *Using plant varieties and rootstocks that resist pests or stock that is certified pest-free and well adapted to local conditions.*

- *Choosing a planting site that is suitable for your trees. Avoid sites where diseased trees have recently been removed and make sure that the soil drains well.*

- *Encouraging naturally occurring biological controls such as predators or parasites.*

- *Adopting cultivation, pruning, fertilization, and irrigation practices that reduce pest problems.*

- *Changing the habitat to make it incompatible with pest development. For instance, you can remove mummy nuts or fruit in which pests survive over the winter to prevent them from emerging in spring and infesting the new crop.*

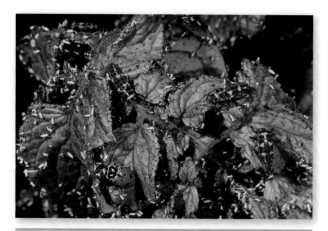

Figure 11.1. Convergent lady beetle adults and larvae are common predators of aphids. The white specks on these leaves are cast skins of aphids. Photo by Jack Kelly Clark.

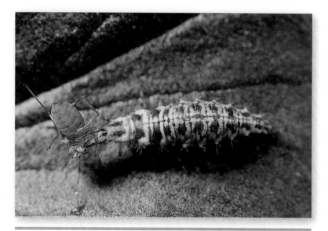

Figure 11.2. Green lacewing larvae feed on many types of insect eggs and soft-bodied insects such as the aphid shown here. Photo by Jack Kelly Clark.

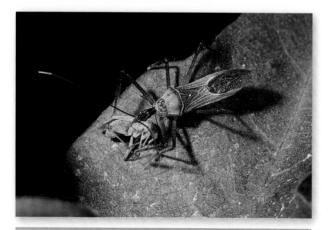

Figure 11.3. Assassin bugs are large predators that capture and feed on many pests, including leafhoppers. Photo by Jack Kelly Clark.

- *Trapping, washing off, pruning, or screening out pests.*

- *Selecting pesticides with lower toxicity to humans, beneficial organisms, and nontarget organisms and applying them when they will be most effective.*

Biological Control

Almost every insect and mite pest that occurs in orchard trees can fall victim to one or more biological control agents. These *natural enemies* often suppress pest populations and may keep them from reaching levels that would cause serious damage to fruit and nut trees. It is important to recognize these beneficial organisms and protect them and encourage their activity. Insect natural enemies can be classified into three groups: predators, parasites, and pathogens. Predators hunt down and kill insects and mites, some killing a hundred or more pest individuals during a lifetime. Parasites (often called *parasitoids*) in biological control are tiny wasps and flies that lay their eggs in or on insects; the larvae that hatch out of the eggs feed on the insect host, killing it by the time the parasite is ready to pupate. Although parasite larvae kill only one individual, adult females may lay many eggs and so have a significant impact on pest populations. Pathogens include the many types of disease organisms, including fungi, bacteria, viruses, and nematodes, that may infect and kill insect and mite pests. *Bacillus thuringiensis* is a bacterium that kills caterpillars and is widely used in pest management programs. While a few biological control agents are available for purchase and release (including *Bacillus thuringiensis*), most biological control involves the use of naturally occurring populations.

Some important general predators present in many orchard trees are pictured here (Figures 11.1 through 11.6). Other important biological control agents are discussed in the specific pest sections later in this chapter. See the *Natural Enemies Handbook* (UC ANR Publication 3386) for more information on biological control.

Cultural Controls

Cultural controls include any modification of normal management practices that can decrease pest establishment, reproduction, dispersal, and survival. To be successful with cultural techniques, you need a good knowledge of plant and pest biology. Changes in irrigation practices, fertilizing practices, and planting or harvest time, and prompt removal of infested material from the garden and surrounding landscape are common cultural practices that can reduce pest problems.

Mechanical and Physical Control

Mechanical and physical control methods include practices that mechanically destroy pests, trap them, or present a physical barrier to pest infestation by creating conditions unsuitable for their entry or survival. Many mechanical and physical methods are labor-intensive but quite suitable for backyard orchard situations. Common methods include hoeing weeds, mulching, mowing, soil solarization, and setting up barriers and traps. Limited infestations of borers, aphids, leafrollers, or other pests can sometimes be pruned out. Hosing a small tree with a strong stream of water is an effective nonchemical way to manage aphids, whiteflies, and spider mites.

Pesticides

Pesticides can be important tools in an integrated pest management program. For certain pests, they may offer the only realistic method for control. There is a great range of pesticide products, and some of them pose only limited risks for health and the environment. The challenge in an integrated pest management program is to recognize when pesticides are needed and when they are not. Once the decision to use a pesticide is made, choose the safest product that provides effective control with the least impact on the environment. Make sure to time the application for the point in the pest's life cycle that will make it most effective. Use proper application equipment and protective clothing. Read the pesticide label carefully, mix the product precisely according to label directions, and be aware of the proper disposal procedures for leftover pesticide and empty containers. Pesticides should be used in combination with other methods. Any application decision should include consideration of the potential for impact on natural enemies and careful attention to cultural practices that reduce pest problems.

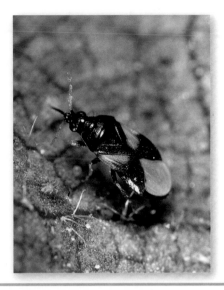

Figure 11.4. The tiny minute pirate bug feeds on insect eggs, small insects, and mites. Photo by Jack Kelly Clark.

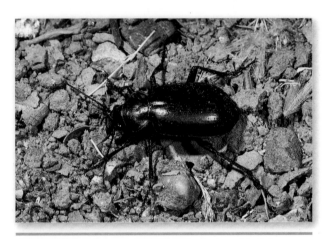

Figure 11.5. Predaceous ground beetles such as this *Calasoma* sp. feed on insects, including larvae and pupae in soil and on the trunks of trees. Photo by Jack Kelly Clark.

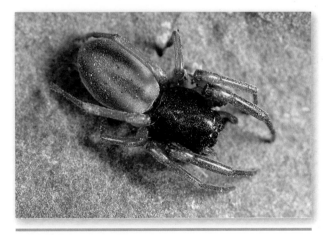

Figure 11.6. Spiders such as *Trachelas pacificus* occur commonly in fruit trees and may be important predators of moth larvae. Photo by Jack Kelly Clark.

Certain insecticides are especially compatible with integrated pest management programs because of their low impact on natural enemies of pests and nontarget organisms. Where possible, consider these safer products. They include

- *Bacillus thuringiensis (Bt), a microbial insecticide that causes disease symptoms in specific insects. Bacillus thuringiensis products are available for caterpillars (the larvae of moths and butterflies) and for flies, and particularly for mosquitoes and fungus gnats. To be effective, the Bt must be consumed by the insect.*

- *Insecticidal soaps provide partial control of soft-bodied insects and mites such as aphids, whiteflies, scale insects, spider mites, and psyllids. They are extremely safe products and in many cases are available in ready-to-use squirt bottles that are convenient for vegetables and annual bedding plants. Because soaps must directly contact the insect's body at the time of application, good coverage of leaf surfaces is essential for good control.*

- *Insecticidal oils, sometimes called horticultural oils or narrow-range or superior oils, are effective against soft-bodied insects and mites including aphids, spider mites, whiteflies, scale insects, psyllids, and the overwintering eggs of a number of pests. They can be applied during the dormant season on deciduous trees or during the growing season. They leave no residues and so have limited impact on natural enemies. Most available oils are petroleum-based, but several plant-based oils such as neem oil are also available. Oils also are active against powdery mildews and some other foliar fungal diseases. Because oils must directly contact the insect's body at the time of application in order to be effective, good coverage of leaf and bark surfaces is essential for good control.*

Virtually all of the petroleum oil products currently available to home orchardists are superior or narrow-range oils that are safe to use throughout the growing season except when temperatures exceed 90°F (32.2°C) or when trees are drought-stressed (an exception is walnuts, which are sensitive to oils, especially in spring.) Prior to the 1980s, many gardeners and growers used heavy oils with high sulfur content, called "dormant oils," during the dormant season. These oils were phytotoxic if they got onto leaves or buds and thus were not safe to use during the growing season. These oils are generally not available

any more. Products currently sold as "dormant oil sprays" are narrow-range/superior type oils containing the same oils as would be applied during the growing season. Narrow-range or superior oils should have a minimum unsulfonated residue (UR) of at least 92 percent. A higher unsulfonated residue indicates less phytotoxicity risk, but any product with 92 percent UR or greater is safe to use. Some products have a minimum UR of 99 percent. Minimum unsulfonated residue ratings are listed on the label of most oil products.

The Safe and Effective Use of Pesticides (UC ANR Publication 3324) is an excellent source of information on application equipment and the safe use of pesticides.

Types of Pests

This chapter provides information on identification, biology and management of some key insect, mite, and pathogen pests in backyard orchard trees. Many other insects and pathogens cause occasional damage in fruit and nut trees. See the integrated pest management books listed at the end of this chapter for information on other pests or look at the UC IPM Pest Management Guidelines on the University of California's Statewide IPM Program Web site (http://www.ipm.ucdavis.edu). In addition to arthropod and pathogen problems, damage may also result from the activities of vertebrate pests such as squirrels, pocket gophers, rabbits, deer, and birds; see the publication Wildlife Pests around Gardens and Homes (UC ANR Publication 21385) for information on identifying and managing vertebrates.

Common Insect and Mite Pests

Aphids

Aphids are common pests on many orchard trees, especially apples, plums, and walnuts. Small, soft-bodied insects that reproduce rapidly in the spring, aphids pierce leaves and young shoots with their sucking mouthparts, removing plant sap and leaving behind copious quantities of sticky honeydew. Some species distort and curl leaves. Different aphid species attack each fruit and nut tree species (Table 11.1).

Table 11.1. Common aphid species on backyard orchard trees

Tree	Aphid species
Apple	Rosy apple aphid, *Dysaphis plantaginea*
	Apple aphid, *Aphis pomi*
	Woolly apple aphid, *Eriosoma lanigerum*
Cherry	Black cherry aphid, *Myzus cerasi*
Peach and nectarine	Green peach aphid, *Myzus persicae*
Pear	Green peach aphid, *Myzus persicae*
	Melon or cotton aphid, *Aphis gossypii*
	Bean aphid, *Aphis fabae*
Plum and prune	Mealy plum aphid, *Hyalopterus pruni*
	Leaf curl plum aphid, *Brachycaudus helichrysi*
Walnut	Walnut aphid, *Chromaphis juglandicola*
	Dusky-veined aphid, *Callaphis juglandis*

Identification

Aphids are small, soft-bodied, pear-shaped insects with long legs and long antennae. Most species have a pair of tube-like structures called cornicles that project backwards out of the rear of their body. The presence of cornicles distinguishes aphids from all other insects.

Most adult aphids are wingless (Figure 11.7), but in most species adults also occur in winged forms, especially when populations are high or during the spring or fall. Although they may be found singly, aphids usually are found in dense groups on leaves or stems. Unlike leafhoppers or plant bugs, they do not move rapidly when disturbed.

Aphids come in many colors including green, yellow, brown, red, or black, depending on species. Some species have two or more color forms. A few aphids, such as the woolly apple aphid and the mealy plum aphid, have waxy or wooly secretions that cover their body surfaces.

Life Cycle

Aphids reproduce rapidly and have many generations a year. Throughout most of the year, the adult aphid population is made up of adult females that give birth to live offspring (as many as 12 a day) without mating. Immature aphids, called nymphs, pass through four instars (growth stages) before becoming adults. Most of the aphids on fruit trees develop into the sexual form in fall. These males and females mate and lay eggs that survive the winter on twigs and branches. Look carefully with a hand lens during the dormant season to find eggs on buds or bark (Figure 11.8). Aphids usually are most abundant on orchard trees in the spring. Many species migrate to herbaceous plants during the summer and come back in fall to lay their eggs on fruit trees (Figure 11.9).

Damage

Low to moderate numbers of aphids usually are not damaging, but large populations can be a problem. High populations of aphids can produce large quantities of a sticky exudate known as honeydew that covers leaves and fruit and often turns black with the growth of a sooty mold fungus. Some aphid species inject a toxin into leaves that causes them to curl or distort (Figure 11.10). Very high populations of these

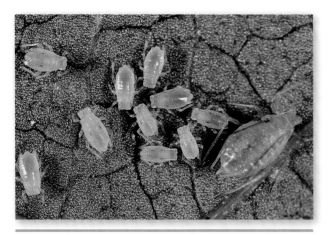

Figure 11.7. This green peach aphid colony contains a wingless adult and several offspring. Photo by Jack Kelly Clark.

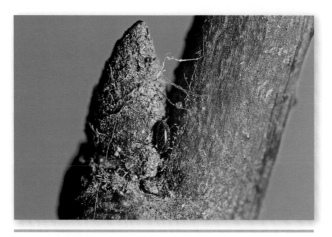

Figure 11.8. Mealy plum aphid egg. Many aphids overwinter in the egg stage on twigs or on bark. Photo by Jack Kelly Clark.

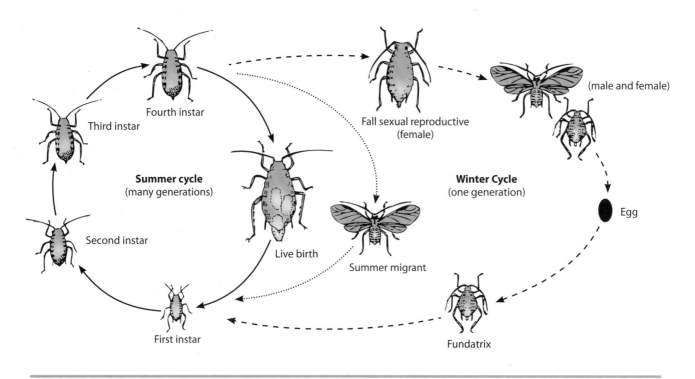

Figure 11.9. General life cycle of aphids.

leaf-feeding aphids may reduce tree vigor and the sugar content of fruit, but they will not kill trees.

Woolly apple aphid infests roots, trunks, limbs, and shoots and produces galls at the site of infestation (Figure 11.11). Root colonies can cause galling so severe that it prevents roots from taking up sufficient water and nutrients. High populations can stunt tree growth or kill young trees.

Management

Because aphids have many natural enemies, insecticide treatments usually are not required for backyard fruit trees. Learn to recognize natural enemies and parasitized aphids (Figure 11.12) and avoid treatments with broad-spectrum insecticides (e.g., organophosphates, carbaryl, or pyrethroids) that will kill these and cause aphid numbers to surge. Common natural enemies include several species of red and black lady beetles (Figure 11.13), syrphid fly larvae (Figure 11.14), lacewing larvae (Figure 11.2), soldier beetles (Figure 11.15), and many species of parasitic wasps. Ants frequently climb up tree trunks to tend aphids and harvest their honeydew for their colonies on the ground. At the same time, ants protect aphids from natural enemies. If you can keep ants out of trees by using sticky barriers or baits and pruning branches where they touch buildings, you will do a lot to enhance the beneficial activities of biological control agents. When using sticky agents on young or sensitive bark, apply it to a trunk wrap rather than directly to avoid damaging the bark.

Aphids thrive on vigorously growing terminals and leaves. Avoid applying more nitrogen than recommended.

An application of supreme or superior type oil will kill a significant number of overwintering eggs if applied as a delayed dormant application just as buds swell and eggs are beginning to hatch in early spring. These sprays probably are not justified for aphid control alone, but they also help control scale insects if these are a problem in the tree. Good coverage of bark and twigs is essential. Delayed dormant sprays of oil will have a minimal negative impact on natural enemies. Sprays later in the season usually are not justified for aphids in backyard fruit trees. Try washing honeydew and sooty mold off the tree with a strong spray of water or a water and soap solution.

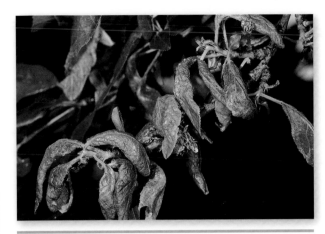

Figure 11.10. Aphids may cause leaves to curl and distort. Photo by Jack Kelly Clark.

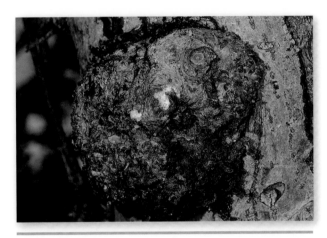

Figure 11.11. This burl at the base of an apple tree was caused by a woolly apple aphid colony. Photo by Jack Kelly Clark.

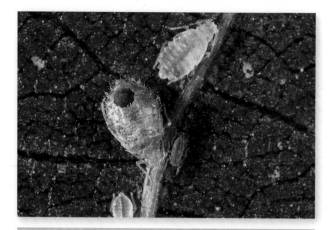

Figure 11.12. The bronze color of this walnut aphid mummy indicates that it has been parasitized by larvae of the parasitic wasp *Trixoys pallidus*. The mature wasps emerge through the round exit hole. A healthy walnut aphid nymph is at top. Photo by Jack Kelly Clark.

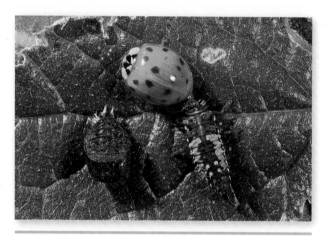

Figure 11.13. The multicolored Asian ladybeetle, shown here in adult, larval, and pupal stages, is a recently introduced predator of aphids. Photo by Jack Kelly Clark.

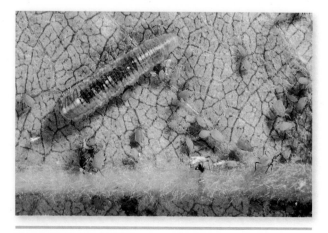

Figure 11.14. Syrphid fly larvae can be important natural enemies of aphids. Photo by Jack Kelly Clark.

Woolly apple aphids are more difficult to manage than leaf-feeding aphids. The parasitic wasp *Aphelinus mali* can completely control populations in aboveground portions of the tree but can't get to root populations. You can also apply insecticides directly to galls on trunks and branches, but root colonies cannot be treated.

Scale Insects

Scale insects can be serious pests on fruit and nut trees when their populations are high. Scales have many natural enemies that in many cases provide adequate control, but these biological control agents can be severely disrupted by broad-spectrum insecticide treatments. Application of insecticidal oils in the dormant or delayed dormant period is usually sufficient to reduce scale populations below damaging levels.

Most scales that cause problems on fruit trees can be divided into two groups: armored scales and soft scales. Armored scales, family Diaspididae, are less than ⅛ inch in diameter and have a flat, plate-like cover. The armored scale cover can usually be removed from the body. Armored scales do not secrete honeydew, but they can cause severe dieback of twigs and limbs and sometimes discoloration of fruit and leaves. The most common armored scale on deciduous fruit and nut trees is the San Jose scale (*Quadraspidiotus perniciosus*) (Figure 11.16).

Mature female soft scales, family Coccidae, are much larger and more rounded and convex than armored scales. Like aphids, they produce large quantities of honeydew when their populations are high. The hard surface of the soft scale is actually its body wall and cannot be removed. Soft scales reduce tree vigor but rarely kill trees or branches. The major problem is honeydew and sooty mold. Common soft scales on fruit trees include black scale (*Saissetia oleae*) and European fruit lecanium (*Parthenolecanium corni*) (Figure 11.17).

Life Cycle

San Jose scale, like most armored scales, has several generations a year, while most of the soft scales require a whole year to complete one life cycle. Eggs of both types of scale are usually hidden under the adult female and hatch into tiny yellow crawlers with legs. Crawlers walk over the plant surface for one or more days and then settle down at permanent feeding sites. Crawlers of armored scales lose their legs and antennae, while immature soft scales retain very tiny legs but rarely move. Once a feeding site has been established, armored scales begin to secrete their hard covers. Soft scale body walls gradually get harder as they grow. Immature scales molt three or four times before becoming adults. Mature females remain immobile and produce eggs under their covers. Male scales, where they exist, are tiny winged insects that superficially resemble parasitic insects. Females of many soft scale species reproduce without mating.

Most soft scales spend the winter as second instar nymphs on twigs and branches, grow rapidly in spring and produce eggs from late May through early July. Eighty percent of San Jose scales spend the winter as first instar nymphs and the rest as adult, mated females. Usually the first San Jose scale eggs hatch in April or May and are followed by three or four more generations before the tree drops its leaves in autumn. The life cycle of a typical armored scale is shown in Figure 11.18.

Damage

Trees that are heavily infested with San Jose scale often look water stressed. Leaves turn yellow and drop, twigs and limbs may die, and bark may crack and produce gum. This scale may also move onto fruit and cause blemishes that look like halos. In contrast, while soft scales may also reduce tree vigor, their most noticeable damage is associated with their production of sticky honeydew, which may coat leaves and fruit and become colonized by black sooty mold. Although unsightly, sooty mold can generally be tolerated on backyard trees. Most soft scales do not move onto fruit.

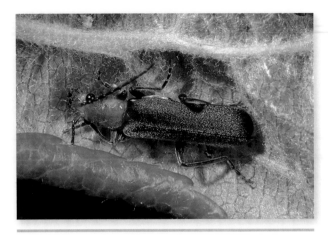

Figure 11.15. Soldier beetles consume large numbers of aphids in many backyards. Photo by Jack Kelly Clark.

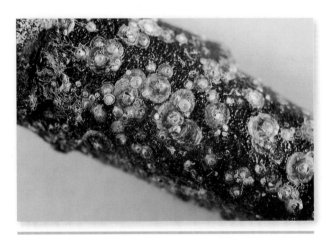

Figure 11.16. San Jose scales are flatter and smaller than soft scales. Photo by Jack Kelly Clark.

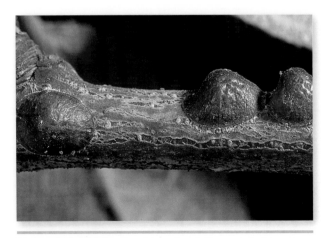

Figure 11.17. Adult females of the soft scale European fruit lecanium. Photo by Jack Kelly Clark.

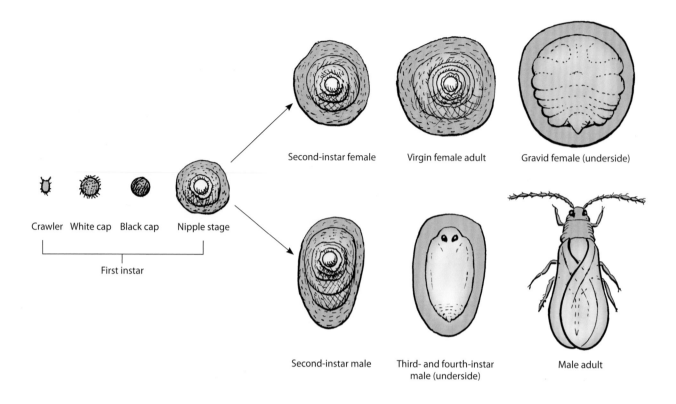

Figure 11.18. Life cycle of a typical armored scale.

Management

Scales have many natural enemies and these beneficial insects often keep populations below damaging levels in backyard trees. Learn to recognize these natural enemies and look for darkening of scales and holes in scale covers that indicate parasite activity. Parasitic wasps in the genera *Aphytis* (Figure 11.19), *Encarsia*, and *Metaphycus* are important control agents, as are several ladybeetle species including the twice stabbed lady beetle *(Chilocorus orbus)*. Lacewings and other general predators may feed on scales as well. Broad-spectrum insecticides such as organophosphates, carbaryl, and pyrethroids will kill them and let scale populations get out of control.

If scale populations are high in spring or summer and little evidence of parasitism is seen, management may be needed the following winter. Also look for evidence of scales when you prune in the winter. Treatment during the growing season in backyard trees is not recommended. A dormant or delayed dormant application of insecticidal oil should provide sufficient control. Never apply oil to water-stressed trees or during fog, rain, or hot or freezing weather.

CODLING MOTH

Codling moth *(Cydia pomonella)* feeds within fruit and nuts and can be a serious pest in apple, pear, quince, and walnut trees. It may also cause occasional damage to plums and other stone fruit. It is one of the most difficult pests to manage in the backyard orchard.

Identification

Adults are small, ½-inch long, mottled gray moths (Figure 11.20). In traps you can distinguish them from other grayish moths that occur on fruit trees by observing a dark brown and coppery band on their wing tips. Eggs are disk-shaped and flattened, about the size of a pinhead, and difficult to see without a hand lens. They are translucent white when first laid and later develop a red ring inside. Just before hatching, the black head of the larva becomes visible. Codling moth caterpillars are white to pink with a mottled brown head and darkened shield on the first segment behind the head. Most caterpillars that are found feeding inside pear or apple fruit are codling moth larvae.

Life Cycle

Codling moth has complete metamorphosis with egg, larva, pupa, and adult stages. Depending on temperatures, there may be two to four generations a year in the orchard.

The pest overwinters as a full-grown larva within a thick, silken cocoon under loose scales or bark, or in soil or debris around the base of the tree. In early spring, the larvae pupate within their cocoons, emerging as moths when temperatures warm up from mid-March to April. Moths are most active in the early evening. During the day they rest on branches and trunks, blending in with the bark. Mating occurs when sunset temperatures exceed 62°F (17°C).

Eggs are deposited singly on fruit, nuts, or nearby leaves. After the eggs hatch, larvae seek out and bore into fruit or developing nuts within hours of hatching. Larvae complete their development within the fruit. When mature, they leave the fruit and drop from the trees to search out pupation sites in the soil, in debris, or in cracks in tree trunks.

Damage

Codling moth larvae bore through the fruit and into the core of apples and pears, leaving brown-colored holes in the fruit that are filled with frass (excrement) (Figure 11.21). Larvae feed on the walnut kernel, leaving it inedible. When plums are attacked, larvae bore all the way to the pit. Fruit or nuts attacked when they are very small will drop off the trees.

Management

Codling moth is difficult to manage because it spends most of its life deep within the fruit or nut, out of the reach of insecticides or natural enemies. It is essential to use an integrated program that takes advantage of the few vulnerable points in the pest's life cycle. In trees with low to moderate numbers, you may be able to keep codling moth populations to tolerable levels by using several nonchemical management methods in combination. It is essential, however, that you implement your program early in the season.

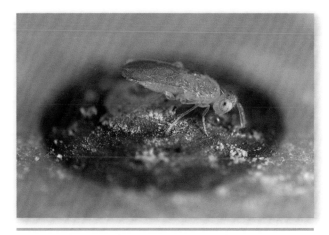

Figure 11.19. Parasites such as this *Aphytis* spp., which is laying its egg in a San Jose scale, often keep scales below damaging levels on unsprayed trees. Photo by Jack Kelly Clark.

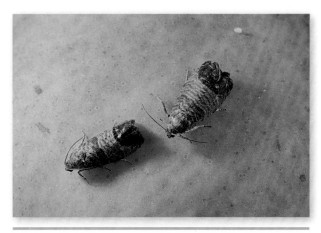

Figure 11.20. The codling moth adult has a bronze band at the tip of its wings. Photo by Jack Kelly Clark.

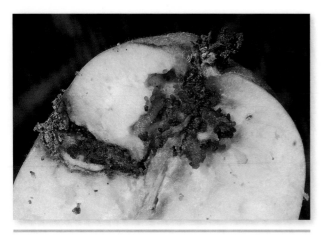

Figure 11.21. Codling moth larvae bore into the center of fruit to feed. Note the excrement, including the frass pushed out of the entry hole. Photo by Jack Kelly Clark.

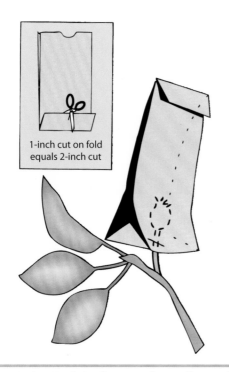

1-inch cut on fold equals 2-inch cut

Figure 11.22. Bagging fruit will protect it from codling moth attack.

Where populations are very high and many infested trees are nearby, it may be necessary to apply insecticides that will rapidly bring populations down to low levels. Insecticides are very difficult to use effectively, though, and most materials that are effective are also very toxic to natural enemies and honey bees. In many backyard situations, the best course of action may be to combine a variety of nonchemical methods such as sanitation, bagging, pheromone traps, and trunk banding. It may take several seasons of diligent practice of these nonchemical methods to reduce codling moth damage to about 10 to 20 percent of the crop every year.

Sanitation

You can reduce overwintering populations of codling moth on your trees if you remove rubbish and loose bark in winter. As soon as small fruit appear on trees, start to keep an eye on them and remove and destroy any infested fruit. Also, rake up and destroy dropped fruit and nuts as soon as they fall—especially in May and June. Many fallen fruit will contain codling moth larvae. If the majority of fruit are infested by midsummer, consider removing and destroying all of the fruit as a way to reduce the next year's codling moth population. These sanitation measures will be most effective in trees that are at least ¼ mile or so away from untreated, infested trees.

Bagging

You can bag apple or pear fruit when they are ½ to 1 inch in diameter to protect them from damage. Use standard paper lunch bags. Cut a 2-inch slit in the bottom of the bag and slip it over the fruit to form a seal around the stem. Staple the open end shut (Figure 11.22). Thin fruit to one per cluster before bagging. You can bag all fruit on a tree or just some of them. Bagging does not affect maturity or quality, but it may result in a loss of color in red varieties. Remove the bag a few days before harvest if you want to allow the fruit to color.

Fruit Thinning

Thinning the fruit load can help control codling moth populations. Thin apples to one apple per cluster (see Chapter 9) to reduce preferred egg-laying sites.

Mass Trapping

Pheromones are chemicals that insects give off to communicate with other individuals of their species. The pheromone that female codling moths use to attract males for mating has been synthesized and is widely used in pest management. In backyard trees you can use this pheromone to lure male moths en masse to sticky traps in an effort to reduce the size of the mating population. In commercial apple, pear, and walnut orchards, pheromone lures are used to inundate the orchard with the female scent, making males unable to find actual females for mating. Although successful in large orchards, this "confusant" approach has not been demonstrated to be useful in single backyard trees.

To mass-trap codling moth males, start hanging traps in mid-March. You can purchase pheromone traps and lures in your nursery or by mail order. Make sure to get traps and lures that are specific to codling moth. The inside of the trap has a sticky coating that traps the moths. Place two to four traps in each large tree and one or two in each small tree, away from the trunk and preferably near the top of every tree. Another strategy is to place traps in non-host trees about 20 to 50 feet away from the apple, pear, or walnut tree, and thus to draw the male moths away from the host trees and reduce their chance of mating before being trapped. Check traps every week or two and remove dead moths. Replace the pheromone lures according to the manufacturer's directions. Mass trapping works best where trees are separated by at least ½ mile from other infested trees, and you can only count on them to control part of the population. Some backyard gardeners have reported success with mass trapping using a solution of 1 cup cider vinegar, ⅓ cup dark molasses, ⅛ teaspoon ammonia, and enough water to make 1½ quarts in a plastic milk jug with a round 2-inch hole cut in the handle. Unlike pheromone traps, this solution catches both male and female moths.

Trunk Banding

One traditional nonchemical method for controlling codling moth is to trap mature larvae in a trunk band made of corrugated cardboard as they seek a refuge for pupation. Use a 2- to 4-inch-wide strip of large-core corrugated cardboard, wrapping it around the trunk so the tubes are vertical and the band is snug. Staple the band to the trunk at least 18 inches from the ground and reinforce it with duct tape. Place bands on trunks and major scaffold limbs after bloom and just before the caterpillars drop from the trees to pupate, generally in early May in the Central Valley and by the end of May along California's coast. Remove the cardboard bands and the pupae they contain before the moths have a chance to emerge, and then burn the bands along with any pupae or caterpillars found underneath them on the trunk. For the overwintering generation, put bands onto the trees in August and destroy them in November or early December. Banding works best on smooth-barked varieties and, even in the best circumstances, will control only a fraction of the codling moths present because many will pupate elsewhere on the tree or on the ground.

Insecticides

Codling moth management with insecticides alone is difficult because they must be applied to kill larvae in the few hours between the time they hatch from eggs and the time they bore into fruit. Once the caterpillar has gone into the fruit or nut, it is protected from pesticides. Unless your insecticide applications are precisely timed, they are unlikely to give satisfactory control. A combination of the nonchemical methods discussed above may be a better approach for many gardeners. Also, most currently available insecticides that are effective for codling moth control in backyard trees are very toxic to natural enemies and honeybees, so they may cause other production problems.

In commercial orchards, growers time insecticide applications by keeping track of daily temperatures and calculating heat unit accumulations, measured in degree-days, that predict the rate of codling moth development. To use degree-day calculations to time applications, you will need a pheromone trap and a way to track daily maximum and minimum temperatures for your backyard. Already this involves more time, effort, and expertise than many gardeners are willing to invest. Details on using degree-days for codling moth management are given in *Integrated Pest Management for Apples and Pears* (UC ANR Publication 3340) and the UC IPM Pest Management Guidelines for apples, pears, or walnuts (online at http://www.ipm.ucdavis.edu).

An alternative way to time sprays is to check fruit two or more times a week for entry holes or stings that indicate that larvae have begun to bore into fruit. Check places where one fruit touches another: this is the most likely entry point. Spray as soon as you see the first sign of damage.

See the Pest Note on Codling Moth (online at http://www.ipm.ucdavis.edu) for specific insecticides suggested for use in the home orchard.

PEACH TWIG BORER

Peach twig borer (*Anarsia lineatella*) larvae bore into the growing shoots and twigs of stone fruit trees in spring. The tips and leaves of young shoots wilt and turn brown (Figure 11.23). Damage to twigs and shoots is the most serious in young trees because it can interfere with the developing shape of the tree. In summer, larvae bore into ripening fruit. Unlike other caterpillars found in fruit, older peach twig borer larvae are chocolate brown with distinct segments (Figure 11.24). Feeding on fruit is usually superficial, less than ⅜ inch deep, distinguishing it from that of oriental fruit moth. Management is not usually needed in backyard trees.

Peach twig borer overwinters in tiny protected cells called hibernacula in limb crotches of two- to three-year-old wood or in pruning wounds or deep cracks in bark (Figure 11.25). Look for hibernacula on your tree in fall and early spring. At about the time blossoms open in spring, the larvae emerge from their hibernacula and migrate up the branches to feed on flower buds and shoots. They bore into shoots and then emerge to pupate, and the first generation of adults may begin flying between March and May to lay their eggs on shoots, leaves, or fruit. It is the larvae that hatch out of these eggs that are the first generation to damage fruit. There are three to four generations a year.

Low levels of peach twig borer can be tolerated in the home orchard. Various predators such as lacewing larvae, minute pirate bugs, assassin bugs and spiders feed on larvae before they bore into shoots or fruit. The gray ant can be an important natural enemy in some locations. Several wasps parasitize high percentages of peach twig borer in untreated trees in some areas, providing good biological control.

A traditional treatment for peach twig borer has been an application of oil and an insecticide (usually an organophosphate, carbaryl, or a pyrethroid) during the dormant season. Oil sprays alone will not be effective. These sprays can disrupt natural enemies of many pests, though, and their drawbacks probably outweigh their benefits in most backyard situations. If you feel a spray is necessary, consider two applications of *Bacillus thuringiensis*, a microbial insecticide that will not disrupt biological control, just as trees are beginning to bloom. The first should be applied when larvae start emerging from hibernacula after popcorn bud stage (examine hibernacula to see if about 20 to 40 percent of larvae have left their shelters). The second should be applied 7 to 10 days later. Good coverage of all buds and surfaces is necessary for good control. Since *Bacillus thuringiensis* needs to be ingested if it is to be effective, it is important to make the application when two to three days of warm, dry weather are forecast so the larvae will be actively feeding.

ORIENTAL FRUIT MOTH

Oriental fruit moth (*Grapholita molesta*) may cause shoot and fruit damage on peach, nectarine, and almond trees. Damage to shoots is similar to that caused by peach twig borer. On fruit, oriental fruit moth caterpillars bore right into the center of green and ripening fruit and feed around the pit, causing fruit damage (Figure 11.26) unlike the superficial sort caused by peach twig borer.

Oriental fruit moths spend the winter as prepupae inside cocoons that they spin in protected areas on the tree or on the ground. First-generation moths emerge in February or March and lay eggs singly on the undersides of leaves near shoot tips. The larva is white with a black head. First-generation larvae bore into shoots causing damage similar to that caused by peach twig borer. If you open up damaged shoots and find larvae, you can distinguish the two species because older larvae of the oriental fruit moth do not have darker body segments like those of the peach twig borer. When mature, the larvae leave shoots to pupate under bark or on the ground, from which they later emerge as adults. The next generation of larvae hatches in May and attacks fruit. There may be up to five or six generations a year.

You should try to tolerate oriental fruit moth in backyard trees to the extent possible. Management with insecticides can disrupt populations of other pests' natural enemies. Dormant treatments with oils or insecticides do not control this pest. To be effective, an insecticide must be applied in spring just as the eggs hatch and before the larvae bore into shoots or fruit. More details on effective treatment timing for commercial orchards are available in *Integrated Pest Management for Stone Fruits* (UC ANR Publication 3389) or the UC IPM Pest Management Guidelines for peach or nectarine (online at http://www.ipm.ucdavis.edu).

Many commercial growers are using pheromone dispensers to manage oriental fruit moth. These dispensers, which disperse female sex lure to confuse male moths in the orchard so they can't mate, are hung out in trees in late February before the first moths appear. These have not been tested in backyard situations and are unlikely to be effective where only a few trees are grown. Pheromones have no known negative impact on natural enemies or the environment.

LEAFROLLERS AND OTHER LEAF-FEEDING CATERPILLARS

A number of leaf-feeding caterpillars may be found in backyard fruit trees from time to time (Table 11.2). The most serious pests are several leafroller species (Figure 11.27) and green fruitworms (Figure 11.28) that may also feed on the surface of fruit. Caterpillars that limit their feeding to leaves are unlikely to cause significant damage to the harvested crop in backyard trees. The colorful larvae of western tussock moth (Figure 11.29) occasionally cause damage to fruit in coastal areas. Treatment is not normally needed.

Because they feed on exposed or semi-exposed leaves or within curled leaves, these caterpillars are both much more vulnerable to natural enemies and easier to control

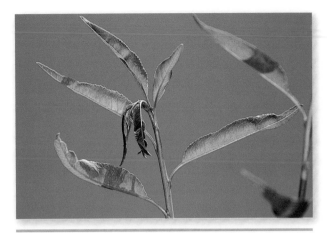

Figure 11.23. Peach twig borers bore into young terminal shoots, causing them to wilt and die. Photo by Jack Kelly Clark.

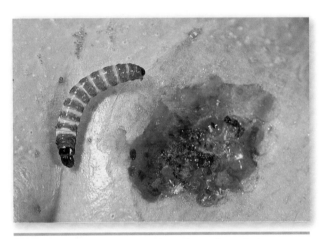

Figure 11.24. Older peach twig borer larvae have distinct darkened segments. They mostly do surface feeding on fruit as shown here. Photo by Jack Kelly Clark.

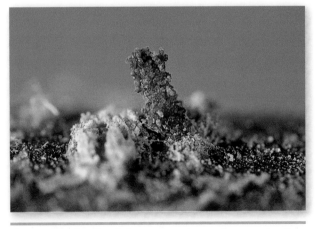

Figure 11.25. Peach twig borers overwinter as larvae on trunks in tiny cells called hibernacula. You can try to find these in winter by looking for the frass that comes out of them. The hibernacula are very difficult to see. Photo by Jack Kelly Clark.

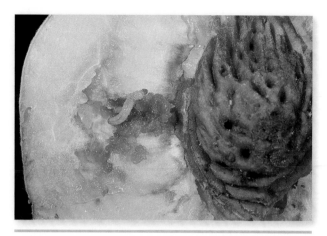

Figure 11.26. Oriental fruit moth larvae bore into fruit and feed near the pit. They lack the dark segments of peach twig borer. Photo by Jack Kelly Clark.

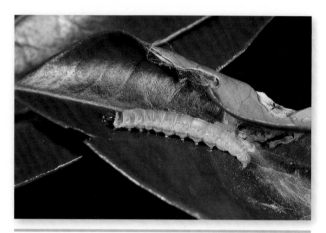

Figure 11.27. This fruittree leafroller larva has been removed from the webbed leafroll at right. Photo by Jack Kelly Clark.

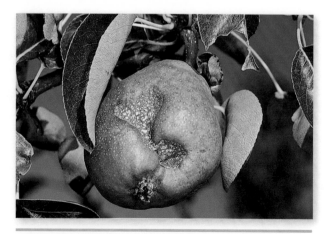

Figure 11.28. Green fruitworms caused this damage early in the season. It later scabbed over and distorted the fruit. Adjacent leaves have also been chewed on. Photo by Jack Kelly Clark.

with insecticide sprays than caterpillars that feed within fruit. General predators such as assassin bugs, lacewings, spiders, and minute pirate bugs may feed on their eggs and larvae. For each species, there usually are several parasitic wasps or flies that can attack and kill them. Preservation of these natural enemy populations by avoiding broadly toxic insecticide sprays is an important part of an IPM program.

Sanitation can be important for reducing leafroller populations. Remove webbed leaves and egg masses as soon as you see them in the spring. Remove trash, mummy fruit, and debris around trees in the fall and winter to eliminate the overwintering pupae of some species.

Dormant oil treatments for scale insects or aphids will kill the eggs of a few of these species, such as fruittree leafroller, that overwinter in the egg stage on branches and twigs. If treatment is needed during the season, *Bacillus thuringiensis* or spinosad sprays are recommended, applied just as eggs hatch. These sprays will have minimal impact on natural enemy species. Young caterpillars must consume treated surfaces within a day of application, so proper timing is essential to success. More-broadly toxic insecticides usually are not warranted in backyard trees and are not recommended because they may cause outbreaks of aphids, scales, and caterpillar pests.

Walnut Husk Fly

The walnut husk fly (*Rhagoletis completa*) is a common pest wherever walnuts are grown. Its larval stages feed inside the husk, turning it black and gooey and staining the walnut shell. The damage is mostly cosmetic, so treatment is generally not required in the home orchard.

Walnut husk flies spend the winter as pupae in the soil and emerge as adults (Figure 11.30) in early to mid-summer, usually between mid-July and mid-August. Female flies lay eggs in groups below the surface of the developing walnut husks, leaving stinglike marks. The stings darken and eggs hatch into white maggots within five days. The maggots (Figure 11.31) feed inside the husk, enlarging the black area, which remains soft, unsunken, and smooth (Figure 11.32). Although the husk surface stays intact, the fleshy parts below decay and stain the nutshell. The kernel within usually is not affected. Maggots mature

Table 11.2. Some common leaf-feeding caterpillars in fruit and nut trees

Common Name	Scientific Name	Common Hosts	Comments
Fall webworm	*Hyphantria cunea*	Plum, prune, walnut, many ornamental deciduous trees	Hairy larvae feed inside silken tents that enlarge to cover. Prune out.
Fruittree leafroller	*Archips argyrospila*	Apple, almond, pear, stone fruit, walnut	Overwinters as an egg, so dormant oils may reduce its numbers.
Green fruitworms	Several species including *Orthosia hibisci* (speckled green fruitworm), *Amphipyra pyramidoides* (humped green fruitworm), and *Xylomyges curialis* (citrus cutworm)	Apple, pear, cherry, apricot, plum, prune	May damage fruit, chewing out small bites on surface.
Obliquebanded leafroller	*Choristoneura rosaceana*	Apple, pear, stone fruit	Causes surface scars to fruit; larvae green with black or light-colored heads.
Omnivorous leafroller	*Platynota stultana*	Most fruit trees	Larvae are light colored with brown or black head.
Orange tortrix	*Argyrotaenia citrana*	Stone fruit, apple	Mostly a coastal pest in California
Redhumped caterpillar	*Schizura concinna*	Most fruit trees, especially plum, prune, and walnut	Mature caterpillars are brightly colored with yellow, black, white, and red markings.
Tent caterpillars	*Malacosoma* spp.	Stone fruit, apple, and pear	Larvae build large webbed nests or mats but feed outside. Prune out.
Western tussock moth	*Orgyia vetusta*	Apple, cherry, apricot, walnut, and other fruit	Most common on California's coast. Colorful caterpillars with prominent tufts of hair.

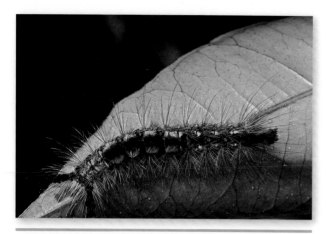

Figure 11.29. Western tussock moth larvae have long hairs and colorful markings. Photo by Jack Kelly Clark.

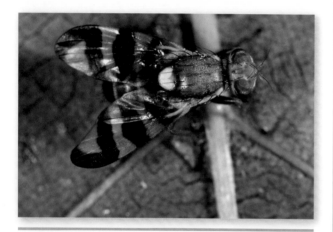

Figure 11.30. The adult walnut husk fly has colorful, striped wings, and is about the size of a house fly. Photo by Jack Kelly Clark.

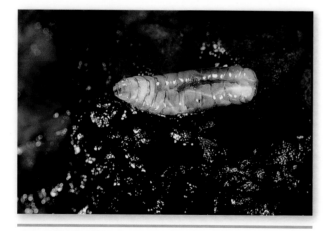

Figure 11.31. Walnut husk fly larvae are maggots that feed under the husk surface. Photo by Jack Kelly Clark.

after about three to five weeks and pupate in the soil. There is only one generation a year.

Sprays are not generally suggested for managing walnut husk fly on backyard walnut trees. You can reduce the number of husk flies overwintering near your tree or orchard by removing and disposing of damaged nuts as soon as possible, before the maggots emerge to pupate. Also, a tarp placed under the tree from July through August may prevent maggots from entering the soil to pupate.

Husk fly damage can make it difficult to remove the husks from nuts. You can remedy this by placing the nuts in a damp burlap bag for a few days before attempting to remove the husks. Be sure to dispose of infested husks in a tightly sealed bag.

Commercial walnut growers apply insecticide-laden baits to control high husk fly populations. Timing of application is critical but difficult. Proper timing requires that you trap and dissect female flies. For details on this method, see the third edition of Integrated Pest Management for Walnuts (UC ANR Publication 3270) or the UC IPM Pest Management Guidelines for walnuts (online at http://www.ipm.ucdavis.edu).

SPIDER MITES

Spider mites may become abundant in fruit trees under hot, dusty conditions, especially when their natural enemies have been knocked out by insecticide treatments applied for other pests. Spider mites feed on the undersides of leaves, destroying chlorophyll and causing a pale stippling of leaves. When spider mite numbers are high, their webbing is easily visible on leaves (Figure 11.33).

The two common spider mites in California, two-spotted spider mite (*Tetranychus urticae*) (Figure 11.34) and Pacific spider mite (*Tetranychus pacificus*), are almost impossible to tell apart; however, biology and management of the two species are the same. They are tiny, about 0.5 mm long when full grown, and they look like pale, moving dots on leaves. Under the hand lens, you can see that they are yellowish with red eyes and a large dark spot on each side. Spider mites overwinter as mature females, which are reddish orange and lack distinct dark spots, in protected places on the trunk and on the ground. Once the trees leaf out, the female lays spherical translucent eggs on the leaves.

Eggs hatch into tiny mites that rapidly mature and reproduce. There are many generations in a year when the weather is warm.

Spider mites have many natural enemies that regularly limit their numbers. Among the most important are the western predatory mite *(Galendromus occidentalis)* (Figure 11.34), the six-spotted thrips *(Scolothrips sexmaculatus)*, the larvae of certain flies such as the cecidomyid *Feltiella acarivora*, the spider mite destroyer lady beetle *(Stethorus picipes)*, and various general predators such as minute pirate bugs, bigeyed bugs, and lacewing larvae. Commercial fruit and nut growers sometimes purchase and release predatory mites in order to re-establish populations in their orchards, but most backyard situations already have adequate numbers of natural enemies if they have not been destroyed by dust or pesticides.

Spider mites are rarely a problem in backyard trees that have been kept adequately irrigated, dust-free, and free from broadly toxic insecticides. If problems do occur, re-evaluate your irrigation program and pesticide application program to make sure your actions are not the cause of the problems. Sometimes regular, forceful spraying of plants with water will adequately reduce spider mite numbers on smaller trees. If insecticide treatments are required, use insecticidal oils or soap sprays. These are more compatible with natural enemies than other types of materials. Don't use oils and soaps on water-stressed trees or when temperatures are above 90°F (32.2°C) or within 30 days of a sulfur spray.

Borers

Several species of boring insects can cause damage on fruit and nut trees. This is a diverse collection of insects grouped together because of a common behavior: they tunnel into tree bark and wood. Borers cause more of a problem if the tree is newly planted or if it has suffered damage from other pests or poor cultural practices. Sometimes you can nurse a tree along with improved irrigation and cultural practices, but often the best solution is to remove the damaged limb or tree entirely. Except for the peachtree borer, insecticide applications are not generally recommended for borer control.

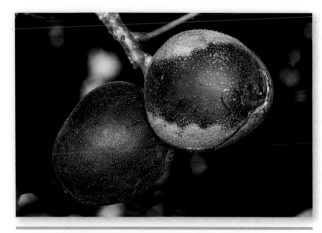

Figure 11.32. Walnut husk fly maggots feed within the husk, causing dark spots that expand over time. Photo by Jack Kelly Clark.

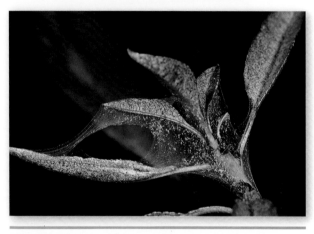

Figure 11.33. Trees with heavy infestations of spider mites may have yellowish stippling and webbing on their leaves. Photo by Jack Kelly Clark.

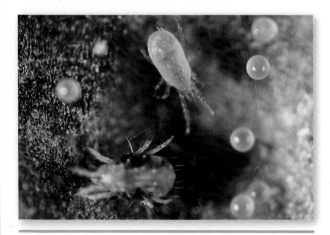

Figure 11.34. The two-spotted spider mite is at the bottom of this photo and the clear-bodied western predatory mite is at top. The eggs shown here are spider mite eggs. Photo by Jack Kelly Clark.

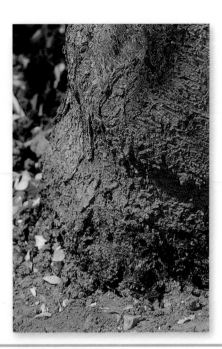

Figure 11.35. The orange, sawdust-like excrement and gumming at the base of this trunk indicate damage by peachtree borer larvae. Photo by Jack Kelly Clark.

Borers are a common problem on young trees that have been sunburned. Protect young trees by whitewashing their trunks with white latex paint from 1 inch below ground level to at least 2 feet above (see Chapter 4). You can also use tree protectors wrapped around the trunk.

Peachtree Borer *(Synanthedon exitiosa)*

The peachtree borer attacks the crown or trunk of stone fruit trees or peach rootstocks on almond trees. The adult is a steel-bluish black moth with clear wings that emerges in late spring and early summer. Female moths lay their eggs during the summer on bark at the base of tree trunks. Hatching larvae tunnel into the tree just at or above ground level, leaving piles of sawdust-like excrement at their burrow entrances (Figure 11.35). The larvae remain inside the tree, feeding and tunneling until the following spring when they leave the tree to pupate on the trunk or in the soil beneath. Peachtree borers can girdle and kill healthy young trees. Older trees are sometimes attacked but they usually tolerate the damage unless borer populations are very high.

It may be possible to control peachtree borer larvae with applications of an insect parasitic nematode, *Steinernema carpocapsae*, if applied directly and deeply into the burrows when larvae are actively feeding in mid- to late summer. See the Pest Note on Clearwing Moth (online at http://www.ipm.ucdavis.edu) for details on using this biological control agent. Insecticide sprays to the trunk to control peachtree borer adults before they lay eggs in early summer can also be used, but application timing can be difficult and you need to choose a persistent material such as a pyrethroid, and it must be labeled for trunk treatments.

Shothole Borer *(Scolytus rugulosus)*

The shothole borer is a pest of many fruit and nut trees, including stone fruit, apple, pear, and almond. It is primarily a pest of trees that have already been weakened by root disease, insufficient irrigation, sunburn, or other maladies. Adults are tiny black beetles, about $\frac{1}{10}$ inch long. Adult females bore small holes in the tree's bark and lay their eggs along a gallery that is 1 to 2 inches long. Hatching larvae feed beneath the bark. Healthy trees exude resin that usually kills shothole borers before they can do much damage, but weakened trees cannot protect themselves. Infested trees are characterized by groups of small shot holes left in branches or trunks after adult beetles emerge (Figure 11.36). Shothole borers can have two to three generations a year.

The key to preventing damage from shothole borers is to keep trees healthy and vigorous. If borers successfully invade, it usually is an indication that the tree has other serious problems. If shothole borers occur in only one limb or scaffold branch, prune it out. If the whole tree is weakened, remove the tree. Burn all infested wood or at the very least remove it from the backyard area. Insecticides are not recommended.

Pacific Flatheaded Borer *(Chrysoborthris mali)*

The adult Pacific flatheaded borer is a large (about ½-inch-long) beetle with a bronze cast. Females lay their eggs on injured areas on tree trunks or limbs. Flatheaded borer larvae have a distinctive flattened enlargement just behind the head and they are large—they may grow up to ¾ inch long (Figure 11.37). Larvae feed under the bark in the rapidly growing outer wood and then bore deeper to pupate.

Prevention is the main way to manage flatheaded borers. Prevent sunburn on young trees with latex paint or trunk wraps. When you prune, leave a few extra twigs to shade the newly exposed limbs beneath. Supply adequate water and fertilizer. Prune out and destroy infested wood. Insecticide sprays are not recommended for this pest.

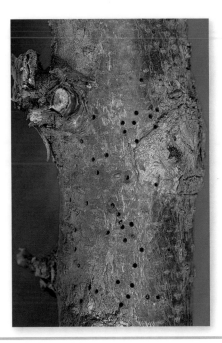

Figure 11.36. These tiny holes are emergence holes of the shothole borer. Photo by Jack Kelly Clark.

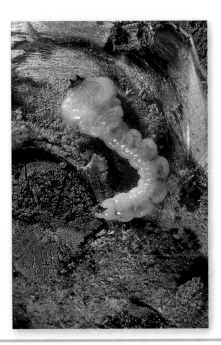

Figure 11.37. The Pacific flatheaded borer larva is large, with an enlarged area behind its head. Photo by Jack Kelly Clark.

OTHER INSECTS

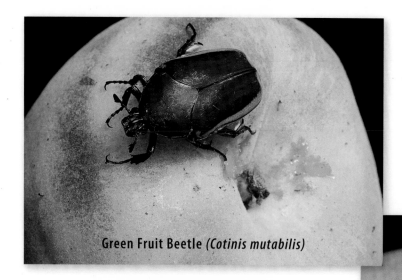

Green Fruit Beetle *(Cotinis mutabilis)*

Figure 11.38. The green fruit beetle, *Cotinis mutabilis*, is a large (1.25-inch-long), metallic green beetle that attacks maturing soft fruit. Its larvae develop in decaying organic material in the soil or partially decomposed compost or manure. To manage it, remove manure piles and other larval food sources and turn the compost regularly. Photo by Jack Kelly Clark.

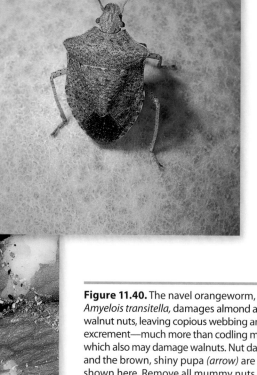

Consperse Stink Bug
(Euschistus conspersus)

Figure 11.39. The consperse stink bug, *Euschistus conspersus*, sucks juices from stone fruits, apples, or pears, often leaving blemishes and excrement that later develop into depressed areas or distortions. Several other stink bug species may cause similar damage, but a few stink bugs are predaceous and beneficial. Other plant bugs such as the lygus bug *(Lygus hesperus)* and *Calocoris norvegicus*, also cause blemishes, gum, cracks, and distortion. Management of weedy areas around the orchard in early spring before plant bug populations build up may help reduce their numbers in trees later in the season. Photo by Jack Kelly Clark.

Navel Orangeworm *(Amyelois transitella)*

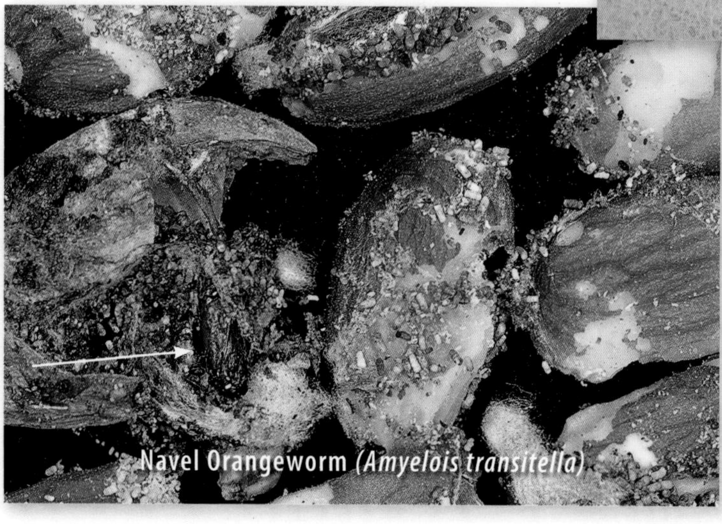

Figure 11.40. The navel orangeworm, *Amyelois transitella*, damages almond and walnut nuts, leaving copious webbing and excrement—much more than codling moth, which also may damage walnuts. Nut damage and the brown, shiny pupa *(arrow)* are shown here. Remove all mummy nuts from trees after harvest in order to keep navel orangeworm at tolerable levels. Photo by Jack Kelly Clark.

Common Diseases in Backyard Orchards

POWDERY MILDEW

Powdery mildew infections are characterized by the white powdery growth that may cover leaves, flowers and or fruit. Many fruit trees are attacked by powdery mildew fungi. Several species of fungi are involved. Common species causing problems on fruit trees are listed in Table 11.3.

Identification and Damage

The powdery mycelial and spore growth that forms on both sides of leaves (Figure 11.41) and sometimes on flowers, fruit and shoots makes powdery mildew easy to recognize. Under a hand lens, powdery mildew spores can be seen growing in chains on the tips of fungal strands. Powdery mildew may cause new growth to be dwarfed or distorted. Weblike russet scars may develop on fruit, leaving a rough, corky skin (Figure 11.42).

Life Cycle

Powdery mildew fungi survive from one season to the next in infected buds or as fruiting bodies called cleistothecia (Figure 11.43). Once tree growth begins in the spring, the fungus grows as thin layers of mycelia over the plant surface. The fungus produces spores that are blown by wind to new hosts. High humidity, moderate temperatures, and shady conditions are generally most favorable for powdery mildew development. Water is not required for, and may even inhibit, spore germination of some powdery mildew species.

Management

Prevention is the first step in any management program for powdery mildew. Avoid planting the most susceptible fruit tree varieties (Table 11.4) and follow good cultural practices. That will be enough to control the disease adequately in many situations. Among the fruit trees, fungicide applications are most often needed on susceptible varieties of apple.

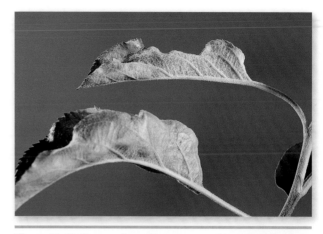

Figure 11.41. The powdery white spores on the underside of these apple leaves are indicative of a powdery mildew. Photo by Jack Kelly Clark.

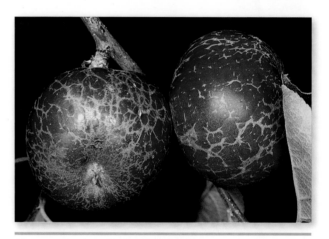

Figure 11.42. Fruit that have been damaged by powdery mildew may develop webs of russet scars. Photo by Jack Kelly Clark.

Table 11.3. Host plants and control measures for powdery mildew species

Hosts	Fungus species	Controls
Apple, nectarine, peach	*Podosphaera leucotricha*	Tolerant varieties; prune out infections in apple trees during dormant season; fungicides if necessary.
Cherry	*Podosphaera clandestina*	Fungicides if necessary.
Apricot, plum, prune	*Podosphaera tridactyla*	Tolerant varieties; fungicides if necessary.
Apricot, nectarine, peach, plum	*Sphaerotheca pannosa*	Fungicides if necessary; remove or treat roses.

Table 11.4. Susceptibility of fruit varieties to powdery mildew

Fruit	Most susceptible	Moderately susceptible	Least susceptible
Apple	Gravenstein Jonathan Rome Beauty Yellow Newtown	Braeburn Golden Delicious Granny Smith Jonagold McIntosh	Red Delicious Stayman Winesap
Cherry	Bing Black Tartarian Rainier		
Nectarine	Most varieties are susceptible.		
Peach	Elegant Lady Fairtime Fay Elberta Summerset		Freestone varieties such as Flame Crest, Flavor Crest, O'Henry
Plum	Black Beaut Gaviota Kelsey Wickson		

Where possible, choose resistant varieties that meet your growing requirements and personal preferences. Fungicide applications may be necessary when you plant more-susceptible varieties. Examples of the most and least susceptible varieties are listed in Table 11.4. Check with your nursery operator about the disease resistance of new varieties when you purchase trees.

Cultural Practices

High temperatures and low humidity provide the best protection against powdery mildew. Plant trees in sunny locations, provide for good air circulation, and avoid excess fertilization. You can wash spores from trees using a hose or sprinkler, but if you do so, avoid causing any sustained rise in humidity, especially at night. On dormant apple trees, infected terminal shoots are stunted and have a bleached appearance. These infected shoots should be removed during winter.

One of the common fungi causing powdery mildew in apricot, peach, nectarine, and plum overwinters on infected roses. The simple removal of rose bushes that are infected with powdery mildew may be all that is needed to manage the problem on these trees in a backyard situation, especially for apricots and plums since the fungus is not known to overwinter on these fruit trees. Powdery mildew spores are, however, known to blow in from neighboring infected roses.

Fungicide Applications

Spraying is not generally necessary in many backyard situations. If you have had serious powdery mildew damage in past years, however, a fungicide application may be advisable. Make applications at two-week intervals beginning when buds just start to open (green tip stage) in early spring and continue until small green fruit are present. Various products are available, including wettable sulfurs, horticultural oils, potassium bicarbonate, and synthetic fungicides. Never use sulfur on an apricot tree and do not apply sulfur within two weeks of an oil spray on any fruit tree. Oils and sulfurs should not be applied when temperatures are above 90°F (32.2°C) or on water-stressed trees. See the Pest Note on Powdery Mildew on Fruits and Berries (online at http://www.ipm.ucdavis.edu) for more information on fungicides.

Peach Leaf Curl

The distorted, reddened foliage typical of a peach leaf curl infection on peach or nectarine trees is an all-too-familiar sight for many backyard orchardists (Figure 11.44). The fungus that causes peach leaf curl, *Taphrina deformans,* is especially active during unusually wet springs, but it can generally be satisfactorily managed with a dormant spray of fungicide in winter. Only peaches and nectarines are affected by this disease.

Identification and Damage

Leaf curl symptoms become apparent in spring about two weeks after leaves emerge from buds. Damage first appears as reddish areas on leaves that rapidly become thick and puckered. Whitish spores develop on affected leaf surfaces. Leaves later turn yellow or brown and may either remain on the tree or fall off. Fallen leaves are usually replaced by new healthy ones, unless wet weather intervenes to foster a second infection. The loss of leaves can take a toll on trees, decreasing tree growth and fruit production. Leaf loss may also lead to sunburn on branches, opening them up to borer attack. Twigs and shoots may be infected and become thickened, stunted, and distorted, and die back. Wrinkled, reddish, warty areas occasionally develop on fruit. If a leaf curl infection builds up on a tree and is left uncontrolled for several years, the tree may decline and may have to be removed.

Life Cycle

The fungus overwinters as spores on the surface of twigs and buds (Figure 11.45). When the buds begin to grow in spring, the spores grow into the developing tissue. The fungus grows between cells just under the leaf, fruit, or shoot surface, causing abnormal cell growth in young plant tissue that results in the characteristic distortion. As the infection progresses, the fungus breaks through the leaf surface, producing a fuzzy gray layer of fruiting bodies called asci, each of which contains ascospores. The ascospores are released into the air and carried to new tissues to produce spores that can infect right away if moist conditions and young tissue are available, or if conditions are not favorable they may remain inactive until the following

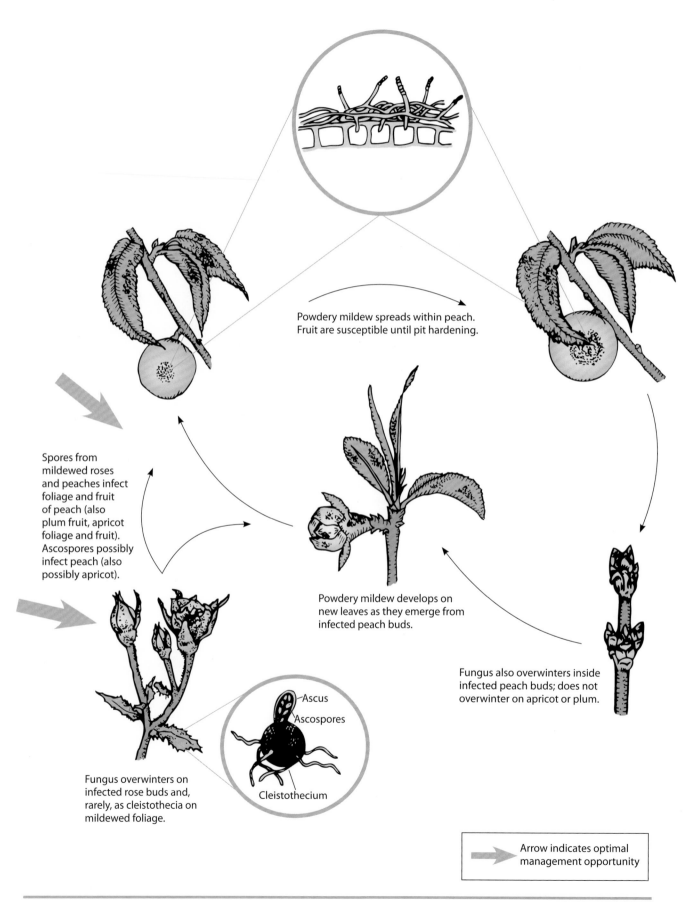

Powdery mildew spreads within peach. Fruit are susceptible until pit hardening.

Spores from mildewed roses and peaches infect foliage and fruit of peach (also plum fruit, apricot foliage and fruit). Ascospores possibly infect peach (also possibly apricot).

Powdery mildew develops on new leaves as they emerge from infected peach buds.

Fungus also overwinters inside infected peach buds; does not overwinter on apricot or plum.

Ascus

Ascospores

Cleistothecium

Fungus overwinters on infected rose buds and, rarely, as cleistothecia on mildewed foliage.

Arrow indicates optimal management opportunity

Figure 11.43. Powdery mildew life cycle diagram.

spring. Only young leaf, fruit, and shoot tissues are susceptible, so the disease becomes less severe as leaves mature. Also cooler (below 80° to 85°F [27° to 30°C]), wet or humid weather is required for spores to germinate, so new infections cease in late spring.

Management

The key to preventing leaf curl infections is to make an annual application of fungicide during the dormant season. There is little you can do during spring when the distorted red leaves are obvious on the tree. Some people remove diseased leaves or prune infected shoots, but this has not been shown to reduce the disease. Diseased leaves will normally fall off on their own. It is also important that you prevent water from sprinkler irrigation from spraying onto the tree. This moisture can enable the disease to continue until temperatures increase in spring.

Make dormant treatments after leaves have fallen off trees, in December or early January. Usually a single treatment will be enough, but in areas of high spring rainfall or where the disease was severe the previous spring it may be advisable to spray a second time just before buds begin to swell. Fixed copper or copper-based fungicides such as Bordeaux mixture, tri-basic copper sulfate, or metallic copper provide good control. Synthetic materials are also effective. Lime-sulfur (calcium polysulfide) can also be used instead of copper. Thorough spray coverage is essential to getting the fungicide to move into all of the buds.

BROWN ROT

Brown rot is probably the most common cause of fruit rot in stone fruit trees. Flowers also are susceptible, but the damage to flowers and shoots usually is minimal except in a year with a very wet spring. When conditions are favorable to the disease, you can lose an entire crop. Fruit may appear healthy when you harvest it, but then develop brown rot shortly after in storage. Susceptibility varies among stone fruit species and their varieties. Generally, plum is least susceptible, and the early ripening varieties of peach and nectarine generally have little trouble with brown rot.

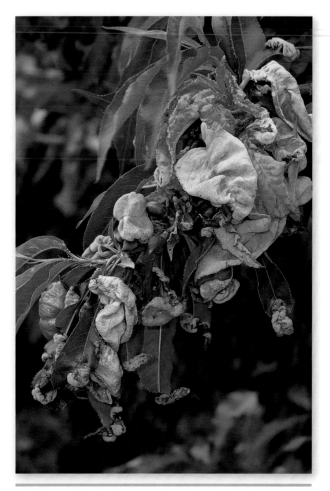

Figure 11.44. Puckered and thickened areas on leaves are typical of a peach leaf curl infection. Photo by Jack Kelly Clark.

Identification and Damage

Two fungi, *Monilinia fructicola* and *M. laxa*, cause brown rot. The two cause similar symptoms but differ in their life cycles. *Monilinia fructicola* is most common on peach and nectarine, *M. laxa* is most common on almond, and both are found on apricot, cherry, and prune. Except for a few varieties, plum trees seldom have brown rot. In spring, the pathogen invades the stigma and stamens of open flowers, causing blossoms to wither, turn brown, and stick to the tree. An amber-colored gum usually is present near the base of the dead flower. If the infection extends into the shoot, the portion of

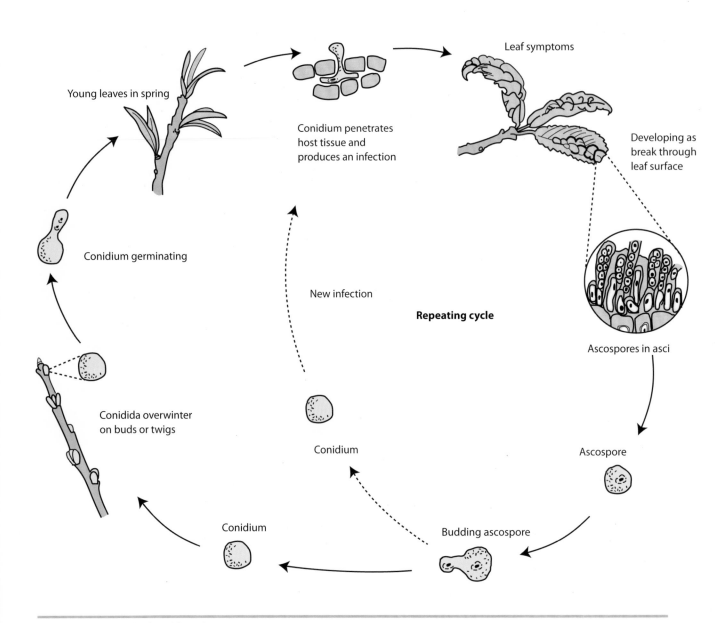

Young leaves in spring

Conidium penetrates
host tissue and
produces an infection

Leaf symptoms

Developing as
break through
leaf surface

Conidium germinating

New infection

Repeating cycle

Ascospores in asci

Conidida overwinter
on buds or twigs

Conidium

Ascospore

Conidium

Budding ascospore

Figure 11.45. Peach leaf curl life cycle.

the shoot above the dead flower may die with wilted dead leaves still attached. In humid or wet weather, the fungus produces visible tan tufts of spores (spore pads) on the dead flowers (Figure 11.46). As fruit ripen in summer, light brown areas of rot appear on the fruit and are followed by more powdery, tan spores over the rotted area (Figure 11.47).

Brown rot and bacterial blast infections are sometimes difficult to distinguish from one another. Shoots and spurs killed by brown rot generally are brown and always have an infected flower present, and spore pads can be found. In contrast, bacterial blast infections are black and do not extend very far into the shoot. Bacterial blast never has spores associated with it.

Life Cycle

Both types of brown rot fungus produce spores on dead flowers or twigs in spring that are carried by wind currents to other flowers or, later, to fruit. In summer, especially when there are rains or dews that moisten the fruit surface, the spores germinate and penetrate the fruit. Some rotten fruit fall from the tree and decay on the ground. Others remain attached to the tree and slowly shrivel into wrinkled, black and tan structures called mummies (Figure 11.48). The mummy is composed of both fungal and plant tissues and is a survival structure for the fungus. During winter rains, the wet mummies become heavy and fall from the tree. Mummies on the ground resulting from infection by *M. fructicola* produce small cup-shaped structures called apothecia. Sexual spores, called ascospores, are produced in the apothecia and released into the air at the same time that trees begin to bloom, beginning the disease cycle again. Both fungi produce vegetative spores on the infected flowers, fruit, and mummies, but only *M. fructicola* is known to produce apothecia and ascospores.

Management

Most backyard trees do not need protection from blossom blight. This is especially true of peach and nectarine trees. If you find infected blossoms, prune them out of the tree to help reduce potential inoculum that will infect the fruit later on. More importantly, remove and destroy all infected fruit from the tree

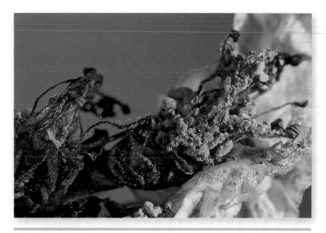

Figure 11.46. Brown rot-infected flower, showing sporulation. Photo by Jack Kelly Clark.

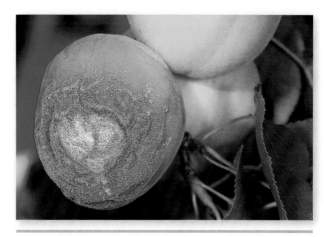

Figure 11.47. Circular brown rot lesions on ripe fruit. Photo by Jack Kelly Clark.

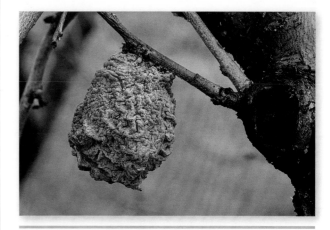

Figure 11.48. Mummies on the tree provide overwintering spots for the disease. Photo by Jack Kelly Clark.

and ground at the end of summer. While pruning out infected flowers and removing infected fruit will not eliminate brown rot, it may help reduce losses from the disease. Avoid overfertilization, since excess nitrogen makes flowers and fruit more susceptible. Any injury to the ripening fruit, such as insect feeding wounds or fruit split, increases the chances for brown rot infection. Harvesting fruit when they are mature but before they are completely ripe also will help reduce the amount of brown rot.

Fire Blight

Fire blight is most serious on pears, but may also damage apple, quince, and loquat trees as well as a few ornamentals, especially pyracantha. The disease gets its name from the characteristic blackening and shriveling of affected shoots, flowers, and young fruit, which truly do look like they have been singed by fire (Figure 11.49). The causal agent is the bacterium *Erwinia amylovora.*

Identification and Damage

The first evidence of a fire blight infection usually is a watery, tan bacterial ooze that begins to seep out of branch, twig, or trunk cankers as soon as tree growth resumes in spring. The ooze turns dark, leaving dark streaks on bark. Cankers and ooze may be inconspicuous, though, and many people may not notice an infection until several weeks later when flowers or shoots begin to shrivel and blacken. The disease spreads from blossoms into wood and the newly infected wood may show pink, orange, or red streaks. Young branches infected with fire blight quickly develop dry, brown leaves and their terminals often wilt over into a shepherd's crook shape (Figure 11.50). Cankers (dead areas) form on the bark of older branches and trunks and may girdle, disfigure, and even kill entire branches or even entire trees of highly susceptible hosts.

Life Cycle

The fire blight bacteria spend the winter in cankers that developed on trunks or branches in previous years' infections. When the tree begins growing in spring and moisture and temperature are adequate, the bacteria begin to multiply and a tan-colored liquid oozes from the canker. Insects (especially flies) or splashing rain move the bacteria to nearby blossoms or succulent new plant tissue, which they easily penetrate. Daytime temperatures in the 75° to 85°F (24° to 30°C) range coupled with rain or humid weather are ideal for infection. Dry conditions inhibit further new infections.

Once in the flowers, the bacteria may only cause a localized infection and then eventually die or, alternatively, they may move into twigs and branches to cause more serious damage in the wood. Insects and rain may also move the bacteria from flower to flower or from flower to succulent shoot. When the bacteria move through the wood, they usually penetrate in a narrow strip about ½ to 1½ inches wide and as far as 3 feet down into the tree. Cankers form where bark has been killed. They ooze bacteria that can then be the source of new infections.

Management

Fire blight management involves choosing less susceptible fruit tree varieties, keeping trees healthy but not over fertilized, removing diseased wood as soon as it appears, and in some cases applying Bordeaux or copper sprays to prevent new infections.

Almost all pear varieties are highly susceptible to fire blight, including Asian pears (with the exception of Shinko). Susceptible apple varieties include Fuji, Gala, Golden Delicious, Granny Smith, Gravenstein, Jonathan, Mutsu, Pink Lady, and Yellow Newtown.

Tree vigor has an influence on the extent of fire blight damage. Once within the tree, the pathogen moves at a rate directly related to the rate of tree growth. Vigorously growing new shoots are most severely affected. High soil moisture and high nitrogen levels thus increase the severity of damage. Do not apply more water or fertilizer than recommended.

Prune out diseased branches as soon as they appear. Always cut an infected branch at least 8 to 12 inches below the visible injury or canker, preferably at its point of attachment, and do not leave a stub. Larger branches may have to be pruned a greater distance below the apparent injury, especially when infections are spreading rapidly in May and June. Trunk and major branch infections can sometimes be removed by scraping the bark down to the cambium layer; in this case, all discolored areas of the cambium must be removed. If the infection completely surrounds the limb (i.e., the limb is girdled), it cannot be saved. Disinfect pruning and scraping tools in a 10 percent solution of household bleach in water after each diseased shoot or branch has been pruned. Many pear varieties continue to produce late or "rat-tail" blooms long after the main bloom is over. Remove these flowers before they open to reduce the chances of late-season fire blight infection.

Sprays may be necessary for pear and susceptible apple trees if fire blight is an annual occurrence and other infected trees are nearby. Sprays will reduce some (but not all) new infections but cannot eliminate existing infections. Start sprays as soon as the blossoms begin to open and the average daily temperature (the midpoint between the daily high and daily low) exceeds 60°F (1.5°C). Reapply at four- to five-day intervals during periods of high humidity until late bloom is over. This may mean between five and twelve applications per season. A very weak (about 0.5 percent) Bordeaux mixture or other copper fungicide is suggested. Be aware that these copper treatments can cause severe russetting of the fruit surface.

Apple Scab

Apple scab, considered the most serious disease of apples in some parts of California, is most severe when conditions are cool and moist and takes its greatest toll in coastal areas. Symptoms do occur on flowers and leaves, but the scabby lesions on fruit are particularly recognizable (Figure 11.51). Apple scab is caused by the fungus *Venturia inaequalis.* A related fungus, *Venturia pirina,* causes a similar disease on pears, but pear scab is not usually a major problem in backyard trees. Its symptoms, development and management are very similar to those discussed below for apple scab.

Identification and Damage

The appearance of dark, velvety or sooty spots on the undersides of leaves in early spring is usually the first noticeable sign of apple or pear scab. The darkened

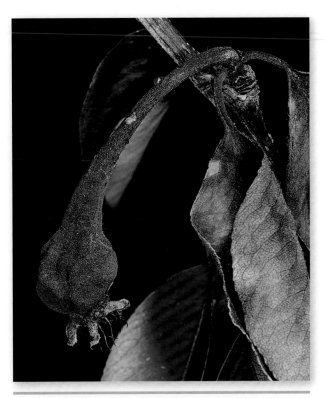

Figure 11.49. Blackened fruit and bacterial ooze are typical of a fire blight infection. Photo by Jack Kelly Clark.

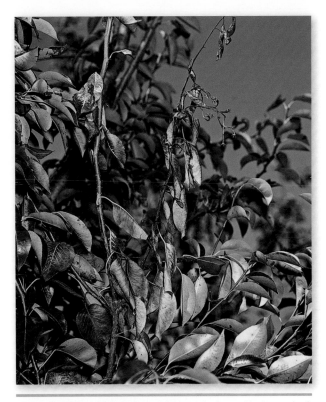

Figure 11.50. Fire blight-infected shoots wilt, dry and look scorched and often are crooked at the top. Photo by Jack Kelly Clark.

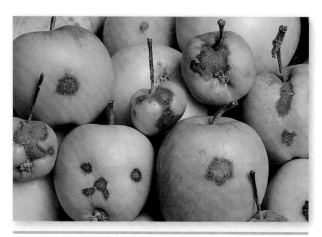

Figure 11.51. Late in the season, fruit damaged by apple scab have dry, cracked spots and often are distorted. Photo by Jack Kelly Clark.

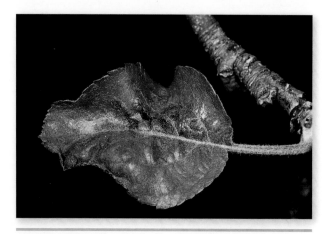

Figure 11.52. Leaves affected by scab are puckered and twisted and have dark circular spots. On the undersides of leaves, spots are dark and velvety. Photo by Jack Kelly Clark.

growth eventually expands over the entire leaf surface and the leaf puckers or twists (Figure 11.52). Severely affected leaves may yellow and drop. Fruit infections begin as dark green spots that eventually turn black. The center of the infected area becomes cracked and scabby. Affected fruit become misshapen or drop from trees. Later infections on fruit may cause small "pinpoint" surface scars that usually are tolerable on homegrown fruit.

Life Cycle

The apple and pear scab fungus spends the winter in infected leaves on the ground beneath the tree where it produces ascospores within fruiting bodies called pseudothecia. When trees begin to grow in spring, ascospores within the fruiting bodies mature and are forcibly discharged into the air. They can be carried long distances on air currents to uninfected flowers, leaves, or young fruit. If the surface of the plant is wet and temperatures are suitable (between 55° and 75°F [13° and 24°C]), the ascospores germinate and penetrate the plant tissue. Once in the plant, the fungus grows and eventually produces secondary spores that can spread the disease further when moisture and temperature conditions are right. Leaves must be continuously wet for a period of 9 hours or more for infection to occur. If spring weather is dry from the green tip stage of bloom through fruit set, scab will not be a problem.

Management

In single backyard trees, removal of leaves from beneath the trees in winter may be sufficient to limit the disease to tolerable levels. In areas where apple scab is a consistent problem, choose apple varieties that are highly resistant to the disease, as indicated in Table 11.5. In plantings of several trees of susceptible varieties in areas with cool, wet spring conditions, you may consider application of fungicides, but careful attention to application timing is critical. See the Pest Note on Apple Scab (online at http://www.ipm.ucdavis.edu) for more information of fungicides and timing of applications.

Shothole Disease

Shothole is a disease of apricot, peach, nectarine, and almond trees. The disease is only very rarely seen on cherry and plum trees. The spots and holes usually seen on plum and cherry leaves have other causes. Leaves, twigs, buds, and fruit affected by shothole show small, scabby lesions (Figure 11.53). The disease is caused by the fungus *Wilsonomyces carpophilus* and is most severe following warm, wet winters when wet weather is prolonged into spring.

Identification and Damage

Shothole disease first appears in the spring as reddish or purplish brown spots about $\frac{1}{10}$ inch in diameter on new leaves and occasionally on shoots. As the spots expand, their centers turn brown. If it rains after the spots are formed, tiny, dark specks visible best with a hand lens form in the brown centers. These dark specks, which are masses of fungal spores, distinguish shothole lesions from other types of spots. Spots on young leaves have a narrow, light green or yellow margin and a center that often falls out as the leaf expands, leaving a hole something like what you would see if a buckshot pellet had passed through; hence, "shothole." Leaves may fall from the tree if the infection is severe, especially if the tree is young when it is infected. Blemishes on fruit become rough and corky, but rarely show dark specks. On peach and to some extent on apricot trees, the fungus infects and kills dormant buds in winter. The dead buds are covered with a sticky exudate that dries to look like lacquer (Figure 11.54). If there are several infections on a twig, they may girdle and kill it.

The part of the tree that is affected by shothole varies from crop to crop. Shothole on almond and apricot primarily takes the form of leaf and fruit infections. On peach and nectarine, shothole is largely limited to buds and twigs and is thus less noticeable than the conspicuous leaf and fruit spotting of apricot.

Life Cycle

The shothole fungus overwinters as spores in infected buds and twig lesions. Twigs and buds can be infected any time between fall and spring when there are 24 hours of wetness. Developing leaves and fruit become

Table 11.5. Apple varieties susceptible and highly resistant to apple scab

Susceptible	Highly resistant
Bellflower	Easy-Gro
Blushing Gold	Enterprise
Fuji	Florina
Gala	Freedom
Golden Delicious	Gold Rush
Granny Smith	Jon Grimes
Gravenstein	Jonafree
Grimes	Liberty
Ida Red	Mac-free
Jonathan	Prima
Monroe	Priscilla
Mutsu	Pristine
Paula Red	Redfree
Red Delicious	Sir Prize
Rome Beauty	Spigold
Stayman Winesap	Williams Pride
Winesap	
Yellow Newtown	
York Imperial	

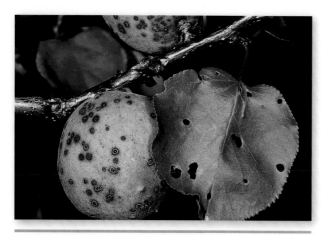

Figure 11.53. Small holes in leaves and brownish scabby spots on fruit are typical of shothole infections on apricot. Photo by Jack Kelly Clark.

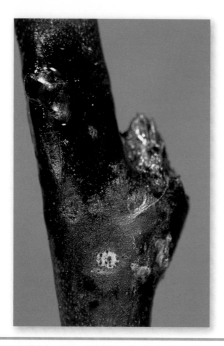

Figure 11.54. This bud was killed by shothole. Note the varnishlike gumming and the shothole lesions with dark spots in the center. Photo by Jack Kelly Clark.

infected during spring when the weather is wet. Spores are produced on leaf, bud, and twig lesions, and, rarely, on fruit infections. The disease cycle stops with the onset of warm, dry weather in the spring, but the pathogen survives inside infected buds and twig lesions until wet weather resumes in fall.

Management

Where incidence of shothole is low, it is often possible to manage the disease in backyard trees by means of cultural practices and sanitation. If sprinklers are used near your trees, it is very important that their angle be low enough to keep the water from getting on leaves. Removal of infected twigs does only a little bit of good, but if practiced it should be done in winter.

If shothole damage is high, you can apply a protectant fungicide such as Bordeaux or some other copper product after leaf fall and before the first fall rains to protect dormant buds, but it will not control spring infections of leaves and fruit. This treatment will help control peach leaf curl, even though it occurs a little earlier than necessary for good leaf curl protection. Additional applications may be useful in commercial orchards, but these should not be necessary for backyard trees. Copper sprays are safe on dormant fruit trees but may burn leaves if the trees are not dormant.

Bacterial Canker and Blast

Bacterial canker and blast are caused by the bacterium *Pseudomonas syringae.* The canker phase of the disease is most common in stone fruits and seldom seen in apples or pears. Symptoms appear in late winter and early spring. Cankers begin as irregularly shaped, water- or gum-soaked areas of bark (Figure 11.55), but may grow to girdle and kill entire branches or trunks. Reddish flecking around canker margins distinguish these cankers from those caused by other pathogens (Figure 11.56). Infected trees have a distinct sour or vinegary odor, and young trees are most severely affected. The disease is active during the winter and ceases when warm weather returns and the trees start to grow. Bacterial canker does not affect roots, so suckering at the rootstock in late spring and summer is a typical symptom on trees that have died aboveground in winter and early spring.

The blast phase of the disease, which may occur in pear and apple as well as in stone fruit and almond trees, causes blossoms and shoots to shrivel, turn dark, and die (Figure 11.57). In pears and apples, bacterial ooze is never present with the blast phase of the disease, distinguishing it from fire blight, which also kills flowers and shoots. Gumming may occur, however, on stone fruit buds and spurs infected with the bacterium. Blast can also cause sunken black spots on pear and cherry fruit. Frost injury and cold, rainy weather increase the incidence of blast.

Pseudomonas syringae bacteria are always present on the surfaces of plants. The bacteria invade trees when the right combination of favorable conditions occurs. It is unclear how the bacteria enter the tree, but lenticels or other natural openings appear to be the most likely places. Infections are not associated with pruning wounds.

Management of bacterial canker must rely on cultural practices. Fungicides and bactericides are not effective. Healthy, vigorous trees suffer less damage from bacterial canker. Choose your planting site carefully, avoiding sites with a history of bacterial canker. Trees grown on sandy, shallow, hardpan, acidic (pH below 5.5), or nitrogen-deficient soils are most susceptible. The presence of ring nematodes in the soil may also predispose trees to infection. Certain stone fruit and pear rootstocks show resistance to bacterial canker (see *Integrated Pest Management for Stone Fruits*, UC ANR Publication 3389). Provide optimum levels of key nutrients, especially nitrogen, to maintain tree vigor without overfertilizing. Although acidic conditions favor the disease, there is no apparent benefit to be had from adjusting the pH through addition of soil amendments. These nutritional and cultural practices have no effect on the blast phase of the disease, but apple and pear trees should be protected from frost during bloom using sprinkler irrigation or shelters. If trees have been damaged by bacterial canker, remove entire affected branches in the summer.

EUTYPA DIEBACK

Eutypa dieback, caused by the fungus *Eutypa lata*, is a special problem on apricots but may also affect cherry and apple trees and is a serious problem in grapevines. Leaves wilt and die early on affected limbs and then

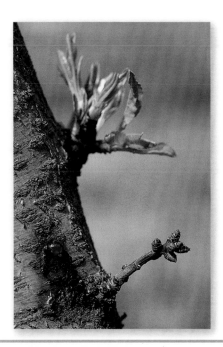

Figure 11.55. The gumming in this photo indicates the initiation of a new bacterial canker. Photo by Jack Kelly Clark.

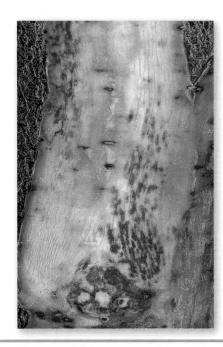

Figure 11.56. The reddish flecking around the margins of a bacterial canker distinguishes this disease from cankers caused by other pathogens. Photo by Jack Kelly Clark.

remain on trees through the following winter. Trees usually have a gum-exuding canker located near a pruning wound or other injury that was the original site of infection (Figure 11.58). Dieback symptoms become apparent 1 to 2 years after infection and advance for many years, often eventually killing the tree.

To manage the disease in areas where it is a problem, restrict pruning of apricots to July and August in California's Central Valley and to August in coastal areas. This will allow pruning wounds to heal before spores are released during fall and spring rains. Existing infections can also be pruned out at least 8 inches below the canker and destroyed. Remove abandoned grapevines and apricot trees in the vicinity, as these can be sources of infection.

WALNUT BLIGHT

Walnut blight is a common disease of walnuts that reduces nut production. It causes darkened or distorted catkins and leaves, dark spots on husks, and shriveled nutmeats (Figure 11.59). The disease does not damage the tree or cause defoliation. Nuts infected by blight serve as a breeding site for the navel orangeworm and may be more difficult to shake from trees.

Walnut blight is caused by a bacterium, *Xanthomonas campestris* pv. *juglandis,* which survives the winter in dormant buds and catkins and to some extent in old cankers. The pathogen enters new plant tissue through natural openings when growth begins in spring. Bacteria are spread to other sites with windblown rain, sprinkler water, or pollen. The severity of the disease each year is directly related to the presence of free moisture, which is required for infection. Infection rates drop sharply when spring rains cease, unless sprinkler irrigation sends water up into the canopy.

The only management measure suggested for backyard walnut trees is to adjust your irrigation program to keep water from getting into trees and keep moisture to a minimum. Make sure that any sprinklers are set at an angle low enough to keep young fruit from becoming wet. Remove low limbs that are likely to become wet and train young trees to allow air movement under the trees. Open up older trees during pruning to increase air movement through the tree. Avoid irrigation during bloom. If winter rains were not adequate, schedule a pre-bloom irrigation instead. If you are planting a new walnut tree, select a variety that blooms late so that most spring rains will be over by the time young fruit are present.

ARMILLARIA ROOT ROT (OAK ROOT FUNGUS)

Most fruit and nut trees and many ornamentals are susceptible to Armillaria root rot. The fungus that causes the disease, *Armillaria mellea,* is often called oak root fungus because it is frequently associated with oak trees. The disease is common in flood plains and along rivers. Trees suffering from Armillaria show the same general symptoms of decline as trees suffering from other root diseases. These include wilting of leaves and a general decline in growth and vigor, often on one side of the tree at first. Trees usually die within a period of one to a few years.

Armillaria-infected trees can be readily distinguished from trees damaged by other root diseases if you search for the distinctive features of the fungus. Thin, white or yellowish mats of mycelium grow beneath the outer layer of infected bark (Figure 11.60) and they have a strong mushroom smell. Also, dark brown to black root-like structures called rhizomorphs spread over the surface of infected roots and beneath the bark of severely decayed roots or crowns. Finally, clusters of light brown or honey-colored mushrooms (Figure 11.61) sometimes appear around the base of infected trees during wet weather in fall or winter.

When a susceptible plant is affected by Armillaria root rot, little can be done except to remove the affected plant, allow the soil to dry out, and replant with a tolerant species. In orchards, it is advisable to remove adjacent trees as well. Destroy all infected tissue, including all roots that are greater than ½ inch in diameter.

Trees that are somewhat tolerant to Armillaria, such as certain rootstock varieties of pear and apple, may be saved if less than half of the crown's circumference is affected. To do this, you must cut away and destroy all infected material and remove soil at the base of the tree to expose the crown and the top of the root system for several months, and you must not overirrigate.

PHYTOPHTHORA ROOT AND CROWN ROT

Almost all fruit and nut trees can develop Phytophthora root and crown rot, caused by *Phytophthora* spp., if soil around the base of the tree remains wet for prolonged periods. Trees infected in the crown may decline rapidly and die within a year. The first noticeable symptom is usually on leaves, which wilt and turn dull green or yellow. Often trees may leaf out normally in spring and then collapse and die suddenly with the first hot weather, retaining dead leaves. If only smaller roots are infected, the trees grow slowly, do not respond to irrigation or fertilization, and may die after several years. Cankers on roots and crowns appear as darkened patches of bark that exude copious quantities of gum that can be amber (on stone fruits) or black (on walnut). Wood underneath the gum is dark, reddish brown on stone fruit and almond trees (Figure 11.62) and mustard brown to black on walnut trees. There is no fungus mycelium as with Armillaria root rot. Positive confirmation of a Phytophthora infection requires laboratory analysis.

A number of *Phytophthora* species are capable of causing root and crown rot. They survive in soil, in plant material, or as resistant spores and are carried to new locations on infected plants, in contaminated soil, or in water. Within the orchard, the pathogen spreads as zoospores that require water to move, germinate, and infect bark at new sites. Under saturated soil conditions, more *Phytophthora* zoospores are produced and new infections escalate. Although the pathogens can form other types of spores that can survive when conditions are dry, *Phytophthora* populations decline with prolonged exposure to dry soil.

The most important factor in reducing the threat of Phytophthora root and crown rot (and other root and crown rots as well) is good water management. Avoid prolonged saturation of soil and do not allow standing water around the base of trees. Irrigate only as much and as often as necessary. Choose an appropriate planting site and provide good soil drainage. In some cases, planting trees on mounds or berms will improve drainage. Don't plant trees deeper than they were planted at the nursery, and never cover the graft union with soil. Don't grow irrigated turf or other plants around the base of trees and do not irrigate crown

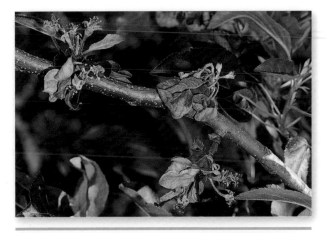

Figure 11.57. Bacterial blossom blast has killed these apple blossoms. Unlike fire blight, damage will not extend below the base of the flower cluster, although fruit spurs can be killed. Photo by Jack Kelly Clark.

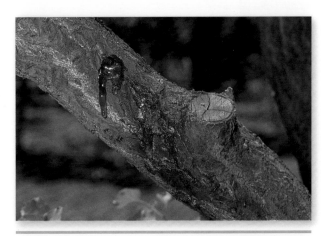

Figure 11.58. Gumming from a Eutypa canker. Notice its location adjacent to a pruning wound. Photo by Jack Kelly Clark.

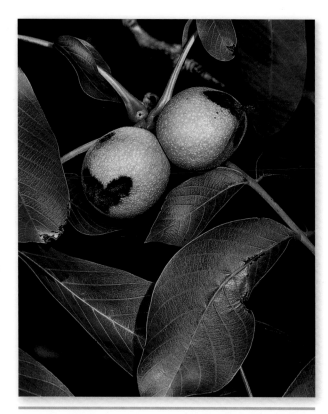

Figure 11.59. The blackened areas on these walnuts are the result of a walnut blight infection. Initial infection sites enlarge, blacken, and often sink. The leaf in the foreground has become distorted around a black lesion that also resulted from a blight infection. Photo by Jack Kelly Clark.

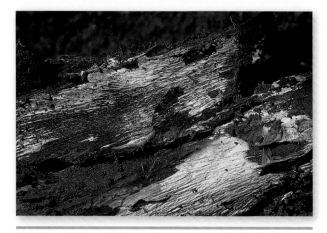

Figure 11.60. Mycelial mats produced by *Armillaria mellea* grow between bark and wood. Photo by Jack Kelly Clark.

areas directly. Some rootstocks are more susceptible to Phytophthora than others; consult your local nursery or the materials listed in this chapter's References section to help you choose more-resistant rootstocks before you plant.

At the first sign of aboveground symptoms, check the tree at the soil line for crown rot. Carefully cut away bark that looks affected. If crown rot is present, you can sometimes save a tree by removing the soil and vegetation from the base of the tree down to the tops of the main roots and allowing the crown tissue to dry out over the summer. If you do this, make sure that you keep ground cover and sprinklers away from crowns and do not allow saturated conditions in the future.

Crown Gall

Crown galls are rough, warty tumors caused by the soil-inhabiting bacterium *Agrobacterium tumefaciens* (Figure 11.63). Galls first appear as smooth swellings but develop rapidly into larger, woody tumors with a cracked appearance. Galls disrupt the normal flow of water and nutrients in the tree's conducting tissue, and can quickly girdle and kill young trees. Older trees can usually tolerate galls, but if the galls are invaded by secondary wood decay organisms, even older trees may be injured.

Most infections start in the nursery. You can greatly reduce problems if you obtain planting material from a reputable nursery. Examine trees for signs of galls before purchase. Established plants are infected only through fresh wounds such as those caused by planting, pruning, cultivation equipment, or growth cracks, so take care not to injure crowns.

New trees planted into sites where crown gall has been a problem in the past can be treated with commercial formulations of the antagonistic K-84 strain of *Agrobacterium tumefaciens,* which is a biological control agent. Galls growing on established young trees can be removed surgically and treated with a bactericide (Gallex) during the dormant season. Rinse soil away from galls before you apply this material and make sure to allow tissue to dry. Young trees with multiple large galls on the crown and upper roots should be replaced.

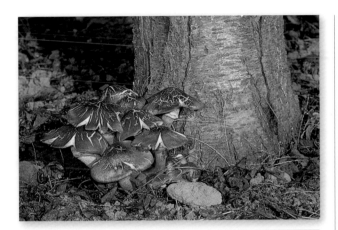

Figure 11.61. Honey-colored mushrooms at the base of the tree may be a sign of an Armillaria root rot infection. Photo by Jack Kelly Clark.

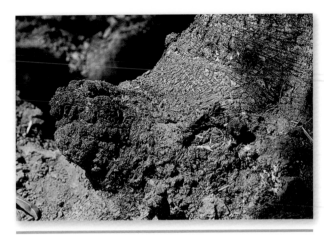

Figure 11.63. Rough galls grow at the base of a plum tree affected by crown gall. Younger trees are the most seriously damaged. Photo by Jack Kelly Clark.

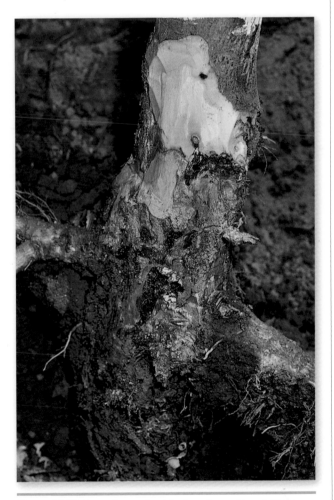

Figure 11.62. Gumming and reddening of wood beneath the crown area of this trunk indicates a Phytophthora infection. Photo by Jack Kelly Clark.

References

Flint, M. L. 1999. Pests of the garden and small farm: A grower's guide to using less pesticide, second ed. Oakland: University of California Division of Agriculture and Natural Resources, Publication 3332.

Flint, M. L., and S. H. Dreistadt. 1998. Natural enemies handbook: An illustrated guide to biological control. Oakland: University of California Division of Agriculture and Natural Resources, Publication 3386.

O'Connor-Marer, P. J. 2000. The safe and effective use of pesticides, second ed. Oakland: University of California Division of Agriculture and Natural Resources, Publication 3324.

Ohlendorf, B. O. 1999. Integrated pest management for apples and pears, second ed. Oakland: University of California Division of Agriculture and Natural Resources, Publication 3340.

Salmon, T. P., D. A. Whisson, and R. E. Marsh. 2006. Wildlife pest control around gardens and homes, second ed. Oakland: University of California Division of Agriculture and Natural Resources, Publication 21385. This is the best book available for identifying and managing vertebrates in gardens and landscapes.

Strand, L. L. 1999. Integrated pest management for stone fruits. Oakland: University of California Division of Agriculture and Natural Resources, Publication 3389.

Strand, L. L. 2002. Integrated pest management for almonds, second ed. Oakland: University of California Division of Agriculture and Natural Resources, Publication 3308.

Strand, L. L. 2003. Integrated pest management for walnuts, third edition. Oakland: University of California Division of Agriculture and Natural Resources, Publication 3270.

University of California Statewide IPM Project Web site: http://www.ipm.ucdavis.edu. Constantly updated. Contains identification, biological, and management information for over 100 home, garden, and landscape pests, pest management guidelines for commercial orchard crops, a weed photo gallery, and a gallery of natural enemy species. See especially the following Pest Notes, available at http://www.ipm.ucdavis.edu or in your county UC Cooperative Extension office:
Aphids
Apple Scab
Codling Moth
Fire Blight
Fruittree Leafroller
Leaf Curl
Powdery Mildew on Fruits and Berries
Redhumped Caterpillar
Scales
Spider Mites
Walnut Husk Fly

CHAPTER 12

Failure to Bear and Abiotic Disorders

Chuck A. Ingels, Maxwell V. Norton, and Pamela M. Geisel

Failure to Bear

Fruit and nut trees normally begin to bear fruit 2 to 5 years after planting, depending on the species, tree vigor, and the method of training and pruning. Most stone fruit and almond trees begin to bear in 2 or 3 years, although cherries may not begin bearing for up to 4 years after planting. Apples often begin to bear in 2 to 4 years, but pears can take 1 to 2 years longer. Walnuts and pecans may take up to 5 years to begin bearing. Fruiting in most species requires pollination as well as adequate sunlight, irrigation, drainage, and fertilization. Certain diseases can also affect fruit set and retention (see Chapter 11). Some rootstocks can also affect when trees begin to bear, mainly because of their effects on vigor (see Chapter 3). For example, Betulafolia rootstock usually imparts more vigorous growth and later bearing than other pear rootstocks, whereas Gisela rootstock usually imparts less vigor and earlier bearing than other cherry rootstocks.

If a tree is properly pruned, free of disease, sufficiently irrigated and fertilized, and getting enough sunlight, but it fails to form flowers or fruit fails to set after several years, consider topworking (grafting) a different variety onto the tree (see Chapter 8) or replacing the tree entirely.

DIAGNOSING FAILURE TO BEAR

When diagnosing why a tree bears few or no fruit, note whether the tree does not bloom at all, blooms but does not set fruit, or blooms and sets fruit, most or all of which falls off before harvest. For more information on the causes listed below, see the appropriate sections in this chapter or other relevant chapters.

- **Tree does not bloom:**

    - *Tree is too young or too vigorous.*

    - *Excessive or improper pruning.*

    - *Excessive nitrogen fertilization.*

    - *Lack of sunlight.*

    - *Alternate or biennial bearing.*

    - *Damage from improperly mixed or timed dormant oil or lime sulfer spray.*

    - *Damage from diseases that kill the dormant buds (shothole or bacterial blast).*

- **Tree blooms but does not set fruit:**

    - *Lack of pollination because of no pollinators (e.g., too cold, wet, or windy for bees) or pollinizers (e.g., no other variety planted nearby).*

    - *Frost damage.*

    - *Lack of sunlight.*

    - *Nutrient deficiencies (especially nitrogen).*

    - *Lack of sufficient chilling hours.*

- **Most or all fruit falls from tree:**

    - *Lack of pollination.*

    - *Frost damage.*

    - *Excessive or insufficient water.*

    - *Root constriction caused by hardpan or compacted soil.*

Normal Flower and Fruit Drop

Over the course of the growing season, it is common for all fruit trees to shed some flowers or fruit. Trees generally produce more flowers than they can maintain; shedding them is the tree's way of balancing its resources between the demands of fruit with the demands of the rest of the tree. Some fruit tree species may shed many fruit in what is known as *spring drop,* which in California usually occurs in May. Natural loss of some flowers and fruit is a normal part of tree growth and development and should not be cause for concern unless it results in few fruit or nuts being left on the tree.

Planting Site

Fruit trees should be planted where they will receive at least 6 to 8 hours of direct sunlight per day. This amount of sunlight allows the tree to produce enough carbohydrates through photosynthesis to support the growth and development of fruit (see Chapter 2). If a tree does not receive enough sunlight, it may conserve energy by not producing buds, flowers, or fruit. Over time, you may need to trim back nearby trees or shrubs if they cast too much shade on a fruit tree. Poor fruit color, size, or sugar may indicate that the tree receives insufficient light.

Pruning

Excessive or improper pruning can reduce the number of flower buds and encourage vegetative growth that shades the fruiting wood. Most fruit and nut trees form flowers on spurs or short branches, although peaches, nectarines, figs, persimmons, and some walnuts bloom on longer branches. When pruning, leave many of the one-year-old spurs and shoots. Also, provide adequate light to these fruiting shoots by thinning out crowded growth, especially by summer pruning (see Chapter 7).

Climate and Weather

Effect on Pollination

Inclement weather is often more of a factor in the fruit production of early-flowering species such as almond and plum. Cold or wet weather conditions prevent the growth of pollen tubes in the female parts of the flower. Also, rain, wind, and cold temperatures can disrupt pollination by limiting the activity of bees and other pollinator insects and by washing pollen off of the flowers.

Chilling Hours

Most fruit trees need a certain amount of cold temperature to end their dormancy and promote spring growth. After a mild winter, flowering and spring growth are delayed and irregular, the flowering period is extended, and fruit set is reduced. The extended bloom period increases the chance that inclement weather will be able to cause blossom diseases such as brown rot or fire blight. (For more information on chilling hours, see Chapters 1 and 2.)

Frost

Frost during or shortly after bloom can cause young flowers, fruits, or nuts to abort, even though no frost damage may be seen. Frost during pistachio bloom in April kills the flowers. When you expect a heavy frost, you can cover the trees with plastic or bed sheets in an attempt to prevent or at least minimize injury to the expanding buds or blossoms, provided that temperatures do not fall too low and the cold weather does not last too long. Adding a heat lamp or Christmas tree lights under the cover can often protect flowers and fruit from even the most severe frosts.

Pollination

Most fruit and nut trees need to be cross-pollinated. Without sufficient pollination, they may bloom abundantly but still fail to bear fruit. A pollinizer is a tree or branch of one variety of a species (e.g., Black Tartarian cherry) that has a similar bloom period to another variety that is grown for fruiting (e.g., Bing cherry). Pollinators (usually bees) or winds (most nut crops) carry pollen from the flower of one variety to the flower of the other.

Trees with flowers that bear fruit through self-pollination are called *self-fruitful*. Some species have perfect flowers (i.e., each flower has both male and female parts) but are unable to produce fruit with their own pollen; they require pollen from another variety (cross-pollination). These are called *self-unfruitful*. Some species do not fit into either category: they are *dioecious*, which is to say that they have male trees that produce pollen and female trees that produce fruit. Pistachio and kiwifruit are both dioecious species. To grow them successfully, you have to have plants of opposite sex near each other.

Self-Fruitful Types

Self-fruitful fruit tree varieties include quince, sour cherry, most apricots, fig (except the Smyrna type), peach (except J. H. Hale and some others), and European-type plums, prunes, persimmons, and pomegranates. Some European pears are also self-fruitful. Bartlett pear is parthenocarpic, which means that it requires no pollination in order to set fruit (a phenomenon that seems to occur only in California). Some cherry varieties are self-fruitful, such as Lapins, Stella, and Sunburst. Many apple varieties are self-fruitful, including Braeburn, Empire, Fuji, Gala, Golden Delicious, and Pippin.

Self-Unfruitful Types

Many almond, apple, Asian pear, sweet cherry, and Japanese plum varieties are self-unfruitful. The nursery label on the tree usually indicates which varieties a self-unfruitful tree can use for a pollinizer. Some cherry varieties have fairly specific pollinizer requirements.

For example, Bing, Lambert, and Royal Ann do not pollinate each other; plant a pollinizer variety near them, such as Black Tartarian or Van, or a sour cherry such as Montmorency.

To pollinate adequately, plant the pollinizer no farther than 20 to 35 feet (6 to 10 m) from the self-unfruitful tree—the closer the better. Alternatively, you can graft a pollinizer variety onto the tree (see Chapter 8). You can improve the pollination rate by taking measures to attract bees to the tree. In the interim before you are able to graft a pollinizer variety or plant one nearby, cut some flowering branches from a pollinizer variety, place the clipped ends of the branches into water in a bucket, jar, or plastic bag, and set them in the tree canopy. Bees will visit these flowers and pollinate the fruiting variety's flowers.

For more information on pollination and varieties, see Chapters 2 and 3 of this book or the UC Fruit and Nut Research and Information Center Web site (http://fruitsandnuts.ucdavis.edu/index.html).

Alternate Bearing

Fruit trees may bear heavily one year and sparsely the next. This is known as alternate or biennial bearing. The spring-flowering buds of most deciduous fruit trees form during the previous year's spring and summer. If a tree has an especially heavy crop one year, the tree may use most of the carbohydrate it produces through photosynthesis to produce that year's fruit rather than form flower buds for the following year. Some species are more prone to alternate bearing than others: for example, alternate bearing is relatively common in apples and apricots but less so in cherries. Among the nut crops, pistachio is notorious for alternate bearing.

Alternate bearing is not difficult to correct. If you thin the fruit early (shortly after petal fall) and heavily during a year in which the tree has produced a large number of fruit, that may encourage the tree to form more flower buds for the next year (see Chapter 9). You can also prune more heavily in the dormant season prior to an anticipated heavy crop year to reduce alternate bearing by selectively removing fruiting wood, or prune less heavily before an anticipated light crop year.

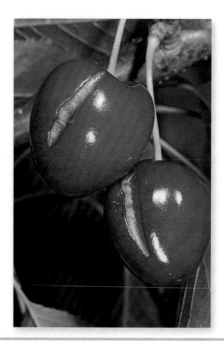

Figure 12.1. During ripening, cherries may crack if they get wet from rain or irrigation. Photo by Jack Kelly Clark.

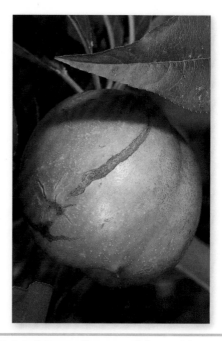

Figure 12.2. As fruit grow, they may split from an injury or sunburn, but splitting is often caused or enhanced by improper irrigation. Photo by Jack Kelly Clark.

IMPROPER IRRIGATION, ROOT PROBLEMS, AND PESTS

Excessive or insufficient water can reduce flowering and fruit set and quality. Too much water creates anaerobic conditions in the soil, reducing root growth. Water stress—a lack of water—during the summer also reduces shoot and root growth and can cause poor fruit size as a result of reduced leaf surface area and reduced photosynthesis. Either of these conditions will also be accompanied by drooping or yellowing leaves.

Root constrictions caused by hardpan or compacted soil can cause trees to become stressed for water and nutrients, and this can lead to fruit drop. Pests and diseases such as soil nematodes, root rot, bacterial canker, brown rot of twigs, powdery mildew, and spider mites can affect individual fruit or weaken the tree as a whole (see Chapter 11).

LATE TO COME INTO BEARING

Species with vigorous, upright growth, such as cherry and pear trees, tend to begin bearing later in life than those with a spreading growth habit, such as peach and apricot. You can encourage such trees to bear earlier, however, by bending vertical branches outward during the growing season before they become too stiff to bend. To hold a bent branch in place, tie it to a stake, to a string attached to a brick or stone on the ground, or to a trellis (espalier). Avoid making excessive heading cuts on these vigorous trees, especially during the dormant season, since heading encourages growth and reduces the development of flowers. Bending unheaded, upright branches outward to about a 45- to 60-degree angle is a proven method for quickly developing spurs and flowers.

Physiological Disorders

SPLITTING AND CRACKING OF CHERRIES

As cherries ripen, accumulate sugar, and begin to color, they become susceptible to cracking or splitting if they get wet from rain or sprinklers (Figure 12.1). Do not allow sprinklers to wet the foliage. If rain is forecast and you have a fairly small tree, you can reduce cracking by covering the top of the tree with plastic to keep most of the fruit dry. Remove the plastic as soon as the threat passes.

SPLITTING AND CRACKING OF OTHER FRUIT

Anything that damages the skin while the fruit is still small will cause the skin to crack or split as the fruit enlarges (Figure 12.2). Sunburn, limb rub, and powdery mildew are a few of the possible causes. Dried plums (prunes and sugar plums) may split on the side or bottom. Side cracking in dried plums occurs about the first two weeks in July and is caused by a combination of fruit exposure to direct sunlight and change in fruit size caused by daily fluctuations in moisture. Cool weather at that time will increase the number of side cracks and large fruit will crack more. End cracking in dried plums is caused by moisture stress followed by a heavy irrigation. End cracks can be reduced by making sure trees have uniform, ample moisture in May and June.

DOUBLING AND SPURRING OF CHERRIES

Two fruit that are attached at the base or the side are often called doubles (Figure 12.3). A fruit with a partially developed fruit attached to its side is called a spur (Figure 12.3). Both disorders are caused by high temperatures the previous summer during the period when the fruit buds began to develop. There is nothing you can do about this deformity.

SPLIT PIT OF PEACHES AND NECTARINES

Most stone fruit grow in three stages. In stage 1, most of the cell division takes place; in stage 2, the pit begins to harden; and in stage 3, rapid cell enlargement occurs. Excessive soil moisture and rapid fruit growth during stage 2 can cause the pit to split in peaches and nectarines (Figure 12.4). By cutting sample fruit each week in late spring or early summer and noticing when the pits just begin to harden, you can avoid overirrigating for a week or so, depending on weather, irrigation method, and soil moisture status. In some years, this may reduce pit splitting.

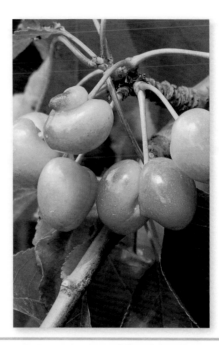

Figure 12.3. Fruit spurring *(upper left)* and doubling *(center)* of cherries. Photo by Joe Grant.

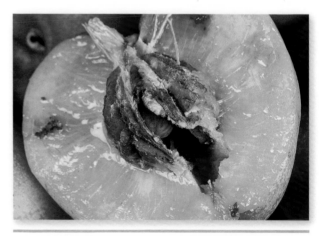

Figure 12.4. Excessive soil moisture during pit hardening can cause peach and nectarine pits to split. Photo by Jack Kelly Clark.

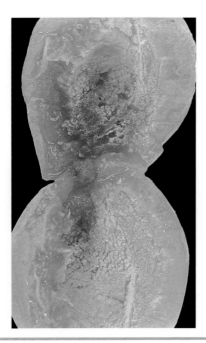

Figure 12.5. Apricot pit burn is caused by excessive heat shortly before harvest. Photo by Bill Coates.

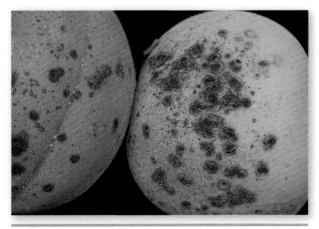

Figure 12.6. Fog spot of apricot appears as small, reddish spots *(left)*, which later turn scabby *(right)*. Photo by Maxwell Norton.

PIT BURN OF APRICOT

In California's Central Valley, high temperatures during the last month before harvest can cause the flesh next to the apricot pit to become dark and watery due to internal breakdown. This is pit burn (Figure 12.5). If it occurs early enough, the whole fruit will begin to rot inside. There is little you can do other than make sure the tree has ample water during this period. Varieties vary in their susceptibility. Blenheim, Wenatchee, Autumn Royal, and Moorpark are most susceptible. Modesto, Patterson, Westley, Castlebright, Katy, Improved Flaming Gold, Helena, Tri Gem, Goldbar, Poppy, Lorna, Robada, Tilton, and Patterson tend to resist pit burning.

FOG SPOT OF APRICOT

In years when apricot fruit get wet during cool, damp weather, fog spot may appear as small, reddish spots on the upper surface of the fruit (Figure 12.6). The spots enlarge and darken and may grow together to create a large scab. The center of each spot may turn dark brown while the margins remain reddish. The persistent red color on the edges of the spots and the lack of spots on the leaves distinguish fog spot from shothole disease. As fruits mature, the spots become scablike and may flake off, leaving roughened areas beneath. The actual cause of fog spot is not known, but a fungal pathogen is suspected.

BITTER PIT OF APPLE

Bitter pit is characterized as small, water-soaked spots on the apple's skin that begin to appear soon after the fruit are picked (Figure 12.7). These spots gradually turn a deeper color than the surrounding fruit surface and later turn brown, while the tissue directly underneath the spots dies. Individual spots are 2 to 10 mm in diameter. The dying tissue underneath may look like a tiny bruise. The spots become sunken and the tissue below becomes spongy. Highly vigorous trees, trees that were heavily pruned the prior winter, and trees with high nitrogen levels are more likely to have bitter pit symptoms. Fruit that is overripe at harvest may also develop more symptoms. Sometimes foliar sprays with calcium applied in June and July will reduce symptoms. Use only calcium that is formulated for foliar sprays. Calcium applied to the soil will not help.

SUNBURN OF ALL FRUIT

Although fruit trees thrive in full sun, any fruit will sunburn if suddenly exposed to hot afternoon sun, as can happen after excessive summer pruning, or if shoot growth is stunted and the fruit are exposed to direct sunlight most of the day (Figure 12.8). Pruning for a rigid framework will stabilize fruit positions in the canopy (see Chapter 7). With the exception of apples in the Central Valley, fruit that are exposed to sun the entire season may not sunburn at all. Weak trees with a sparse canopy will have more sunburned fruit, as will trees that become water-stressed or stunted from root diseases or soil compaction.

LACK OF FRUIT SWEETNESS

Low sugar may be a symptom of insufficient light, excess crop, excess vigor, or excess nitrogen. Fruit trees usually need full sun in order to fully mature a large crop. Pruning back nearby shade trees may be necessary to provide the fruit tree with full illumination. Thin the fruit enough to allow the tree to sustain and mature the fruit that remain. This may mean eliminating more than half of the tree's fruit early in the spring while they are still quite small (see Chapter 9). Trees that were stunted much of the year may have too few leaves to support the fruit load or sweeten the fruit. Make sure the tree is adequately irrigated (but not overirrigated) throughout the spring. Mature fruit trees in the home landscape usually do not need nitrogen fertilizer and in most cases you should limit its use.

FALL BLOOM

On rare occasions, a tree that became very dry during late summer or early fall may begin to bloom after it is irrigated later in the fall, if the weather is favorable. While this is not harmful to tree health, it will use up many of the flower buds that have developed during the current year, and thereby reduce the crop the following spring. A fall bloom does not result in fruit or nut production.

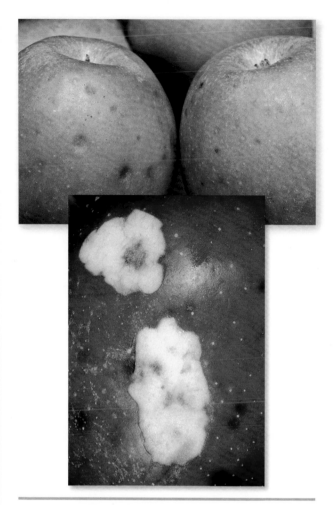

Figure 12.7. Bitter pit of apple is caused by calcium deficiency. Photos by Jack Kelly Clark.

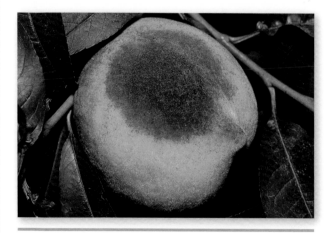

Figure 12.8. Fruit are exposed to hot afternoon sun if insufficient foliage is present, as is the case with this peach. Apples are particularly susceptible. Photo by Jack Kelly Clark.

References

Costello, L. R., E. J. Perry, N. P. Matheny, J. M. Henry, and P. M. Geisel. 2003. Abiotic disorders of landscape plants. Oakland: University of California Division of Agriculture and Natural Resources, Publication 3420.

LaRue, J. H., and R. S. Johnson, eds. 1989. Peaches, plums, and nectarines: Growing and handling for fresh market. Oakland: University of California Division of Agriculture and Natural Resources, Publication 3331.

Retzel, K. 1995. Why fruit trees fail to bear. Pullman: Washington State University Cooperative Extension, Publication EB0838. Available online at http://cru.cahe.wsu.edu/CEPublications/eb0838/eb0838.html

Vossen, P., and D. Silva. 2002. Temperate tree fruit and nut crops. Pages 449–530 in D. Pittenger, ed., California master gardener handbook. Oakland: University of California Division of Agriculture and Natural Resources, Publication 3382.

Useful Web Sites

Dave Wilson Nursery Web site (http://www.davewilson.com/)

University of California Fruit and Nut Research and Information Center Web site (http://fruitsandnuts.ucdavis.edu/index.html)

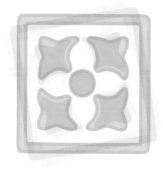

APPENDIX

Crop–by–Crop Calendars

Pamela M. Geisel

These crop-by-crop calendars give you a typical year's timing for important crop-care activities. The calendars run from November to October, left to right, with each cultural or pest control practice appearing as a line underneath the appropriate months to show when that activity would typically occur. A green line indicates the primary period for an activity and an orange line indicates a secondary period of activity. There is an explanatory footnote for each activity at the end of each table.

It is important to note that the timing of various cultural and pest management activities may vary slightly in your climate zone. Pest management operations may also require more-specific, more-accurate timing. In some cases, the pest may not even be a problem in your area. Please see the UC IPM Pest Notes or Pest Management Guidelines (http:// www.ipm.ucdavis.edu/) for further, more-detailed information. Additional useful information is available in other publications from UC ANR (http://anrcatalog.ucdavis.edu).

	NOV	DEC	JAN	FEB	MAR	APR	MAY	JUNE	JULY	AUG	SEPT	OCT
A L M O N D		Plant bare-root trees*										
	Pruning and dormant oil sprays†				Fertilize young trees‡						
	Remove old nuts¶				Fertilize mature trees§						
					Irrigation#						
				Trunk paint**				Harvest††			
	Shothole disease control‡‡										

Plant bare-root trees: Plant bare-root trees during the dormant season. ■ †*Dormant pruning:* Prune out any dead, diseased, or broken branches. Prune off about 10 to 20% of last year's wood to thin the crop, usually thinning cuts of larger wood. Almonds can carry a heavy crop, so heavy pruning to moderate the crop is not required. *Dormant sprays:* For San Jose scale, mite, or aphid management, spray trees with dormant oil late in the dormant season, just prior to bud break. Provide thorough coverage including the trunk. ■ ‡*Fertilize young trees:* Fertilize with nitrogen fertilizers three times: in March, May, and July. ■ §*Fertilize mature trees:* Fertilize if necessary, applying one-half of total fertilizer in spring and the second half in August or September or any time after harvest. See Table 6.4 for specific rates. ■ ¶*Remove old nuts and husks:* Remove and destroy all old husks and nuts on the ground and on tree branches to reduce future pest problems. ■ #*Irrigation:* Drip irrigate several times per week, or for sprinkler or flood irrigation, water about every one to two weeks during the heat of summer and provide enough water to wet the soil to a depth of 18 to 24 inches (45 to 61 cm) depending upon soil type and environmental conditions. Irrigate at the drip line, well away from the trunk of the tree. ■ **Trunk paint:* In hot regions, paint the trunk and lower branches of young trees that are exposed to afternoon sun with a 50:50 mixture of white interior latex paint and water to prevent sunburn injury and reduce borer infestations. ■ ††*Harvest:* Harvest fruit as soon as the hulls begin to split. Clean up fallen nuts quickly to minimize infestations of navel orangeworm and ants. Store hulled, dry kernels in airtight containers or freeze them. ■ ‡‡*Shothole disease control:* Spray copper or lime sulfur fungicide twice, with the first application around November 15 or after the leaves have fallen and the second around February 1 to 15.

Periods of primary activity:		Periods of secondary activity:	

APRICOT

NOV	DEC	JAN	FEB	MAR	APR	MAY	JUNE	JULY	AUG	SEPT	OCT
	Plant bare-root trees*										
Dormant oil spray†				Fertilize young trees‡							
Remove fruit mummies¶					Fertilize mature trees§				Pruning#		
				Irrigation**							
					Fruit thinning††						
Shothole fungus‡‡				Prevent brown rot§§							
			Trunk paint¶¶				Harvest##				

Plant bare-root trees: Plant bare-root trees during the dormant season ■ †*Dormant sprays:* To control San Jose scale, mites, or aphid eggs, spray trees with dormant oil late in the dormant season, just prior to bud break. Provide thorough coverage including the trunk. Do not use sulfur products on apricot trees. ■ ‡*Fertilize young trees:* Fertilize with nitrogen fertilizers three times: in March, May, and July. ■ §*Fertilize mature trees:* Fertilize if necessary, applying the total fertilizer amount in spring. See Table 6.4 for specific rates. Water the fertilizer in immediately to avoid nitrogen loss. ■ ¶*Remove fruit mummies:* Remove and destroy all mummified fruit hanging on tree branches to reduce future pest problems. ■ #*Pruning:* Prune before the onset of winter rains to prevent Eutypa fungus infections in the pruning wounds. Prune out about 20% of last year's growth and remove dead, diseased, or broken branches. ■ **Irrigation:* Drip irrigate daily, or for sprinkler or flood irrigation, water about every two to three weeks and provide enough water to wet the soil to a depth of 18 to 24 inches (45 to 61 cm) depending upon soil type and environmental conditions. ■ ††*Fruit thinning:* Thin fruit to about 4 to 6 inches apart when it is 1/2 to 5/8 inch (1.3 to 1.6 cm) in diameter. This will help to increase the size of the remaining fruit and prevent limb breakage. ■ ‡‡*Shothole fungus:* If shothole fungus has been a problem during the growing season, apply Bordeaux or a fixed-copper fungicide during or just after leaf fall but before the onset of winter rains. ■ §§*Prevent brown rot:* Prune out infected blooms if observed. If brown rot was a serious problem on fruit the previous year or if there is excessive rainfall during bloom, spray with a fungicide as flowers start to open. One to three applications may be required if weather is rainy. ■ ¶¶*Trunk paint:* In hot regions, paint the trunk and lower branches of young trees with a 1:1 mixture of white interior latex paint and water to prevent sunburn injury and reduce borer infestations. ■ ##*Harvest:* Harvest fruit when fully ripe. Some varieties are harvested over a period of weeks; others ripen all at one time. Clean up fallen fruit immediately to minimize brown rot and infestations of dried fruit beetles. Store fully ripe fruit under refrigeration or sun-dry, can, or freeze.

CHERRY

NOV	DEC	JAN	FEB	MAR	APR	MAY	JUNE	JULY	AUG	SEPT	OCT
	Plant bare-root trees*										
Pruning and dormant oil sprays†‡				Fertilize young trees§							
								Fertilize mature trees¶			
			Irrigation#								
			Prevent brown rot**			Summer pruning††					
							Cover trees with netting‡‡				
		Trunk paint§§				Harvest¶¶					

Plant bare-root trees: Place trees in areas that have good soil texture and good drainage. Use raised beds or mounds if you are planting where soils are heavy or compacted. ■ †*Dormant pruning:* Prune out any dead, diseased, or broken branches. Prune out about 10% of last year's growth on mature trees to let light into the tree. ■ ‡*Dormant sprays:* For scale, mite, or aphid management, spray trees with dormant oil late in the dormant season, just prior to bud break. Provide thorough coverage including the trunk. ■ §*Fertilize young trees:* Fertilize with nitrogen fertilizers three times: in March, May, and July. Water the fertilizer in immediately to avoid nitrogen loss. ■ ¶*Fertilize mature trees:* If necessary, fertilize mature trees just after harvest. See Table 6.4 for specific rates. ■ #*Irrigation:* Drip irrigate several times per week, or for sprinkler or flood irrigation, water about every one to three weeks during the heat of summer and provide enough water to wet the soil to a depth of 18 to 24 inches (45 to 61 cm) depending upon soil type and environmental conditions. ■ **Prevent brown rot:* If brown rot has been a problem in the past, apply Bordeaux or fixed copper at the popcorn stage of bud development (when the unopened flower buds have matured and the petal color is discernible, so they resemble partially popped corn kernels). Apply again at the full bloom stage if high moisture conditions exist. ■ ††*Summer pruning:* Remove the strong, vigorous shoots from the interior portion of the canopy to improve light penetration and air circulation in the tree's interior. Regular summer pruning will be required for those fruit trees being trained to fruit bushes. ■ ‡‡*Cover trees with netting:* Netting will help protect the fruit from birds. ■ §§*Trunk paint:* In hot regions, paint the trunk and lower branches of young trees that are exposed to afternoon sun with a 1:1 mixture of white interior latex paint and water to prevent sunburn injury and reduce borer infestations. ■ ¶¶*Harvest:* Harvest cherries when fully ripe and avoid damaging the fruit spurs as the fruit are picked. Keep the stems attached to the cherries to keep the tearing of the fruit's flesh to a minimum. Cherries may be stored for several days under refrigeration. They may be sun-dried, canned, or frozen for longer storage.

FIG

NOV	DEC	JAN	FEB	MAR	APR	MAY	JUNE	JULY	AUG	SEPT	OCT
		Plant bare-root trees*									
	Pruning and dormant oil sprays†			Fertilize young trees‡							
Remove fallen or over-ripe fruit§						Fertilize mature trees¶					
				Irrigation#							
						Smyrna-type fig caprification**			Annual pruning††		
		Trunk paint‡‡					Harvest§§				

Plant bare-root trees: Plant bare-root stock during the dormant season. ■ †*Dormant pruning and sprays:* Prune out any dead, diseased, or broken branches. Prune off about one-half of last year's wood to thin the crop and ensure good shoot growth. If scale insects are a serious problem and treatment is necessary, spray with dormant oil when leaves are off during the dormant or delayed dormant period. If a large number of the scales have parasite exit holes, treatment may not be needed. ■ ‡*Fertilize young trees:* Fertilize with nitrogen fertilizers three times: in March, May, and July. Water the fertilizer in immediately to avoid nitrogen loss. ■ §*Remove fruit mummies:* Remove and destroy all mummified fruit on the ground and hanging on tree branches to reduce future pest problems. ■ ¶*Fertilize mature trees:* Mature trees do not require significant nitrogen fertilization. If tree growth is less than 1 foot (30.5 cm) per year and irrigation is adequate, fertilize with half of the total fertilizer in spring and the second half just after harvest or in August or September. See Table 6.4 for specific rates. ■ #*Irrigation:* Drip irrigate several times per week, or for sprinkler or flood irrigation, water about every one to three weeks during the heat of summer and provide enough water to wet the soil to a depth of 18 to 24 inches (45 to 61 cm) depending upon soil type and environmental conditions. Irrigate within the drip line, well away from the trunk of the tree. ■ **Caprification:* On Smyrna-type figs, caprification is done during May. Two to four caprifigs are placed in a brown lunch sack with a small hole in the bottom of the bag. The bag is then placed out in the tree and replaced weekly with fresh caprifigs during the pollination period. Caprifigs are hard to find unless there is a tree growing nearby. If grown in the same yard, over-caprification *(over-pollination)* may occur, making the fruit overly seedy. ■ ††*Annual pruning:* Figs are best pruned in late summer or fall after you harvest the main crop. Remove broken, drooping, crossed, or diseased limbs. Once a fig tree has strong framework, it requires only minimal pruning. ■ ‡‡*Trunk paint:* In hot regions, paint the trunk and lower branches of young trees that are exposed to afternoon sun with a 1:1 mixture of white interior latex paint and water to prevent sunburn injury and reduce borer infestations. Apply the paint mixture from 2 inches (5.1 cm) below the soil line to 2 feet (61 cm) above. ■ §§*Harvest:* Figs must be fully tree-ripened before picking. If picked immature, they will not ripen further after harvest. The fruit is ready to harvest when it becomes somewhat soft and the neck of the fruit begins to bend. Most varieties can be eaten fresh, pickled, or sun-dried. Some varieties may have more than one crop each season depending upon the degree and time of pruning.

Periods of primary activity: Periods of secondary activity:

PEACH & NECTARINE

NOV	DEC	JAN	FEB	MAR	APR	MAY	JUNE	JULY	AUG	SEPT	OCT

Plant bare-root trees*

Pruning and dormant oil sprays†‡

Remove fruit mummies#

Fertilize young trees§

Fertilize mature trees¶

Irrigation**

Scaffold support††

Fruit thinning‡‡

Prevent brown rot§§

Summer pruning¶¶

Trunk paint##

Harvest***

Shothole and peach leaf curl†††

*Plant bare-root trees: Plant bare-root trees during the dormant season. ■ †Dormant pruning: Prune out any dead, diseased, or broken branches. Prune off about one-half of last year's wood to thin the crop and ensure good shoot growth. Early varieties are pruned more severely than later-maturing varieties. ■ ‡Dormant sprays: For San Jose scale, mite, or aphid management, spray trees with dormant oil late in the dormant season, just prior to bud break. Provide thorough coverage including the trunk. ■ §Fertilize young trees: Fertilize with nitrogen fertilizers three times: in March, May, and July. ■ ¶Fertilize mature trees: Fertilize mature trees with one-half of the total fertilizer in spring and the second half in August or September or any time after harvest. See Table 6.4 for specific rates. ■ #Remove fruit mummies: Remove and destroy all mummified fruit hanging on tree branches to reduce future pest problems. ■ **Irrigation: Drip irrigate several times per week, or for sprinkler or flood irrigation, water about every one to two weeks during the heat of summer and provide enough water to wet the soil to a depth of 18 to 24 inches (61 to 91 cm) depending upon soil type and environmental conditions. Irrigate at the drip line, well away from the trunk of the tree. ■ ††Scaffold support: To prevent limb breakage from heavy fruit loads, rope scaffold branches of open center trees loosely with cotton fiber rope. As the weight of the fruit pulls the scaffold branches down, the rope will tighten and provide adequate support. Alternatively, you can prop up heavy limbs in summer to prevent breakage. ■ ‡‡Fruit thinning: Thin fruit to about 6 inches (15 cm) apart when they are about 1 inch (2.5 cm) in diameter. ■ §§Prevent brown rot: Prune out infected blooms if observed. If brown rot is a serious problem on fruit, or if there is excessive rainfall during bloom, spray with a copper fungicide when flowers show pink color but have not yet opened. One to three applications may be required. ■ ¶¶Summer pruning: Remove the strong, vigorous shoots from the interior portion of the canopy to improve light penetration and air circulation in the tree's interior. Two or three summer prunings will be required for those fruit trees being trained to fruit bushes. See Chapter 7 for details. ■ ##Trunk paint: In hot regions, paint the trunk and lower branches of young trees that are exposed to afternoon sun with a 1:1 mixture of white interior latex paint and water to prevent sunburn injury and reduce borer infestations. Apply the paint mixture from 2 inches (5.1 cm) below the soil line to 2 feet (61 cm) above. ■ ***Harvest: Harvest fruit as soon as it is firm ripe. Clean up fallen fruit immediately to minimize brown rot and infestations of dried fruit beetles. Store fully ripe fruit under refrigeration or sun-dry, can, or freeze them. ■ †††Peach leaf curl and shothole control: Spray copper or lime sulfur fungicide twice, with the first application around November 15 or after the leaves have fallen and the second about February 1 to 15. The later spray should coincide with bud swell but should occur before the flowers open.

PECAN

NOV	DEC	JAN	FEB	MAR	APR	MAY	JUNE	JULY	AUG	SEPT	OCT

Plant bare-root trees*

Pruning†

Remove old nuts§

Fertilize young trees‡

Apply zinc to foliage¶   Fertilize mature trees¶

Irrigation#

Summer training of young trees**

Trunk paint††

Harvest‡‡

Aphid control§§

*Plant bare-root trees: Dormant bare-root trees are available for planting in December and January. ■ †Dormant pruning: Prune out any dead, diseased, or broken branches. Once trees have been trained to a modified central leader, mature tree pruning is confined to the removal of broken or dead branches and crossing limbs. Also, remove any branch originating from the central leader that has a narrow crotch angle, preferably when the branch is young. ■ ‡Fertilize young trees: Fertilize with nitrogen fertilizers three times: in March, May, and July. ■ §Remove old nuts: Remove and destroy nuts left on the tree as well as those on the ground following harvest to reduce future pest problems. ■ ¶Fertilize mature trees: Pecans need very little nitrogen in the home garden. If necessary, fertilize mature trees in small amounts from mid-May to August. Water well after each application. See Table 6.4 for specific rates. Some trees may occasionally have zinc deficiency. Apply chelated or liquid zinc to the foliage in April. ■ #Irrigation: Drip irrigate several times per week, or for sprinkler or flood irrigation, water about every one to two weeks during the heat of summer and provide enough water to wet the soil to a depth of 24 to 36 inches (61 to 91 cm) depending upon soil type and environmental conditions. Keep the trunk and crown area around the trunk dry in summer to reduce root and crown rot problems. ■ **Summer training of young trees: Light summer pruning is helpful during the training phase of young pecans. Promote the development of a strong central leader and wide-angled scaffold branches. ■ ††Trunk paint: In hot regions, paint the trunk and lower branches of young trees that are exposed to afternoon sun with a 1:1 mixture of white interior latex paint and water to prevent sunburn injury and reduce borer infestations. ■ ‡‡Harvest: Harvest begins as soon as the hulls begin to split and the kernels have filled in the shell. The hulls will begin to loosen from the shell and gradually dry over a period of several weeks. Nuts can be shaken or knocked off of the tree with a pole. The hulls should be removed from the nuts as soon as possible after harvest. Wear gloves to avoid staining your hands. ■ §§Pecan aphid control: Aphids are common on pecans and high populations are bothersome because of the copious honeydew excreted by the aphids. Treatment may be required if there are more than 20 aphids per leaf in summer or more than 10 per leaf from August 15 to leaf fall.

PERSIMMON

NOV	DEC	JAN	FEB	MAR	APR	MAY	JUNE	JULY	AUG	SEPT	OCT

Plant bare-root trees*

Pruning and dormant oil sprays†

Remove decayed and fallen fruit§

Fertilize young trees‡

Fertilize mature trees¶

Irrigation#

Harvest‡‡   Trunk paint††   Summer pruning**   Harvest‡‡

*Plant bare-root trees or container stock: Bare root trees are available in December and January. ■ †Dormant pruning: Prune out any dead, diseased, or broken branches. To keep trees small enough to allow harvesting without a ladder, top the trees or head them back to a height of about 8 feet (244 cm) every year. Once the scaffold structure is in place, minimal pruning is required except to maintain structure and remove suckers. Dormant sprays: For mealybug, scale, mite, or aphid management, spray trees with dormant oil late in the dormant season, just prior to bud break. Provide thorough coverage including the trunk. ■ ‡Fertilize young trees: Fertilize young trees in April and July. Water the fertilizer in immediately to avoid nitrogen loss. ■ §Remove fruit mummies: Remove and destroy all fallen fruit. ■ ¶Fertilize mature trees: If necessary, fertilize mature trees over the course of the growing season. To prevent fruit quality problems, do not apply excess nitrogen fertilizer. See Table 6.4 for specific rates. ■ #Irrigation: Drip irrigate several times per week, or for sprinkler or flood irrigation, water about every one to three weeks during the heat of summer and provide enough water to wet the soil to a depth of 18 to 24 inches (45 to 61 cm) depending upon soil type and environmental conditions. Irrigate within the drip line, well away from the trunk of the tree. ■ **Summer pruning: Thin shoots to open the canopy and remove any broken or dead limbs. ■ ††Trunk paint: In hot regions, paint the trunk and lower branches of young trees that are exposed to afternoon sun with a 1:1 mixture of white interior latex paint and water to prevent sunburn injury and reduce borer infestations. ■ ‡‡Harvest: Harvest astringent varieties when they are hard but fully colored. They will soften on the tree and improve in quality. Non-astringent persimmons are ready to harvest when they are fully colored, but for best flavor, allow them to soften slightly after harvest. To harvest, clip the fruit stem rather than pulling the fruit from the tree.

PISTACHIO

NOV	DEC	JAN	FEB	MAR	APR	MAY	JUNE	JULY	AUG	SEPT	OCT

Plant container-grown trees*

Pruning and dormant oil sprays†

Fertilize young trees‡

Fertilize mature trees§

Remove mummies and fallen nuts¶

Apply chelated zinc#

Irrigation**

Trunk paint††

Harvest‡‡

*__Plant container-grown trees:__ Plant container-grown trees during the dormant season through early spring for optimum establishment. ■ †__Dormant pruning:__ Remove broken, dead, or diseased limbs. To prune mature trees, head back terminal branches to stimulate the development of lateral shoots and new fruiting wood. The degree of pruning should be based on tree vigor and how low you want the canopy to be. Dormant sprays: If soft scale insects are a serious problem and treatment is necessary, spray with dormant oil when leaves are off during the dormant or delayed dormant period. ■ ‡__Fertilize young trees:__ Fertilize with nitrogen fertilizers three times: in March, May, and July. Water the fertilizer in immediately to avoid nitrogen loss. ■ §__Fertilize mature trees:__ Mature trees do not require significant nitrogen fertilization in the home garden. ■ ¶__Remove fruit mummies:__ Remove and destroy mummified fruit on the ground and hanging on tree branches to reduce future pest problems. ■ #__Apply chelated or liquid zinc:__ Some trees may occasionally have a zinc deficiency. Apply chelated or liquid zinc to the foliage in April. ■ **__Irrigation:__ Drip irrigate several times per week, or for sprinkler or flood irrigation, water about every two to three weeks during the heat of summer and provide enough water to wet the soil to a depth of 6 feet (183 cm) depending upon soil type and environmental conditions. Irrigate within the drip line, well away from the trunk of the tree. ■ ††__Trunk paint:__ In hot regions, paint the trunk and lower branches of young trees that are exposed to afternoon sun with a 1:1 mixture of white interior latex paint and water to prevent sunburn injury and reduce borer infestations. ■ ‡‡__Harvest:__ To minimize insect damage, harvest nuts as early as possible when mature. Harvest when the skin changes from translucent to opaque or from greenish to yellowish red color. The hulls will begin to loosen from the shells and gradually dry over a period of several weeks. The shells will begin to crack at the same time. Knock the nuts down with a pole. It is best to have the nuts drop onto a tarp to prevent contamination from soilborne pathogens.

PLUM (incl. CHERRY-PLUM, PLUOT, & PRUNE)

NOV	DEC	JAN	FEB	MAR	APR	MAY	JUNE	JULY	AUG	SEPT	OCT

Plant bare-root trees*

Pruning and dormant oil sprays†

Remove fruit mummies¶

Fertilize young trees‡

Fertilize mature trees§

Irrigation#

Fruit thinning**

Summer pruning††

Trunk paint‡‡

Harvest§§

Plum aphid management¶¶

*__Plant bare-root trees:__ Place trees in areas that have good soil texture and good drainage. Use raised beds or mounds if you plant where soils are heavy or compacted. ■ †__Dormant pruning:__ Prune out any dead, diseased, or broken branches. Thin branches out (usually about 20% of last year's growth) to allow light into the canopy. Avoid making heading cuts except on young trees. Some heading cuts might be appropriate if you are trying to establish branching in a gap. __Dormant sprays:__ For San Jose scale, mite, or aphid management, spray trees with dormant oil late in the dormant season, just prior to bud break. Provide thorough coverage including the trunk. ■ ‡__Fertilize young trees:__ Fertilize with nitrogen fertilizers three times: in March, May, and July. Water the fertilizer in immediately to avoid nitrogen loss. ■ §__Fertilize mature trees:__ Fertilize mature trees with one-half of the total amount of fertilizer in spring and the second half in early August or September. Use lower rates or no fertilizer at all for vigorous trees. See Table 6.4 for specific rates. ■ ¶__Remove fruit mummies:__ Remove and destroy all mummified fruit hanging on tree branches to reduce future pest problems. ■ #__Irrigation:__ Drip irrigate several times per week, or for sprinkler or flood irrigation, water about every one to two weeks during the heat of summer and provide enough water to wet the soil to a depth of 18 to 24 inches (45 to 61 cm) depending upon soil type and environmental conditions. Irrigate within the drip line, well away from the trunk of the tree. ■ **__Fruit thinning:__ Thin fruit to about 4 to 6 inches apart when they are 1/2 to 3/4 inch (1.3 o 1.9 cm) in diameter. ■ ††__Summer pruning:__ Remove the strong, vigorous shoots from the interior portion of the canopy to improve light penetration and air circulation in the tree's interior. Two or three summer prunings will be required for those fruit trees being trained to fruit bushes. ■ ‡‡__Trunk paint:__ In hot regions, paint the trunk and lower branches of young trees that are exposed to afternoon sun with a 1:1 mixture of white interior latex paint and water to prevent sunburn injury and reduce borer infestations. ■ §§__Harvest:__ Harvest fruit when firm ripe. Early varieties may need to be harvested over a period of weeks, while fruit of later varieties are usually harvested all at once. Clean up fallen fruit immediately to minimize pest problems. Store fully ripe fruit under refrigeration or sun-dry, can, or freeze them. ■ ¶¶__Plum aphid management:__ Plum aphids often cause curling of the young leaves in spring, but will only require control when 50% of the leaves are curled and live aphids are present.

Periods of primary activity:		Periods of secondary activity:	

POMEFRUIT (APPLE, PEAR, & QUINCE)

	NOV	DEC	JAN	FEB	MAR	APR	MAY	JUNE	JULY	AUG	SEPT	OCT

Plant new bare-root trees*

Pruning and dormant oil sprays†

Fertilize young trees‡

Fertilize mature trees§

Remove mummified fruit/Clean up fallen fruit and leaves¶

Irrigation#

Fruit thinning**

Fire blight management††

Trunk paint‡‡

Harvest§§

Control codling moth¶¶

Plant dormant bare-root trees. ■ †*Dormant pruning:* Thin out 15 to 20% of last year's growth to let light into the tree center. Remove broken, crossed, or diseased limbs, as well as water sprouts and root suckers. *Dormant sprays:* For scale, mite, or aphid management, spray trees with dormant oil late in the dormant season, just prior to bud break. Provide thorough coverage including the trunk. ■ ‡*Fertilize young trees:* Fertilize with nitrogen fertilizers three times: in March, May, and July. Water the fertilizer in immediately to avoid nitrogen loss. ■ §*Fertilize mature trees:* If necessary, fertilize mature trees with one-half of the total amount of fertilizer in spring and the second half just after harvest. To avoid fruit quality problems, avoid excessive nitrogen applications. ■ ¶*Remove fallen fruit and leaves:* Remove and destroy overwintering fruit in the tree and on the ground. Picking up fallen fruit reduces codling moth, and picking up fallen leaves reduces scab infections the following spring. ■ #*Irrigation:* Drip irrigate several times per week, or for sprinkler or flood irrigation, water about every one to three weeks during the heat of summer and provide enough water to wet the soil to a depth of 24 to 36 inches (61 to 91 cm) depending upon soil type and environmental conditions. ■ **Fruit thinning:* When 3/4 inch in diameter, thin them to one fruit per 6 inches (15 cm) of shoot growth or one fruit per cluster. Pears are not usually thinned unless fruit set is especially heavy. Asian pears, however, should be thinned about 30 to 60 days after bloom to increase fruit size. The fruit should ultimately be 5 to 7 inches (13 to 18 cm) apart on the branch. Quince do not typically need to be thinned. ■ ††*Fire blight management:* Prune out affected shoots, making pruning cuts into healthy wood at least 12 inches below the dead portion of the branch. Remove and destroy all diseased wood. A spray application of fixed copper every five to seven days during the bloom period may help to control the disease, but it may also cause some russetting of fruit. ■ ‡‡*Trunk paint:* In hot regions, paint the trunk and lower branches of young trees that are exposed to afternoon sun with a 1:1 mixture of white interior latex paint and water to prevent sunburn injury and reduce borer infestations. Apply the paint mixture from 2 inches below the soil line to 2 feet (61 cm) above. ■ §§*Harvest:* Harvest when fruit is fully mature and has full color. Note that in hot summer climates, red fruit may not fully show red at maturity. European pears such as Bartlett are harvested when green and hard and should be stored in the refrigerator before ripening. They are then allowed to soften at room temperature. Asian pears are allowed to ripen on the tree. Quince should be harvested when fruit turn from green to yellow. Leave them on the tree as long as possible to get the best flavor, but harvest before frost. Clip fruit from the tree to avoid damaging the fruit. ■ ¶¶*Control codling moth:* Control should begin in spring at petal fall and may be required all season. One of the most reliable control methods that does not involve spraying is to cut a small hole in the bottom of a brown paper lunch sack and slip the hole over a small developing fruit. Staple the mouth of the bag shut to exclude adult moths.

POMEGRANATE

	NOV	DEC	JAN	FEB	MAR	APR	MAY	JUNE	JULY	AUG	SEPT	OCT

Plant bare-root trees*

Pruning†

Fertilize young trees‡

Remove split and decayed fruit§

Fertilize mature trees¶

Irrigation#

Trunk paint**

Harvest††

Plant bare-root trees or container stock: Bare-root trees are available in December and January and containerized nursery stock is available for planting out in later spring. ■ †*Dormant pruning:* Prune out any dead, diseased, or broken branches. Pomegranates tend to sucker heavily. These suckers and water sprouts should be removed. To keep trees smaller such that harvesting can be done without a ladder, top the trees or head them back to a height of about 8 feet (244 cm) every year. Once the scaffold structure is in place, minimal pruning is required except to maintain structure and remove suckers. ■ ‡*Fertilize young trees:* Fertilize with nitrogen fertilizers three times: in March, May, and July. Water the fertilizer in immediately to avoid nitrogen loss. ■ §*Remove fruit mummies:* Remove and destroy all split and decayed fruit. ■ ¶*Fertilize mature trees:* If necessary, fertilize mature trees over the course of the growing season. To prevent fruit quality problems, do not apply excess nitrogen fertilizer. See Table 6.4 for specific rates. ■ #*Irrigation:* Drip irrigate several times per week, or for sprinkler or flood irrigation, water about every one to three weeks during the heat of summer and provide enough water to wet the soil to a depth of 18 to 24 inches (45 to 61 cm) depending upon soil type and environmental conditions. Irrigate within the drip line, well away from the trunk of the tree. ■ **Trunk paint:* In hot regions, paint the trunk and lower branches of young trees that are exposed to afternoon sun with a 1:1 mixture of white interior latex paint and water to prevent sunburn injury and reduce borer infestations. ■ ††*Harvest:* Harvest fruit when they develop full color and before they crack. Pomegranates have a long storage life when held in cold storage and at high humidity. They improve in juiciness and flavor. Clip the fruit stem at harvest rather than pulling the fruit from the tree.

WALNUT

	NOV	DEC	JAN	FEB	MAR	APR	MAY	JUNE	JULY	AUG	SEPT	OCT

Plant bare-root trees*

Pruning†

Fertilize young trees‡

Remove and destroy old and fallen nuts§

Fertilize mature trees‡   Remove and destroy fallen nuts§

Irrigation¶

Trunk paint#

Harvest**

Plant bare-root trees: Place trees in areas that have deep soil with good texture and drainage. ■ †*Dormant pruning:* Prune out any dead, diseased, or broken branches. Prune mature trees by thinning out limbs in crowded parts of the canopy to let light into the whole tree. ■ ‡*Fertilize young trees:* Fertilize young trees monthly with nitrogen fertilizer beginning in April prior to first irrigation. *Fertilize mature trees:* Fertilize mature trees in spring. Water after application to avoid nitrogen loss. Use lower rates for vigorous trees. See Table 6.4 for specific rates. ■ §*Remove and destroy old and fallen nuts:* Remove and destroy all nuts hanging on tree branches to reduce future pest problems. In May and June, clean up fallen nuts to reduce incidence of codling moth and navel orangeworm. ■ ¶*Irrigation:* Drip irrigate several times per week, or for sprinkler or flood irrigation, water about every one to two weeks during the heat of summer and provide enough water to wet the soil to a depth of 24 to 36 inches (61 to 91 cm) depending upon soil type and environmental conditions. Irrigate within the drip line, well away from the trunk of the tree. ■ #*Trunk paint:* In hot regions, paint the trunk and lower branches of young trees that are exposed to afternoon sun with a 1:1 mixture of white interior latex paint and water to prevent sunburn injury and reduce borer infestations. ■ **Harvest:* Harvest nuts as early as possible. Shake or pole the trees when the green hulls begin to crack and separate from the shells. Remove the hulls as soon as possible after harvesting and discard them. Wear gloves to avoid staining your hands.

Glossary

abiotic disorder. A disorder or disease that is not caused by a living organism such as fungus or bacterium, but instead has an environmental or physiological cause.

acaricide. See *miticide.*

advective freeze. A phenomenon that occurs when wind moves a sub-freezing air mass into an area, displacing warmer air.

adventitious bud. A bud that arises in a place on a branch other than a leaf axil; usually refers to a bud that sends out vigorous growth from a relatively large branch.

alternate (biennial) bearing. The habit of alternating heavy fruit production on a given tree in one year with light fruit production the following year; can be corrected with proper pruning and fruit thinning.

anion. A negatively charged ion (e.g., sulfate, nitrate).

anther. The tip of the stamen (male flower part) that contains the pollen grains.

anvil lopper. Pruning tool in which one blade cuts down against a flat surface. Compare with *bypass lopper.*

apical dominance. Hormonal influence, primarily influenced by gravity, through which a terminal bud suppresses the growth of lateral buds.

apical meristem. The tissues at the tip of roots and shoots where cells divide, giving rise to new growth. Compare with *vascular cambium.*

arborsculpture. A horticultural art form in which the shoots of young trees are trained and grafted together to create tree structures.

arthropod. Any member of a large group of invertebrate animals with jointed legs and a segmented body, including insects, spiders, and mites.

auxin. A generic term for a group of plant hormones that are active at low concentrations and regulate plant growth and development, particularly cell division, cell elongation, adventitious root initiation, and bud dormancy.

axil. See *leaf axil.*

bacteria. One-celled microscopic organisms that lack chlorophyll and may be parasites on plants or animals; examples include the fire blight pathogen and the beneficial *Bacillus thuringiensis.* (singular: bacterium)

bactericide. A pesticide used for control of bacteria and the diseases that they cause.

banding. The placement of fertilizer in one or more strips near trees or in a circle under the drip line of the tree.

bare-root tree. A tree that is dug from a nursery field and sold with no soil around the roots.

bark. Tissues outside the vascular cambium that consist of inner bark (phloem) and outer bark.

bark grafting. A technique in which the scion is inserted between the bark and the wood of the stock.

bark lifter. A part of a budding knife used to separate the bark from the wood to insert a bud; located on the opposite side of the blade from the cutting edge or as a separate fold-out element on the same knife.

bark slipping. The ability to easily peel back the bark of a young shoot or branch for budding or grafting; it is greatest when vegetative growth is most active.

basal. Lower portion of shoot or branch near the point of attachment with another shoot or branch.

beneficials. Organisms that provide a benefit to crop production. The term is applied especially to natural enemies of pests and to pollinators such as bees.

biological control. The action of parasites, predators, pathogens, or competitors in maintaining another organism's density at a lower population than would occur in their absence.

bitter pit. A physiological disorder of apple fruit, associated with low levels of calcium in the fruit tissue.

blade. The broad, expanded part of a leaf, also called a *lamina,* which is attached to the petiole.

blast. The sudden death of buds, flowers, or young fruit.

blight. Any disease causing sudden, severe leaf damage or general killing of stems or flowers.

Bordeaux mixture. A mix of copper and hydrated lime, used for dormant season spraying to control fungal diseases such as peach leaf curl. The addition of lime enhances the steadfastness of copper on the tree.

branch. Any woody extension growing from the trunk or limb of a tree.

branch (crotch) angle. The angle formed between the trunk and a main limb or between two branches.

branch bark ridge. A thin, crescent-shaped area of raised bark in the branch crotch that marks where the branch wood and trunk wood meet. It is usually darker than the surrounding bark.

branch collar. The distinct, enlarged portion of woody tissue formed at the base of a branch where it attaches to the trunk.

breba crop. The first of two fig crops produced each year. Breba figs begin as enlarged lateral buds that develop in the fall and ripen in early to mid summer.

bud. A plant organ at the base of the leaf axil or the tip of a shoot from which a shoot, flower, or flower cluster develops.

bud grafting. Grafting by inserting a single bud (scion) onto a branch of the rootstock. Also called budding.

bud scales. Thin, papery or leathery structures that cover dormant buds.

bud swell. The enlargement of buds before growth starts, signaling the beginning of the growing season.

budding. See *bud grafting.*

budding rubber. A specialized rubber strip used to hold a recently inserted bud in the bark of a stock.

budstick. See *budwood.*

budwood. Current-season shoots or one-year-old branch collected for the purpose of bud grafting.

bypass lopper. Pruning tool in which two blades pass each other, like scissors; sometimes called eagle-beak loppers Compare with *anvil lopper.*

caliche. A naturally occurring hardpan cemented by lime (calcium carbonate).

callus. Undifferentiated tissue that forms a protective covering around a wounded plant surface.

calyx. The usually green outer whorl of sepals of a flower.

cambium. See *vascular cambium.*

canker. A localized area of diseased tissue on a stem, often sunken or swollen, and surrounded by healthy tissue.

canopy. The leaf-bearing portion of the tree.

caprification. Pollination of the flowers of certain figs by the blastophaga wasp using pollen from the caprifig.

carbohydrates. Organic compounds, including sugars, starches, and cellulose, that are produced as a result of photosynthesis.

caterpillar. Immature form of butterflies and moths; a type of larva.

cation. A positively charged ion (e.g., potassium, iron).

catkin. The pollen-bearing male flower of walnuts, pecans, chestnuts, and filberts.

central leader system. A method of tree training in which the trunk is encouraged to form a central axis with branches distributed laterally around it; used primarily for apples and pears.

chilling hours. The number of hours of temperature below 45°F (7°C) that accumulate during the dormant season.

chilling requirement. The cumulative chilling hours required by fruit or nut trees in order to overcome bud dormancy and provide satisfactory growth and fruit or nut production. The requirement may vary considerably between species and varieties.

chip budding. A method of budding in which a section of bud and wood is removed from one branch and inserted onto a branch of another plant on which a similar cut was made.

chlorophyll. The green pigment of plant cells that absorbs light energy necessary for photosynthesis.

chlorosis. Yellowing of foliage that results from a loss of or deficiency in chlorophyll; can be caused by nutritional deficiency, disease, insufficient light, or other factors.

clay. *1.* A soil particle less than 0.002 mm in diameter. *2.* A textural class of soil that is characterized by an ability to hold relatively large amounts of water and nutrients, but may be poorly drained and difficult to cultivate.

cleft grafting. A method of grafting in which the scion is inserted into the split-open stub on a branch of the stock.

clingstone. A stone fruit in which the flesh (pulp) clings to the pit. Compare with *freestone*.

cocoon. A sheath, usually mostly of silk, formed by an insect larva as a chamber for pupation.

collar. See *branch collar*.

compatibility. *1.* Of sex cells, the ability of pollen and egg cells to unite and form a viable embryo. *2.* Of grafting, the ability to form a successful, long-lived stock/scion union.

compound leaf. A leaf divided into two or more parts, or leaflets, all attached to the stem by a single petiole.

controller. See *irrigation controller*.

cornicles. The pair of tube-like structures that project backward out of the rear of an aphid's body.

crawler. The active first instar of a scale insect.

crop load. The relative amount of fruit on a tree.

cross-pollination. The transfer of pollen from the anther of one plant to the stigma of another plant.

crotch. Junction formed between the trunk and a main limb or between two limbs.

crown. The area of a tree where the trunk and large roots join. (Arborists usually refer to the upper portion of a tree [canopy] or the branches and leaves as the "crown.")

crown rot. Disease of the (root) crown, usually caused by the fungus *Phytophthora*, in which cambium tissues are killed and the tree becomes stunted or dies.

cultivar. *Culti*vated *var*iety, e.g., 'Fuji' apple; a variety that was developed or discovered and is now maintained under cultivation. In common horticultural usage, *cultivar* is synonymous with *variety*.

deciduous. Of trees or shrubs, those that typically drop their leaves at the end of each growing season.

devigoration. A decline in the overall growth rate of shoots, caused by any of a number of factors.

delayed dormant period. The late dormant period when buds are beginning to swell. This timing is important when spraying for peach leaf curl, aphids (eggs), scale, and some spider mites.

dichogomous. A phenomenon in which the male and female flower parts of a plant mature at different times, preventing self-pollination.

dioecious. Of plants, species that have male flowers on one plant and female flowers on another, such as kiwifruit and pistachio. Compare with *monoecious*.

disease. Any disturbance of a plant that interferes with its normal structure or function, usually caused by a microorganism (e.g., fungus or bacteria).

dormancy. A state of inactivity or prolonged rest, such as that of deciduous fruit trees in winter.

dormant bud. Usually refers to a bud on a one-year-old branch that is inactive during the dormant period. Compare with *latent bud*.

dormant pruning. Pruning during the dormant season. Invigorates tree growth the following spring. Compare with *summer pruning*.

dormant season. The period from late fall, just before leaves fall off, through bud swell.

dormant spray. Pesticide treatment applied during the dormant period.

drip line. The imaginary vertical line extending downward from the outermost branch tips of a tree to the soil directly below.

drip irrigation. A low-volume irrigation system in which drip emitters are connected to or embedded within drip tubing, with discharge rates of 1/2 to 4 gallons of water per hour.

drupe. Botanical name for a one-seeded fruit derived entirely from an ovary with a stony endocarp containing the seed. Stone fruit and almonds are drupes.

dwarfing rootstock. A rootstock that imparts reduced vigor in a tree. Compare with *standard rootstock*. Produces a semidwarf tree.

embryo. The rudimentary juvenile plant usually contained in the seed.

endocarp. The hard, inner ovary wall of a ripened fruit; the stony part of the pit containing the seed of stone fruits and almonds.

espalier system. A method of tree training in which the main branches of a tree are trained along a wall or trellis.

ethylene. A plant hormone that regulates flowering and ripening; emitted as a gas from ripening fruit and damaged plant tissues.

evapotranspiration (ET). The loss of water through evaporation from the soil and transpiration from the leaves. A technical term referring to the amount of water used by a tree.

exocarp. The skin or the outermost layer of a fruit.

fall budding. Bud grafting performed in late summer or early fall, in which a bud from a current-season's shoot is inserted into a current season's shoot on another tree, and that bud is not forced to grow until the following spring. Compare with *June budding*.

"feel method" for soil. A technique for estimating the amount of sand, silt, and clay in a soil sample by squeezing a moist, well-mixed sample of the soil between the thumb and forefinger.

fertilization. *1.* The process by which a pollen grain germinates and unites with an ovule to form an embryo (See also *pollination*). *2.* The application of nutrient fertilizers to the soil or a plant's leaves.

fertilizer. A substance added to soil or sprayed onto foliage to provide plants with essential nutrients.

fertilizer analysis. A statement, usually on the label of a fertilizer container, of the percentages by weight of nitrogen, phosphoric acid, and potash contained in the material.

field capacity. The amount of water a soil can hold against gravity.

fine roots/feeder roots. The youngest roots with root hairs, usually less than 1/16 in (2 mm) diameter; important in the absorption of water and minerals.

flesh. The soft, pulpy portion of a fruit.

flower bud. A bud containing a single flower (e.g., in stone fruit, almond) or a cluster of flowers (e.g., in pome fruit).

foliar fertilizer. A fertilizer mixed with water and sprayed onto the leaves of a plant.

forcing. Causing a bud (flower or shoot) to grow at a time when it would normally not be growing. This is done by cutting the branch off just above the bud (heading cut), girdling or notching above the bud, applying a growth-promoting hormone, or significantly modifying the ambient temperature around the plant.

frass. The solid fecal material produced by insect larvae.

freestone. A fruit in which the pit does not cling to the flesh of a ripened fruit. Compare with *clingstone*.

fruit bush. A fruit tree that is kept small through pruning to develop scaffold branches near the ground and periodic removal, throughout the growing season, of shoots that grow above a certain height.

fruit doubling. A phenomenon on stone fruit in which a single ovary produces two fruit, connected near the stem end, instead of one.

fruit set. The persistence and development of the ovary (fruit) after flowering.

fruit spurring. A phenomenon on stone fruit, particularly cherries, in which a small spur-like inedible protrusion forms near the stem end of the fruit, arising from a semi-aborted double.

fruit thinning. The removal of a portion of the immature fruit on a tree in order to increase fruit size, reduce insect and disease problems, reduce limb breakage, and reduce alternate bearing.

fruiting body. In fungi, a reproductive structure containing spores.

fungicide. A pesticide used for control of fungi and the diseases that they cause.

fungus. Multicellular organism lacking chlorophyll, such as a mold, mildew, rust, or smut. The fungal body normally consists of filamentous strands called mycelia and reproduces through dispersal of spores. (plural: fungi)

gall. Localized swelling or outgrowth of plant tissue, often formed in response to the action of a pathogen or other pest.

genus. The second division of classification, above the species and below the family; the first name of a binomial scientific plant name (e.g., *"Prunus"* in *"Prunus persica"*).

genetic dwarf. A scion that produces a small tree (usually due to short internode growth) even if grafted onto a standard rootstock.

girdle. To damage or remove a ring of bark tissue around a stem or root; such damage temporarily interrupts the downward transport of hormones and carbohydrates.

grafting. The process of joining a part of one plant to another plant in such a way that the two will unite and continue growth as a single unit.

grafting over. See *topworking*.

grafting tape. Specialized tape used to hold a scion piece onto the stock. It may or may not be adhesive.

grafting wax. A specialized wax used to prevent a new graft union from drying out.

graft union. The point on a trunk or branch where a scion (bud or stick) was grafted onto the stock (trunk or branch).

gummosis. A general disorder, particularly of stone fruits, characterized by the exudation and deposit of sap.

hand thinning. Thinning of fruit by hand. Compare with *pole thinning*.

hanger. Fruiting branch on a peach or nectarine tree that hangs downward from the weight of fruit.

hardpan. A subsurface layer of cemented soil that is formed by the chemical bonding of certain ions and soil particles.

heading cut. A pruning cut that takes a shoot or branch back to a bud, a stub, or a lower lateral branch that is too small to assume apical dominance. This technique is used to produce lateral branches, to stiffen a branch, or to reduce the amount of fruit that a gardener will have to thin from a one-year-old branch. Compare with *thinning cut*.

heartwood. The nonliving, darker-colored wood in the center of a trunk, branch, or root. Compare with *sapwood*.

heavy pruning. Removal of a relatively large number of branches when pruning. Compare with *light pruning*.

heel in. To temporarily cover the roots of a bare-root tree in preparation for planting.

herbicide. A pesticide used to control weeds.

honeydew. An excretion from insects such as aphids, mealybugs, and soft scales that consists of modified plant sap.

horizon. See *soil horizon*.

hormone. See *plant hormone*.

horticultural oil. A highly refined petroleum or seed-derived oil that is manufactured specifically to control pests on plants.

host. A plant or animal species that provides sustenance for another, often parasitic organism.

hull. The dry, external coating common to most nut crops.

humus. The decayed residues of organic matter derived from plants and animals.

husk. See *hull*.

infection. The entry of a pathogen into a host and the establishment of the pathogen as a parasite in the host.

infestation. The presence of one or more insects or mites feeding on plant tissues.

inoculum. A pathogen or its parts (spores, mycelium, etc.) that can cause infection.

inorganic. Containing no carbon; generally used to indicate materials (e.g., fertilizers, pesticides) that are of mineral or synthetic origin.

insecticidal oil. See *horticultural oil*.

insecticide. A pesticide that kills insects. Many insecticides also function as *miticides*.

instar. The period between molts in young insects.

integrated pest management (IPM). A pest management strategy that focuses on long-term prevention or suppression of pest problems through a combination of techniques such as biological control, resistant varieties, alternative cultural practices, modification of pest habitat, or the use of pesticides (as a last resort).

internode. The portion of a stem between two nodes or buds.

interveinal. On a leaf, referring to the space between the veins.

ion. An atom or group of atoms that carries a negative (anion) or positive (cation) charge. Ions can be formed by the breakup of molecules, as when certain molecules or compounds are dissolved in water.

irrigation controller. The electronic timer used to schedule and control irrigations.

June budding. Bud grafting performed in spring or early summer, in which a bud from a current-season's shoot is inserted into the current season's shoot of another tree, and that bud is forced to grow during the same season. Compare with *fall budding*. In California, June budding is usually practiced in the month of May.

kernel. The edible portion of a nut within the shell.

larva. The worm-like immature form of an insect that develops through the process of complete metamorphosis including egg, several larval stages, pupa, and adult; examples include the caterpillars of moths, the grubs of beetles and the maggots of flies. (plural: larvae)

latent bud. A bud, often concealed, that remains dormant for an indefinite period. Under certain conditions such as after severe pruning, it may grow. Compare with *dormant bud*.

lateral branch. A branch that arises from the side of a larger branch but is not a strong upright branch.

lateral bud. A bud on the side of a shoot, spur, or branch.

leaching. *1.* Removing salts, ions, or other soluble substances from soil through application of abundant irrigation combined with drainage. *2.* The movement of soluble materials downward through the soil with percolating water.

leader. A dominant, upright stem that usually becomes the main trunk in a tree trained to a central leader or modified central leader. Some branches also have a single leader.

leaf axil. The upper angle formed by the petiole (leaf stem) with the shoot.

lesion. A well-defined area of diseased tissue, such as a canker or fruit spot, usually sunken and having a different color than the surrounding tissue.

light pruning. Removal of a relatively small number of branches when pruning. Compare with *heavy pruning*.

limb. A large branch of a tree.

loam. A soil that contains defined portions of sand, silt, and clay and as such has an ideal soil structure for cultivation and plant growth.

macronutrients. Plant-essential elements required in relatively large amounts by plants: nitrogen (N), phosphorous (P), potassium (K), magnesium (Mg), sulfur (S), and calcium (Ca). Compare with *micronutrients*.

maggot. The legless larva of certain fly species.

marginal. Pertaining to the edges of a leaf.

mass trapping. Trapping of male moths (e.g., codling moth) in large numbers in an attempt to reduce populations and reproduction and to control fruit damage.

meristem. The undifferentiated plant tissue from which new cells and new plant tissues arise. The main meristems in a plant are the apical meristems, which form terminal shoot and root growth, and vascular cambium, which causes thickening of stems.

mesocarp. The flesh of a fruit or hull of most nuts.

metamorphosis. A change in form during development. Some insect families undergo complete metamorphosis, in which the larval, worm-like stage creates a protective cocoon where it transforms first into a pupa and then into a winged adult form that emerges from the cocoon. Other insect families undergo incomplete metamorphosis, in which the young nymphs look like small adults.

microclimate. A local variation from the general or regional climate resulting from slight differences in one or more factors that may include elevation, direction of slope, sun exposure, soil type, density of vegetation, fog pattern, and other conditions.

micronutrients. Plant-essential elements that are required by plants in very small amounts (e.g., boron [B], chlorine [Cl], copper [Cu], iron [Fe], manganese [Mn], molybdenum [Mb], and zinc [Zn]). Compare with *macronutrients*.

microsprinkler. A low-volume sprinkler, usually connected to drip tubing, that discharges about 6 to 30 gallons of water per hour.

mineral oil. See *horticultural oil*.

miticide. A pesticide that controls spider mites.

modified central leader system. A training system in which the central leader is removed or no longer promoted after several lateral branches have been developed along the central leader; often used for walnut, chestnut, pistachio, and persimmon trees.

molt. In insects and other arthropods, the shedding of skin before entering another stage of growth.

monoecious. Of a plant, bearing both male and female flowers separately on the same plant, as with walnuts, pecans, filberts, and chestnuts. Compare with *dioecious*.

mulch. A layer of organic or inorganic material, such as wood chips or landscape fabric, placed on the soil surface to prevent weed growth, conserve moisture, prevent erosion, and moderate soil temperature.

mummy. A dried, shriveled fruit or nut that adheres to the tree.

mycelium. The vegetative body of a fungus, consisting of a mass of slender filaments called hyphae.

natural enemies. Naturally occurring beneficial organisms that attack harmful organisms, and as such can be used to enhance pest or disease control.

necrosis. The death of plant tissue, usually at the edges or tip of a leaf.

nematode. A microscopic, plant-parasitic worm with a long, cylindrical, unsegmented body.

node. The point on a shoot or branch where a leaf is attached and one or more buds arise in the leaf axil.

notching. Dragging a small file in a single stroke across a branch above a bud, cutting only through the bark; a technique used to stimulate the growth of the bud below.

nurse limb. A limb allowed to remain temporarily on a tree that is being topworked or severely cut back, the function of which is to maintain sufficient leaf area for photosynthesis to provide carbohydrates for roots.

nymph. The immature stage of insects such as aphids that hatch from eggs and gradually acquire adult form through a series of molts without passing through a pupal stage; essentially, a smaller version of the full-sized adult.

open center (vase) system. A method of training in which three to five primary scaffold branches are developed low in the tree and the center of the tree is kept open.

organic. *1.* Of, relating to, or derived from living organisms. *2.* Of a material (e.g., a fertilizer), being made up of molecules that contain carbon and hydrogen atoms. *3.* Of crops, those that are grown with organically acceptable rather than synthetic fertilizers or pesticides.

ovary. The swollen flower part at the base of the pistil containing the ovule or seed. As a fertilized ovary grows, it becomes the fruit.

overcropping. Allowing too many fruit to remain on a tree, to the detriment of the tree's vigor.

ovule. The part of the ovary that becomes fertilized and grows to become the seed.

parasite. An organism that lives in or on the body of another living organism (its host). In this publication, the term mainly refers to tiny wasps and flies (technically known as parasitoids) that spend their immature stages on or within the body of a single host and also kill the host. Compare with *predator.*

parthenocarpic fruit. Fruit produced without fertilization and seed development (e.g., in California, the Bartlett pear).

pathogen. Any disease-producing organism.

peduncle. The stem of an individual flower or fruit.

perfect flower. A flower with both male and female parts.

perianth. The outer envelope of the flower, including petals and sepals.

pesticide. Any product sprayed onto a plant to control insects (*insecticide*), mites (*miticide*), fungal diseases (*fungicide*), weeds (*herbicide*), rodents (*rodenticide*), etc. Pesticides can be chemical-based (synthetic), such as malathion, or natural (organic), such as soaps and oils.

petal. A flower part, usually conspicuously colored.

petiole. The stalk connecting a leaf to a stem.

pheromone. A chemical given off by an insect to attract other insects of the same species; used in trapping of insects or, in commercial orchards, disruption of insect mating.

pheromone trap. A sticky trap with a pheromone lure that attracts male insects.

phloem. Inner bark tissue that conducts carbohydrates, hormones, and other organic compounds from the site of production to tissues and organs throughout the tree. Compare with *xylem.*

photosynthesis. The production of carbohydrates from carbon dioxide and water in the presence of chlorophyll, using light energy.

phytotoxic. Causing injury to plants. Usually refers to sprays that burn the leaves.

pinching. See *tipping.*

pistil. The female portion of a flower, typically consisting of ovary, style, and stigma.

pistillate. Of flowers, having one or more pistils but no stamens. Compare with *staminate.*

pit. See *endocarp.*

pit burn. Softening and darkening of the fruit flesh around the pit, usually as a result of excessive heat; mainly affects apricots.

plant hormone. A substance produced in minute amounts in one part of a plant and transported to another part where it evokes a response.

pole thinning. Removal of a portion of the immature fruit on a tree by striking them with a pole. Compare with *hand thinning.*

pollen (grain). Tiny, grain-like male sex cells formed in the anther of a flower's stamen.

pollen tube. The growth extension of the pollen grain in the style following the pollen grain's germination on the stigma.

pollination. The transfer of pollen from the anther to the stigma of the same flower or another flower. See also *fertilization.*

pollinizer. The producer of pollen; the variety used as the pollen source for cross-pollination.

pollinator. The agent of pollen transfer, usually bees.

pome. A fleshy fruit, the outer portion of which is formed by the floral parts that surround the ovary (e.g., apple, pear, quince, or pomegranate).

pomology. The branch of science dealing with fruit and nuts and with fruit and nut culture; derives from the Latin *pomum,* meaning "fruit."

popcorn stage. The stage of flowering in stone fruit and pome fruit just before the petals fully open.

potash. Potassium oxide (K_2O), containing 83 percent potassium.

precocious. Of a tree, bearing fruit early in its life.

pre-cut. The first step in a two-step pruning process that prevents damage to the branch collar or tearing of the bark of the trunk or parent stem when pruning off a large branch.

predator. Any animal (including insects and mites) that kills other animals (prey) and feeds on them. Compare with *parasite.*

primary scaffold branch. A main structural limb arising from the trunk.

propagate. To generate or to multiply, whether by sexual or asexual means.

pupa. The nonfeeding, inactive stage between larva and adult in insects such as moths and beetles with complete metamorphosis. (plural: pupae)

radiation frost. A frost that occurs on calm, clear nights as heat is lost from the earth's surface into the atmosphere, causing cold air to collect near the soil surface and move into low spots.

receptacle. The enlarged upper end of the stalk that supports or surrounds the main floral parts. The edible portion of the fruit of some species consists of a fusion of receptacle tissue with the calyx (apples and pears) or the ovaries (fig).

reference evapotranspiration. The maximum evapotranspiration rate as determined from local weather station data; based on how hot, dry, windy, and sunny it is.

resistant. Able to tolerate conditions (such as pesticide sprays, temperature extremes, soil moisture, or pest damage) that are harmful to other species or other strains of the same species. Plants can be resistant to certain pests and diseases, and pests can be resistant to certain pesticides.

resistant variety. A strain of a plant species that is able to resist or tolerate damage from an insect pest or disease that normally would be damaging to plants of that species.

respiration. The process by which oxygen and carbohydrates are assimilated by an organism to produce energy, resulting in the release of carbon dioxide and water.

rodenticide. A pesticide that kills rodents.

root hair. The elongated extension of a single epidermal cell on a plant's root, which serves to absorb water and minerals. Compare with *fine roots.*

rootstock. The lower portion of most fruit and nut trees, onto which the desired fruiting variety (scion) is grafted. Rootstocks are propagated either by seed or vegetatively through cuttings.

rosetting. A cluster of leaves with short internodes.

russetting. Brownish, roughened areas on the skin of fruit that results from abnormal production of cork tissue. May be caused by diseases, insects, certain pesticides, temperature fluctuations, or changes in humidity, or it may be a natural characteristic of some varieties or strains.

sand. *1.* Soil particles that are finer than gravel but coarser than silt, ranging in size from 2.0 to 0.5 mm in diameter. *2.* Any soil class that contains 85 percent or more sand and not more than 10 percent clay.

sanitation. Orchard cleanliness that is practiced in order to prevent the spread of insect or disease pests; can include the removal and destruction of fruit infested with insects or infected with disease.

sapwood. The outer wood of a stem or tree trunk, usually light in color and physiologically very active. Compare with *heartwood.*

scaffold branch. A main structural limb.

scion. A branch, shoot, or bud removed from one plant and grafted onto another (the stock or rootstock). Also, the aboveground portion of a tree that is asexually produced from a single parent by budding or grafting.

secondary scaffold branch. A limb arising from a primary scaffold limb.

self-fruitful. Of a fruit or nut tree, able to set fruit with pollen from the same tree. Some varieties are only partially self-fruitful.

self-unfruitful. Of a fruit or nut tree, unable to produce fruit without a nearby pollinizer tree.

semidwarf. A specific tree size that is usually between 40 and 90 percent of the size of a standard large tree as a result of its having a dwarfing rootstock. Usually an intermediate-sized tree that reaches about 10 to 15 feet (3.0 to 4.6 m) in height. See also *dwarfing rootstock.*

sepal. One of the outermost flower structures; usually encloses the outer flower parts in the bud. Part of the calyx.

shield budding. See *T-budding.*

shoot. A stem with leaves, referred to as "current season's growth" during the growing season. Compare with *branch.*

silt. *1.* Small, mineral soil particles ranging from 0.05 to 0.002 mm in diameter. *2.* Textural class of soils that contains 80 percent or more silt and less than 12 percent clay.

slipping. See *bark slipping.*

soaker hose. Low-volume irrigation hose made with numerous small pores along its entire length through which water can seep out.

soil. The upper, arable layer of earth in which plant roots can grow; the soil provides a medium for plant support and the storage and release of water and nutrients.

soil aggregate. Clusters of soil particles that vary in shape, size, and degree of association, such as granules or clods, giving a soil its structure.

soil amendment. A substance added to soil in order to alter one or more of its physical or chemical properties.

soil horizon. A layer of soil with well-defined physical and chemical characteristics produced through the soil-formation processes.

soil organic matter. The fraction of the soil consisting of decomposing plant and animal residues.

soil pH. A measure of the acidity or alkalinity of the soil.

soil profile. A vertical section of the soil through its horizontal layers.

soil structure. The arrangement of soil particles (sand, silt, and clay) naturally arranged into soil aggregates; soil structure varies mainly on the basis of the amount of pores within and between the aggregates.

soil texture. The relative proportion of the various soil separates (sand, silt, and clay) that make up the soil classes as described by the textural triangle (Figure 1.2).

soil texture triangle. A triangular graph (Figure 1.2) used to determine the soil textural name after one has determined the percentages of sand, silt, and clay through laboratory analysis.

sooty mold. Fungus that grows on honeydew.

species. The scientific or taxonomic identity of a specific type of fruit or nut tree, written out as a binomial made up of the genus and species names (e.g., *Malus domestica* = domesticated apple, *Juglans regia* = English walnut).

spore. A reproductive body produced by certain fungi and other organisms and capable of growing into a new individual under proper conditions.

spring drop. The natural dropping of immature fruit by a tree during the late spring, believed to be caused by embryo abortion or the plant's response to an extremely large crop load. Also known as June drop.

spur. A short branch that is specialized for flower and fruit production on most fruit species.

spur-type tree. A fruit tree (primarily apple and cherry) that has shortened internodes and a greater number of spurs; a spur-type tree grows to about one-half to two-thirds the height of a standard non-spur-type tree.

stamen. The male part of the flower producing pollen, composed of anther and filament (stalk).

staminate. Pertaining to flowers that have stamens but no pistil. Staminate flowers of several nut species are called *catkins*. Compare with *pistillate*.

standard rootstock. A rootstock that imparts relatively high vigor in a tree. Usually originates from a seed (seedling). Compare with *dwarfing rootstock*.

stigma. The female portion of a flower, located at the tip of the style, that receives pollen.

stock. The rootstock or tree onto which the scion (bud or stick) is grafted.

stomate. An opening or pore in a leaf through which the plant exchanges gases and loses water vapor. (plural: stomates or stomata)

stone fruit. Any of the *Prunus* spp. fruits with a hard pit surrounding the seed (e.g., peach or cherry).

strain. A genetic mutation within a variety that results in the expression of some different characteristics, such as fruit color, skin smoothness, fruit size, precocity, etc.

stratified soil. A soil consisting of one or more layers of different textures or structures, usually limiting the penetration of water, air, and roots.

style. The female portion of the flower that connects the ovary and stigma, and through which the pollen tube grows to reach the ovule.

subsoil. The layer of soil immediately under the surface soil. The texture or structure of the subsoil often differs from that of the surface soil and the subsoil may contain restrictive or impermeable layers.

sucker. A vigorous shoot arising from a tree's base or roots, below the soil line. Compare with *water sprout*.

summer pruning. Pruning done at any time from early spring through summer in order to train young trees, maintain tree height, and/or improve the availability of light for lower fruiting wood. Reduces tree growth to some extent. Compare with *dormant pruning*.

syconium. A type of multiple fruit in which the flowers are borne on the inside of a balloon-like receptacle (e.g., figs).

T-budding. Bud grafting performed between spring and midsummer, in which a shield-shaped bud patch from a current-season's shoot is inserted underneath a **T**-shaped cut in the bark of a shoot of another tree (the rootstock). Also called *shield budding*.

taproot. The primary root growing vertically downward from a seedling tree; lateral roots arise from the taproot and the taproot usually becomes insignificant.

temperate zone. The part of the Earth between the Tropic of Cancer and the Arctic Circle in the Northern Hemisphere or between the Tropic of Capricorn and the Antarctic Circle in the Southern Hemisphere. Characterized by a climate that is warm and dry in the summer, cold and wet in the winter, and moderate in the spring and fall.

terminal bud. A bud that develops at the tip of a shoot or branch when growth stops.

thinning. Selective pruning to improve branch spacing, direct growth, eliminate weak and defective branches, and reduce the end weight of branches. (For thinning of fruit, see *fruit thinning*.)

thinning cut. The complete removal of a branch or cutting back of a branch to a lateral branch that is one-third or more the size of the main branch. Used to encourage light penetration or allow access for fruit thinning, harvest, and other cultural operations. Compare with *heading cut*.

tilth. The physical condition of the soil in relation to its ability to cultivate and/or support plant growth.

tipping. Removing the growing tip of a shoot to slow elongation growth or promote lateral branching.

tissue. A group of organized plant cells that perform a specific function.

tolerant. Able to withstand the effects of an adverse condition (e.g., temperature extremes, high salt concentrations, high humidity, drought, or little chilling) without suffering serious injury or death.

topping. Reducing a tree's size, often through the use of heading cuts to shorten limbs or branches to a predetermined length.

topsoil. The fertile upper part of the soil.

topworking. Severely cutting back a tree (except for a temporary nurse limb) or main branch and grafting one or more other species or varieties onto the cut limbs.

training. Directing the growth of a young plant to a desired shape through pruning, bending, and/or tying.

translocation. The movement of water, nutrients, and other dissolved substances through the conducting systems of a plant.

transpiration. The loss of water vapor from plant surfaces, mainly through the stomates of leaves; transpiration keeps the plant cool and prevents the leaves from sunburning.

tree trunk topiary. See *arborsculpture*.

tree water use. The amount of water used by a tree, through both evaporation from the soil and transpiration through the leaves; expressed either in gallons (liters) or inches (centimeters) of water.

trunk. The main supporting stem of a tree, connecting the roots to the branches.

trunk banding. *1.* The placement of a band of corrugated cardboard around a tree's trunk to trap mature larvae as they seek refuges for pupation. *2.* Wrapping a tree's trunk with various wrapping materials to protect it from sunburn.

variety. A taxonomic group of plants that have unique characteristics within a species. In common horticultural usage, *variety* is synonymous with *cultivar*.

vascular. Pertaining to the conducting tissues of a plant (the *xylem* and *phloem*).

vascular cambium. An actively dividing layer of cells found between a plant's bark and its wood that generates new sapwood (*xylem*) to the inside and new bark (*phloem*) to the outside. The cambium causes stems and roots to grow in diameter and it forms a tree's annual rings. In grafting, at least a portion of the scion's vascular cambium must match up with that of the stock. Compare with *apical meristem*.

vegetative bud. A bud that produces only a shoot with leaves.

vegetative growth. The growth of shoots, roots, and leaves, as opposed to flowers and fruit.

vigorous. Of a plant, healthy and producing fast-growing shoots.

water sprout. A vigorous shoot arising from a tree's trunk or a branch, often from an adventitious bud. Compare with *sucker*.

waterlogged soil. An improperly drained soil in which the water content is too high to allow normal plant growth.

wet feet. Lack of oxygen in a tree's root zone. Wet feet may lead to root and crown diseases such as Phytophthora rot.

whip grafting. A method of grafting in which a one-year-old branch is attached to the branch of another tree using both a long, angled cut and a vertical cut on the scion and stock.

wood. A hard, fibrous substance that makes up most of the stem and branches of the tree, consisting of living and inactive xylem tissues surrounded by the vascular cambium.

wound. A mechanical injury that creates an opening in the tree's protective bark, damaging living tissue and allowing the entry of pathogens that can cause wood decay or diseases.

xylem. The complex vascular tissue located at the inner edge of the vascular cambium through which most of the water and nutrients in a tree are conducted in an upward direction. Younger xylem tissues are termed *sapwood* and older, inactive xylem tissues are termed *heartwood*. Compare with *phloem*.

Index

Photographs are indicated with *italicized* page numbers. Tables are indicated by the letter "t".

abiotic disorders, 182–185
absorption process, nutrients, 18, 57–59, 60
acidic soils, 7, 60
     See also pH levels
Adriatic figs, 37
advective freezing, 4
adventitious buds, 12
aggregates, soil, 6
Akane apples, 24
alkaline soils, 7, 60
     See also pH levels
All-in-One almonds, 34
almonds
     overview, 33–34, 187
     bearing age, 179
     diseases, 165, 171
     grafting compatibility, 100
     growth characteristics, 19, 74
     harvest and storage guidelines, 129, 136, *137*
     insect pests, 152
     pollination, 14, 33, 181
     training and pruning, 79–81, *82, 83*
alternate bearing, 12, 181
Ambrosia pomegranates, 26
amendments, 6, 41
     See also fertilizers
ammonium sulfate, 7
Anna apples, 23
anthers, 13
antique varieties, apples, 23
ants, 26, 145
anvil loppers, 71
aphids, 22, 24, 25, *140,* 142–146
apical dominance, 74
apical meristems, 11, 12
apples
     overview, 21–24, 191
     bearing age, 179
     bearing cycles, 181
     bitter pit, 184–185
     flowering habits, *15*
     flower parts, *13*
     fruit characteristics, 15–16
     fruit thinning, 123–126
     grafting compatibility, 100
     harvest and storage guidelines, 129, 131
     insect pests, 142, *143, 145,* 148
     pollination, 21, 181
apples, disease management
     bacterial canker and blast, 172–173, *175*
     Eutypa dieback, 173
     fire blight, 168
     powdery mildew, 161–163, 164
     scab, 169–170, *171*
apples, training and pruning
     central leader system, 86–87, *89, 90*
     espalier, 90–91
     newly planted trees, 45
     overgrown trees, *96, 98*
apple scab, 169–170, *171*
apricots
     overview, 26–27, 188
     bearing cycles, 181
     calendar for crop-care activities, 188
     flowering habits, *15*
     fruit thinning, 123, *124,* 125, *127*
     grafting compatibility, 100
     harvest and storage guidelines, 129, 130, 132
     physiological disorders, 184
     pollination, 26, 181
     training and pruning, 77, 79–80, *90,* 98
apricots, disease management
     Eutypa dieback, 77, 173–174
     powdery mildew, 162, 163, 164
     shothole disease, 171, *172*

apriums, 33, 125, 132
arborsculpture, 120–122
Arctic Glo nectarines, 29
Arctic Rose nectarines, 30
Armillaria root rot
     overview, 174, 176, *177*
     pome fruit susceptibility, 24, 26
     stone fruit susceptibility, 27, 31
     walnut susceptibility, 34
armored scale insects, 146–148
arthropod. *See* insects
Asian pears
     overview, 25–26
     fire blight, 168
     fruit thinning, 123–125, *126*
     harvest and storage guidelines, 133, 134
     pollination, 181
     training and pruning, *77,* 90–91, *94*
assassin bugs, *140*
Autumn Gem peaches, 31
autumn growth cycle, 20
Autumn Rosa plums, 32
Autumn Royal apricots, 27, 184
auxin, 12, 74, 109–110
avocados, storage temperatures, 130

Babcock peaches, 30
Bacillus thuringiensis (Bt), 140, 142, 152, 154
bacterial blast and canker
     overview, 167, 172–173, *175*
     almond susceptibility, 33
     stone fruit susceptibility, 26, 27, 28, 31, 33
bagging fruit
     codling moth management, 150
     ripening process, 131
banding, 151
Barcelona filberts, 34
bare-root trees, 39, 41, 42
bark grafting method, *113–114,* 115–117
Bartlett pears, 24, 25, 123, 181
bearing cycles and patterns
     failure factors, 12, 179–182
     figs, 36–37, 95
     nut crops, 33–35, 36, 179
     pome fruits, 22–26, 179
     pruning guidelines generally, 72–73, 76, *77*
     stone fruits, 26–27, 28, 29, 31, 32–33
Beauty plums, 32
bees, 14, 181
bending branches, 12, 77, 120–122, 182
beneficial organisms, defined, 139
     See also biological control
berms, *40,* 41, 42
Betulaefolia rootstock, 25, 179
biennial bearing, 12, 181
Bing cherries, 28, 181
biological control
     overview, 139, 140
     aphids, 145
     crown galls, 176
     leafrollers, 153–154
     peachtree borer, 158
     peach twig borer, 152
     scale insects, 146, 148, *149*
     spider mites, 157
birds, nut harvesting, 136–138
bitter pit, apples, 22, 184–185
blackberries, post-harvest changes, 129
Black Jack figs, 37
Black Mission figs, 36
black scale, 146
Black Tartarian cherries, 28
Black walnut rootstock, *10,* 35
Blenheim apricots, 27, 184

blights
     overview, 168–169
     pome fruit susceptibilities, 22, 23, 24, 25, 26
     walnuts, 174, *176*
blooming stage, chilling requirements, 2–3, 180
blueberries, 60, 129
Blue Damson plums, 32
Bonfante Gardens, 121, *122*
Bordeaux mixture, 165, 169, 172
borers, 26, 152, 157–159
boron, 59, 65
Bosc pears, 25
Braeburn apples, 181
branches, 10–11
breba crop, 36
Brooks cherries, 28
brown rot, 27, 123, 165, 167–168
Brown Turkey figs, 36
Bt (*Bacillus thuringiensis),* 140, 142, 152, 154
buckskin virus, 28
budding
     overview, 10, 99, 102–103
     chip-budding method, *106,* 107–109
     compatibility chart, 100
     follow-up care, 119
     forcing bud growth, 109–110
     supplies, 101–102
     T-budding method, 103–107
     See also grafting
buds, 12–13, 19
bud union, defined, 10
Burgundy plums, 32
Butler filberts, 35
bypass loppers, 71

calcium, 58, 60, 64t, 185
calendars for cultural activities, 187–191
Calimyrna figs, 37
Calleryana rootstock, 25
calluses, 74, 99
cambium, 11, *12,* 99
canker. *See* bacterial blast and canker; fire blight
caprification, defined, 36
carbohydrates
     overview, 17–18
     bearing cycles, 12
     plant organ functions, 9, 10, 13
     pruning timing, 76
     seasonal changes, 19, 20
carbon dioxide, 17, 18
Carmel almonds, 34
Castlebright apricots, 27, 184
catkins, 15
cecidomyid flies, 157
Central Coast zone, climate characteristics, 2, *4*
central leader training system, 86–88, *89, 90*
Chandler walnuts, 36
chemical problems, generally, 6–7
     See also nutrients; pH levels
cherimoyas, 129, 130
cherries
     overview, 27–29, 188
     bearing age, 179, 182
     bearing cycles, 181
     fruit thinning, 123
     grafting, 100, 108, *118*
     growth characteristics, *15,* 74, 75
     harvest and storage guidelines, 129, 130, 132, *133*
     insect pests, 143t
     physiological disorders, 182–183
     pollination, 27–28, 181
     training and pruning, 77, 79–80, 98
cherries, disease management
     bacterial canker and blast, 173

brown rot, 165
Eutypa dieback, 77, 173
powdery mildew, 162
shothole, 171
cherry-plums, 32–33, *92*, 135, 190
chestnuts
overview, 34
flower structures, 14
pollination, 15, 34
training and pruning, 42, 86–87, 93
chilling hours, *4*
chilling requirements
overview, 2–3, 180
nut crops, 33
stone fruits, 27, 28, 30, 31, 33
chilling requirements, pome fruits
apples, 21, 22, 23
pears, 24, 25
pomegranates, 26
Chinese apricots, 27
chip-budding method, *106, 107*–108
chlorophyll, 17, 20
chlorosis, 58, 63–66, *67*
Chocolate persimmons, 37
Choctaw pecans, 35
Chojuro Asian pears, 25
Citation rootstock, 27, 29, 30, 32
citrus fruits, 129, 130
clay soils, 5–6, 40, 41
cleft grafting, 117–118
climate zones, 1–5, 49, 180
codling moth, 26, 148–152
Colossal chestnuts, 34
Colt rootstocks, 28
Comice pears, 25
compaction, 6, *40*, 41
complete flowers, defined, 14
compost, 7, 60–61
compound leaves, 13
conserpse stink bugs, *160*
container-grown trees, 39, 42, 43, 44
copper treatments, 165, 168, 172
cover crops, 6
cracking problems, 182–183
Craig Crimson cherries, 28
cross-pollination. *See* pollination
crown galls, 36, 176, *177*
crown rot
overview, 175–176, *177*
planting guidelines, 41, 42
stone fruit susceptibilities, 27, 31
walnut susceptibilities, 36
cultivar. *See* varieties
cultivation, 6, 41
cultural practices
calendars for, 187–191
pest management generally, 140–141
See also specific practices, e.g., irrigation practices; sanitation practices
current season's growth, defined, 10

damage characteristics, diseases
Armillaria root rot, 174
bacterial blast, 172–173
blights, 168, 174
brown rot, 165, 167
crown galls, 176
Eutypa dieback, 173–174
peach leaf curl, 163, *165*
Phytophthora root and crown rot, 175
powdery mildew, 161
scab, 169–170
shothole, 171, *172*
damage characteristics, insects
aphids, 143, 145
borers, 152, 158, 159
codling moth, 149
conserpse stink bug, 160, *160*
navel orangeworm, *160*
oriental fruit moth, 152–153
scale, 147
walnut husk fly, 154

D'Anjou pears, 25
Dapple Dandy pluot, 33
Davianna filberts, 34
degree-day calculations, 151–152
Delight cherry-plums, 33
dioecious flowers, 14, 181
Diospyros spp., persimmon rootstocks, 37
disease management, generally
fertilizer applications, 57
fruit thinning, 123
graft unions, 10
irrigation practices, 47
nut crop susceptibilities, 33, 34, 35
pome fruit susceptibilities, 22, 23, 24, 25, 26
pruning practices, 74, 77
soil pH, 60
stone fruit susceptibilities, 26, 27, 30, 31
storage practices, 130
disease management, specifically
blights, 168–169
brown rot, 165, 167–168
crown rot, 41, 42, 175–176, *177*
Eutypa dieback, 77, 173–174, *175*
peach leaf curl, 163, 165, 166, 172
powdery mildew, 161–163, 164
root rot, 174, 175–176, *177*
scab, 169–170, *171*
shothole disease, 171–172
dormant oils. *See* oil treatments
dormant pruning, 76–77
See also pruning guidelines; training systems
dormant stage, 12, 19
Double Delight nectarines, 29
doubling problems, 183
Doughnut peaches, 31
drip irrigation, 43, *46*, 53–54, 67
drop, fruit, 123, 180
drupe fruits, defined, 16
See also stone fruits, generally
dry ice method, pest management, *136*
dry limit, determining, 55
Du Chilly filberts, 35
Dunstan chestnuts, 34
dwarf trees. *See* pruning guidelines; rootstocks

Earligrande peaches, 30
Early Burlat cherries, 28
Early Richmond cherries, 29
Early Ruby cherries, 28
Eastern Black walnuts, 36
El Dorado plums, 32
Elephant Heart plums, 32
Empire apples, 181
English Morello cherries, 29
English walnut rootstock, *10*, 35
Ennis filberts, 35
Enterprise apples, 24
espalier training system, 44, 90–91, 93, *94*
ethylene, 131
European fruit lecanium, 146, *147*
European pears, 25, 123–125, 129, 133, 181
European plums, 31, 32, 181
Eutypa dieback, 77, 173–174, *175*
Eversweet pomegranates, 26

failure to bear, 179–182
Fairtime peaches, 31
fall bloom problem, 185
fall budding, defined, 103
fall growth cycle, 20
Fantasia nectarines, 29
Fay Elberta peaches, 31
feeder roots, 9, 193
feel method, soil moisture, 55
feijoas, storage temperatures, 130
fertilization. *See* pollination
fertilizers
overview, 57–63
application guidelines, 19, 66–69
disease management, 168, 173
insect management, 145

planting preparations, 41
sweetness failures, 185
field capacity, 55
figs
overview, 36–37, 188
bearing habits, 36–37, 95
flowering habits, *17*
frost vulnerability, 4–5
fruit thinning, 123
harvest and storage guidelines, 129, 130, 132
plant structures, *14*, 16
pollination, 36, 181
propagation, 10
training and pruning, 79, 86, 88, *91*, 95
filberts, 14, 15, *16*, 34–35
filing bark, 12, 109–110
fine roots, 9
fine soils, 5
fire blight
overview, 168–169
pome fruit susceptibilities, 22, 23, 24, 25, 26
Flamekist nectarines, 29
Flavor Delight aprium, 33
Flavor Grenade pluot, 33
Flavor King pluot, 33
Flavor Queen pluot, 33
Flavor Supreme pluot, 33
Flavortop nectarines, 29
flow control devices, 51
flower buds, 12–13, 20
flower drop, 180
flowers, 13–15, 16, *17*
fog spots, apricots, 184
foliar applications, 67, 184–185
forcing bud growth, 109–110
Forty-Niner peaches, 31
Franquette walnut variety, 93
frass, defined, 149
Freedom apples, 24
French Improved plums, 32
French seedling rootstock, 24
Friar plums, 32
frost
overview, 4–5, 180
bacterial canker and blast, 173
climate zone differences, 2
nut crop vulnerabilities, 33, 35
stone fruit vulnerability, 26
Frost peaches, 31
fruit, 15–16, 18, 19
See also specific topics, e.g., disease entries; harvest guidelines
fruit beetle, green, *160*
fruit beetles, *133*
fruit bush training system, 44, 88, 90, *91*–92
fruit flies, 26
fruit set, defined, 14
fruitworms, green, 153–154
Fuji apples, 23, 181
fungicides
apple scab, 170
bacterial canker, 173
fire blight, 169
peach leaf curl, 163, 165, 172
powdery mildew, 161–163
shothole disease, 172
Fuyu persimmons, 37, 134

Gala apples, 22, 181
galls, 145, 176, *177*
garden hose irrigation, 50–51
genetic dwarf trees, 78
Giant Babcock peaches, 30
girdling, 12, 109–110
Gisela Series rootstock, 28, 179
glossary, 192–196
Goldbar apricots, 184
Golden Amber apricots, 27
Golden Delicious apples, 22, 181
Golden Nectar plums, 32
Goldmine nectarines, 29
Goldrush apples, 24

gophers, 7, 28, 36
grafting
  overview, 10, 11, 99–100, 102–103
  arborsculpture methods, 120–122
  bark grafting method, *113–114*, 115–117
  compatibility chart, 100
  follow-up care, 119
  supplies, 101–102
  whip grafting method, 110–114
  See also budding
grafting over, defined, 115
graft union, defined, 10
Granada pomegranates, 26
Granny Smith apples, 23
grapes, post-harvest changes, 129
Gravenstein apples, 22
green fruit beetle, *160*
green fruitworms, 153–154
Green Gage plums, 32
green lacewings, *140*
green peach aphids, *143*
growth of plants, stages, 16–20
gypsum, 7

Hachiya persimmons, 37
Hall's Hardy almonds, 34
hand thinning, 126, 193
Harcot apricots, 27
hardpan, 6, 41, 50, 182
Hartley walnuts, 35, 93
harvest guidelines
  overview, 129–130
  fruit crops, 131–135, 168
  nut crops, 135–138
hazelnuts, 14, 15, 34–35
heading cuts
  defined, 11
  and bearing habits, 76
  method of, 12, 74–75
  newly planted trees, 42
heartwood, 11, *12*
heat units, ripening period, 3
Heavenly White nectarines, 30
heavy soils, 5
Helena apricots, 184
herbicides, 7
honeydew, 142, 143, 145–146, 147
horizons, soil, 6
horticultural oil, defined, 142
  See also oil treatments
hose irrigation, 50–51, 53–54
hose spraying, pest management, 141, 145–146
Hosui Asian pears, 25
Howard Miracle plums, 32
humid conditions, diseases
  bacterial canker and blast, 173
  blights, 168, 174
  brown rot, 167
  peach leaf curl, 165
  powdery mildew, 163
  scab, 169, 170
  shothole, 171
  See also wet feet tolerance
humidity, storage guidelines, 130, 132
humus, defined, 5

identifying pests, diseases
  apple scab, 169–170
  Armillaria root rot, 174
  bacterial blast, 167, 172–173
  blights, 168, 174
  brown rot, 165, 167
  peach leaf curl, 163
  Phytophthora root and crown rot, 175
  powdery mildew, 161
identifying pests, insects
  aphids, 143, *144*
  borers, 158, 159
  codling moth, 148–149
  oriental fruit moth, 152
  scale, 146
  spider mites, 156

Imperial plums, 32
Improved Flaming Gold apricots, 184
incomplete flowers, defined, 14
Independence nectarines, 29
Indian Free peaches, 31
indoleacetic acid, 12
inorganic fertilizers, 62–63
  See also fertilizers
insecticidal oils. *See* oil treatments
insecticides
  overview, 141–142
  aphids, 145, 146
  borers, 152, 157, 158, 159
  codling moth, 150, 151–152
  leafrollers, 154
  oriental fruit moth, 153
  peach twig borer, 152
  scale insects, 146, 148, 154
  spider mites, 157
  walnut husk fly, 156
insect management, generally
  fertilizer applications, 57
  fruit thinning, 123
  harvest guidelines, 129, 132, 136–138
  irrigation practices, 47
  pome fruit susceptibilities, 22
insect management, specifically
  aphids, 142–146
  borers, 152, 157–159
  codling moth, 26, 148–152
  consperse stink bug, 160
  green fruit beetle, 160
  leafrollers, 153–154, 155
  navel orangeworm, 160
  oriental fruit moth, 152–153
  scale, 145, 146–148, *149*
  spider mites, 156–157
  walnut husk fly, 154, 156
integrated pest management (IPM)
  defined, 139
  diseases, 161–177
  insects, 142–160
  methods for, *136*, 139–142
IPM. *See* integrated pest management (IPM)
iron, 58, 60, 63, *65, 67*
irrigation practices
  overview, 47
  bearing failures, 182
  calculating, 48–50
  evaluating, 54–55
  fertilizers, 58, 67
  methods, 50–54
  newly planted trees, 42, 43, 44, *46*
  physiological disorders, 182–184, 185
  salinity management, 60
  site selection factors, 40
  spider mites, 157
irrigation practices, disease management
  bacterial canker, 173
  blights, 168, 174
  peach leaf curl, 165
  Phytophthora root and crown rot, 175–176
  shothole disease, 172
Italian Everbearing figs, 37
Italian plums, 32
Izu persimmons, 37

Japanese plums, 31, 32, *81, 84,* 181
Jonamac apples, 24
Jonathan apples, 22
June budding, defined, 103
June drop, 123

Kadota figs, 37
Katy apricots, 184
Kelsey plums, 32
Kerman pistachios, 35
Kikusui Asian pears, 25
King cherries, 28
kiwifruit, 14, 129, 181
knives for grafting, 101–102

lacewings, *140,* 145, 148
lady beetles, *140,* 145, *146,* 148, 157
La Feliciana peaches, 30
Lambert cherries, 28, 181
Lapins cherries, 28, 181
Laroda plums, 32
late bearing problems, 182
latent buds, 12
lateral branches, defined, 10
  See also pruning guidelines; training systems
Late Santa Rosa plums, 32
leaf appearance
  disease damage, 163, 174, 175
  insect damage, *145,* 147, 156
  nutrient deficiencies, 57, 58, 59, 63–66, *67*
  sunlight deficiency, 17
  water insufficiency, 182
leaf axil, 12
leaf-feeding caterpillars, 153–154, 155, *156*
leafhoppers, *140*
leafrollers, 153–154, 155
leaves, functions, 13, 19
  See also leaf appearance
Liberty apples, 24
light soils, 5
limbs, 10–11
lime applications, 7, 60
loam soils, 5
loppers, types of, 71
loquat trees, fire blight, 168
Loring peaches, 31
Lorna apricots, 184
Lovell peach rootstock, 27, 29, 30, 31
low-chill varieties
  pome fruits, 23, 25
  stone fruits, 27, 28, 29, 30, 31, 33
lygus bug, 160

Macoun apples, 22
macronutrients, 57–58
magnesium, 58, 60, *65*
Mahaleb rootstocks, 28
Mahan pecans, 35
manganese, 58, 60, *65, 67*
mangoes, 129, 130
manures, 61
Marianna 2624 plum rootstock, 27, 31
Mariposa plums, 32
massive structure, soils, 6
mass trapping, 151
maturity dates. *See* ripening periods
Mazzard rootstocks, 28
McIntosh apples, 22
mealy plum aphids, 143, *144*
mechanical control of pests, 141
medium soils, 5
Mericrest nectarines, 29
meristems, 11
Meteor cherries, 29
Meyers walnuts, 35
microclimates, 1
micronutrients, 58–59
microsprinkler systems, 53–54
mildew, powdery, 24, 161–163
Mission almonds, 34
Modesto apricots, 184
modified central leader training system, 88, *89, 90,* 95
Mohawk pecans, 35
moisture levels, soil, 44, 54–55
monoecious flowers, 14
Montmorency cherries, 29
Moorpark apricots, 27, 184
M rootstocks, apples, 22
mulches
  overview, 7, 60–61
  irrigation practices, 50
  newly planted trees, 41, 44
  soil structure improvement, 6
mummies, 167
Myrobalan rootstocks, 27, 31
narrow-range oils, defined, 142
  See also oil treatments

natural enemies, defined, 140
    See also biological control
natural enemies, insecticide cautions
        generally, 141
        codling moth management, 151
        leafroller management, 154
        peach twig borer management, 152
        scale management, 146, 148
        spider mite management, 157
natural fruit drop, 123, 124
navel orangeworm, *160*, 174
nectarines
        overview, 29–30, 189
        bearing habits, 76
        disease management, 162, 163, 165, 171
        dwarf trees, 78
        fruit thinning, 123–125
        grafting compatibility, 100
        harvest and storage guidelines, 129, 130,
                132–133
        insect pests, 143*t*, 152
        pit splitting, 183
        training and pruning, 79, 81, 82–86, 98
Nectar peaches, 30
Nemaguard peach rootstocks, 29, 30
nematodes
        and bacterial canker, 173
        parasitic, 158
nematodes, resistant rootstocks
        nut crops, 35
        pome fruits, 24, 25
        stone fruits, 27, 28, 29, 30, 31
Ne Plus Ultra almonds, 34
Nevada chestnuts, 34
Newton Pippin apples, 23
Niitaka Asian pears, 26
Nijisseiki Asian pears, 25
nitrogen
        overview, 57
        application methods, 66–69
        deficiency and toxicity symptoms, 63, *64, 66*
        in fertilizer types, *61–62*, 63
        planting preparations, 41
        seasonal changes, 19, 20
        soil pH, 60
Nonpareil almonds, 34
North Coast zone, climate characteristics, 2, *4*
Northern California Black walnut, 35, 36
North Star cherries, 29
notching, *12*, 109–110
Nubiana plums, 32
nurse limbs, 98, 115, 119
nut crops, generally
        bearing age, 179
        calendar for crop-care activities, 187, 189,
                190, 191
        climate zones, 1–5
        fruit thinning, 123
        harvest and storage guidelines, 129, 135–138
        plant growth, 16–20
        tree organs, 9–16
        varieties, 33–36
        See also specific topics, e.g., irrigation practices;
                pistachios; training systems
nutrients
        absorption process, 18, 57–59, 60
        deficiencies and toxicities, 63–66
        in photosynthesis process, 17
        plant organ functions, 9–10, 11
        recycling, 59
        winter storage, 19

oak root fungus. *See* Armillaria root rot
O'Henry peaches, 31
Ohio walnuts, 35
oil treatments
        overview, 142
        aphids, 145
        leafrollers, 154
        oriental fruit moth, 153
        peach twig borer, 152
        powdery mildew, 163

scale insects, 146, 148, 154
        spider mites, 157
Old Home × Farmingdale rootstock, 25
olives, 10, 130
open-center training system, 79–81, *91, 94, 95*
Orange quinces, 26
organic fertilizers, 7, 60–61, 67
oriental fruit moth, 152–153, *154*
Osborn Prolific figs, 37
ovaries, 13, 15–16
overgrown trees, pruning, *96,* 97–98

Pacific flatheaded borer, 159
Pacific spider mites, 156–157
Panachée figs, 37
Panamint nectarines, 29
papayas, 129, 130
Paradox walnut rootstock, 36
parasite, defined, 140
parasitic nematodes, 158
parasitic wasps, 140, 145, 146, 148
parthenocarpic fruit, 14, 181
pathogen, defined, 140
        See also disease *entries*
Patterson apricots, 27, 184
Paulared apples, 23
Pawnee pecans, 35
peach aphids, green, *143*
peaches
        overview, 30–31, 189
        bearing habits, 76, *77*
        budding and grafting, 100, *104–105*
        dwarf trees, 78, *79*
        fruit thinning, 123–125
        growth characteristics, *15,* 74
        harvest and storage guidelines, 129, 130,
                132–133
        insect management, 143*t*, 152, *153,* 158
        nitrogen deficiency, *66*
        physiological disorders, 183, *185*
        pollination, 181
        seed structures, *14*
        selecting trees, *39*
        training and pruning, 45, 79–86, 98
peaches, disease management
        brown rot, 165
        peach leaf curl, 30, 163, 165, 166, 172
        powdery mildew, 162–163, *164*
        shothole, 171
peach leaf curl, 30, 163, 165, 166, 172
peachtree borer, 158
peach twig borers, 152, *153*
pears
        overview, 3, 24–26, 191
        bearing age, 179, 182
        disease management, 168, 169–170, 172–173
        fruit thinning, 123–126
        grafting, 100, *111*
        growth characteristics, *15,* 74
        harvest and storage guidelines, 129, 133–134
        insect management, 143*t*, 148
        phosphorus deficiency, *66*
        plant structures, *14, 15*–16
        pollination, 24, 181
pears, training and pruning
        central leader system, 86–87, *89*
        espalier system, 90–91
        open-center system, 79–80
        overgrown trees, *96,* 98
        spreading branches, *75–76,* 182
pear scab, 169–170
pecans
        overview, 35, 189
        bearing age, 179
        flowering habits, *16*
        flower structures, 14
        harvest and storage guidelines, 129, 136–137
        pollination, *15,* 35
        training and pruning, 42, 86–87, 93
pedestal, defined, 41
Pedro walnuts, 36
Peento peaches, 31

perennial weeds, 7
perfect flowers, 14, 181
perpendicular **V** system, 82–86
persimmons
        overview, 37, 189
        bearing habits, 76, *77*
        flowering stage, 19
        flowering structure, *17*
        fruit thinning, 125, *126*
        harvest and storage guidelines, 134
        pollination, 37, 181
        training and pruning, 79, 86, 88, 93–94
pesticides, 67, 140, 141–142
        See also insecticides
Peters pistachios, 35
pheromone dispensers, 153
pheromones, 151, 153
pH levels
        overview, 6–7
        bacterial canker, 173
        fertilizer effects, 62, 69
        managing, 60
        nutrient absorption, 58
phloem, 11, *12*
phosphorus
        overview, 58
        application methods, 67–69
        deficiency and toxicity symptoms, 63, *64t, 66*
        in fertilizer types, *61–62,* 63
        planting preparations, 41
        soil pH, 60
photosynthesis, 11, 13, *17*–18, 180
physical control of pests, 141
physiological disorders, 182–185
Phytophthora root and crown rot. *See* crown rot
Pineapple quinces, 26
Pink Lady apples, 23
Pippin apples, 181
pirate bugs, *141*
pistachios
        overview, 35, 190
        bearing cycles, 181
        flowering habits, *16*
        flower structures, 14
        frost vulnerability, 180
        harvest and storage guidelines, 137
        pollination, 15, 35, 181
        training and pruning, 79, 86, 88, 95
Pistacia spp., rootstocks, 35
pistillate flowers, 14
pistils, 13
pit burn, apricots, 27, 184
pit splitting, 183
Placentia walnuts, 36
plant growth
        pruning considerations, 72–73, *74–75*
        role of fertilizers, 57–60
        stages, 16–20
planting guidelines
        overview, 39–43
        apples, 21, 22
        frost protection, 4–5
        graft unions, 10
        for perpendicular **V** training system, 82
        See also spacing requirements
plumcots, 33, 135
Plum Parfait plumcot, 33
plums
        overview, 31–33, 190
        cracking problems, 183
        disease management, 162, 163, 164, 165, 171
        flowering habits, *15*
        flowering stage, 19
        fruit thinning, 123, 125
        grafting compatibility, 100
        harvest and storage guidelines, 129, 130, 135
        insect pests, 142, 143*t*, 148, 149
        pollination, 31, 181
        training and pruning, 79–80, *81, 83, 84,* 90
pluots, 33, 135, 190
pole thinning, 126–127

pollination
    overview, 13–15, 181
    climate influences, 180
    figs, 36, 37
    nut crops, 33, 34–36
    persimmons, 37
pollination, pome fruits
    apples, 21, 22, 23
    Asian pears, 25
    pears, 24
    quinces, 26
pollination, stone fruits
    apricots, 26–27
    cherries, 27–28
    nectarines, 29
    peaches, 30
    plumcots, 33
    plums, 31, 32
pollinators, defined, 14
pollinizer, defined, 181
pollution, water, 57
pome fruits, generally
    calendar for crop-care activities, 191
    climate zones, 1–5
    fruit thinning, 123–128
    plant growth, 16–20
    rootstocks and varieties, 21–26
    tree organs, 9–16
    See also specific topics, e.g., apples; irrigation
        practices; training systems
pomegranates
    overview, 26, 191
    flowering stage, 19
    fruit characteristics, 15–16
    fruit thinning, 123
    harvest and storage guidelines, 135
    pollination, 181
    propagation, 10
    training and pruning, 79, 94–95
Poppy apricots, 184
potassium
    overview, 58
    absorption process, 57
    application methods, 66–69
    deficiency and toxicity symptoms, 63, 64*t*, *66*
    in fertilizer types, *61–62*, 63
    planting preparations, 41
powdery mildew, 24, 161–163, 164
precipitation. *See* rainfall
predaceous ground beetles, *141*
predator, defined, 140
preemergent herbicides, 7
President plums, 32
Price almonds, 34
primary scaffold branches, 79
Priscilla apples, 24
Pristine apples, 24
propagate. *See* budding; grafting
prunes
    overview, 31–33, 190
    diseases, 162, 164, 165
    harvest and storage guidelines, 135
    insect pests, 143*t*
    pollination, 31, 181
    potassium deficiency, *66*
    training and pruning, 79
pruning guidelines
    basic principles, 11, 12–13, 14–15, 71–76
    bearing failures, 12, 180, 181, 182
    central leader, 86–88
    disease management, 167–169, 173, 174
    dwarf trees, 78
    espalier system, 90–91, 93, *94*
    fruit bush system, 88, 90, *91–92*
    insect management, 145, 159
    newly planted trees, 42, *45*
    open-center system, 79–81, *82*
    overgrown trees, *96*, 97–98
    perpendicular **V** system, 82–86
    seasonal timing, 19, 20, 76–77
    sweetness failures, 185
    See also training systems

Prunus besseyi rootstock, 27, 29, 30, 32
Puget Gold apricots, 27

quince
    overview, 24, 26, 191
    codling moth, 148
    fire blight, 168
    flowering habits, *15*
    fruit characteristics, 15–16
    fruit thinning, 125
    grafting compatibility, 100
    harvest and storage guidelines, 135
    pollination, 26, 181
Quince rootstock, 24, 25

radiation frosts, 4
rainfall
    climate zone differences, 1–2
    salinity levels, 59–60
    stone fruit problems, 26, 182–183
Rainier cherries, 28
raspberries, post-harvest changes, 129
Red Delicious apples, 22
Red Haven peaches, 30
reference evapotranspiration, 48
resources and references
    bearing failures, 186
    budding and grafting, 99, 121, 122
    climate characteristics, 1, 2, 8
    fertilizers, 61, 70
    fruit thinning, 128
    harvest and storage guidelines, 138
    irrigation, 56
    physiological disorders, 186, 188
    plant growth, 20
    planting guidelines, 46
    pollination, 181
    soils, 8
    training and pruning, 98
    varieties and rootstocks, 38
resources and references, pest management
    generally, 178, 187
    biological control, 140
    diseases, 163, 170, 178
    insects, 152, 153, 156, 158, 178
    pesticide use, 142
respiration, 17–18
rind grafting, defined, 115
ring nematodes, 173
Rio Oso Gem peaches, 31
ripening periods
    overview, 3
    figs, 36–37
    nut crops, 33–36
    persimmons, 37
    pome fruits, 21–26
    stone fruits, 26–34
Riverside example, chilling hours, 3
Robada apricots, 184
Rome Beauty apples, 23
root aphid, 24, 25
root knot nematode, 27, 28, 31
root rots
    overview, 174–176, *177*
    nut crop susceptibilities, 34, 36
    pome fruit susceptibilities, 24, 25
    stone fruit susceptibilities, 27, 28, 31
    See also crown rot
rootstocks
    defined, 99
    bearing age, 179
    nut crops, 35, 36
    persimmons, 37
    pest control, 139
    pome fruits, 21–22, 24–25
    See also grafting
rootstocks, stone fruits
    apricots, 27
    cherries, 28
    nectarines, 29
    peaches, 30
    plumcots, 33

plums and prunes, 31–32
root systems
    overview, 9–10, 18
    aphid damage, 145
    irrigation practices, 47, 50, 182
    planting guidelines, 41–42, *43*
    seasonal growth stages, 18, 19, 20
    tree selection guidelines, 139
rose bushes, 163
Royal Ann cherries, 28, 181
Royal apricots, 27
Royalty apricots, 27
Ruby Red pomegranates, 26

Sacramento Valley, climate characteristics, 1, *4*
salinity levels, 7, 59–60, 63
sandy soils, 5–6
sanitation practices
    pest control generally, 139, 141
sanitation practices, disease management
    Armillaria root rot, 174
    brown rot, 167–168
    Eutypa dieback, 174
    fire blight, 169
    powdery mildew, 163
    scab, 170
    shothole, 172
sanitation practices, insect management
    borers, 159
    codling moth, 150
    consperse stink bug, 160
    green fruit beetle, 160
    leafrollers, 154
    navel orangeworm, 160
    walnut husk fly, 156
San Joaquin Valley, climate characteristics, 1, *4*
San Jose scale, 146, 147, *148*
Santa Rosa plums, 32
sapwood, 11, *12*
Satsuma plums, 32
Saucer peaches, 31
saws, pruning, 71
scab, 22, 24, 25, 169–170
scaffold branches, defined, 10, 79
    See also training systems
scale insects, 145, 146–148, *149*
Scharsch Franquette walnuts, 36
scion, 10, 99
    See also budding; grafting
Seckel pears, 25
secondary scaffold branches, defined, 79
seedling rootstock, 21, 34, 36
seed structures, *14*
selecting trees, 39
self-fruitful trees, 14, 181
    See also pollination
self-unfruitful trees, 14, 181
    See also pollination
semidwarf trees. *See* pruning guidelines; rootstocks
sepal, defined, 15
Shinko Asian pears, 26
Shinseiki Asian pears, 25
Shiro plums, 32
shoots, 10–11, 18, 19, 20
shothole borers, 159
shothole disease, 171–172
Sierra Nevada foothills, climate characteristics, 2, *4*
silt soils, 5–6
simple leaves, 13
site selection factors, 40, 139, 173, 180
six-spotted thrips, 157
slugs, 7
Smyrna quinces, 26
Snow Giant peaches, 31
Snow Queen nectarines, 30
soaker hoses, 54, 195
soaps, insecticidal, 142, 145, 157
sodium, 7
soft scale insects, 146–148
soil
    overview, 5–7
    fertility management, 59–60

moisture evaluation, 44, 54–55
planting preparations, 40–41
soil analysis, 63, 66
soil application, fertilizers, 67
soil reaction. *See* pH levels
soldier beetles, 145, *147*
sooty mold, 145–146, 147
sour cherry varieties, 27–28, 29
Southern California zone, climate characteristics, 2–3, *4*
spacing requirements
nut crops, 35
persimmons, 37
pome fruit varieties, 22, 24
site selection factors, 39
spacing requirements, stone fruits
apricots, 26
cherries, 27, 28
nectarines, 229
peaches, 30
plums and prunes, 31
spider mites, 156–157
spiders, *141*
splitting problems, 182–183
spreading of branches, 75, *76*
spring budding, defined, 103
Springcrest peaches, 30
spring drop, 180
spring growth cycle, 19
sprinkler systems, 51–53
Sprite cherry-plums, 32–33
spurring/doubling problems, 183, 193
spurs, 76, 81
See also pruning guidelines; training systems
squirrels, 129, 136–138
stamens, 13
staminate flowers, 14
Stanley plums, 32
Stella cherries, 28, 181
sticky barriers, ant control, 145
sticky traps, codling moth, 151
stigmas, 13, 14, 15
stink bugs, 160
stomates, 13, 17, 18
stone fruits, generally
bearing age, 179
calendar for crop-care activities, 188, 189, 190
climate zones, 1–5
fruit thinning, 123–128
plant growth, 16–20
rootstocks and varieties, 26–34
tree organs, 9–16
See also specific topics, e.g., irrigation practices; peaches; training systems
storage guidelines, 130, 131, 132–134, 135
strawberries, postharvest changes, 129
Strawberry Freestone peaches, 30
styles, 13
subsoils, 6
suckers, defined, 12
sulfur, 7, 58, *65*, 142, 163
summer growth cycle, 20
summer pruning, 76–77
See also pruning guidelines; training systems
summer varieties, apples, 23
sunburn protection
overview, 185
grafts and buds, 119
insect management, 158, 159
newly planted trees, 43, *45*
pruning guidelines, 77, 82
Sunburst cherries, 181
Suncrest peaches, 30
sunlight requirements, 17, 180
superior oils, defined, 142
See also oil treatments
sweet cherry varieties, 27–28
sweetness failures, 185
syconium, defined, 16
synthetic fertilizers, 62–63
See also fertilizers
syrphid flies, 145, *146*

taproots, 10
T-budding, 101, 103–107
Tehama walnuts, 36
temperatures
bearing failures, 180
climate zone differences, 1–2
disease development, 161, 163, 165, 168, 170
fig preferences, 36
fungicide applications, 163, 169
insecticide applications, 142, 148
nut crop preferences, 33, 34, 35
oil treatments, 157, 163
physiological disorders, 183, 184
spider mites, 156, 157
See also chilling requirements
temperatures, storage
fruit crops, 25, 130, 132, 133, 135
nut crops, 136, 137, 138
terminal buds, 12
Texas Mission almonds, 34
thinning cuts
defined, 11
dwarf trees, 78
method of, *74, 75*
overgrown trees, 97
summer pruning, 77
thinning of fruit
overview, 123–128
bearing failure prevention, 181
sweetness failure prevention, 185
young trees, 12–13
Thomas walnuts, 35
thrips, 29, 157
tilth, soil, 6
Tilton apricots, 27, 184
tissue analysis, 63, 66
topsoils, 6, 196
topworking methods, 115–118
toxicities, nutrient, 63–66
training systems
overview, 71, *72–73*
central leader, 86–88, 89, *90*
espalier, 90–91, 93, *94*
fruit bush, 88, 90, *91–92*
newly planted trees, 42, 43–44, *45*
open-center, 79–81
perpendicular **V**, 82–86
spreading branches, 75, *76*
See also pruning guidelines
translocation, 18, 20
transpiration, 18
trapping pests, 151
tree organs, 9–16
trees, generally
biological processes, 16–18
growth cycles, 18–21, 180
organ functions, 9–16
tree trunk topiary, 120–122
tree water use units, 48–50
trellises, 22, 90–92
Tri Gem apricots, 184
trunk banding, 151
trunks, 10
Tsu Li Asian pears, 26
Tulare cherries, 28
Twentieth Century Asian pears, 25
twig borers, 26
two-spotted mites, 156–157

Utah Giant cherries, 28

Van cherries, 28
varieties
figs, 36–37
nut crops, 33–39
persimmons, 37
pome fruits, 21–26
stone fruits, 26–33
vascular cambium, 11, *12,* 99
vascular tissues, 11
vegetative buds, 12–13
Verticillium wilt, 35

Veteran peaches, 30
Vista Bell apples, 23

walnut aphids, *146*
walnut blight, 174, *176*
walnut husk fly, 154, 156, *157*
walnuts
overview, 35–36, 191
bearing age, 179
disease management, 174, *176*
grafting compatibility, 100
growth characteristics, *16,* 19
harvest and storage guidelines, 129, 138
insect pests, 142, 143*t*, 148, 149, 154, 156
plant structures, 14
pollination, 15, 35
training and pruning, *10,* 42, 86–87, *88,* 93
wasps, parasitic, 140, 145, 146, 148
water, plant functions, 9–10, 11, 18
See also irrigation practices
waterspouts, defined, 12
water use units, 48–50
waxing materials
arborsculpture methods, 121
bark grafting, *114,* 115, *116*
cleft grafting, 117, *118*
follow up care, 119
types of, 102
whip grafting, *111, 112,* 113
weeds, 7, 44, 50
Wenatchee apricots, 184
western flower thrips, 29
western predatory mites, 157
Western Schley pecans, 35
western tussock moth, 153, *156*
Westley apricots, 184
wet feet tolerance
figs, 36
nut crops, 33, 34, 36
persimmons, 37
Phytophthora root and crown rot, 175
pome fruits, 24–25, 26
stone fruits, 27, 29, 30, 31–32
wet limit, determining, 55
wet soil tolerance. *See* wet feet tolerance
whip grafting method, 110–114
White Genoa figs, 37
Wichita pecans, 35
Wickson plums, 32
Williams Pride apples, 24
wind pollination, 15
winds, climate zone differences, 1–2
winter growth cycle, 19
Winter Nelis pears, 25
winter pruning, 76–77
See also pruning guidelines; training systems
Wonderful pomegranates, 26
wood chips, mulches, 7
woolly apple aphids, 22, 143, 145, 146
wrapping materials
budding methods, *103, 105, 106,* 107, *108*
grafting methods, *110, 112,* 113, *116,* 117, *118*
types of, 102

xylem, 11, 18

Ya Li Asian pears, 26

zinc
overview, 58–59
application methods, 67, 68, 69
deficiency and toxicity symptoms, 63, *65, 67*
soil pH, 60
zones. *See* climate zones